Foreclosure Investing

2nd Edition

by Ralph R. Roberts with Joe Kraynak and Kyle Roberts

for
dummies®
A Wiley Brand

Foreclosure Investing For Dummies®, 2nd Edition

Published by: **John Wiley & Sons, Inc.,** 111 River Street, Hoboken, NJ 07030-5774, www.wiley.com

Copyright © 2022 by John Wiley & Sons, Inc., Hoboken, New Jersey

Published simultaneously in Canada

For general information on our other products and services, please contact our Customer Care Department within the U.S. at 877-762-2974, outside the U.S. at 317-572-3993, or fax 317-572-4002. For technical support, please visit https://hub.wiley.com/community/support/dummies.

Wiley publishes in a variety of print and electronic formats and by print-on-demand. Some material included with standard print versions of this book may not be included in e-books or in print-on-demand. If this book refers to media such as a CD or DVD that is not included in the version you purchased, you may download this material at http://booksupport.wiley.com. For more information about Wiley products, visit www.wiley.com.

Library of Congress Control Number: 2022934231

ISBN 978-1-119-86098-3 (pbk); ISBN 978-1-119-86099-0 (ebk); ISBN 978-1-119-86100-3 (ebk)

SKY10033722_031922

Foreclosure Investing

2nd Edition

by Ralph R. Roberts with Joe Kraynak and Kyle Roberts

A Wiley Brand

Foreclosure Investing For Dummies®, 2nd Edition

Published by: **John Wiley & Sons, Inc.**, 111 River Street, Hoboken, NJ 07030-5774, www.wiley.com

Copyright © 2022 by John Wiley & Sons, Inc., Hoboken, New Jersey

Published simultaneously in Canada

For general information on our other products and services, please contact our Customer Care Department within the U.S. at 877-762-2974, outside the U.S. at 317-572-3993, or fax 317-572-4002. For technical support, please visit https://hub.wiley.com/community/support/dummies.

Wiley publishes in a variety of print and electronic formats and by print-on-demand. Some material included with standard print versions of this book may not be included in e-books or in print-on-demand. If this book refers to media such as a CD or DVD that is not included in the version you purchased, you may download this material at http://booksupport.wiley.com. For more information about Wiley products, visit www.wiley.com.

Library of Congress Control Number: 2022934231

ISBN 978-1-119-86098-3 (pbk); ISBN 978-1-119-86099-0 (ebk); ISBN 978-1-119-86100-3 (ebk)

SKY10033722_031922

Contents at a Glance

Introduction 1

Part 1: Prepping Yourself for Foreclosure Success 7

CHAPTER 1: Wrapping Your Brain around Foreclosure Investing 9

CHAPTER 2: Getting Up to Speed on the Foreclosure Process 29

CHAPTER 3: Picking Your Point of Entry in the Foreclosure Process 41

Part 2: Laying the Groundwork for Maximized Profit and Minimized Risk 57

CHAPTER 4: Building a Powerful Foreclosure Investment Team 59

CHAPTER 5: Filling Your Foreclosure Tank with Financial Fuel 77

CHAPTER 6: Networking Your Way to Foreclosure Success 95

Part 3: Creating Win–Win Situations in Pre-Foreclosure (Before Auction) 107

CHAPTER 7: Discovering Homeowners Facing Foreclosure 109

CHAPTER 8: Performing Your Due Diligence 125

CHAPTER 9: Contacting the Homeowners and Lenders 145

CHAPTER 10: Analyzing the Deal and Presenting Your Offer 173

Part 4: Finding and Buying Foreclosure and Bankruptcy Properties 187

CHAPTER 11: Bidding for Properties at a Foreclosure Sale 189

CHAPTER 12: Buying Repos: Bank Foreclosures and REO Properties 207

CHAPTER 13: Finding and Buying Government Repos 225

CHAPTER 14: Banking on Bankruptcies 241

CHAPTER 15: Sampling Some Other Foreclosure Strategies 255

Part 5: Cashing Out Your Profit . . . After the Sale 277

CHAPTER 16: Assisting the Previous Homeowners Out the Door 279

CHAPTER 17: Repairing and Renovating Your Investment Property 291

CHAPTER 18: Cashing Out: Selling or Leasing Your Property 305

CHAPTER 19: Checking Out Other Cash-Out Strategies 319

Part 6: The Part of Tens 329

CHAPTER 20: Ten Common Beginner Blunders. 331

CHAPTER 21: Ten Ways to Maximize Future Leads by Acting with Integrity. 337

CHAPTER 22: Ten Tips for Avoiding Common Foreclosure Minefields 345

Appendix: Foreclosure Rules and Regulations for the 50 States 353

Index 367

Table of Contents

INTRODUCTION 1
   About This Book. 1
   Foolish Assumptions. 2
   Icons Used in This Book 4
   Beyond the Book. 4
   Where to Go from Here 4

PART 1: PREPPING YOURSELF FOR FORECLOSURE SUCCESS 7

CHAPTER 1: **Wrapping Your Brain around Foreclosure Investing** 9
   Investigating the Foreclosure Process from Start to Finish. 10
   Picking Your Point of Entry. 12
      Scooping other investors during the pre-auction stage 12
      Bidding on properties at foreclosure auctions 13
      Buying properties after the sale 15
   Assembling a Team of Experts and Advisers. 16
   Getting Your Financial Ducks in a Row. 17
   Finding Foreclosures and Seized Properties 18
   Performing Your Due Diligence. 19
      Investigating the property's title and other documentation 20
      Inspecting the property with your own eyes. 21
      Guesstimating a property's true value 22
      Investigating the situation and the homeowners. 22
   Setting and Sticking To Your Maximum Bid. 23
   Taking Possession of the Property 24
      Completing the essential paperwork 24
      Paying property taxes and insurance. 25
      Persuading the current residents to move on 26
   Cashing Out: Realizing Your Profit 26
      Repairing and renovating the property to maximize its value 27
      Marketing and selling to get top dollar 27
      Cashing out equity by refinancing 28
      Profiting in other ways 28

CHAPTER 2: **Getting Up to Speed on the Foreclosure Process** 29
   Identifying the Foreclosure Process in Your Area. 30
      Foreclosure by trustee sale 30
      Foreclosure by judicial sale 31

Exploring the Missed-Payment Notice Stage 31
Getting Serious: The Notice of Default 32
Proceeding to the Foreclosure Sale 32
Halting the Foreclosure Process 33
        Reinstating the mortgage 34
        Requesting and receiving a forbearance 35
        Mortgage modification or repayment plan 35
        Filing for bankruptcy 36
        Agreeing to a deed in lieu of foreclosure 36
        Getting one last chance during the redemption period 37
Finalizing the Foreclosure: Ushering the Previous Owners
Out the Door 39

CHAPTER 3: **Picking Your Point of Entry in the
Foreclosure Process** 41
Dipping In at the Pre-Auction Stage 42
        Exploring the pros and cons of pre-auction foreclosures 42
        Guiding homeowners to good decisions 43
        Dealing with anger and angst 44
        Assessing your ability to deal with pre-auction scenarios 45
Pursuing Foreclosure Notices 46
        Knowing the benefits of waiting for the foreclosure notice 47
        Weighing the drawbacks of waiting for the foreclosure notice . . .48
        Wrapping up your deal before the sale .48
Bidding for a Property at a Foreclosure Auction 49
        Weighing the pros and cons of buying at auctions 50
        Setting a maximum bid well in advance 51
        Putting on your poker face 51
Acquiring Properties after the Auction 52
        Scoping out REO properties 52
        Finding and buying government properties 53
        Buying properties from other investors 54
Waiting Out the Redemption Period — If Necessary 54

PART 2: LAYING THE GROUNDWORK FOR
MAXIMIZED PROFIT AND MINIMIZED RISK 57

CHAPTER 4: **Building a Powerful Foreclosure Investment
Team** 59
Lawyering Up with a Real Estate Attorney 60
Teaming Up with a Good Moneyman or Woman 61
Consulting a Title Company to Cover Your Back 63
Hiring a Tax-Savvy Accountant 64
Lining Up a Home Inspector 65

Contacting Contractors and Subcontractors...........................66
    Hiring a general contractor — or not........................67
    Tracking down top-notch contractors and subcontractors.......68
    Contracting with contractors and subcontractors..............68
    Finding skilled and unskilled help..........................70
    Insuring your helping hands.................................70
Selling Your Property for Top Dollar through a Seller's Agent.......71
    Recognizing the value of a seller's agent...................72
    Picking an agent with the right stuff.......................73
Assessing the Pros and Cons of Partnerships.......................74

CHAPTER 5: **Filling Your Foreclosure Tank with Financial Fuel**...77

Estimating Your Cash Needs..78
Finding a Cash Stash: Knowing Your Financing Options.............79
Financing with Hard-Money and Gap Loans..........................81
    Weighing the pros and cons of hard money....................81
    Making up the difference with a gap loan....................83
    Finding private lenders.....................................83
Partnering with Investors...84
Shaking Your Piggy Bank: Tapping Your Own Resources..............84
    Examining the pros and cons of using your own money........85
    Totaling your sources of investment capital.................85
    Planning for contingencies..................................88
Financing Your Venture with Conventional Loans...................88
    Exploring conventional loan types...........................89
    Making yourself look good on paper..........................90
    Gathering the paperwork and records you need................93
Comparison Shopping for Low-Cost Loans...........................93

CHAPTER 6: **Networking Your Way to Foreclosure Success**.....95

Grasping the Power of Networking..................................96
    Generating leads on profitable pre-auction properties........96
    Securing your financing.....................................97
    Tracking down reliable, affordable professionals............98
    Selling your house for more money in less time..............98
Realizing the Importance of Being Good............................99
    Acting with integrity — always..............................99
    Investing in quality craftsmanship.........................100
    Building thriving communities..............................100
Marketing Yourself...101
    Gathering your marketing tools.............................101
    Starting with your inner circle............................103
    Keeping in touch: A daily chore............................103

Managing Contact Information 104
Rewarding Good Deeds and Good Leads 104

PART 3: CREATING WIN–WIN SITUATIONS IN PRE-FORECLOSURE (BEFORE AUCTION) 107

CHAPTER 7: **Discovering Homeowners Facing Foreclosure** 109

Networking Your Way to Promising Properties 110
   Identifying your personal lead generators 110
   Getting the word out on the streets 114
Scoping Out the Neighborhood for Dontwanners 114
Searching for FSBO Properties 115
Finding Foreclosure Notices 116
   Tracking down local publications 116
   Getting on the mailing list 117
   Subscribing to commercial foreclosure information
   services . . . or not 117
   Deciphering a foreclosure notice 118
Teaming Up with Attorneys to Help Distressed Clients
Sell Their Homes 119
   Acquiring properties in probate 119
   Adopting homes orphaned by divorce 121
   Teaming up with bankruptcy attorneys 122

CHAPTER 8: **Performing Your Due Diligence** 125

Collecting Essential Information about the Property 126
   Honing your title acquisition and reading skills 126
   Picking up details from the foreclosure notice 127
   Digging up details at the Register of Deeds office 132
   Gathering tax information at the assessor's office 138
   Getting your hands on the property worksheet 138
   Gathering additional information 139
Doing Your Fieldwork: Inspecting the Property 140
   Doing a drive-by, walk-around inspection 140
   Snapping some photos 142
Assembling Your Property Dossier: A Checklist 142
Recognizing the Most Common and Serious Red Flags
and Big Mistakes 144

CHAPTER 9: **Contacting the Homeowners and Lenders** 145

Scheduling Your Foreclosure Activities 146
Contacting the Homeowners Directly 150
   Tracking down the homeowners 150
   Kicking off your mail campaign 151
   Getting in touch over the phone 156

Adding the Homeowners' Profile to Your Property Dossier 159
Presenting All Available Options 160
    Reinstating the loan 162
    Negotiating with the lenders for a forbearance 162
    Refinancing the mortgage 162
    Listing the property. 163
    Selling short 164
    Accepting your cash offer. 164
    Refinancing through you 164
    Selling the home and leasing it with an option to buy it back
    later 165
    Selling the home and leasing it without an option to buy. 166
    Giving a deed in lieu of foreclosure 166
    Filing for bankruptcy. 167
    Waiting (and saving) during redemption 167
    Doing nothing 168
Getting Inside to Take a Look Around 168
Contacting the Lenders 169
    Contacting the senior lienholder. 170
    Contacting the junior lienholders 171

CHAPTER 10: Analyzing the Deal and Presenting Your Offer 173
Completing the Deal Analysis Worksheet 174
    Calculating the homeowners' equity in the property. 174
    Calculating your top cash offer 177
    Logging the loan status. 178
    Determining options based on LTV 178
    Assessing the homeowners' credit health 179
    Gauging the homeowners' wants 180
    Determining the homeowners' gross monthly income 180
Assessing the Homeowners' Options. 181
Presenting Your Offer: The Purchase Agreement 183
Closing Time. 185

**PART 4: FINDING AND BUYING FORECLOSURE
AND BANKRUPTCY PROPERTIES** 187

CHAPTER 11: Bidding for Properties at a Foreclosure Sale 189
Tracking Down Auction Dates, Times, and Places 190
Preparing Your Maximum Bid. . . . . . . : 191
    Guesstimating the property's improved value 192
    Estimating repair and renovation costs .192
    Figuring in holding costs. 192
    Subtracting agent commissions and closing costs. 193
    Arriving at your maximum bid amount 194

Bidding at a Foreclosure Auction 197
    Packing for an auction 198
    Sitting in on a few auctions 198
    Crafting a winning bidding strategy 199
    Submitting sealed bids 199
Playing the Role of Backup Buyer 201
Following Up After the Auction 202

CHAPTER 12: **Buying Repos: Bank Foreclosures and**
REO Properties 207
Acknowledging the Drawbacks of REO Opportunities............208
Getting Up to Speed on the REO Process 209
Shaking the Bushes for REO Properties.......................210
    Positioning yourself as an attractive investor 210
    Connecting with REO brokers 211
    Getting connected with REO A-listers...................211
    Tracking the property through the REO stage 214
    Working your way to the better deals 215
    Following up with homeowners during redemption 216
Inspecting the Property 216
Timing Your Offer for Optimum Results 217
    Acting quickly after the auction.......................217
    Timing your move with the redemption period 218
    Tuning in to the lender's fiscal calendar..............218
    Waiting for the broker to list the house 219
Pitching an Attractive Offer 220
    Sizing up the lender's needs 220
    Reevaluating your needs 221
    Putting your offer in writing..........................222
    Closing on the deal 224

CHAPTER 13: **Finding and Buying Government Repos** 225
Bargain Hunting for HUD Homes 227
    Weighing the pros and cons of HUD homes................227
    Hooking up with a HUD-approved agent...................228
    Finding HUD homes online 229
Finding and Buying VA Repos 230
Profiting from Fannie Mae and Freddie Mac Properties........231
    Tapping into Freddie Mac's home clearinghouse..........232
    Shopping for Fannie Mae properties 233
    Buying FDIC properties.................................234
Finding and Buying Government-Seized Properties 234
    Buying properties at tax sales 235
    Avoiding the tax lien sales gurus......................236

Buying properties from the IRS 236
Contacting your county treasurer's office 237
Taking a trip to the state department of transportation 237
Finding government-seized property online 238

CHAPTER 14: Banking on Bankruptcies 241
Brushing Up on Bankruptcy Laws. 242
Selling assets through Chapter 7 bankruptcy 242
Restructuring debt through Chapter 13 bankruptcy 243
Knowing When to Purchase. 244
Tracking Down Houses in Bankruptcy 245
Skimming publications for bankruptcy notices. 246
Researching bankruptcy filings 246
Networking with the gatekeepers. 247
Dealing with the Gatekeepers 248
Cooperating with bankruptcy trustees. 249
Teaming up with bankruptcy attorneys 249
Getting the homeowners on your side. 250
Getting the creditors on your side 250
Dealing with Bankruptcy Delays on a House You Bought. 251

CHAPTER 15: Sampling Some Other Foreclosure Strategies 255
Negotiating Short Sales 256
Knowing the lienholder pecking order. 256
Wheeling and dealing with lienholders 259
Recognizing a short-sale opportunity. 260
Teaming up with the homeowners. 261
Gathering payoff amounts. 262
Crunching the numbers 263
Negotiating with the lienholders. 265
Buying and Selling Junior Liens 269
Buying junior liens to foreclose for a quick payday 269
Buying seconds to protect the first mortgage. 271
Selling a junior lien for a profit 272
Profiting from Property Tax Sales. 272
Tracking down property tax sales. 273
Finding golden tax sale opportunities 274
Buying tax deeds and tax certificates. 275
Getting redeemed out of your position 275
Profiting from the tax lien or deed 276

PART 5: CASHING OUT YOUR PROFIT . . . AFTER THE SALE 277

CHAPTER 16: **Assisting the Previous Homeowners Out the Door** 279

Tying Up the Loose Ends after the Purchase 280
    Closing on a pre-auction purchase 280
    Tying up the loose ends after the auction 282
Protecting Your Investment through Redemption 282
    Maintaining the property's status quo 282
    Securing the property 283
    Keeping hungry investors at bay 284
Planning Repairs and Renovations 287
Evicting the Residents When Time Runs Out 287

CHAPTER 17: **Repairing and Renovating Your Investment Property** 291

Choosing a Renovation Strategy 292
Planning Repairs and Renovations 293
    Calculating the return on your investment 293
    Roughing out your budget and schedule 294
Giving Your Property a Quick Makeover 297
    Freshen the exterior 297
    Gussy up the interior 298
    Tidy up the kitchen 298
    Scour the bathrooms 299
    Spiff up the bedrooms 299
    Make the basement tolerable 300
    Attend to the mechanicals 300
Investing in High-Profile Rooms: Kitchens and Baths 301
    Cooking up a remodeled kitchen 301
    Updating the bathrooms 303
Adding Valuable Features 303

CHAPTER 18: **Cashing Out: Selling or Leasing Your Property** 305

Selling Through a Qualified Real Estate Agent 306
    Selling faster for a higher price 306
    Choosing a top-notch seller's agent 308
Staging Your House for a Successful Showing 309
    Jazzing up the front entrance 309
    Decluttering the joint 310
    Adding a few tasteful furnishings 310
    Appealing to the senses 311

Generating Interest Through Savvy Marketing.................312
Negotiating Offers and Counteroffers......................313
    Comparing offers.....................................313
    Mastering the art of counteroffers...................315
Closing the Deal..316
Becoming a Landlord.......................................317

CHAPTER 19: **Checking Out Other Cash-Out Strategies**.........319
Refinancing to Cash Out the Equity........................320
Reselling the Property to the Previous Owners or Their Family.....320
    Reselling to the previous owners.....................321
    Financing the buyback through insurance-policy
    proceeds and other means.............................323
Leasing the Property to the Foreclosed-on Homeowners......324
Offering a Lease-Option Agreement.........................325
Assigning Your Position to a Junior Lienholder............327

PART 6: THE PART OF TENS..................................329

CHAPTER 20: **Ten Common Beginner Blunders**...................331
Having Insufficient Funds on Hand.........................331
Overestimating a Property's Value.........................332
Underestimating Your Holding Costs........................333
Overbidding in the Heat of Battle.........................333
Failing to Investigate the Title.........................333
Failing to Inspect the Property with Your Own Eyes........334
Bidding on a Second Mortgage or Junior Lien...............335
Renovating a Property before You Own It...................335
Trusting What the Homeowners Tell You.....................336
Getting Greedy..336

CHAPTER 21: **Ten Ways to Maximize Future Leads
by Acting with Integrity**................................337
Stopping the Bleeding: Providing Basic Financial Advice...........338
Assisting Homeowners in Their Job Search..................338
Suggesting That the Homeowners Seek Help from
Family and Friends..338
Encouraging the Homeowners to Contact Their
Lenders . . . and Soon....................................339
Suggesting Short Sales and Other Debt Negotiations........340
Assisting Homeowners in Assessing Their Refinance Options......340
Suggesting the Option of Selling the House before Foreclosure....341
Bringing Up the Bankruptcy Option.........................341
Offering a Helping Hand...................................342
Revealing the Option to Walk Away.........................343

CHAPTER 22: **Ten Tips for Avoiding Common Foreclosure Minefields**...........................345

Steer Clear of Foreclosure Investment Scams 346
Research the Title Yourself 346
Inspect the Property with Your Own Eyes 346
Know What You're Bidding On 347
Set Realistic Goals 347
Muffle Your Emotions...348
Invest with Integrity..348
Anticipate Delays...349
Foresee Unforeseen Expenses 350
Deal with the Blame and Guilt.................................351

APPENDIX: FORECLOSURE RULES AND REGULATIONS FOR THE 50 STATES 353

INDEX..367

Introduction

When most people think about foreclosure investing, they envision a process of buying a property at auction for much less than it's worth, fixing it up (or not), and then immediately putting it back on the market for tens of thousands of dollars more than they paid for it. They think it's a quick and easy way to earn big bucks in real estate.

Truth is, the process is far more complex and risky. Do you know, for example, that when you "buy a house" at a foreclosure sale, you may not actually be getting the house? You may end up paying $100,000 for a junior lien against a property (such as a construction lien) and have your position wiped out by the buyer of the senior lien (the first mortgage)! What you thought you'd be getting for your $100,000 investment is actually a worthless piece of paper. Or maybe you get the house and find out that the current residents are legally allowed to live there for a year or whenever the latest government mandate prohibiting foreclosure expires. You're stuck paying the mortgage, insurance, and property taxes, and you're awake all night worrying about what the current residents are doing in (and to) your property.

When it comes to foreclosure investing, what you don't know *can* hurt you. I've seen it happen time and time again to very intelligent but ill-informed investors. They miss opportunities by not fully understanding the foreclosure process and get burned by not fully understanding what they're buying or what they need to do after buying a property in foreclosure.

To capitalize on foreclosure opportunities while minimizing your risk, you need the guidance of an experienced professional. In *Foreclosure Investing For Dummies*, I serve as your guide, providing the information and direction necessary for your success.

About This Book

Foreclosure Investing For Dummies isn't a quick-cash, no-risk, no-work guide to building wealth through foreclosure investing. People who want that sort of thing can stay up late at night and watch real estate investment "gurus" peddle their products, or they can attend any of the readily available "free" foreclosure investment seminars that make the rounds.

This book guides you in the methods of making money the old-fashioned way: earning it fairly. I've been investing in foreclosures and assisting distressed homeowners for more than 30 years. I've achieved great success and experienced my fair share of failures. I've had homeowners provide glowing testimonials of how much I've helped them, been accused of trying to steal homes from "little old ladies," and assisted homeowners when con artists have tried to steal their homes. Sad to say, even lost property in foreclosure myself.

In *Foreclosure Investing For Dummies*, I show you how to invest in foreclosures the right way. I steer you clear of the many pitfalls inherent in foreclosure investing. I show you how to properly and thoroughly research properties so you know what you're getting into before you buy or bid on a property. I step you through the process of finding the best opportunities with the maximum potential profit and lowest risk. I lead you through the process of buying foreclosures before auction, bidding for them at auction, and purchasing them after the auction from the lenders that have foreclosed on them. I present various ways to cash out and realize your profit after the sale. And I show you how to do all this without misleading and cheating distressed homeowners.

I wrote this book so you could approach it in either of two ways: You can flip to any chapter for a quick, stand-alone mini-course on a specific foreclosure-investing topic, or you can read it from cover to cover. At the end of the book is an appendix of the foreclosure rules and regulations across the 50 states. Although I encourage you to research the foreclosure process in your local area carefully, you can flip to the appendix to get up to speed on the basics.

Foolish Assumptions

In some books that cover advanced topics, authors must assume that their readers already understand some basic topics or have acquired beginning-level skills. If this book were about molecular biology, for example, you'd have to know what a molecule is.

The biggest foolish assumption I make in this book is that you own the home you live in. You've been involved in at least one closing and signed the documents that the closing agent passed around. When you own a home, you instantly become a real estate investor. You begin to grasp the value of real estate as an investment. You gain firsthand knowledge of the benefits of owning a home, understand the challenges of maintaining it, and take on the responsibility of making mortgage payments. You can empathize with homeowners who are about to lose their homes in foreclosure.

If you're not a homeowner, sell this book, and put the proceeds toward a down payment on a house. If you live in the Detroit metropolitan area, contact me, and I'll find the perfect house for you and your family. I'll even give you credit on the purchase of the book. Or stop by the office, and I'll personally sign your copy. After you've purchased a house and have lived in it for a few months, pick up the book. I'll be waiting for you.

Other foolish assumptions I make include, but aren't limited to, the following:

>> **You're committed to success.** Investing in foreclosures is hard work and requires *sticktoitism* (pronounced stik-to-it-izm) — a word I've been using since the 1970s to describe the determination and dogged perseverance required to build wealth in real estate. I could use *stick-to-itiveness*, which happens to appear in the dictionary, but I like my word better.

>> **You can talk to people.** You don't need to be a social butterfly (although that helps), but you do need to be able to network, ask questions, and haggle with people. If you don't have some basic people skills, you should team up with someone who does. Effective word-of-mouth networking leads to the best opportunities, and in almost every situation, you'll need to talk with home-owners, county clerks, sheriffs, lenders, and a host of others involved in the foreclosure process.

>> **You're dedicated to developing mutually beneficial solutions.** I hate to see "investors" ripping off homeowners, and I'd really hate to see anyone use the information in this book to take advantage of distressed homeowners. You can earn plenty of money investing in foreclosures by acting with integrity and presenting reasonable solutions that meet the needs of all parties involved.

>> **You're able to treat foreclosure investing as business.** Understand that you're not the cause of the homeowners' distress. More than likely, you can't solve their problems. Very likely, many others have tried to help the home-owners solve the root cause of the problem (and failed) before you came along. What you can offer are truth and useful information. You must be empathetic without jumping in to save a drowning family that may drag you under both financially and emotionally.

Keep in mind that a *real* problem is something that money can't fix, such as an untreatable illness or a death in the family. Most families, if they choose to, can move on after experiencing a financial calamity. Foreclosure isn't the end of the world, although at the time, homeowners may perceive it to be.

Icons Used in This Book

Throughout this book, I've sprinkled icons in the margins to cue you in on different types of information that call out for your attention. Here are the icons you'll see and a brief description of each.

REMEMBER

I want you to remember everything you read in this book, but if you can't quite do that, remember the important points I flag with this icon.

TIP

Tips provide insider insight from behind the scenes. When you're looking for a better, faster, cheaper way to do something, check out these tips.

WARNING

"Whoa!" This icon appears when you need to be extra-vigilant or seek professional help before moving forward.

Beyond the Book

In addition to the priceless information and guidance you'll find in the nearly 400 pages of this book, you can access the *Foreclosure Investing For Dummies* Cheat Sheet online. Just go to www.dummies.com, and enter "Foreclosure Investing For Dummies Cheat Sheet" in the search box. The Cheat Sheet includes a complete checklist of everything you should have before you bid or make an offer on a foreclosure property, step-by-step instructions for buying properties in pre-foreclosure, step-by-step instructions for buying properties at foreclosure auctions, a list of foreclosure auction websites, and a list of the ten most common mistakes to avoid when investing in foreclosure properties.

Where to Go from Here

Foreclosure Investing For Dummies is constructed in a way that's similar to the foreclosure process itself. It presents you with opportunities and with information to capitalize on those opportunities in three key entry points in the foreclosure process: pre-foreclosure, foreclosure, and post-foreclosure.

For a quick course on foreclosure investing, check out Chapter 1, which provides an overview of the foreclosure process along with some tidbits on how to profit from the various stages of the process. Skip to Chapter 3, where I guide you in selecting your preferred entry point. The chapters in Part 2 are indispensable in preparing you for a successful investment venture. If you choose to invest in pre-foreclosures, skip to Part 3, were you discover how to research properties and deal directly with homeowners. Part 3 also contains a chapter (Chapter 8) that's essential for all foreclosure investors: properly researching a property. If you're interested in purchasing properties at auction or after they've been repossessed, Part 4 provides all the information you need to know. And when you're ready to cash out on your investment, skip to Part 5.

TIP

In a few chapters, I include fill-in-the-blank forms and worksheets. Although you can fill them out in the book, consider making copies to write on. These forms and worksheets are indispensable for gathering research data, evaluating properties, and presenting options to homeowners facing foreclosure.

1

Prepping Yourself for Foreclosure Success

Get up to speed on finding, researching, bidding on, buying, and selling foreclosure properties at all stages of the foreclosure process, from pre-foreclosure to post-sale.

Tell the difference between judicial and nonjudicial foreclosure, and figure out which approach your state follows.

Identify the different stages of the foreclosure process, and discover the benefits and drawbacks of opportunities for acquiring properties at each stage.

Find profitable opportunities by connecting directly with homeowners in pre-foreclosure; wheeling and dealing when foreclosure notices are posted; bidding at auctions; or buying properties after a foreclosure sale from banks, government agencies, and other investors.

Chapter **1**

Wrapping Your Brain around Foreclosure Investing

Whenever you're developing a new skill, having an overview of what's involved provides you a framework for understanding. In the case of investing in foreclosures, that framework must include the basics of the foreclosure process, the importance of having a strong team, the benefits of thoroughly researching properties, and a general idea of the different ways to realize your profit (because selling isn't the only option).

A general knowledge of the foreclosure process and the rules and regulations that govern it can reveal opportunities for purchasing properties below market value. Understanding the necessity of having a strong investment team in place enables you to begin thinking about the people who would be best qualified to assist you. Realizing the benefits of thorough research can prevent you from buying a property that's destined to send you to the poorhouse. And knowing your options for extracting equity from a property enables you to optimize your overall investment strategy.

In this chapter, I provide an overview of the foreclosure process, stress the necessity of building a competent investment team, introduce you to essential property research techniques and resources, briefly explain the process of buying and taking possession of properties, and touch on various options you have to cash out your profit when you own the property. In a nutshell, I give you a framework for investing in foreclosed properties. As you proceed through the book and gain experience, you'll develop a deeper and more detailed understanding.

Investigating the Foreclosure Process from Start to Finish

A common misconception of foreclosure is that after the homeowners miss a payment or two, the lender immediately takes possession of the property, and then turns around and auctions it off at a foreclosure sale. But the process is more drawn out than that, and it follows this typical scenario:

1. The homeowners stop making mortgage payments.

2. After about 15 to 30 days, the lender sends a payment reminder.

3. If the homeowners don't respond, the lender continues to send notices and may start to call the homeowners.

4. If the homeowners still don't contact the lender, the lender turns the matter over to its collection department, which specializes in hassling homeowners.

5. After about three missed monthly payments, the lender transfers the matter to outside counsel, which is normally handled regionally. The attorney sends an official notice, warning that foreclosure proceedings are about to begin.

6. The homeowners don't reply or present a solution that the lender deems to be unsatisfactory. At this point, the homeowners can usually stop the foreclosure by negotiating a suitable solution with the lender.

7. The attorney begins the foreclosure process by posting a foreclosure notice in the county's legal newspaper or in the local newspaper. The homeowners can still reinstate the mortgage at this point by catching up on the payments and paying any additional late fees and penalties, which occurs quite often. See Chapter 8 for details on how to track foreclosure notices. (The county legal newspaper serves the public and provides the legal community an automated system, but it's not free.)

8. Foreclosure paperwork for the property arrives at the civil division of the sheriff's office, which is assigned the task of handling the sale. The trustee or attorney handling the foreclosure sets the opening bid and typically advertises it in the foreclosure notice. The opening bid is the balance of the mortgage plus penalties, unpaid interest, attorney fees, and other costs that the lender has incurred during the process.

9. The sheriff or a deputy may visit the house before the sale to post a foreclosure notice and inspect the property, because redemption rights sometimes change if the homeowners abandon the property. (Some states have a *redemption period* after the sale, during which time the homeowners can buy back the property by paying the full amount of the loan along with taxes, interest, and penalties. This period can last up to a year.)

10. The day before the auction, the lender may adjust the opening bid up or down but may not artificially inflate it. Frequently, lenders reduce the opening bid to make the property more appealing to investors and to rid themselves of it.

11. The property goes on the auction block for sale to the highest bidder or is turned over to a trustee to liquidate the property and pay the lender.

12. An investor purchases the property at auction or from the trustee or the lender buys the property. If nobody bids higher than the opening bid which the foreclosing lender submits, control is handed over to the lender, who can take possession of the property following any redemption period, as explained next.

13. In some states, the high bidder (or lender, if nobody bids more than the opening bid) takes immediate possession of the property. In states with a redemption period, the new "owner" must wait until the expiration of the redemption period and a final court hearing with the homeowners before they can do anything with the property. If the lender takes possession of the property, the lender transfers the property to its Real Estate Owned (REO) department which prepares it for sale.

14. The previous owners move out or are evicted, and the new owner takes possession of the property.

The foreclosure process is a lose–lose situation for both the homeowners and the lender. The homeowners lose the property, and the lender takes a loss on the loan and often pays additional costs to resell the property to recoup a portion of its loss.

REMEMBER

If you or a loved one is ever facing a foreclosure, contact the lender immediately to explore your options. Seek help sooner rather than later. Shame, anger, and denial may discourage you from seeking help, but the longer you wait, the fewer your options will be. Educate yourself, and communicate with your lender. Homeowners who panic become very vulnerable to foreclosure rescue schemes designed to strip them of any equity built up in the home. (*Equity* is the profit the owners would realize if they were to sell the property and pay off the mortgage.) Do your research, know your options, and don't deal with someone who's claiming to be your friend. A good place to start is the USA.gov Foreclosure page at www.usa.gov/foreclosure.

For more in-depth coverage of the foreclosure process, including variations in different areas of the country, see Chapter 2. For details about the foreclosure rules and regulations in your state, check out the appendix. If you're investing in foreclosures outside the United States, search online for a reliable government website that contains details about the foreclosure process in your area.

Picking Your Point of Entry

As a real estate investor, you can step in at any stage of the foreclosure process to acquire properties and enact other profitable transactions:

>> **Presale:** Before the property is auctioned or transferred to the trustee

>> **Sale (or auction):** When the sheriff or the court auctions the property or after control of the property is placed in the hands of the trustee

>> **Postsale:** After the lender repossesses the property, when you can purchase the property from the lender or from its REO broker

In the following sections, I describe these three entry points. For more advice on how to select the entry point that's right for you, see Chapter 3.

TIP

Begin tracking properties early in the process, even if you choose to buy properties later. By tracking properties early, you pick up on the history of what's going on and develop a clearer idea of how much to pay for the property.

Scooping other investors during the pre-auction stage

As soon as homeowners realize that they can't make their payments, you can mediate between them and their lenders to work out a mutually acceptable solution. In a few cases, you can help the homeowners keep the property, such as by negotiating a *forbearance* with the lender that provides the homeowners extra time to catch up on their payments.

Did I just say "help the homeowners keep the property"? Yes. Your long-term interest is best served by doing what's best for the homeowners. Sometimes, that means you receive no profit from your efforts. In a huge percentage of cases, however, the homeowners' best option is to sell the property and find more affordable housing arrangements. By being sincerely concerned with their best interests, you place yourself in a position to acquire the property if the homeowners can't or won't take the action necessary to keep it.

TIP

Your goal during the pre-foreclosure stage is to present the distressed homeowners all the options and enable them to make well-informed decisions. See Chapter 9 for a complete list of options.

Stepping into the foreclosure process during the pre-auction stage provides you some of the best opportunities to assist the homeowners and purchase a property at an attractive price. In Part 3, I show you exactly how to research and buy homes before homeowners lose them in foreclosure.

Bidding on properties at foreclosure auctions

Some investors prefer to step into the process at the auction stage, because they're uncomfortable dealing with distressed homeowners, who are often in a state of denial and unwilling to sit down with an investor to discuss their options. At the auction stage, you buy the property in a less-emotional atmosphere. In most cases, however, you still have to deal with the homeowners when the time comes to take possession of the property.

Now, don't run out and start scooping up properties at foreclosure auctions just yet. Uninformed investors often get burned by diving in before they learn to dog paddle. Foreclosure auctions are packed with peril, often trapping novice investors into making costly mistakes such as these:

>> **Buying a property without researching the title:** A title history reveals who really owns the property, the amount currently owed on the property, and the priority of the mortgages: tax lien (top priority), first mortgage (next in line), second mortgage, and so on. Do your research, as explained in "Performing Your Due Diligence" later in this chapter and in greater detail in Chapter 8.

>> **Buying a junior lien thinking that it's a senior lien:** When you buy properties at a foreclosure sale, you're really buying mortgages. The first mortgage on a property is called the *senior lien,* which gives the buyer the most control of the property. Additional claims against the property are called *junior liens,* which often get wiped out during foreclosure. Buy a junior lien by mistake

and you may have just bought yourself a worthless piece of paper. Only thorough research of the title, as explained in Chapter 8, can steer you clear of making this common and potentially very costly mistake.

>> **Buying a property without inspecting it:** A house may look valuable on paper, but until you see it with your own eyes, you won't know for sure. The house may have significant fire damage, toxic materials, foundation problems, or a host of other defects. Check out Chapter 8 for details.

REMEMBER

Your eyes or no buys. Never, ever buy a property without seeing it. Later, you may have a trusted member of your team check out properties for you, but when you're getting started, do the checking yourself.

>> **Paying more for a property than it's worth:** In the heat of an auction, your enthusiasm to outbid other investors can make you highly susceptible to paying more for a property than it's worth. This approach almost guarantees that you'll end up taking a loss on the property.

A MORATORIUM ON FORECLOSURES?

The COVID-19 pandemic gave foreclosure investors something new to think about: moratoriums on foreclosures and evictions. The Coronavirus Aid, Relief, and Economic Security (CARES) Act, signed into law on March 27, 2020, prohibited banks from foreclosing on government-backed loans. That prohibition expired on July 31, 2021.

The CARES Act also gave homeowners with government-backed loans the right to ask for and receive forbearance, which enabled them to stop making payments for a specified period. Although, officially, the relief applied only to federally owned or federally backed loans, many private lenders followed suit. As a result, foreclosure investors had far fewer opportunities, and some were trapped in limbo; they owned the property but couldn't evict the previous owners or move forward with repairs and renovations, and they were still responsible for paying property taxes and insurance.

Although the COVID-19 foreclosure and eviction moratoriums may be over by the time you're reading this book, keep in mind that they're always a possibility, and they're probably more likely to occur now that there's a precedent for them. They can happen at the federal, state, and local levels. This warning shouldn't discourage you from investing in foreclosures; it's just another risk to keep in mind.

>> **Failing to account for the redemption period:** Most states have a mandatory redemption period, during which time the homeowners retain possession of the property and can redeem the title by paying off the mortgage in full, along with any penalties and back taxes. You need to have enough cash reserves on hand to pay the property taxes on the property and to insure the property during this time. If you don't pay the property taxes, another investor may be able to purchase a tax lien or deed at a tax sale and take control of the property; tax liens have priority (even over first mortgages). You also need to insure the property, because you're not covered by the homeowners' insurance policy (if they have one).

REMEMBER

Never bid on a property at auction until you've done your homework. Reading this book from cover to cover is a start. Brush up on the foreclosure rules and regulations in your area, and always research a property thoroughly before bidding. Research the title, and inspect the house as closely as possible with your own two eyes, as shown in Chapter 8.

Buying properties after the sale

If working with homeowners before auction and bidding against other investors at an auction don't appeal to you, you can profit from investing in foreclosures after the foreclosure sale.

If nobody at the auction offers the minimum acceptable bid, the lender buys back the mortgage. If the state has a mandatory redemption period, the lender waits until the period expires and then passes the property to its REO department (sometimes referred to as the *OREO* [Other Real Estate Owned] department, not to be confused with the cookie), which prepares the property for resale and typically hires a mortgage broker to place it back on the market. By dealing with a lender's REO department or its mortgage broker, you may be able to purchase the property at a price that's discounted far enough below market value to turn a profit of 20 percent or more.

The chapters in Part 4 explain how to find and buy REO properties and the following other properties that government institutions and law enforcement agencies take possession of and then often sell at deep discounts:

>> Properties seized due to nonpayment of taxes

>> Properties seized by customs and law enforcement agencies because they were paid for with profits from illicit activities

- Houses that were repossessed when homeowners defaulted on HUD (U.S. Department of Housing and Urban Development) or VA (U.S. Department of Veterans Affairs) loans

- Fannie Mae and Freddie Mac properties that were repossessed and then turned over to these government-sponsored loan programs

- Bankruptcy properties that are being liquidated to pay off loans

- Properties that the U.S. Department of Transportation purchased for road improvements and must dispose of after completing the improvements

WARNING

When you buy a property from the government or a bank, don't assume that you're getting a good deal. Homes are typically sold in their "as is" condition. You must still research the title carefully and inspect the property with your own two eyes. If you see ads or late-night infomercials selling lists of bank-owned properties, don't fall for the hype; these lists are usually outdated long before they arrive in your mailbox.

Assembling a Team of Experts and Advisers

Flying solo on foreclosures may seem like a good idea. After all, any professional help you get will eat into your profits, right? Flying solo, however, is a good way to go bust or at least to limit your potential profit. Developing synergistic relationships with top-performing specialists has been a key to my success (and to the success of almost all the top real estate investors around the world).

In addition to providing expert guidance and advice for seizing opportunities and avoiding common pitfalls, experts deliver leads to potentially profitable properties, affordable financing, and quality contractors. They can assist you in managing your finances and in renovating and selling your property for top dollar after you purchase it. And, by delegating some of the workload to others who are better equipped to handle it, you free up time and resources for finding the most profitable opportunities.

In Chapter 4, I explain how to assemble a solid foreclosure investment team consisting of the following members:

- Real estate agent

- Real estate attorney

>> Mortgage broker

>> Accountant

>> Title company

>> Home inspector

>> Contractors

In Chapter 5, I lead you to sources of financial capital to fuel your investments, and in Chapter 6, I lead you through the process of developing a strong support network that virtually ensures that you'll never run out of leads on profitable foreclosure properties.

REMEMBER

With a solid team in place, you take on the role of manager and decision-maker, and you can create an efficient system that minimizes risk while maximizing profit.

Getting Your Financial Ducks in a Row

In real estate, cash is king. In foreclosure investing, cash is the grand, high-exalted mystic ruler. Investment capital enables you to step in at any stage of the foreclosure process and buy out anyone who has a claim on or an interest in the property.

REMEMBER

When I say *cash*, I'm not talking about the money you have stuffed in your mattress. I'm talking about borrowing certified funds from a bank or other lending institution or from a private investor. See Chapter 5 for details.

Cash gives you the upper hand with the four Cs:

» **Credibility:** With cash, you have instant credibility that you can deliver on your promises without hesitation. In most cases, homeowners need cash to escape their current financial crisis. Lenders need cash to cut their losses. With cash on hand, you can give homeowners and lenders what they need to achieve their goals while you take possession of a profitable property.

» **Confidence:** Cash provides you the confidence to pitch offers to homeowners and lienholders, knowing that you can deliver in a timely manner.

» **Creativity:** Putting together a foreclosure deal that satisfies all parties often requires a great deal of creativity. With sufficient capital, you liberate your imagination from financial limitations.

» **Competitiveness:** Multiple real estate investors often compete for the same property. Cash gives you a competitive edge because it enables you to execute a deal much more quickly. Both homeowners and lenders are eager to put the current crisis behind them. An ability to act quickly often separates the successful investor from the wannabes.

The question "Where am I going to get the money?" often derails the novice investor before the train leaves the station, but many of the most successful investors started with only a few bucks in their pockets, including yours truly.

REMEMBER

Don't let a lack of investment capital discourage you. In Chapter 5, I explain how to estimate just how much money you need to get started; then I steer you toward sources of capital that can fuel your foreclosure investments. At first, the cost of investment capital (mostly interest) may chip away at your profits, but as you develop a stronger financial position, the cost of money gradually decreases.

Finding Foreclosures and Seized Properties

The first step in foreclosure investing — finding potentially profitable properties — is often the most difficult for first-time investors. Plenty of foreclosures and seized properties are available, but where do you look for them? The answer to that question varies depending on which part of the foreclosure process you choose to focus on, but here's a list of where you can find leads on foreclosure properties:

- The neighborhood grapevine, including neighbors, churches, cafes, clubs, and even people who contact you directly for assistance when they know that you buy distressed properties

- Auctioneers

- County offices, especially the sheriff's office

- Drive-bys (driving through neighborhoods looking for *dontwanners* — homes that are unkempt, indicating that the owners don't want them)

- Foreclosure notices in local papers or legal publications

- Bankruptcy notices in local papers or legal publications

- Divorce filings and decrees in publicly accessible court documents

- Foreclosure listing services (websites that list foreclosure and government-seized properties)

- Government-owned listings (see a list of links to the top government sites at www.hud.gov/topics/homes_for_sale)

- Real estate agents

- Attorneys, particularly bankruptcy, divorce, and probate attorneys

- Banks and other lenders

Online foreclosure information services range from excellent to total rip-off. Some services deliver timely information; others deliver out-of-date information that's totally useless. In the beginning, dig up leads the old-fashioned way: through networking and research.

TIP

Word-of-mouth leads are often the best leads. Make sure that everyone you know and meet knows that you purchase distressed properties and work with people who are facing foreclosure. Some investors have so many distressed homeowners contacting them for assistance in foreclosure that they don't even need to look for properties. See Chapter 6 for networking tips.

Performing Your Due Diligence

After you find a potentially profitable foreclosure property, the real work begins: performing your due diligence to avoid getting burned. To protect yourself from the many inherent risks of foreclosure investing, dig up the essential facts and figures so that you know what you're buying and what it's worth, as well as your options for purchasing the property for less to maximize your profit.

Thorough research requires you to dig up the following essential information:

» Names of the homeowners

» Amount owed on the property

» Lienholder names and contact information

» Physical condition of the property

» Homeowners' current situations and motivations

» Market value of the property

The following sections introduce you to the types of research to perform as part of your due diligence, but proper research requires much more than I can cover in this chapter. For additional details, see chapter 8.

Investigating the property's title and other documentation

Before you commit to purchasing a property, you need to know who really owns it, how much the current owners owe on it, to whom they owe the money, how much they owe (if anything) in back taxes, and whether the property has any *encumbrances* (liens, judgments, or zoning restrictions). In short, you need to know what you're getting yourself into before you get yourself into it.

Fortunately, most of the following critical documentation about a property is publicly and easily accessible if you're working with a title company (which I recommend):

» **Title:** The title shows the names of the property owners and lienholders and any legal judgments on the property. I once purchased a property from a mother and daughter, only to discover later that the daughter from whom I bought the property wasn't the daughter who owned it. The owner daughter eventually took possession of the property, and I was left with some nasty, time-consuming legal battles. By checking the title, you can avoid similar mistakes.

» **Title history:** A title company can provide you with a title history that shows the change of ownership over the years. In some cases, this history reveals gaps in the transfer of the property from one homeowner to the next. A gap in the history may be a warning that someone else can lay claim to the property later and take you to court.

>> **Property history:** Your town or city keeps a history of every property, including all building permits issued on the property. If the property has an additional structure that was built without a permit, it may not have been built to code. Any information you can gather about the history of the property can assist you later in evaluating its market value and spotting any red flags.

WARNING

Never purchase a property without fully researching its title and any other public documents recorded on that property. In Chapter 8, I guide you through the process of researching a property and assembling a detailed dossier, which is essential for making sound investment decisions.

Inspecting the property with your own eyes

Tattoo the following message on your forehead: *My eyes, or no buys.* You can look at the title work and other property documents until your eyes cross, but you don't know the condition of the property unless you see it for yourself. I recommend that you do the following:

>> **Visit the property and the neighborhood it's in.** Never try to assess the value of a property in a vacuum. The condition of the neighborhood affects the sale price.

>> **Walk around the property and inspect it from all four sides.** The front of the house can look like the Taj Mahal while the back or sides look more like a bombed-out bunker. See Chapter 8 for additional suggestions on doing drive-by and walk-around inspections.

>> **If possible, get inside and look around.** You don't want to get arrested for trespassing or run off by an angry homeowner, but if the homeowner invites you in, accept the invitation.

TIP

If the house is currently listed with a broker, make an appointment to view it. This approach is an excellent way to get the inside scoop without being accused of trespassing or voyeurism! You don't have to tell the broker what you know about the property, why you're interested in it, or anything else that might increase the asking price.

See Chapter 8 for more tips on inspecting the property with your own two eyes.

TIP

This cursory inspection offers you only a glimpse of the property, and in foreclosure investing, that's all you get sometimes, especially if you're buying the property at an auction. When buying a property directly from the homeowners before auction, make your offer conditional upon a satisfactory inspection, and have the property professionally inspected before closing. This inspection will uncover any costly defects and give you a ballpark estimate of the cost of repairs and renovations needed to bring the property up to market value. If the property requires repairs, try to negotiate a price reduction instead of canceling the deal. If the estimated cost of repairs is $5,000, for example, try to get a reduction of $6,000.

Guesstimating a property's true value

An essential component of successful real estate investing is developing an exit strategy or endgame. Before you agree to pay a certain price for a property, you must have a fairly accurate estimate of what you can sell it for. Otherwise, you risk overpaying and losing money on your investment.

Estimating the market value of a house is easiest with the assistance of a real estate agent who's knowledgeable about property values in the area. A qualified agent can pull up Multiple Listing Service (MLS) sheets on comparable homes that have recently sold in the same neighborhood and quickly provide you a good idea of how much you can sell the property for, assuming that it's in marketable condition and the market remains relatively stable.

Don't let your agent or the word on the street pump up your expectations or estimates. Tell your agent that you want an estimated sales price based on reality, not hope. Provide your agent as many details as possible about the property to ensure that the estimate is based on truly comparable properties.

REMEMBER

Never enter into a real estate deal unless you have at least two exit strategies: Plan A, typically for selling the property at a profit, and Plan B, just in case Plan A doesn't pan out. Your Plan B may be to lease the property, live in it, or sell it for slightly less than you planned to sell it for, but you should always have a Plan B, because real estate transactions and markets aren't always predictable.

Investigating the situation and the homeowners

The more you know about the homeowners and their situation, the better able you are to assist them in extricating themselves from their current predicament. Unfortunately, homeowners who are facing foreclosure often feel isolated, ashamed, resentful, and defensive. They may not be very forthcoming about the details that landed them in their current situation, and they may see you as merely an opportunist who's trying to sell their property out from under them.

In a way, they're right. You *do* want the property, and you want to make a profit. But that doesn't change the fact that the homeowners are trapped and need to explore their options. Your job at this stage is to convince the homeowners that they'll see better results working with you than with someone who's not quite on the level. In Chapter 9, I show you how to approach distressed homeowners and explain their options.

When you meet with homeowners, listen at least twice as much as you talk, and try to gather the information like the following that can enable you to provide more valuable guidance and assistance:

>> The total amount owed on the first mortgage and all other liens on the property, including any back taxes owed

>> The current monthly payment on the house and on any other outstanding loans

>> The names and contact information for all lienholders (lenders, contractors, and others who have a claim on the property)

>> The amount of time before the property goes up for auction

>> The value of any possessions the homeowners have that can be liquidated

>> A list of any family members who may be able to help

>> A clear idea of what the homeowners see as their options, such as selling the house, moving to a rental unit, relocating, or scaling down to a smaller house

This brief list can start you on your information–gathering mission, but as you talk with the homeowners, other issues and opportunities often present themselves. Create a thorough record of your discussions with the homeowners so that you can begin to paint a portrait of them in your mind. The more information you have, the more creative you can be in developing viable solutions. See Chapter 9 for additional details.

Setting and Sticking To Your Maximum Bid

Even the coldest and most calculating real estate investors become enthusiastic about properties. They may fall in love with a particular house or simply get so caught up in the heat of an auction that they bid too much for a property. Then they have to work twice as hard to make a profit on it.

REMEMBER

Before you bid on a property or make an offer to the homeowners, you should have a clear idea of how much you can afford to pay for a property to earn the desired return on your investment — usually, no less than 20 percent. Write down the amount, and make a firm commitment to yourself to stick to it. Bid or offer no more than your upper limit, no matter how hyped you become during the bidding or negotiations.

In Chapter 10, I show you how to set the maximum price you'll pay for a property when preparing an offer to purchase directly from homeowners. In Chapter 11, I lead you through the process of preparing a maximum bid for an auction and let you in on some strategies for effective bidding.

Taking Possession of the Property

When you buy a house, you usually expect to move into it on the agreed-upon date. You and the seller sign a purchase agreement in which the seller agrees to vacate the premises and turn over the keys on a specified date. Sometimes, the buyer requests possession at closing. In other cases, the seller agrees to move out one or two weeks later.

With foreclosures, the transfer of a property can be a long, drawn-out, and messy affair. In some areas, you take immediate possession of a property as soon as you offer the winning bid and pay the trustee or courtroom clerk. In other cases, the homeowners retain possession of the property for the duration of the redemption period, which can last up to a year in some areas.

WARNING

While you're waiting for the redemption period to expire, you may be tempted to start working on the house. Don't. You may invest $10,000 in renovations only to have the property owners decide to redeem the property just before you wrap up the project. They may thank you for the free $10,000 in renovations, but don't count on it.

Even when the redemption period is over, you have no guarantee that the previous homeowners are going to vacate the premises in a quiet, orderly fashion when their time runs out. In some cases, you can gently encourage the homeowners to move out. In other cases, you must have them forcibly evicted (by the sheriff, not you), which is always a painful process for all parties.

In the following sections, I provide an overview of what to do to take formal ownership of a property and eventually take possession of it. In Chapter 16, I reveal your responsibilities as the new owner and cover the eviction process in more detail.

Completing the essential paperwork

When you purchase a property directly from the homeowners, you and the sellers attend a closing in which a title company's agent or an attorney shuffle all the paperwork and file the necessary records.

When you purchase a property at an auction or sheriff's sale, however, you receive the deed, which you must then record at the Register of Deeds office to have your name officially added to the title. See Chapter 11 for details.

TIP

After dropping off the deed to have it recorded, make sure that you obtain title insurance to protect you from any hidden claims against the property. Some title companies don't offer title insurance for foreclosure properties or properties you pick up at a sheriff's sale.

Paying property taxes and insurance

As soon as you purchase a property, either from the homeowners or at an auction, you become the official owner of the property, even though you may not be able to take immediate possession of it. As owner, you're in charge of insuring the property and paying property taxes. Be sure to do the following:

>> Call your insurance agent to obtain a homeowner's insurance policy for the property.

>> Pay the property taxes as soon as they're due. (You may need to pay back taxes when you purchase the property.)

DON'T FORGET THE INSURANCE

As soon as you buy a foreclosure, even if you can't take possession of it right away, call your insurance agent and buy a homeowner's insurance policy for the property.

I once purchased for $75,000 a house that was worth $150,000. By the time I took possession of the property, the previous owners had taken the carpeting, the entire kitchen (including the sink), the bathroom fixtures, the furnace, the central air conditioning unit, the doors, and everything else they could carry out, hoping to stick it to the next owners. I turned the claim in to my insurance carrier, received $25,000, and sold the house to another investor for $100,000. After expenses and holding costs, I walked away with about $35,000.

The investor who bought the property decided to rent it instead of selling right away. He refinanced to pull about $50,000 equity out of the property, used the equity to cover repair and renovation costs, and still had a little money left over. Then he rented the property to cover his mortgage payments.

>> File an affidavit proving that you paid the insurance and property taxes. If the homeowners decide to redeem the property, an affidavit enables you to recover any taxes and insurance payments you made during the redemption period.

See Chapter 16 for details concerning your responsibilities as a homeowner during the redemption period.

Persuading the current residents to move on

As the official owner and soon-to-be possessor of the property, your goal is to encourage the homeowners to move out without trashing the place or forcing you to evict them. You want the property to be broom-clean and in the same condition it was in when you first inspected it — or better. The key to success in this area is providing the homeowners an easy exit. Following are some suggested perks for assisting the homeowners out the door:

>> Offer cash for keys and a *nonredemption certificate* — a signed agreement that the homeowners promise not to redeem the property.

>> Provide a dumpster in which the homeowners can toss anything they don't want to move.

>> Offer to pay for a moving van, or pay a portion of their relocation costs.

>> Offer to pay the first month's rent on a rental unit.

WARNING

Don't hand over the cash until you get what you need. I've experienced several incidents in which homeowners took cash, agreed to move out, and then stayed put. Chapter 16 offers some additional suggestions along with instructions on how to have homeowners who resist moving out evicted.

Cashing Out: Realizing Your Profit

Assuming that you purchase a property for the right price, you've already profited from it, but you won't see that profit until you cash out your chips. Various cash-out strategies are available, as I discuss in Part 5. The following sections provide a brief overview of your cash-out options.

Repairing and renovating the property to maximize its value

The most common way to maximize your profit is to repair and renovate the property and then place it back on the market in the shortest possible time. Time is of the essence, because every day you hold a property costs you — in monthly payments (if you financed the purchase), property taxes, insurance, and utilities.

TIP

The trick to repairing and renovating a property cost-effectively, as I explain in Chapter 17, is planning well in advance and improving the property only enough to meet or slightly exceed the going price. Transforming a $150,000 property into a $250,000 property in a neighborhood where most homes sell for around $150,000 is a huge mistake. Buyers who want a $250,000 house buy in a $250,000 neighborhood.

Marketing and selling to get top dollar

Your goal in selling a house is to sell it quickly at a price that's close to its market value. To accomplish that goal, follow these marketing guidelines:

- » **Set the price right the first time.** Don't set a super-high price hoping that the fish will bite. Your investment property is likely to linger on the market, during which time holding costs will continue to chip away at your profit. An asking price that's in line with comparably priced homes is best.

- » **Get the word out through a successful real estate agent.** If you're thinking of saving money on real estate commissions by selling the house yourself, think again. Homes sell in about half the time and for more money through a real estate agent. What you may save in commissions, you end up losing through holding costs and by having to sell for a lower price.

- » **Begin marketing as soon as you take possession.** Marketing begins as soon as you begin your renovations, especially if you start renovating the exterior first. Neighbors notice and begin to gossip, and word-of-mouth advertising begins to take off.

- » **Plant a For Sale sign on the front lawn when renovations are nearing completion.** A For Sale sign removes all doubt that the house is for sale.

- » **Stage the house impeccably.** Clean and scrub inside and out, mow the lawn, freshen the landscape, remove the clutter, tastefully furnish and decorate the interior, set out fresh bouquets of flowers, and let the buyers stream in.

For additional tips and strategies to sell your property quickly and for top dollar, check out Chapter 18.

Cashing out equity by refinancing

When you purchase a property for less than its market value, you automatically have equity in the property. Renovations that bring the property up to its market value may add more equity, assuming that you don't overspend.

You can cash out the equity by refinancing it for more than you paid for it to real-ize your profit almost immediately. Keep in mind, however, that by refinancing for more than the purchase price, you take on a larger mortgage, and the increased interest chips away at your total profit over time. Refinancing, however, does pro-vide you capital to fuel your next investment or cover the cost of renovations. For more about refinancing to cash out equity, see Chapter 19.

Profiting in other ways

Selling and refinancing are two of the quickest and most common ways to realize the profit from foreclosures, but other strategies are available:

>> Negotiate a short sale. With a short sale, you persuade lenders to accept less than they're owed, which increases equity in the property, providing you creative ways to help the distressed homeowners out of their jam. (See Chapter 15.)

>> Lease the property to renters other than the previous homeowners. (See Chapter 18.)

>> Lease the property back to its previous owners. (See Chapter 19.)

>> Sell the property to the homeowners' family members. (See Chapter 19.)

>> Sell your position in the property to another lienholder. If you control the first mortgage, for example, you can sell it at a markup to a construction company that has a lien against the property so that the company can protect its interest in the property; otherwise, it risks losing all the money it's owed. (See Chapter 19.)

how foreclosures are handled

» **Investigating the early missed-payment pre-foreclosure period**

» **Finding opportunities in the Notice of Default stage**

» **Arriving at the foreclosure auction stage**

» **Waiting out post-foreclosure, from redemption to eviction**

Chapter **2**

Getting Up to Speed on the Foreclosure Process

A common foreclosure myth is that it's a one-time event. Homeowners miss a mortgage payment or two, and the lender swoops in and scoops up the property. The fact is that foreclosure is typically a long, drawn-out legal process that begins with missed payments, proceeds through some sort of legal system, and often results in homeowners losing their homes.

An understanding of the foreclosure process reveals the various stages at which you can purchase properties. By knowing what to expect, you can often maximize your opportunities while minimizing costly mistakes.

This chapter provides a road map of the foreclosure process, beginning with a notice to the homeowners and the public of missed mortgage payments and ending with the homeowners relinquishing possession of the property. Anywhere along the way, the homeowners have options to interrupt the process and regain control of the property. I point out these opportunities to help you better assist homeowners in making choices and to warn you about what homeowners can do to derail your plans.

TIP

Homeowners find themselves facing foreclosure for any number of reasons, including long-term illness or disability, overspending, substance abuse, divorce, and gambling, to mention only a few. As a real estate investor, you gain nothing by judging people in foreclosure. The best way to approach homeowners in foreclosure is with respect and empathy, offering solutions that enable them to leave the past behind and build a more solid financial future.

Identifying the Foreclosure Process in Your Area

The end result of foreclosure is that the homeowners lose ownership and ultimately lose possession of their property. That's true no matter where you're buying foreclosure properties. But different states and counties follow different foreclosure procedures. The two main procedures are

» Foreclosure by trustee sale, also referred to as *foreclosure by advertisement*

» Foreclosure by judicial sale, also referred to as *judicial foreclosure*

The following sections describe these two types of foreclosure. To find out which process your state follows, check the appendix at the back of this book. Counties may also have their own local rules for how the sale is carried out, so visit your county courthouse (the Register of Deeds office), and ask for an explanation of the rules and regulations. I also recommend that you sit in on a few auctions before bidding on anything.

Foreclosure by trustee sale

A few more than half the states follow the trustee-sale route. When the homeowners purchase a property in one of these states, the county issues a sheriff's deed that the trustee (which may be the sheriff in some areas) holds in trust until the mortgage is paid in full. After paying off the mortgage, the trustee releases the deed to the homeowners.

If the homeowners default on the payment, the lender can notify the trustee to initiate foreclosure proceedings. Then the trustee can sell the property and transfer the proceeds to the lender as payment of the loan. Because the foreclosure doesn't need to progress through the courts, foreclosure by trustee sale is typically much faster than foreclosure by judicial sale.

Foreclosure by judicial sale

Fewer than half the states follow a judicial foreclosure process. As the name implies, judicial foreclosure passes through the justice system: the state (circuit) or district court. When the homeowners default on their mortgage, the lender files a claim to recover the unpaid balance of the loan from the borrowers. The courts decide the case, which usually takes a long time to resolve — typically four to six months, but sometimes up to a year. During this time, unless the homeowners work out a payment plan or some other solution with the lender, they're almost guaranteed to lose their home.

Exploring the Missed-Payment Notice Stage

Some lenders initiate foreclosure proceedings as soon as the homeowners miss one or two payments. Other lenders start sending reminder notices, often following a predictable timeline:

>> **Two-week notice:** Some lenders give homeowners a two-week grace period, after which they begin to start calling the homeowners or sending them letters.

>> **30-day notice:** When a payment is so late that it's time for the next payment, the lender gets a little jittery and ramps up its efforts. The lender may even begin levying late-payment fees.

>> **45-to-60 days' notice:** Unless the homeowners contact the lender and work out some new payment agreement, the lender typically sends out a certified letter insisting that the homeowners pay up.

>> **90-day limit:** If the homeowners still haven't contacted the lender or shown any commitment to make good on the loan, the lender typically initiates formal foreclosure proceedings. At this point, the lender transfers the matter to outside legal counsel (an attorney), and the attorney in charge posts a foreclosure notice, sometimes referred to as a Notice of Default (NOD). As soon as the attorney starts foreclosure by advertisement, these legal notices or advertisements begin to attract investors.

REMEMBER

The missed-payment notice stage, before the start of foreclosure proceedings, is the best time for homeowners to act and the best time for you to step in to assist them. In 90 percent or more of the foreclosures I've been involved in, the homeowners' best option is to sell the property, cut their losses, and find more-affordable housing. With your assistance, the homeowners still have time at this stage to take advantage of this option.

Getting Serious: The Notice of Default

For investors, the foreclosure process officially kicks off with the posting of the NOD or foreclosure notice in the county's legal newspaper or the local newspaper — private, for-profit publications that get the word out to prospective bidders. At this point, distressed homeowners usually realize the inevitability of losing their property. Some remain in denial; others become resigned to the fact, even though they may have several options to abort the foreclosure process and regain control of their property . . . and their finances.

TIP

If you plan on purchasing properties before the foreclosure sale, your best chance is to contact the homeowners before the NOD is posted. After the NOD appears in the papers or in legal publications, competition for the property begins to heat up. The only way to find distressed homeowners before the NOD is posted is through word-of-mouth networking. See Chapter 3 for additional guidance on choosing the stage of the foreclosure process that's right for you, and see Chapter 6 for word-of-mouth networking tips.

Proceeding to the Foreclosure Sale

Before the foreclosure sale, the homeowners can work with the lender or their attorney to delay or cancel the foreclosure sale. In other words, just because you see a foreclosure notice in the local paper doesn't mean that if you show up for the sale, that property is going to be auctioned off.

TIP

Calling the attorney who's in charge of the foreclosure before the sale is a great way to find out whether the property is going to be offered at the sale. The attorney's name is usually listed on the foreclosure notice. In Chapter 7, I show you how to pick out important details on the foreclosure notice.

At the foreclosure sale, you have an opportunity to bid against other investors for any properties that are being auctioned off. As I explain in Chapter 11, some auctions have open bidding; others use a sealed bid system. However your county chooses to hold its auctions, a few words of advice can assist you in acquiring properties and not losing your shirt:

>> Sit in on at least five auctions before bidding to get a feel for the process and to gather information.

>> Research the property thoroughly before you bid. In Chapter 8, I explain how to build a file for each property, packed with useful details.

>> Buy only senior liens (first mortgages). You can really get burned buying junior liens, because foreclosure typically wipes them off the books. When you have more experience and knowledge, you can start working the junior-lien circuit and tax liens, as I discuss in Chapter 15.

>> Set a maximum bid, and never ever exceed that amount, no matter how juiced up you get at the auction. See Chapter 11 for details on calculating your maximum bid.

>> When you plan to bid, show up with a cashier's check. Most auctions require payment at time of purchase or within an hour. For additional information on paying for a property after the auction, check out Chapter 11.

Halting the Foreclosure Process

Distressed homeowners are plagued by a swarm of emotions, ranging from disbelief and resentment to shame and guilt. They may have several options to stop the foreclosure process, but they're too upset and confused to think clearly or explore their options, and they're so angry or fearful that they hesitate to contact the lender to work out a solution.

In the following sections, I introduce various ways that homeowners in foreclosure can stop or delay the foreclosure process. Use this information not only to better assist distressed homeowners, but also to prepare yourself for the possibility that the homeowners may choose to cut you out of a promising deal by successfully negotiating with the lender or another investor.

TIP

Encourage the homeowners to contact their lender, even if this action results in your losing a prospective property. Never supply misleading information to discourage homeowners from taking the action that's best for them. Be a real estate investor, not a con artist. In addition to keeping you out of legal trouble, acting with integrity establishes goodwill with the homeowners and leads to future referrals, as I point out in greater detail in Chapter 21.

A SMOOTH OPERATOR

I once purchased a property at a sheriff sale and did everything I could to contact the homeowner. I even tried to drop in for a personal visit, but she slammed the door in my face as though she knew who I was and had been expecting me.

Later, I discovered that a con artist named Brian had gotten to her during the redemption period. He established some sort of emotional connection with the homeowner, took her to the county building to pick up the overbid (the money I paid for the property at auction in excess of what was owed on it), and convinced her that he could save her house for her.

Brian bought her a vacuum cleaner and a few groceries in exchange for her signature on a *quitclaim deed* — a document signing away her rights to the property. He video-taped her making statements that he thought would protect him legally.

With quitclaim deed in hand, Brian redeemed the property, and I got my money back. Then he sold the property to an investor named Ray. Ray came to my office. Without knowing what had transpired, I bought the property and sold it to another investor. When that investor showed up at the homeowner's house to work out a rental agreement with her, he learned about the con job and wanted nothing to do with the property.

Eventually, the matter wound up in court. I bought the property back from the other investor and gave the homeowner some money so that she could move to a more-affordable home. While in court, I got a $100,000 judgment against Brian. Last I heard, Brian was scheduled for a creditors' hearing.

Never take advantage of homeowners for your own benefit. After all, this property is their home, and any equity they have in that home is theirs. Commit to becoming a champion of the homeowners. If you can help them and earn some compensation for your assistance, everybody wins. Quick money never lasts. By acting with integrity and in the best interest of the homeowners, you provide a much-needed service to a suffering portion of your community.

Reinstating the mortgage

Before the foreclosure auction, homeowners who can get their hands on enough cash may have the option to *reinstate the mortgage*, which consists of making up for all missed payments and paying any late fees or other penalties.

To reinstate the mortgage, the homeowners must contact the lender before the auction date to verify that reinstatement is an option. If the option is available, the homeowners must work out a payment schedule with their lender.

TIP

If you're trying to assist distressed homeowners in finding a solution and you're running out of time, the homeowners can file for bankruptcy to buy more time. See "Filing for bankruptcy" later in this chapter for details.

Requesting and receiving a forbearance

When homeowners have a temporary loss of income with the promise of regaining their financial footing, the lender may agree to a *forbearance*, in which the homeowners can delay payment for a short period or negotiate a payment plan to make up for missed payments over the course of several months, as explained in the following section.

The lender may also offer some sort of combination between a forbearance and reinstatement, enabling homeowners to delay payment for a short period and then bring their payments current by a specific date.

TIP

The phone number on the mortgage payment coupons may put you in contact with the loan servicer that processes the payments instead of the lender that actually owns the loan. The loan servicer may not offer much assistance, so ask the loan servicer who the lender is and contact the lender directly.

Mortgage modification or repayment plan

To enable financially strapped homeowners to make up missed payments slowly, a lender may agree to a mortgage modification or repayment plan:

>> A *mortgage modification* consists of adding the past-due payments and penalties to the remaining principal, so the homeowners pay off the past-due amounts and penalties over the life of the loan. This arrangement is commonly known as adding amounts due to the back of the loan.

>> A repayment plan enables the homeowners to submit payment of a portion of their past-due amount and penalties with future payments until the past-due amount and penalties are paid off.

When homeowners are already having trouble making their monthly mortgage payments and don't have the resources to cover higher payments, mortgage modification and repayment plans are rarely ideal solutions. Often, these options simply delay the inevitable.

Filing for bankruptcy

Filing for bankruptcy sounds like a permanent solution to a significant financial predicament like foreclosure, but it's not the ideal solution. It destroys the homeowner's credit rating for seven years or so and doesn't exactly wipe all debt off the books. Bankruptcy simply relieves some of the debt burden and provides homeowners some extra time to restructure their remaining debt.

Bankruptcy is one more option for distressed homeowners, however, and it's certainly something you should know about as a foreclosure investor. By filing for bankruptcy at least a couple of days before the auction date, a homeowner can delay the foreclosure process and leave a property that you've already purchased in limbo — at least until the foreclosure trustee and the courts sort out all the legal issues.

TIP

Bankruptcy is another opportunity for real estate investors. As the trustee or courts decide how to liquidate the property, you may be able to step in and work with the lawyers and trustee to purchase the property and make their lives a little easier. Chapter 14 explains how to acquire properties in bankruptcy.

Agreeing to a deed in lieu of foreclosure

When homeowners have very little to no equity or even negative equity built up in their property, and they have no hope of turning the financial tide, they may offer the lender a *deed in lieu of foreclosure.* The homeowners agree to sign their deed over to the lender and give them the keys to the property without having to go through a messy public foreclosure process.

Although this approach may give the homeowners a less-embarrassing escape route, it often leaves the lender with a property that it doesn't want, along with the expense of repairing and rehabbing the property and then selling it. As an investor, you may be able to step in as the ultimate middleman, negotiate with the lender, getting it to accept less than the full loan amount due (what real estate insiders call a *short sale*), and still provide the homeowner a clear escape route.

TIP

Some investors around the country make a really good living just working short sales. If you can't purchase a foreclosure property for a low-enough price to make a profit, negotiating a short sale can make the deal more profitable. Keep in mind, however, that lenders won't agree to short sales if they foresee the homeowners walking away with money, and you shouldn't negotiate a lower payoff to put money in the pockets of the homeowners. See Chapter 15 for details.

Getting one last chance during the redemption period

Reasonable people would assume that when they buy a property at a foreclosure sale, it's automatically their property, but that's not always the case. Many areas of the country have a mandatory redemption period, which can last from a few months to an entire year. Check out the appendix at the back of this book to find out about the redemption period in your area.

During the redemption period, the person who purchased the property at the sale is responsible for insuring the property and paying the property taxes, but the foreclosed-upon homeowners have the right to redeem the property. To do so, the homeowners must come up with enough cash to pay off the mortgage in full, along with any interest and penalties and, in some cases, the investor's expenses.

WARNING

Depending on the rules that govern redemption in your area, the buyer may or may not have the right to recover expenses (including property taxes and insurance) from the homeowners. Consult your real estate attorney to find out exactly what you're allowed to recover if the homeowners redeem the property.

If you purchase a property at a foreclosure sale in an area that has a mandatory redemption period, you end up with the property about 50 percent of the time. The only sure way to end up with the property is to buy in markets that don't have redemption periods. (Check out the appendix at the back of the book to determine whether your state has a mandatory redemption period.) To protect your investment in areas that have a redemption period, take the following precautions:

>> If possible, repair any defects in the house that may be considered to be unsafe or lead to further deterioration of the property. If the property is vacant and unsafe, and you don't take care of the problem immediately, the property is likely to lose value. Avoid investing any more money in repairs than is absolutely necessary; if someone redeems the property, you stand to lose that money.

>> Insure the house and file an affidavit of payment so that if the homeowners redeem the property, you have a better chance of recouping your expenses. Consult your real estate attorney to determine your rights to recover expenses.

>> Pay the property taxes, and file an affidavit proving payment.

>> Don't invest in any renovations. If the homeowners redeem the property, you could lose all the money you invested in the renovations. Generally, you perform repairs only to protect your investment if the house is vacant or if you've worked out an arrangement with the occupants to ensure that you won't lose any money you invest in the property. Different states may have different abandonment laws that may restrict you from doing anything. Your real estate attorney can provide guidance here.

>> Keep an eye on the property to protect it from vandalism and theft. Some disgruntled homeowners may strip the property before vacating it.

For additional advice on surviving the redemption period, see Chapter 16.

TIP

All sales aren't final in areas with redemption periods. If you miss out on an opportunity during the foreclosure sale, you haven't necessarily lost the property for good. The homeowners still control the property, and you can work with them to bump the investor who purchased the property out of the deal. The knife cuts both ways, of course: You could end up getting bumped. You get your money back, but you lose out on the property.

LOSING OUT ON A JUNIOR LIEN

I bought a first mortgage (senior lien) at the first foreclosure sale on a property for $25,000. Another investor bought the second mortgage (junior lien) for $25,000. Thinking that he had the property in the bag, he spent another $25,000 during the redemption period renovating the house, so now he had $50,000 invested in a property that was worth about $100,000.

That sounds like a good deal, but the investor made a huge mistake: He failed to pay off the senior lien, which I held. He could have redeemed the $25,000 senior lien that I held, sold the property for $100,000, and made a $25,000 profit, but he forgot to redeem the senior lien.

I took possession of the house and put it up for sale. The other investor called, understandably upset because he was convinced that the house was his. I had to explain that due to his oversight, the house was not in fact his, but mine.

The moral of the story is that if you buy a junior lien attempting to control the senior lien, be sure that you redeem that senior lien.

Finalizing the Foreclosure: Ushering the Previous Owners Out the Door

Eviction is an unpleasant experience for both the evictor and the evictee, so you want to do everything you can, within reason, to encourage the previous homeowners to vacate voluntarily. Offer them an incentive package — a free dumpster, use of a moving van, relocation expenses, or whatever else they need — to put this problem behind them and move on to a potentially rosier future.

If that approach doesn't work, you have no option but to file a request with the district court to have the homeowners evicted. After you file your request, assuming that it's approved, the sheriff's office delivers the homeowners an eviction notice stating the date on which the eviction will occur. On that date, if the homeowners haven't vacated the premises, the sheriff shows up to forcibly remove them and their belongings, and you formally take possession of the property.

PUTTING SOME EMPATHY IN EVICTION

I knew an investor who reveled in evictions. He would drive to the eviction site, park his red Porsche in front of the house, and make fun of the people being evicted. He even went so far as to take photographs and hang them on his office wall. The company he worked for was doing a billion dollars' worth of business annually, so maybe that fact made this cold-hearted investor feel justified, but the only real justice was what finally happened to him and all the senior management at his company: The U.S. Securities and Exchange Commission investigated its business practices and found the company guilty of several counts of mortgage fraud. The investor received a four-year sentence in a federal prison.

When you have to evict homeowners, do it with heart. Put yourself in their shoes and try to appreciate how you'd feel in a similar situation or how you'd feel if one of your family members was being evicted. If possible, rent a moving truck for the homeowners, and help them pack and load their possessions. Whatever you do, don't cause additional pain while you're getting your gain.

» Chasing foreclosure notices: pros and cons

» Scoping out properties at foreclosure auctions

» Tracking down bank- and government-owned properties

Chapter 3

Picking Your Point of Entry in the Foreclosure Process

Foreclosure investing encompasses much more than simply buying properties for pennies on the dollar at a foreclosure auction. The foreclosure process often takes three months to a year to run its course, and investors can step in at any time to scoop up a property. In fact, investors can even step in before official foreclosure proceedings begin and (in some areas) months after they wrap up.

TIP

Although you can buy properties at numerous stages in the foreclosure process, I recommend that you become a specialist in one area first. Focus on pre-auction properties, auctions, or post-auctions so you can become an expert in one area. You can branch out later, as you become more experienced, develop better connections, and strengthen your investment team and your financial position.

In this chapter, I reveal the various entry points in the foreclosure process, covering everything from pre-auction to post-redemption, also known as Real Estate Owned (REO) opportunities. I point out the pros and cons of investing at each stage so that you can make a well-informed decision about where you'd like to begin your journey in foreclosure investing.

Dipping In at the Pre-Auction Stage

Homeowners often feel reluctant to take action when they first get an inkling of financial foreboding. Instead of contacting their lenders, an attorney, or a real estate agent who specializes in foreclosures to seek advice and try to work out a solution, they often stick their heads in the sand and hope the problem goes away. By the time they act, they're usually too late. Behind on their house payments, drowning in credit card debt, and unable to pay back taxes, they sealed their fate months before the bank initiated foreclosure proceedings.

When the bank finally moves forward to foreclose, the homeowners are often in a panic. They don't know what to do or where to go for reliable information. As a foreclosure investor, you can step into the process, provide homeowners options to cut their losses, and perhaps even help them retain possession of their property.

TIP

You may think that doing everything you can to enable homeowners to retain possession of their property is contrary to the idea of profiting from foreclosures. In about 90 percent of pre-auction foreclosures, however, the homeowners are too deep in debt and must sell their home. By acting with integrity, you give yourself a much better chance of obtaining the property . . . and doing some good at the same time. See Chapter 21 for specific ways you can assist distressed homeowners.

Exploring the pros and cons of pre-auction foreclosures

Although you can certainly wait for the foreclosure auction to roll around, the pre-auction stage offers several benefits to foreclosure investors:

>> Less competition from other investors.

>> More options for negotiating deals with homeowners and their lenders.

>> More time to put together a deal and close on the house.

>> Increased opportunity to inspect the condition of the house, inside and out.

>> No redemption period or other legal issues at the end that can sink the deal. When you close on the property, it's yours. You may have to wait a week or two to take possession, depending on your agreement with the homeowners, but you don't have to wait three months to a year for the redemption period to expire. For more about redemption, skip to the section at the end of this chapter called "Waiting Out the Redemption Period — If Necessary."

At this point, you're probably ready to dive into the pre-auction stage and start scooping up properties from homeowners who are eager to shed the financial burden. But before you leap, consider some of the following drawbacks of buying directly from homeowners:

>> Emotional fallout, including anger and resentment, from the loss of a home

>> Complications of dealing with other people's financial messes

>> Misleading information or outright lies from homeowners who are desperate or still in denial

>> Indecisiveness of homeowners who change their minds at the last minute because they really don't know what they want

>> Legal issues concerning just how far you can go to persuade homeowners to sell their property at less than market value without committing fraud

Carefully consider the pros and cons before investing in anything, and honestly assess your ability to deal with the negative aspects of certain investment options. Buying foreclosure properties in the pre-auction stage isn't for everyone.

Guiding homeowners to good decisions

When helping homeowners, you can't try to pass yourself off as an attorney, accountant, financial adviser, or therapist unless you really *are* one. But you're often called on to play some of these roles. Like a therapist, you have to be able to listen to the homeowners. Like an accountant, you need to be able to look at the homeowners' finances to assess their options. And, like an attorney, you need to know the foreclosure and redemption laws in your area.

WARNING

Make it very clear to the homeowners that you're not an attorney, real estate agent, or accountant unless you are one. State up front that you're an investor representing *yourself*. Full disclosure is the best policy. Passing yourself off as something you're not is fraud.

A TYPICAL DAY IN THE FORECLOSURE OFFICE

As a real estate broker, I once met with a couple facing foreclosure. The husband worked two jobs and the wife took care of the bills. Though the husband was working hard to make ends meet, the couple had fallen behind in their mortgage payments and were receiving notices from their lender. We set up a meeting at my office to do a conference call with the lender to negotiate a solution.

When the couple arrived at my office, I immediately saw the nature of the problem. The wife was decked out in designer clothes and adorned in jewelry that would have made the queen of England jealous. After looking over their finances, I explained that to avoid foreclosure, the couple would need to slash expenses and sell some of their more valuable assets.

Upon hearing my words, the wife was visibly upset. Angry and near tears, she stood up and asked, "What do you want me to do . . . take the clothes off my back and the rings off my fingers?"

I said, "You can leave your clothes on, but let's take a closer look at those rings." The couple were $10,000 behind on their mortgage payments. I agreed to take the jewelry and give them $10,000 in return so they could sell the house and move on. The next day, I took the jewelry to a friend of mine who owned a jewelry store. He appraised the rings at $5,000. So I took a $5,000 loss, but I scored a great Valentine's Day gift for my wife!

REMEMBER

You can't offer legal advice if you're not a licensed lawyer, but you can inform homeowners of their options and recommend professionals who can help. If the homeowners can refinance their way out of a foreclosure, you may be able to steer them to a loan officer or financial adviser who can provide additional assistance. In Chapter 4, I explain how to assemble a team of experts who can help you buy and sell foreclosure properties so that you'll have plenty of experts on hand to recommend to the homeowners.

Dealing with anger and angst

Understandably, when people are in a financial bind, they're often upset, anxious, and angry. Parents have the daunting task of facing their kids and telling them, "We can no longer afford to live here." They're embarrassed about what their neighbors, friends, and family may think. They may be angry at their boss for laying them off or firing them. In many cases, the husband or wife has just found out about the pending foreclosure from their significant other who spent the family into the poorhouse. During the COVID-19 pandemic, many homeowners struggled with the financial fallout from family illness, job loss, business closures, and mandatory shutdowns.

When you show up at the home of a couple or person facing foreclosure, and you tell the homeowners that you want to help them by buying their property, all that fear, frustration, and anger is likely to get unleashed on you. Even if you can manage to avoid direct conflict, you may be recruited into refereeing a domestic dispute or witnessing emotional outpourings that you're just not used to seeing.

Distressed homeowners are often most upset about something that happened in the past — something they can't go back in time and fix. One of your first jobs when dealing directly with homeowners is encouraging them to put the past behind them and address the current situation. Shifting focus to the present can reduced the emotional energy significantly.

TIP

You can often relieve some of the pain of foreclosure by letting the homeowners know that they're not alone. Know the foreclosure statistics for your area, share this information with them, and let them know about their options. This information can often defuse a tense situation and remove some of the anger that may be causing a rift in a couple's relationship. Ask at your county's Register of Deeds office; sometimes, the office tracks foreclosure numbers for the county and may be able to provide city, county, and state statistics.

Assessing your ability to deal with pre-auction scenarios

The most successful pre-auction investors are people who are well versed in local foreclosure laws and procedures and who can quickly and accurately assess the average homeowner's financial predicament. To determine whether you have the qualities to invest successfully in properties in the pre-auction stage, place a check mark next to any of the following statements that you feel are true:

- ❑ People generally like me and trust me right off the bat.
- ❑ I feel comfortable talking with people I've never met.
- ❑ I'm a good listener.
- ❑ I'm diplomatic, often acting as the mediator when friends, family members, or co-workers have issues with one another.
- ❑ I never met a problem I couldn't solve.
- ❑ I'm good with math, especially dollars and cents.

- ❑ I can tell people the truth even when they don't really want to hear it.

- ❑ I can handle disappointment. Even if I've invested a great deal of time and effort in helping a homeowner, I won't get terribly upset if I don't get the house.

- ❑ I can let people fail even after I offer them outstanding advice on how to avoid a catastrophe.

Having every single one of these qualities isn't essential for success in investing in pre-auction properties, but if you checked only two or three items, you may want to consider stepping into the foreclosure process at the auction or post-auction stage. The more of these qualities you have, the more successful you're likely to be in dealing directly with homeowners.

Pursuing Foreclosure Notices

Whether you buy properties directly from homeowners before auction or wait until the auction, the weekly foreclosure notices in your area are required reading. In almost all areas of the country, the lender must post a weekly foreclosure notice or Notice of Default (NOD) in a publicly accessible publication several weeks before the auction. In my area, the foreclosure notice must be posted for four consecutive weeks before the sale in any public newspaper that serves the area. The appendix at the back of this book explains each state's requirements for posting foreclosure notices.

The posting of the foreclosure notice is almost an entirely separate stage of the foreclosure process — after negotiations between the homeowners and lender break down, but before the property is sold at auction. At this stage, every foreclosure investor in your area probably knows about the property, and any investors who are interested in buying the property before auction are likely in the process of trying to contact the homeowners.

The investor who arrives first and whom the homeowners trust most is typically the investor who stands to get the property.

TIP

As you discover in Chapter 7, you can find foreclosure properties even before the foreclosure notice is posted by keeping your ears open, networking effectively (as explained in Chapter 6), and getting the word out that you buy properties.

Knowing the benefits of waiting for the foreclosure notice

Many foreclosure investors don't like dealing with distressed homeowners until the official foreclosure notice is posted because until that point, homeowners may be unwilling to accept the fact that foreclosure is imminent. The posting of the foreclosure notice removes most of the lingering doubt and acts as a wake-up call, spurring the homeowners to take action.

The foreclosure notice offers several additional benefits:

>> Contains the location of the property (usually a legal address, not a street address, but you can use the legal address to obtain the street address, as discussed in Chapter 8)

>> Lists the names of the homeowners being foreclosed on so you can refer to them by name instead of addressing them as "sir" or "madam"

>> Specifies the name of the lender foreclosing on the property, so you have the information you need to gather more information from the lender

>> Provides the name of the attorney or trustee in charge of liquidating the property, so you have someone to call for additional details

As you'll discover throughout your experience as a foreclosure investor, every bit of information you have about a property is a valuable puzzle piece that clarifies the situation and enables you to put together an attractive deal that benefits all those involved.

REMEMBER

Just because the lender posts a foreclosure notice doesn't mean that the property is destined for the auction block. Any time before the sale, the homeowners can strike a deal with the lender, refinance with another lender, or sell the property. As soon as the foreclosure notice is posted, the clock starts ticking for any investor who's looking to buy the property before auction.

TIP

Keep track of properties from the day they're advertised to the time they're sold. Very often, a particular foreclosure sale is adjourned, so the property doesn't go up for auction on the scheduled day. By following the adjournments, you often find that the property goes up for sale later. If you're prepared, you may be able to grab the property without facing any competing bids.

Weighing the drawbacks of waiting for the foreclosure notice

Although the posting of the foreclosure notice delivers some valuable benefits to foreclosure investors, it also heats up competition among investors, all of whom are looking for the best deal. As soon as that foreclosure notice is published, every foreclosure investor working the pre-auction circuit catches the scent and heads out to research the property and contact the homeowners.

REMEMBER

When you're buying properties from distressed homeowners pre-auction, finding out about prospective foreclosure properties before the posting of the notice often gives you a competitive edge. Networking (discussed in Chapter 6) provides the earliest leads. Reading the notices as soon as they're posted and acting quickly to contact the homeowners is the next-best option.

Wrapping up your deal before the sale

Buying a property from the homeowners before the sale is a standard seller-to-buyer transaction. If you've ever bought a house (and you should be a homeowner if you're investing in real estate), you know the drill:

1. Present your offer to the homeowners in the form of a purchase agreement.

You may need to work through a series of counteroffers to agree on a price and terms.

2. Have the property professionally inspected.

3. Order title insurance to protect yourself if the title has any hidden claims against it.

4. Sign the papers at closing.

5. Take possession of the property on the agreed-upon date.

REMEMBER

Because you purchased the property directly from the homeowners, they have no right of redemption, so you don't have to wait around for several months. You can move into the property immediately, renovate and sell it, or turn it into a rental unit. See Part 5 for details on profiting from a property after you take possession of it.

Bidding for a Property at a Foreclosure Auction

Foreclosure investors often choose to do their bidding at auctions. A common misconception about foreclosure auctions is that investors bid on properties. The truth is that investors bid on mortgages (also called *liens*). What's the difference? When you buy a property from homeowners, you own the property. When you buy a lien at a foreclosure sale, you may or may not eventually take possession of the property; if your area has a redemption period, the homeowners or someone else who has a legal claim to the property can redeem it. Check the appendix at the back of this book, and consult your county's Register of Deeds office to find out more about the redemption period in your state.

For a better understanding of what you're actually buying at a foreclosure auction, brush up on the following types of liens:

>> **Senior lien:** The *senior lien,* or *first mortgage,* is the loan that the homeowners took out to purchase the property. I recommend that novice investors always buy first mortgages, because owning the senior lien gives you the best opportunity to take possession of the property eventually.

>> **Junior lien:** The *junior lien* is any other loan the homeowners took out, using their home as collateral. A junior lien is usually a second mortgage, but it can be a home-equity loan, line of credit, or contractor financing provided for home improvements. Junior liens are often wiped off the books during the foreclosure process, so they can be very risky investments.

>> **Tax lien:** A *tax lien* is a claim against the property for unpaid tax bills. Unlike junior liens, which foreclosure typically erases, a tax lien remains in place after foreclosure. If the tax lien is for overdue property taxes, the buyer must pay the taxes. If the lien is for income taxes, the Internal Revenue Service or other taxing agency may choose to forgive the taxes, but make sure that the foreclosing attorney notifies the IRS, as explained in Chapter 11. Buying a property tax lien is usually a safe investment, because if someone else purchases the property, you stand to get your money back and perhaps even earn a small profit. For more about profiting from tax liens, see Chapter 15.

WARNING

Don't bid at auctions until you fully understand the process and know what you're buying. Whenever a foreclosure guru stages a foreclosure seminar in my area, my office begins receiving calls from angry novice investors who purchased junior liens, thinking that they were buying senior liens. One investor purchased more than $100,000 in junior liens only to find out later that those liens were useless pieces of paper. Chapter 11 shows you how to prepare for an auction so that you know what you're bidding for before you place your bid.

STANDING AFAR FROM THE MADDENING CROWD

I always recommend that first-time foreclosure investors sit in on at least five auctions before bidding. When you begin sitting in on auctions, you're likely to notice the same people showing up week after week, a majority of whom never bid on properties. Some people attend for the entertainment value, and that's fine, but others consider themselves to be the resident foreclosure experts. A new face in the crowd draws their attention, and they offer what they're convinced is solid investment advice.

Steer clear of these foreclosure-investor phonies. The people you want to seek advice from are the people who show up every week, bid on properties, buy them, and turn them over for a profit. Unfortunately, these knowledgeable people aren't likely to share their wisdom with a novice investor who's looking to compete with them. But if you can earn their trust and offer something of value in exchange, they may be willing to pass along some advice.

Weighing the pros and cons of buying at auctions

The foreclosure auction provides you an opportunity to purchase a controlling interest in a property without having to deal directly with the homeowners in often-uncomfortable situations. In a way, the auction simplifies the process of acquiring properties. You show up, submit the winning bid, and walk away with the sheriff's deed.

Buying at auction, however, presents several additional challenges, including the following:

>> You may not have the opportunity to inspect the property thoroughly, although you should at least inspect the property from the outside, as I advise in Chapter 8.

>> Properties are often sold as is, so you're more likely to take possession of a property that requires costly repairs.

>> Cash payment is usually required at the time of purchase, so you need to show up with a cashier's check. In some cases, you have a few hours or days to come up with the cash, but you still need ready access to cash to close on the deal.

>> Depending on the number of investors at the auction who actually bid on properties, you may face some stiff competition.

>> When you buy a property at an auction in an area that has a mandatory redemption period, you may need sufficient funds to hold the property for several months to a year until you see your profit. (If you're using your own money, you need just enough cash to insure the house and pay the property taxes. If you borrowed the money, you may need additional cash to cover the monthly payments. For more about financing your purchase, see Chapter 5.)

REMEMBER

Throughout this book, but especially in Chapter 8 and Chapter 11, I reveal tips and techniques for meeting these challenges and minimizing the risks of bidding at auctions. Only by being thoroughly prepared going into an auction can you confidently purchase properties that are almost sure to turn a profit.

Setting a maximum bid well in advance

One big mistake to avoid at an auction is getting caught up in the excitement of the bidding experience. I know the risks of overbidding firsthand, because I have trouble restraining myself at auctions. I hate to lose, so if someone's bidding against me, I always win — the bid, that is. Only later do I realize that my obsession with winning made me the big loser for having spent too much for a property.

TIP

The trick to effective bidding is to research the property thoroughly and set the highest price you can afford to pay for the property and still make a profit of 20 percent or more. That's your ceiling. You can bump your head on it, but don't crash your head through it; if you do, you'll have serious headaches in the future. For auction bidding tips and tricks, see Chapter 11.

Putting on your poker face

Bidding on a property at foreclosure is a bit like sitting around a poker table and trying to figure out why a particular investor is bidding on a specific property for a certain amount of money. In some cases, the other investor may know more about the property than you do. In other cases, the investor knows less. The person may be bidding on instinct to drive up bidding or simply to toy with other investors.

The comparison of bidding on foreclosure properties with playing poker ends there, however. Bidding on properties is a high-stakes game in which you stand to lose as much as you stand to gain — or more. You may never know why a particular investor bids a specific amount on the property, but you always need to know why *you're* bidding a specific amount, what you're bidding on, and how high you're willing to bid.

With a fully fleshed-out property dossier, which I show you how to assemble in Chapter 8, you hold all the cards in the deck. This dossier enables you to put on the dispassionate poker face required to win the bidding game. You know exactly how much you can afford to bid to earn the desired profit. Not everyone who's bidding against you will have the same advantage.

Acquiring Properties after the Auction

The auction close doesn't signal the end of your opportunity to acquire foreclosure properties. For investors who choose to focus on post-auction properties, an auction's close signals the beginning. These investors don't want to deal directly with homeowners, and they prefer to avoid the sometimes-messy auction process. They'd rather buy properties from the new owners.

In the following sections, I list various opportunities and resources for tracking down post-auction properties, from bank-owned and government-owned repos to properties that have been seized because they were paid for with ill-gotten gains. You can make a good profit by focusing on any one of the categories I describe.

REMEMBER

The opening bid at an auction is typically the amount owed on the property, plus attorney fees, plus a dollar. Contrary to what many people think, banks don't want to be in the real estate business, so they rarely bid up a property to take possession of it. A bank holding a second lien, however, may bid on the first lien to protect the bank's interest.

Scoping out REO properties

Auctions typically start with a minimum bid. If nobody in the room bids high enough, a representative for the bank that's foreclosing offers a bid and takes possession of the deed. The bank transfers the property to its REO or Other Real Estate Owned (OREO) department, which prepares the property for sale.

Because preparing properties for sale and selling them costs banks additional money, they're often willing to negotiate sales with investors rather than place the properties on the market.

Admittedly, the process sounds pretty easy, but it can be very challenging for any or all of the following reasons:

>> Banks don't like to sell properties at bargain-basement prices just to unload them.

>> REO managers often pass the best deals on to their closest contacts and to investors with proven track records, so you may need to invest some time in building fruitful relationships.

>> REO managers may require you to buy two or more properties as a package deal. You must agree to take one not-so-promising property along with another that has more potential.

>> Properties are sold as is, so you can get stuck with a lemon, especially if you don't do your homework.

Chapter 12 brings you up to speed with the REO process, reveals ways to contact and work with REO managers, and suggests timing your offer to coincide with the REO department's fiscal calendar.

Finding and buying government properties

The U.S. government sponsors several programs to encourage home ownership, including Department of Housing and Urban Development (HUD) and Department of Veterans Affairs (VA) financing. Often, borrowers default on these loans, and the government ends up with a property that it doesn't need or want. In addition, state and local governments may seize properties for infrastructure improvements or as a result of unpaid taxes or criminal activities.

As a citizen, you have the right to purchase these government properties, and you can often pick them up at deep discounts. Following is a list of common resources for government-owned properties:

>> **HUD and VA repos:** When homeowners default on a HUD or VA home loan, like any lender, the government can choose to foreclose on the property. These deals aren't always best for investors because HUD and VA homes are commonly listed at or just below market value, but by being persistent, you can often find some pretty good deals.

>> **State department of transportation:** The department of transportation commonly buys up property for road improvements and disposes of the property after completing the project.

>> **State or county drug enforcement agency:** If a homeowner is paying for a property with illicit funds, or if the house is home to criminal activity, the

government may step in, take possession of the property, evict the homeowners, and sell the house.

>> **County sheriff's office:** When your county sheriff's office seizes a property, perhaps because it was purchased with proceeds from criminal activity, it may offer the property for sale through a broker or at auction.

TIP

A condominium association can also foreclose on a property to collect unpaid condominium fees. Remember, however, that a condo lien is just another lien. The senior lien (first mortgage) takes precedence.

Buying properties from other investors

Some foreclosure investors are more interested in discovering and acquiring foreclosure properties than they are in fixing them up and reselling them. These investors consider themselves to be *foreclosure wholesalers* who find and buy properties and then sell them to other investors.

WARNING

Generally, I advise against buying properties from foreclosure wholesalers (or whatever they call themselves). Whenever someone tries to sell you on some great investment opportunity, ask yourself this question: "If the property were as profitable as they want me to think, why don't *they* fix it up and sell it?" Another reason not to buy from other investors is that by doing so, you're usually paying a markup or finder's fee. Plenty of foreclosure properties are available, and they're not that difficult to track down, so pocket the markup, and use that money for renovations or the purchase of your next property. But if you've done your research (as explained in Chapter 8), and the price is right, I certainly wouldn't tell you to pass on the deal.

Just as I advise against buying properties from foreclosure wholesalers, I strongly discourage you from becoming a foreclosure wholesaler yourself. You can make more money by working the foreclosure from start to finish: buy, renovate, and sell. For details about renovating and selling a house for more than you paid for it, check out *Flipping Houses For Dummies*, 4th Edition (John Wiley & Sons, Inc.).

Waiting Out the Redemption Period — If Necessary

Many areas of the country give foreclosed-upon homeowners one last chance to get their homes back — through redemption. If the homeowners can come up with enough money to pay off the balance of their loans and all penalties and back taxes, they get to keep the property. In some cases, homeowners have up to a year to redeem their property before the high bidder at the auction takes possession.

The redemption period can affect you in any of several ways:

>> If you purchased the property at auction, you must wait to do anything to the property until the redemption period expires. Otherwise, you may invest heavily in renovations only to see the homeowners or another investor redeem the mortgage that you bought and cut you out of the deal. You may need to secure the home (particularly if it's vacant) and perform repairs to make the property safe and prevent deterioration, such as from a leaky roof, but invest as little as possible during this period.

>> The homeowners may still be able to file for bankruptcy during the redemption period to buy themselves some additional time, which can throw your plans for renovating and selling the property for a loop.

>> If another investor purchased a property and is waiting for the redemption period to expire, you still have an opportunity to purchase the property. You can work with the homeowners to bump the other investor out of the deal, redeem the property, and buy it directly from the homeowners.

Surviving the redemption period can be tricky, especially if other investors take interest in the property. Chapter 16 shows you what you should be doing during this time to protect your interest. Flip to the appendix at the back of this book to find out whether your state has a redemption period and, if it does, how long the redemption period is.

2

Laying the Groundwork for Maximized Profit and Minimized Risk

Build a successful foreclosure investing team, complete with an attorney, a mortgage broker, a title company, a tax specialist, building contractors, and a top-notch real estate agent.

Estimate the amount of money you'll need to buy, fix, and sell an investment property and the profit you can expect.

Figure out how to get the money you need to finance your foreclosure investments and increase your leverage while reducing the risk to your own assets.

Evaluate financing options, including hard-money loans (from private lenders), conventional bank loans, self-directed Individual Retirement Accounts, and partnerships.

Develop a strong reputation and the kinds of relationships that lead to the best foreclosure investment opportunities so that opportunities come looking for you.

IN THIS CHAPTER

» Lawyering up for leads and legal protection

» Tracking down investment capital through a mortgage broker

» Covering your back with a title company and home inspectors

» Contracting out home repairs and renovations

» Weighing the pros and cons of partnerships

Chapter **4**

Building a Powerful Foreclosure Investment Team

At first glance, investing in foreclosures can seem daunting. You need to know how to find a foreclosure property, finance the purchase and renovations, fix it up, and then sell it . . . all on schedule and typically within a tight budget.

The good news is that you can get by with a moderate amount of knowledge and expertise, as long as you know where and how to find good help. With a list of contacts, a phone, and some people skills, you can delegate your way to investing successfully in foreclosures.

In this chapter, I guide you through the process of building a top-notch team of real estate professionals, consisting of an agent, attorney, mortgage broker, accountant, title company, home inspector, contractors, and additional support personnel.

What role do you play on your investment team? You're the resident foreclosure expert. This book — along with the guidance of your real estate attorney, title company, real estate agent, and other real estate professionals — can get you up to speed on the process. But when decision time arrives, you're in the hot seat, deciding how much to offer, scheduling the work, and handling the money.

Lawyering Up with a Real Estate Attorney

Real estate deals are primarily legal and financial transactions. Buying foreclosures involves even more legal complexities, so you should never move forward on a deal without competent legal assistance or sign any purchase agreements without the benefit of an attorney's legal eagle eye.

Don't hire just any old attorney. Look for an attorney with the specialty you need and other qualifications that make that person a perfect candidate for the job:

>> **Specialty in foreclosures:** Foreclosure laws can be tricky. Choose a real estate attorney who has plenty of experience working the foreclosure circuit.

>> **Specialty in bankruptcy:** A real estate attorney who also specializes in bankruptcies is a big plus. In addition to providing expertise on investing in bankruptcy properties, your attorney may deliver some great leads from their less-fortunate clients.

>> **Positive personal referrals:** If possible, find a real estate attorney recommended by a friend or relative instead of simply picking the first attorney you come across in the phone book.

>> **Efficient and affordable:** For a lot of foreclosure-action services, look to pay a flat fee, not by the hour or (gasp) minute. An attorney might quote $600 for an eviction action, or more if the case turns out to be complicated; they'll let you know. Look for affordable, not necessarily cheap, because you often get what you pay for.

>> **Supportive:** Someone who second-guesses your decision to invest can paralyze you with doubt. You want an attorney to steer you clear of potential legal pitfalls, not one who nitpicks every transaction.

>> **Available:** A good lawyer is available when you need them.

>> **Experienced:** A real estate attorney who owns real estate and rentals or even buys foreclosures is better than one who doesn't.

>> **Generous:** A lawyer who shares their leads can help you find properties that you can't find on your own. Be careful to avoid sloppy seconds — properties that the attorney sends your way because those properties aren't profitable enough for them.

TIP

If your friends, relatives, real estate agent, title company, and other people you know can't recommend an excellent real estate attorney, call the local bar association for the names and contact information of a few real estate attorneys or bankruptcy lawyers, and start there. In some cases, the attorney you call may not be the right one for you, but they may refer you to someone who is. If all else fails, inquire at a firm mentioned in a foreclosure notice.

Teaming Up with a Good Moneyman or Woman

Money not only makes the world go 'round, but also moves houses. You need money to purchase a property. Your foreclosure clients may need financing to take action on one of the options you present. And people who are buying property from you often require financing to close on the deal.

Where do you find all this money? Hunt down someone who specializes in home financing: a *mortgage broker* (commonly called a *loan officer*). By teaming up with a loan officer, you not only have the means to secure financing for your investments, but also have someone on call when distressed homeowners need advice or when someone who's interested in purchasing the property from you needs financing.

All mortgage brokers are not necessarily equal; some may not even be licensed. So shop carefully for a quality, licensed mortgage broker. A qualified broker can save you thousands in finance fees and interest. Look for the following qualities in a mortgage broker:

>> State-licensed.

>> Member of the National Association of Mortgage Brokers (NAMB), the Mortgage Brokers Association (MBA), or both.

>> Positive personal referrals from people who have worked directly with the mortgage broker. Ask your attorney, bank, friends, family members, and colleagues for references.

>> An understanding of foreclosures, because you need to borrow money based on the future value of the property, not the purchase price. By borrowing on the *future value* (or *repaired value*) of the property, you gain access to more cash for repairs, renovations, and other investment properties.

>> No conflicting relationships. A mortgage broker who works in the foreclosure arena may have relationships with homeowners in foreclosure or other investors that may create a conflict of interest.

REMEMBER

Laws require anyone who wants to loan money to work through a licensed mortgage broker, so if you want to use other people's money to finance your investment, you almost always need to work through a mortgage broker or directly with a lending institution such as a bank.

To obtain assistance from a mortgage broker, consider writing a letter of introduction, like the letter shown in Figure 4-1. Let the broker know that you're going to be investing in foreclosures, and you may run into clients who require the broker's assistance.

<Your Name>
<Your Address>
<City>, <State> <Zip>
<Date>

<Mortgage Broker's Name>
<Company>
<Address>
<City>, <State> <Zip>

Dear Mr./Ms. <Last Name>:

My name is <Your Name>. I am a real estate investor, planning to work with individuals who are going through foreclosure.

I am seeking financing for my investments and will also be exploring various ways to assist distressed homeowners with refinancing into non-conventional mortgages. In many cases, I may need to refer future clients to you for consultation. I believe we can create a win-win situation by working together.

At your earliest possible convenience, I would like to meet with you to discuss financing options for purchasing and renovating investment properties and services you could offer my future clients who may require your assistance.

Please give me a call at <Your Phone Number> or email me at <your email address> if you have any questions or when you have time to meet with me. I look forward to speaking with you soon.

Sincerely,

<Your Signature>

FIGURE 4-1:
Sample letter to a
mortgage broker.

<Your Name>

Foreclosure Specialist

Consulting a Title Company to Cover Your Back

Although you should hone your own title-inspection skills, a title company offers additional assurance and insurance that the title is accurate and doesn't have any gaps in its history that could cause problems down the road. Here's what a good title company can do for you:

>> Provide a second set of well-trained eyes to inspect the title and ensure that it's in recordable form.

>> Deliver a title commitment and chain of title, showing the history of ownership and any claims against the property. This document ensures that the person selling the property is the person who owns it and makes you aware of any liens against or property taxes owed on the property.

REMEMBER

A *title commitment* is a promise by the title company to insure the title against any future disputes concerning ownership. It typically states who is being insured, the amount of the insurance, a description of the property, conditions that must be met to secure title insurance, and a list of what's not insured.

>> Provide title insurance when you purchase the property to protect you from any financial loss if someone has a legitimate claim against the property that the title company missed. The title company also makes sure that any rights to the property, such as mineral rights, are transferred to you (if they're owned by the seller).

>> Highlight any homeowner-association liens against the property.

>> Inform you of any restrictions on the property or covenants on the land. If you're buying a home in a historic area, for example, the renovations may have restrictions. Certain covenants may prohibit you from removing living trees from the land or limit the total square footage of the house. If these restrictions are valid, and you violate them, adjacent property owners can sue you.

>> Further educate you concerning foreclosure laws and regulations in your area.

>> Provide additional leads on foreclosure opportunities.

>> Refer you to other real estate professionals who can assist you with your investments.

Look for a title company that provides title insurance for the foreclosing attorneys in your area. A company that handles foreclosures regularly knows the common problems to look for in the title. Reputation and location are your two other main considerations. Pick a company that's nearby and has the best reputation for smooth closings. Your real estate attorney or agent can recommend a title company that has a solid reputation in the area. Smaller towns may have only one title company.

TIP

Meet with one of the title company's representatives to explain that you're going to be investing in foreclosure policies. The company may provide you free title commitments on a few properties in the hope of gaining your business when you close on a property and need title insurance.

WARNING

One of the first questions to ask a title company representative is whether the company does title work on foreclosure properties. Many times, underwriters don't do title work on foreclosures. If the company you're considering doesn't work on foreclosures, keep looking for one that does.

Hiring a Tax-Savvy Accountant

Most of the accounting that applies to investing in foreclosures is basic math. Add up the costs of buying, renovating, and selling the house, and subtract those costs from the amount you receive when you sell the house. If you come up with a positive number, you made money.

REMEMBER

Unfortunately, reality is more complex, and having a professional accountant on hand can help you avoid unnecessary expenses and legal woes. Your accountant can take all your money and receipts out of your shoebox, sort through them, and figure out whether you made any money. If you *did* make money, they can calculate the amount of tax you owe. An experienced accountant also delivers the following benefits:

>> Saves you money on income tax while remaining in compliance with often-complex tax laws

>> Ensures that you pay your property taxes on time

>> Evaluates your real estate investment activities to determine whether you're considered to be an investor or a self-employed dealer — essentially, the difference between a part-time and full-time investor

>> Pays your quarterly estimated taxes if you're considered to be a self-employed dealer

>> Pays your quarterly estimated taxes on your capital gains if you're considered to be an investor

>> May assist you in keeping your renovation expenses within budget

>> Manages your payroll, and calculates and pays your payroll taxes if you hire people to work for you

Go with an accountant who has plenty of experiencing keeping the books for real estate investors. If you already have a general accountant who files your state and federal tax returns but has little experience in the real estate arena, consider hiring a different accountant to keep the books for your real estate investments. Ask your real estate attorney or agent for recommendations. Your current accountant may also know someone who's more qualified to deal with real estate. Interview at least three candidates.

TIP

If you're good with numbers and have a solid understanding of tax laws that apply to real estate investments, you can take on this job yourself. If you're not real estate tax–savvy, however, you can avoid legal headaches and worries by hiring a professional.

Lining Up a Home Inspector

When you buy a property at auction or from a bank, you often agree to purchase it as is. In these cases, you don't have the benefit of a home inspection before you lay your money down. When you're buying pre-auction properties from distressed homeowners, however, the purchase agreement should state that the transaction is conditional upon the home's passing inspection.

By lining up an inspector or team of inspectors ahead of time, you're less likely to pick a substandard inspector later in a rush to get the home inspected.

TIP

In the area where I buy most of my investment properties, city inspectors are available to inspect homes before purchase. I prefer using city inspectors, because they tend to be thorough and are well-versed in local building codes. The city inspectors in my area show up as a team that typically includes a plumber, an electrician, a heating and air-conditioning specialist, a builder, and someone who specializes in zoning. You get a thorough inspection and a complete write-up for about the same price you'd pay a private inspector. Not all towns and cities offer inspections, however, or they offer them only for new homes.

You can search online to find listings for dozens of home inspectors in just about any area of the country. Finding a *qualified* home inspector, however, is a challenge. Begin by asking your real estate agent or other real estate professionals you know for references. Another good resource is the National Association of Certified Home Inspector (NACHI) website at www.nachi.org. To track down city inspectors, call your town hall, and ask for the building or building code enforcement department. Some counties publish a free county guide that includes all the contact information for city and township offices. You may also be able to access the information on your county's or town's website.

When you have a few leads, contact your candidates, and ask them the following questions:

>> **Are you certified, licensed, and insured?** Certification and licensing ensure that the inspector has the basic qualifications for the job. Insurance may cover any serious defects the inspector overlooks or only the cost of the inspection, depending on state laws.

>> **How long have you been a home inspector?** Length of service is often, but not always, a good indication of experience and expertise.

>> **How many homes have you inspected?** "One or two" isn't the answer you're looking for. A busy home inspector is usually busy because they're good.

>> **What did you do before becoming a home inspector?** Someone who's a retired carpenter or home builder is typically a good candidate.

>> **Do you have references I can call?** If the inspector has a good track record, people don't hesitate to provide positive references.

>> **Do you recommend repairs or merely identify problems?** Look for an inspector who can recommend repairs and renovations, and provide rough estimates for the work.

A homeowner who's selling a property at a clearance price often does so to avoid the costs and headaches of making repairs. Nitpicking can ruin your chances of acquiring a great piece of property. Choose an inspector who focuses more on big-ticket items than on minor defects.

Don't hire your inspector as your contractor. Such a move only tempts your inspector/contractor to find more problems with the property.

WARNING

Contacting Contractors and Subcontractors

When homeowners are facing foreclosure, they don't have a whole lot of money in the cookie jar to maintain their home. In some cases, the homeowners trash the place and even gut the house as a final act of retribution. You usually end up with a property that requires a moderate to major overhaul.

You can do as much of the fixing up as you're qualified, comfortable, and willing to do. For everything else, hire professionals:

>> A *contractor* (or general contractor) is the boss. This person manages the budget and workflow, hires subcontractors, coordinates the work from start to finish, and hands you the bill.

>> *Subcontractors* perform specific tasks, such as wiring, plumbing, installing ductwork, replacing roofs, and laying carpet.

>> *Skilled laborers* handle general repairs, landscaping, and minor renovations.

In the following sections, I explain the duties of a general contractor and methods for finding and hiring contractors, subcontractors, and handymen.

Hiring a general contractor — or not

On isolated jobs — jobs that require only one or two subcontractors — you can often do the general contracting yourself, just as though you were having your furnace replaced or hiring someone to replace the roof on you house. For more-extensive projects that require the coordination of multiple subcontractors, a general contractor may be a better fit.

TIP

To me, a general contractor represents additional overhead I shouldn't need to pay for. By working closely with the subcontractors to coordinate the work, you should be able to handle the general contracting yourself, but if you have any doubts about your own ability to manage a complex renovation project, hire a qualified contractor. You should also consider using general contractors if you're working on more than a couple of projects. You have enough to do just managing your portfolio.

If you choose to do the general contracting yourself, you assume the following responsibilities:

>> Budgeting

>> Hiring

>> Scheduling

>> Supervising

>> Firing

>> Negotiating costs

When you're acting as contractor, obtain a permit before starting work on any project that requires a permit, such as a room addition, a deck, a garage, or even a fence. If you don't obtain a required permit, and something bad happens, you may ultimately be responsible, even after you sell the property. You can usually pick up an application for a building permit at the office of the municipality in which the property is located. Call town hall to find out which office you need to visit, or consult your handy-dandy county guidebook (if you have one) or your county's website.

If you decide to hire a general contractor to manage a big project, such as a room addition, kitchen or bathroom overhaul, or adding a second story to a house, provide a detailed description of the work you want done, and let the contractor know that you expect the final cost to be in line with the estimate. Some contractors are notorious for presenting low estimates and then performing additional work to jack up the cost. Contractors want repeat business, so let them know that if you have any problems, you won't be calling them back. Have this conversation before the work begins and before you award the contract to them, so you can remind them of that conversation if any issues crop up.

Tracking down top-notch contractors and subcontractors

Ask other homeowners and real estate professionals to recommend the contractors and subcontractors they've used. A good person to start with is your real estate agent. Agents typically have a computer packed with references for affordable, honest contractors who do high-quality work, because agents often need to call in a contractor to whip a home into shape before placing it on the market. Your local hardware store may also be a good source for recommendations. Don't rely on ads in your local newspaper, on the grocery-store bulletin board, or online without checking references.

To lessen the risks of getting ripped off, do your due diligence. Check references, workmanship, and the amount of time the contractor has been in business. Ask the contractor whether they're licensed and insured. Finally, check with the state or your local Better Business Bureau to see whether anyone has filed a recent complaint against the contractor.

Contracting with contractors and subcontractors

When you're hiring a contractor or subcontractor, you have three goals: You want the job to be completed to your satisfaction, on budget, and on schedule.

When you get the contractor's estimate and proposal, attach a one-page agreement that includes the following:

>> Start and end date.

>> A $50 penalty for every day that the project runs over schedule. If the contractor's proposal indicates that the work can be completed in 30 days, you may add a clause stating that if the work isn't completed in 45 days, $50 per day will be deducted from the final cost.

>> A condition that the contractor must notify you before performing any additional work that's not stipulated in the original proposal. Contractors who have been in business for a while know pretty darn close to how much a job is going to cost. By steering clear of any changes or upgrades, you should be able to remain within budget.

Your job's not over when you sign the agreement. Remain vigilant to keep the project on schedule and within budget by doing the following:

>> Let your contractors know when the For Sale sign is going up.

>> Give them what they need to succeed, including deposits and supplies.

>> Have them give you receipts for their purchases.

>> Show up unannounced at the worksite to see whether they're working.

>> If the workers are doing a good job, tell them so, and do it often.

>> Don't strive for perfection, but don't overlook shoddy work just to keep the peace, either. You're paying for a job done well, not just a job done.

WARNING

Whenever you must rely on someone else to do work for you, you take some risk. To limit your exposure to risk with contractors, take the following precautions:

>> When hiring a contractor or subcontractor, make sure that the person is insured against both property damage and personal injury. An average hospital bill can wipe out your profit.

>> Be careful about deposits, especially when you're dealing with a contractor you don't know. Contractors have been known to take the deposit and disappear. A 25–50 percent deposit is normal — generally, the smaller the contractor, the larger the deposit. You can pay most handymen weekly.

>> Be careful about handing huge chunks of money to a contractor. If the contractor needs a costly supply of materials to get started, consider paying the supplier directly.

MY CONTRACTOR WENT AWOL!

You can reduce your risks of losing money to a contractor, but you can't eliminate those risks. I had a great contractor for a long time. After hiring him to rehab dozens of houses, I gave him a $3,500 deposit on a Thursday for a roofing job he promised to complete by the following Tuesday.

The contractor failed to mention that he had planned a weekend trip to Las Vegas. When he returned, the deposit was gone — gambled away in Lost Vegas. "What happens in Vegas, stays in Vegas" must be true, because my money stayed in Vegas, along with the reputation of my contractor. I lost a good contractor, and he lost a good account. He wanted to do business with me again, but I just couldn't allow it.

TIP

Pay your contractors as soon as they complete their work to your satisfaction. My father was a builder, and my brother Jeff, who's now my property manager, worked very closely with him. Jeff has a pay-as-they-go policy: He pays contractors when they're pulling out of the driveway. This approach is one of the best ways to show your appreciation for a job well done.

Finding skilled and unskilled help

You don't necessarily need a licensed subcontractor to do odd jobs around the house. A skilled laborer (someone who's handy with power tools and hand tools) can often complete small jobs for a fraction of the cost. If the house needs new wiring or plumbing or has structural damage, pay a little extra for a licensed expert. For smaller jobs such as leaky faucets, clogged drains, replacement windows, and new doors, a skilled laborer is a more affordable choice. Unskilled laborers are useful for decluttering, cleaning, general landscaping, and other basic tasks that don't require any specialized knowledge or experience.

Insuring your helping hands

Your contractor should supply a separate *proof of insurance* form attached to the bid, verifying that the contractor and workers are insured for this particular job. If you're hiring people who are moonlighting from their day jobs, they may be covered under their company's insurance policy, but they may *not* be covered during a stint as a moonlighter.

WARNING

When you're hiring a contractor or handyman who can't provide proof of insurance, contact your insurance company and take out a separate workers' compensation policy (or add coverage to your current policy on the house you're renovating) that covers anyone who's working on your house. Added insurance takes a little extra time and costs a few hundred dollars, but if you're not covered, and an injured worker sues you, you can lose your entire profit and even some of your own personal savings.

Selling Your Property for Top Dollar through a Seller's Agent

If you plan on selling the properties you buy, a top seller's agent can assist you in marketing the property and selling it quickly and for top dollar. I strongly encourage you to enlist the aid of an agent in selling your investment properties. What you pay in commissions, you usually earn back with interest, because a great agent can sell the property for more money in significantly less time than you can on your own.

In the following sections, I explain the beneficial services that agents can provide and offer guidance on finding the best agent for your flipping needs.

SELLER'S AGENT VERSUS BUYER'S AGENT

Real estate agents often excel in one area: buying or selling homes. Buyer's agents are better at finding the right homes at the right price for home buyers. Seller's agents are more skilled at selling homes quickly for top dollar. A good agent may also have access to information that can help you find and evaluate properties in the foreclosure process. Some agents may even specialize in working with investors. Others may be experts in property management and relocations, and can help buy-and-hold investors find tenants for their rental units.

When you're buying foreclosure properties at auction, you don't need an agent to assist you in finding the right home for your needs. You need an agent who can sell the property quickly for a price that's in line with, or slightly higher than, the going price in your market.

When you're headhunting for an agent to work with, ask whether the agent specializes in certain locations or property types — and then ask around to make sure that you're getting one of the top seller's agents in your area.

Recognizing the value of a seller's agent

A seller's agent who has plenty of experience working with investors can assist you with more than selling the property. A top-selling agent also helps you do the following:

>> Evaluate the value-add and cost-effectiveness of renovations.

>> Locate experienced and reputable contractors, subcontractors, and other professionals.

>> Stage your house (make it look pretty) for showings. A properly staged home, on average, sells in half the time for 7–10 percent more than an unstaged home.

>> Market your rehabbed home to every real estate agent in the neighborhood via the Multiple Listing Service (MLS) — a list of homes for sale that goes out to all the real estate agents in your area.

REAL ESTATE AGENT OR REALTOR: WHAT'S THE DIFFERENCE?

A *real estate agent* is anyone who has a state license to negotiate the sale or purchase of a property and works for a real estate broker or brokerage company. A *Realtor* is a real estate agent who's also a member of the National Association of Realtors. The United States has more than 3 million real estate agents, but only 1.5 million are Realtors.

Because the qualifications for obtaining a real estate license vary from state to state, the quality of real estate agents varies much more than the quality of Realtors. The National Association of Realtors requires its members to complete additional training and testing to improve their knowledge and abilities, and it encourages members to follow a strict code of ethics. The association also provides its members additional resources and tools to help them find and market properties effectively. Being a Realtor costs more, so when you hire a Realtor, you know you're getting someone who's invested substantially in getting established in the profession.

This association membership doesn't mean that a particular Realtor is more qualified than a given real estate agent, of course, but the odds are pretty good that you'll receive superior advice and service from a Realtor. To find a bona-fide Realtor, look for the Realtor logo on business cards and stationery. Almost all Realtors make a point of proudly displaying this logo. You also can find a Realtor in your area by checking out www.realtor.com.

>> Evaluate offers on the rehabbed home, and guide you in picking the best of the bunch.

>> Navigate the closing to ensure smooth sailing.

>> Advise you on how much rent you can charge for a property if you want to hold on to it for a while and you need some cash flow.

On average, you take twice as long selling a property yourself than you do when you work with a real estate agent, and every day your home sits on the market costs you money in the form of interest, property tax, insurance, and utilities.

Picking an agent with the right stuff

Any licensed real estate agent can sell your house for you, but you want someone whose experience and training are rooted in sales. A top agent typically has the following credentials:

>> Five or more years' experience.

>> Graduate Realtor Institute (GRI) certification.

>> Certified Residential Specialist (CRS) certification.

>> Realtor status (not simply a real estate agent).

>> A consistent top-5-percent performance in the marketplace.

>> Is assisted by a clerical staff.

>> Is well connected with other agents.

>> Works for a real estate company that has a website.

>> Maintains a personal website or blog.

>> Is closely involved with the community. (The more the agent is involved, the more committed the person is to excellence.)

To find Realtors in your area, visit www.realtor.com/realestateagents, where you'll find an online form that you can fill out to search for agents, teams, or companies in your area by city or zip code.

Another way to find an agent is through referrals from other homeowners (buyers and sellers), other investors, or your real estate attorney or title company. When you have a list of 10 to 15 names, start calling around and interviewing candidates to compare their experience, education, and certifications, as described in the preceding list.

The size of the real estate company doesn't matter. Whether the agent is with a large franchise, a regional company, or an independent office makes no difference. Interview several agents. If their qualifications seem to be about equal, pick the person you're most confident in and comfortable with.

TIP

Many books on real estate investing recommend that you try to convince the agent to accept a lower percentage in commissions or a flat fee for helping you buy or sell a property, but this approach can backfire. I suggest that you find the best agent and then pay the going rate or a little more. When you pay less, your agent is going to work harder for the clients who are paying more.

Assessing the Pros and Cons of Partnerships

Taking on a partner is like getting married, so if you don't trust a person as much as you trust your spouse, you probably shouldn't become partners. Great partnerships are rare, but when they work, they enable both parties to achieve more than they could achieve individually. All too often, however, a partner runs off with the cash, fails to pay the contractors, cashes checks made out to the water company or building-supply store and pockets the money, files an insurance claim to collect for damages without your knowledge, or figures out some other way to pick your pocket.

TIP

If you're considering partnering with someone, think about having the person work for you for a fee first. That trial period removes one possible area of conflict, and if the relationship doesn't work out, you're out only the money you paid the person up to that point.

Thriving partnerships require continuous attention and nurturing. To establish a productive partnership, take these seven steps:

1. **Pick energetic, talent, and determined partners whose personalities and talents complement yours.**

2. **Address financial concerns upfront.**

   Don't partner with someone who has little or no income, a poor credit rating, or lousy cash flow or is in a precarious financial position. Each of you should fully disclose upfront your financial situation and how the money is to be handled.

3. **Build a common vision with shared goals.**

   You both need to be on the same page.

4. **Communicate, communicate, communicate.**

   Communications should be frequent, open, and honest.

5. **Promise only what you can deliver and then deliver on those promises.**

   This approach builds trust.

6. **Share decisions, work, and rewards equally.**

7. **Be prepared to compromise.**

   "My way or the highway" doesn't always work. Try on your partner's ideas and approach every once in a while to see how it works.

REMEMBER

If you partner with someone, have your attorney write up a contract that details the responsibilities of each party and how profits are to be divided. A partnership that's based only on a handshake often ends in a bitter battle.

» **Sampling your financing options**

» **Using your investment property as collateral**

» **Exploring conventional loans**

» **Comparing the cost of two or more loans**

Chapter **5**

Filling Your Foreclosure Tank with Financial Fuel

When the average homeowners purchase a home, they typically finance their purchase with a conventional loan, but in the land of foreclosure investing, cash is king. Cash gives you a competitive edge over other investors who have to wait around for loan approvals, appraisals, and other delays that can quickly sink a deal. With cash in hand, you can offer distressed homeowners immediate solutions, scoop up properties at auctions, and get the best deals on Real Estate Owned (REO) properties, also referred to as *bank-owned properties.*

In this chapter, I explain how to estimate how much cash you need and how to assess a variety of conventional and creative financing options.

REMEMBER

When I say that you need cash to invest in foreclosures, I don't mean that all the cash must be your own. You can borrow the money, but you need to borrow it in a way that makes the cash readily accessible. Ready cash enables you to wrap up a transaction quickly.

Estimating Your Cash Needs

The standard way of buying a house is to figure out how much house you can afford, get prequalified for a loan, and then start shopping for homes in your price range. You don't need cash. You simply need enough income coming in every month to cover the loan payments.

When you're buying foreclosure properties, the process is reversed by the need for cash. First, you gather the cash you need then you go shopping. So the first step is figuring out how much cash you really need.

Pick a price range that's comfortable for you. Are you planning on buying homes in the $100,000, $200,000, $500,000, or $1 million range? Choosing a price range in a particular neighborhood benefits you in two ways: It enables you to estimate your cash needs more accurately, and it helps you evaluate the worth of comparable properties in that price range.

WARNING

When you're picking a price range, stay in your comfort zone. Sure, you stand to earn a higher profit with pricier properties (a 20 percent profit on a million-dollar home is $200,000, whereas it's only $20,000 on a $100,000 home), but a 10 percent loss on a million-dollar home is $100,000, whereas it's only $10,000 on a $100,000 home. In addition, repairs, holding costs, and other expenses are exponentially higher for million-dollar homes. When you're starting out, make your expensive mistakes with smaller amounts of money.

To calculate a ballpark figure for the amount of cash you need to buy, hold, and renovate a property, account for the following costs:

>> Purchase price of the property.

>> Loan costs — upfront costs for securing a loan, such as loan origination fees or points.

>> Monthly holding costs (loan payments, insurance, property taxes, and utilities) multiplied by the number of months you plan to own the house. You're better off calculating your holding costs, but holding costs generally run about 10 percent of the purchase price for the duration of the project.

>> Repair and renovation expenses, which typically hover around 10 percent of the purchase price.

>> Another 10 percent or so for marketing and selling the property.

>> Miscellaneous costs, including title insurance and closing costs at time of purchase.

Here's a short form you can use to calculate a rough estimate of the amount of cash you need:

Purchase price:	$_____
Loan costs:	$_____
Holding costs:	$_____
Renovation expenses:	$_____
Selling expenses:	$_____
Miscellaneous expenses:	$_____
Total:	$_____

After you come up with a rough estimate of the amount of money required to buy, hold, and sell a foreclosure property, you're ready to evaluate your financing options and then start shaking the bushes for the financing you need to fuel your investment.

Finding a Cash Stash: Knowing Your Financing Options

People often talk themselves out of buying a house or investing in real estate, falsely believing that they "can't afford it." The truth is that money is readily available. You just need to know where to look for it, and the first place to look is a mortgage broker. In Chapter 4, I show you how to find a qualified mortgage broker (or loan officer).

A mortgage broker can quickly assess your situation and your investment plans and then reveal your financing options. These options include the following:

» **Hard-money loans:** High-interest, short-term loans that are often attractive to investors who can't qualify for conventional loans. For more about hard-money loans, check out "Financing with Hard-Money and Gap Loans" later in this chapter.

» **Your own money:** Cash and savings, equity you've built up in your home (your home's value minus what you owe on it), and retirement savings. See "Shaking Your Piggy Bank: Tapping Your Own Resources" later in this chapter for details.

>> **Personal loans:** Cash from family members or friends who are willing to help you or want to profit from foreclosure investing without having to do all the work.

>> **Conventional loans:** Money you qualify to borrow from a bank or other conventional lending institutions based on your income, net worth (the value of what you own minus the value of what you owe), and credit history. To find out more about conventional loans, check out "Financing Your Venture with Conventional Loans" later in this chapter.

>> **Government loans:** If you're buying properties from government-sponsored programs, you may qualify for government loans, even as an investor. See Chapter 13 for details.

>> **Credit-card loans:** Some investors shore up their investments or pay for renovations by using their credit cards. If you can flip the house quickly and pay off your credit-card charges within a few months, this option isn't as risky as you may think. I discuss the credit-card option later in this chapter in "Maxing out your credit cards."

TIP

Whenever you're using your own money to finance real estate investments, you place your personal savings and your home at risk. As much as possible, choose financing options that expose you to fewer risks:

>> **Least risky:** Borrowing money against the foreclosure property you're buying. If the deal goes belly-up, you stand to lose only that property, not your own home. See the next section, "Financing with Hard-Money and Gap Loans."

>> **Moderately risky:** Refinancing your home or taking out a home-equity loan. By cashing out the equity in your home, you lose one of the best buffers you have to get you through hard times if you encounter financial hardship. See "Unlocking the equity in your home" later in this chapter.

>> **Very risky:** Burying yourself in credit-card debt is risky, but it may be a good last resort for covering the cost of repairs and renovations. Instead of losing money in holding costs as the house sits there, you can get the repairs and renovations completed and then place the house back on the market, sell it, and pay off your credit-card charges. See "Maxing out your credit cards" later in this chapter for details.

In the following sections of this chapter, I describe these options in greater detail, provide tips on how to make yourself a more attractive borrower (so you can borrow more money at lower interest rates), and compare the costs of various loans.

TIP

When you buy a home to reside in with your spouse, I recommend that you own the home jointly, but when buying investment properties, only one of you should sign the mortgage and promissory note (the promise to pay), if possible. This approach puts the property you own jointly at less risk. Consult your attorney and accountant to discuss strategies for lowering your exposure to risk.

Financing with Hard-Money and Gap Loans

Lenders always require some *collateral* to secure a loan — something of value they can take from you and sell if you happen to default on the loan. You can use your own house, possessions, and retirement savings as collateral, but you'll be placing your current possessions at risk. Safer, though more expensive, financing is available in the form of hard-money and gap loans:

>> **Hard money** is a high-interest, short-term loan that enables you to use the house you're buying as collateral for the loan. A hard-money loan is typically less than the total you'll need to complete the project, which is where gap loans come into play.

>> **Gap loans** cover any costs, such as holding costs and the cost of repairs and renovations, not covered by the hard-money loan. Gap loans are typically smaller than hard-money loans and offered in exchange for a percentage of the profit, unlike a hard-money loan, which is secured by the property.

Weighing the pros and cons of hard money

Hard money loans offer three big benefits:

>> You get access to cash you may not be able to get through a conventional lender.

>> Hard-money lenders often accept the future value of a property as collateral, so you don't have to borrow against your own home.

>> You can often set up a separate escrow account with a hard-money lender to pay for repairs and renovations.

Now for the bad news. Hard money is called "hard" for several reasons. Before choosing the hard-money option, be aware of the following key features of hard-money loans:

>> **Points or discount points:** You can expect to pay anywhere from 2–10 points for the loan upfront. A *point* is 1 percent of the loan amount, so if you're

paying 6 points on a $200,000 loan, you're paying $12,000 up front just to get your hands on the money.

>> **Interest rates:** Hard-money lenders often charge double or triple the interest rate of conventional loans. If the going interest rate for conventional loans is 4 percent, for example, a hard-money lender may charge 8–12 percent.

>> **Loan to value (LTV):** Hard-money lenders typically approve you for a loan of only 50–70 percent of the expected sale price of the property, so you need to be sure that you're buying the property for 30 percent or more *below* what you expect to sell it for. When you're buying into a declining market, LTV becomes even more critical, because your loan amount stays the same while housing values are declining. If the value of the house dips below what you owe on it, you place yourself in the situation of owing more on a property than you can sell it for.

>> **Amortization:** Hard-money lenders often want to amortize the loan over 5–15 years instead of the standard 30 years, which ends up increasing your monthly payments because you're paying down the principal on the loan faster.

TIP

To lower the monthly payments, amortize over 30 years, or negotiate for interest-only payments. You want to have enough free-flowing cash to finance renovations and cover your holding costs.

>> **Balloon payment and cash calls:** Hard money typically has a balloon payment and cash calls. A *balloon payment* is a large payment at the end of the loan's term that pays off the balance. *Cash calls* are substantial, usually quarterly, payments. Cash calls and balloon payments aren't problems as long as you have a solid plan in place and sufficient funds on hand when these payments come due. But if you miss a payment, you risk losing the property in foreclosure. Hard-money lenders usually want their money back ASAP.

>> **Prepayment penalties:** Avoid any loans that stipulate a *prepayment penalty* — extra money that you're required to pay if you choose to pay off the loan early. I've seen investors lose thousands of dollars when they sold a house because they agreed to pay a 2–3 percent prepayment penalty.

>> **Closing costs:** As with any lender, you have to close on a loan from a hard-money lender. Figure in the cost of the title insurance, closing fee, credit report, and appraisal survey. Be particularly careful of any discount points or loan-origination fees — areas in which the lender and mortgage broker can really jack up the cost of the loan.

>> **Cross-collateralization:** If you're investing in two or more properties, the hard-money lender may want to *cross-collateralize* the properties. If you sell one property for a $10,000 profit, for example, the lender may want to use the profit to pay down the loan on the other property. This arrangement isn't

terrible and may even benefit you by reducing your interest on the second loan, but it's something you should be aware of. Cross-collateralization simply secures the lender's position.

Some hard-money lenders offer something called a *bullet loan*, in which you make no monthly payments. Interest accrues and is rolled back into the loan's principal, which increases the total amount required to pay off the loan and can significantly increase the total amount of interest you end up paying. But a bullet loan frees up your cash flow, so you have more money on hand for renovations and other investment properties.

WARNING

Don't borrow money from a hard-money lender and give them a deed in advance in case you don't perform, which takes away some of your rights. Hard-money lenders normally aren't licensed to provide loans; they purchase loans through others. If you default on the loan, they won't send Guido to break your legs; they'll just take possession of the rehabbed property you put up as collateral.

Making up the difference with a gap loan

One of the big drawbacks to hard-money loans is that they often come up short; you may not get all the money you need to buy, hold, and fix the property. This situation is where gap loans come into play. With a gap loan, a private investor or partner puts up the rest of the money, often in exchange for interest, a cut of the profits, or both. The gap loan covers any remainder of the purchase price, all carrying costs (including payments to the hard-money lender), and the costs of repairs and renovations.

The benefit of a gap loan is that you get to flip a property with zero out-of-pocket expenses. The drawback is that it can cost you another chunk of any profit you earn.

REMEMBER

To get gap lenders to partner with you, you need to convince them that your project will be profitable enough to generate a return on investment (in the form of interest or a percentage of the profit) that's significantly better than the percentage they can earn from a bank or from other investment options.

Finding private lenders

You can often locate private lenders through real estate agents and mortgage brokers, by attending landlord meetings and investment seminars, or by joining a real estate investment group and networking. Most private lenders loan money through mortgage brokers because most states require lenders to be licensed.

WARNING

Remain cautious of experienced investors, landlords, or real estate gurus who agree to loan you money only so that they can sell you their dontwanners (properties they got stuck with and *don't want*). As a foreclosure investor, you typically look for properties that owners don't want, but properties that these people don't want could be real lemons; otherwise, they'd probably keep the properties for themselves.

Partnering with Investors

Partnering with one or more friends, family members, or business associates can be a great way to finance your foreclosures, especially if you have rich friends whose real estate knowledge and skills complement yours, or if you have the skills and they have the money. With their financial backing and your combined knowledge and skills, you may be able to form a long-lasting and financially rewarding partnership. You may also consider taking on a partner in the following situations:

>> Your credit is damaged, and you need someone who has a better credit rating to help you secure the loan.

>> You can obtain a loan for purchasing the property, but you need a partner to provide funds for renovating it.

If you partner with someone for access to cash, you typically split the profits — 50/50 at best when you're getting started. With each successful investment, you strengthen your position and eventually can offer the people who front you the money slightly more than what they can make by investing their money elsewhere, so you keep most of the profit.

REMEMBER

If you partner with someone, have your attorney write up a contract that details the responsibilities of each party, how profits are to be divided, and when they'll be paid out. Need an attorney? Head to Chapter 4 for help in finding one.

Shaking Your Piggy Bank: Tapping Your Own Resources

You may be one of the few fortunate investors who has enough cash in your piggy bank to fuel your investments. The amount of money you can get your hands on may be a little difficult to see and to calculate at first. If the cash is readily available — just sitting in your bank account — that's easy, but you may have other cash locked up in your house, other investments, or retirement accounts.

In the following sections, I explore the pros and cons of using your own money to finance your investments and then I assist you in identifying sources of cash that may be locked up in other assets.

WARNING

When you start investing in foreclosures, keep your day job. A steady income enables you to qualify for loans and keeps you afloat in the event that your investments prove to be less profitable than expected.

Examining the pros and cons of using your own money

If you're single, or if you and your significant other are on the same page about this foreclosure-investing thing, cracking into your nest egg to finance your investments may be the quickest way to get your fingers on some investment capital. Be aware, however, of the potential benefits and drawbacks of using your own money:

>> Tapping your cash reserves places you at greater financial risk, because if anything goes wrong — you get laid off or fired, become too ill to work, or encounter unexpected expenses — you may have less reserves to remain afloat. But using your own money also reduces your risk, because you're not signing a promissory note agreeing to pay back a loan by a specific date.

>> Limiting your investment capital to the amount of cash you have on hand saps your purchasing power. You have to buy houses in a lower price range and may not have sufficient cash to renovate the property properly.

WARNING

A great way to ruin a relationship is to bet the farm on big profits without the knowledge and complete agreement of your spouse or significant other. If your investment doesn't pan out, and even if it does, your spouse may take offense at not being consulted.

Totaling your sources of investment capital

You may have more money than you realize, especially if you own your own home and have done a good job of managing debt. In the following sections, I reveal several sources of personal investment capital that may provide you a solid chunk of the cash you need.

Counting your money in savings

The most obvious source of cash is sitting in your bank accounts: savings and checking. Tally up your personal savings and see how much money you have on hand.

WARNING

Wiping out your savings and checking accounts is never a good idea. If you don't have enough in savings to cover the next three months' worth of bills, seek investment capital elsewhere. Keep a sufficient cash reserve on hand just in case you experience a financial setback.

Unlocking the equity in your home

Your home is not only a place to live; it may also be a cash cow. If you've been paying down the principal for several years and the value of your home has appreciated significantly, you have equity in the home. *Equity* is a measure of your home's currently appraised value minus the amount you owe on the home. If your home appraises for $200,000, for example, and you owe $125,000 on it, you have $75,000 in equity.

You can unlock the equity in your home in one or both of the following ways:

>> **Refinance the mortgage.** Take out a new mortgage on the home for the amount of its currently appraised value and pay off the old mortgage. (You can refinance for less than the appraised value to cash out only a portion of your equity.)

>> **Take out a home-equity loan or line of credit.** A home-equity loan, separate from the mortgage, enables you to take out a loan up to the amount of equity in the home. With a home-equity line of credit, you have an account from which you can draw money at any time. You pay interest on only the money you draw from that account.

See "Financing Your Venture with Conventional Loans" later in this chapter for tips on finding the lowest-cost loans available.

Maxing out your credit cards

Maxing out your credit cards to purchase a car, clothes, electronics, groceries, and other items that provide no return on your "investment" is never a good idea. Using your credit cards to purchase investment properties that offer a solid, relatively quick return on your investment, however, can be a savvy financial move. Following are some tips to maximize the use of credit-card debt when investing in real estate:

- » **Shop for credit cards with the lowest interest rates.** Don't look at the low introductory rates; read the fine print to find the rate after the introductory period expires.

- » **Check your credit-card statements to determine your current limits.** Depending on your credit history and the credit-card company, you may have a credit limit in excess of $10,000 per card.

- » **Pay off your charges as quickly as possible.** Paying off your credit-card debt quickly not only saves you from paying high finance charges, but also raises your credit rating, so you'll qualify for future loans at lower interest rates.

Real estate investors rarely use credit-card debt to finance a purchase. They use it more often to finance repairs and renovations so that they can re-sell the property quickly and pay off their credit-card charges in full.

REMEMBER

If you can purchase and sell the property quickly and pay off your charges in a month or two, credit-card interest is unlikely to consume a big chunk of your profit. Years ago, when I started, when the Bank of Grandma was running low, I bought houses with credit cards. I even attended a seminar that recommended accumulating lots of credit cards. I'd never suggest this strategy today. Use a credit card only for emergencies.

Tapping into your retirement savings with a self-directed IRA

More and more investors are choosing to set up *self-directed* Individual Retirement Accounts (IRAs) and other types of retirement accounts that enable them to invest in real estate rather than in stocks and bonds. The reasoning is that real estate often provides a better and sometimes even more secure return on your investment.

With a self-directed IRA, you can buy and sell properties out of your retirement account. Setting up a self-directed IRA, however, is no simple matter. Typically, a trust company manages the money and properties in the account, and all profits and losses from your investments must stay in that account. Withdrawing money from the account results in the same tax penalties that you have to pay if you withdraw money from any type of retirement account.

TIP

Consult your financial adviser and accountant for details about using a self-directed IRA to finance your foreclosure investments. If a self-directed IRA isn't a viable option, you may be able to borrow money against your retirement account. Keep in mind, however, that borrowing against your retirement savings places those savings at risk.

Planning for contingencies

For every plan you have to buy a foreclosure property, have a Plan B. Your Plan B should cover contingencies in the event that the deal doesn't quite proceed according to Plan A. Your contingency plan should cover the following unexpected events:

>> **Delays:** Homeowners can work out a deal with the lender at the last minute or file for bankruptcy. Courts can add further delays. If your area has a mandatory redemption period, this requirement can be a huge delay. You may also have trouble selling the property after you fix it up; do you have enough money to hold on to the property if it lingers on the market?

>> **Mistakes:** What if you pay too much for a property? What if the market dips right after you buy the property, so you can't sell it at a profit? Plan on making a few costly mistakes, especially when you're starting.

>> **Cost overruns:** Rarely do renovations cost *less* than you expect. Undetected defects in the property can increase repair bills. Irate homeowners can trash the property and steal the kitchen sink and cabinets on their way out the door. Contractors may overcharge you. Do you have enough money to cover unexpected expenses?

TIP

To protect yourself against unexpected expenses and scheduling delays, take the following precautions:

>> Buy properties for at least 25 percent less than you know you can sell them for. If you make a mistake, a 25 percent buffer can usually bail you out.

>> Don't get in over your head. Assume that your total investment is going to be at least 20 percent more than you anticipate, and that you have access to enough cash to cover that additional 20 percent.

WARNING

Hope for the best, but plan for the worst. Without an effective contingency plan in place and a sufficient financial buffer, *you* may end up in foreclosure.

Financing Your Venture with Conventional Loans

To get a conventional loan, you hand your bank or mortgage broker your financial records — including pay stubs, tax returns, bank statements, and documents showing how much you own and owe — and then your bank or mortgage broker does a little extra research to determine how much you qualify to borrow. A *conventional loan* is a mortgage loan that's not backed by a government agency, such as the Federal Housing Administration (FHA) or Department of Veterans Affairs (VA).

In the following sections, I explain common conventional loan types, explain how to make yourself an attractive borrower (so you can borrow more money at lower interest rates), and lead you through the process of gathering the paperwork you need to apply for a loan.

WARNING

Although I'm a big proponent of financing investments with other people's money, always treat that money as though it were your own money, and don't get addicted to it. I've seen business owners use other people's money to finance drug habits, personal purchases, and other indulgences, and it always turns out badly. Show respect for the right to borrow other people's money by choosing smart investments and paying back those loans on time.

Exploring conventional loan types

Conventional loans differ in many ways, but for the purpose of investing in foreclosure properties, you should be aware of the following types of conventional loans:

>> **Fixed-rate mortgage:** The interest rate stays the same over the life of the loan.

>> **Adjustable-rate mortgage (ARM):** The interest rate remains fixed for a specified number of years and then is subject to increase or decrease based on a financial index (typically, the percentage the bank pays to borrow the money it lends). When evaluating ARMs (also referred to as *variable-rate mortgages*), consider the following factors:

- The initial interest rate and how long it lasts, such as 4 percent for 3 years.

- The adjustment period — the frequency with which the rate can change after the initial rate expires. The rate may be subject to change annually or every six months, for example.

- The index the lender chooses. One index may have generally lower interest rates than another.

- The margin — the percentage the lender charges above the index. The lender might charge 3 percent above the index, so if the index increases from 4 to 6 percent, the rate you'd pay would increase from 7 to 9 percent.

- Interest-rate caps, indicating the maximum amount that the interest rate can change in a given adjustment period (the *periodic adjustment cap*) and the maximum interest rate you'll ever be required to pay (the *lifetime cap*).

- Payment caps, indicating the maximum percentage your payments can increase in a given adjustment period. If your interest rate increases more than your payment cap allows, the excess interest is added to the principal of the loan.

WARNING

I often caution homeowners about ARMs because they can cost an arm and a leg. As interest rates increase, so do the monthly payments, often driving homeowners into foreclosure, which is what happened during the mortgage meltdown of 2008. As long as you're aware of the cost and plan to pay off the ARM quickly, however, these loans can be useful for investors who need access to cash.

>> **Low-down-payment mortgage:** The loan requires less than the conventional 20 percent down payment. You may be able to find low-down-payment loans that require a down payment of 5, 3, or even 0 percent.

>> **Rehab loan:** The loan amount covers the purchase price and renovations, making it a great choice for buy, fix, and flip investors. You're essentially borrowing against the fixed-up value of the property instead of its valuation in its current condition.

>> **Home-equity loan:** This type of loan allows you to borrow against the equity in the home. It's great for financing renovations or pulling equity out of an investment property to buy another investment property.

>> **Home-equity line of credit (LOC):** This loan is the same as a home-equity loan, but instead of getting a lump sum, you draw money from your LOC account as you need it and pay interest only on the amount you draw from the account.

Making yourself look good on paper

Real estate investors with proven track records have no problems finding lenders eager to loan them money. Until you achieve platinum status, however, you'd better look good on paper. You need to demonstrate that you have a solid income from your day job, money in the bank, investments, or assets that you can sell. You need proof that you pay your bills on time. And you need to show that you're not so heavily burdened by debt that one more loan is likely to push you into bankruptcy.

In the following sections, you take a snapshot of your financial picture and get up to speed on the details that lenders commonly consider before approving a loan. By identifying areas for improvement, you can hammer out the dents to make yourself look as good as possible to prospective lenders.

Determining what you're worth in dollars and cents

The first question a lender is going to ask you is "What's your net worth?" *Net worth* is simply whatever money you'd have if you sold all your stuff and then paid off all your debts, including your taxes. Officially, the equation goes like this:

Net Worth = What You Own – What You Owe

To prove to a lender that you're a worthy borrower, type up a page that lists your assets and liabilities and calculates your net worth. Don't forget about your personal and household belongings, art collection, model-train collection, jewelry, antiques, and so on. Ideally, the result is a positive number.

TIP

A strong net worth can help you borrow money at competitive interest rates, but you can still borrow money with a low or even a negative net worth. If you have a solid investment strategy and the energy and commitment to implement it, you can secure the capital you need to get started. You may simply have to settle for a hard-money loan, as explained in "Financing with Hard-Money and Gap Loans" earlier in this chapter.

Obtaining your credit report

Your bank or mortgage broker is going to inspect your credit history before approving a loan, so you should know ahead of time what that credit history says about you. Check your credit report every three months or so, correct any errors, and take steps to improve your credit rating. No irregularity is too small to correct.

You can obtain your credit report through any of the following three credit-reporting services, but because lenders may report to only one service, you should check all three (Equifax, Experian, and TransUnion). You can request any or all three reports online at www.annualcreditreport.com/index.action.

Read on for details about obtaining, inspecting, and correcting your credit report.

Examining your credit reports

When you receive your credit reports, inspect them carefully for the following red flags:

>> Addresses of places you never lived.

>> Aliases you never used, which may indicate that someone else is using your Social Security number or the credit-reporting agency has mixed someone else's data into yours.

- » Multiple Social Security numbers, flagging the possibility that information for someone with the same name has made it into your credit report.

- » Wrong date of birth.

- » Credit cards you don't have.

- » Loans you haven't taken out.

- » Records of unpaid bills that you either know you paid or have good reason for not paying.

- » Records of delinquent payments that weren't delinquent or for which you have a good excuse for not paying on time.

- » Inquiries from companies with which you've never done business. (When you apply for a loan, the lender typically runs an inquiry on your credit report, and that inquiry shows up in the report.)

WARNING

An address of a place you've never lived or records of accounts, loans, and credit cards you never had may be a sign that somebody has stolen your identity. Contact the credit-reporting company immediately, and request that a fraud alert be placed on your credit report.

Boosting your credit score

Last but certainly not least, your credit report should contain your credit score. (If it doesn't, contact the credit-reporting agency to request your score.) Credit-reporting agencies often assign you a credit score that ranges roughly between 300 (you never paid a bill in your life) and 900 (you've had a credit card for a long time, borrow small amounts often, always pay your bills on time, and don't carry any huge balances). Each credit-reporting agency may use a different scoring method and range of scores, so you can expect some variation.

Your credit score determines not only whether you qualify for a loan, but also how much you're qualified to borrow and at what interest rate. A high credit score lets you borrow more money at a lower interest rate.

TIP

A credit score of 700 or higher is superb. Anything below about 680 raises red flags. If your credit rating dips below 700, take steps to improve it, such as the following:

- » Dispute any erroneous items on your credit report. You may be allowed to submit your dispute online, or you may be required to mail a letter of dispute.

- » Apply for fewer loans and credit cards. Applying for several loans or credit cards in a short period of can make you appear to be financially desperate and may significantly lower your credit rating.

>> Pay off your credit-card balances or at least pay off enough that the balance is 50 percent or more below your available credit limit. If you have sufficient equity built up in your home, you can refinance or take out a home-equity loan to pay down your credit-card debt.

TIP

If your credit score is lower than you want it to be, consider using a credit-repair smartphone app to monitor and improve your score, such as Credit Karma, Credit Sesame, or CreditWise. Experian and TransUnion also have credit apps that you may find useful.

Gathering the paperwork and records you need

Prepare for your meeting with your bank or mortgage broker. Call and ask for a list of the documents and records they need and make copies to bring with you to your first meeting. Most banks and mortgage brokers typically require the following documents:

>> Two or three recent pay stubs showing your income

>> Your two most recent federal income tax returns

>> Your two most recent bank statements

>> Recent loan statements that show how much you currently owe on your car, credit cards, or other purchases you've had to finance

TIP

If your net-worth statement shows that you own much more than you owe, bring it along too. Banks and mortgage brokers like to see people who have a positive net worth, know the importance of net worth, and care enough to monitor it.

Comparison Shopping for Low-Cost Loans

Whenever you borrow money, comparison-shop to find the loan that costs the least amount of money over the life of the loan. Take the following steps to calculate loan cost:

1. **Start with the amount the bank charges you upfront in loan origination fees, discount points (interest you pay upfront, typically a percentage of the loan, to lower the interest rate), and other fees.**

2. Multiply the monthly payment by the number of months you plan to pay on the loan.

3. Add the two amounts to determine your total payment.

4. Total the amount of each payment that goes toward paying the principal of the loan.

Your lender can tell you how much of each payment goes toward principal.

5. Subtract the total that you determined in step 4 from the total in step 3.

Suppose that you're considering two loans, each for $100,000. You plan on using the loan to buy and renovate a home over two years and then sell it and pay off the remaining principal on the loan. You have a choice between a 30-year, fixed-rate mortgage at 6 percent or a 30-year, interest-only loan at 5 percent. Look at the 6 percent, fixed-rate mortgage first:

Loan origination fee and discount points:	$1,000.00
Plus monthly payment of $599.55 × 24 months:	$14,389.20
Equal total payments:	$15,389.20
Minus total paid toward principal:	$2,531.75
Equal total cost of loan:	$12,857.45

Here are the numbers for the 30-year, interest-only loan at 5 percent:

Loan origination fee and discount points:	$1,000.00
Plus monthly payment of $416.67 × 24 months:	$10,000.08
Equal total payments:	$11,000.08
Minus total paid toward principal:	$0.00
Equal total cost of loan:	$11,000.08

As you can see, even though you're not paying down the principal on the interest-only loan, over the life of the loan, you pay about $1,700 less. In addition, the interest-only loan has much lower monthly payments, freeing up cash to use for renovations and other investments.

TIP

As a general rule for quick flips (buying and selling a property in less than six months), opt for loans with low (or no) closing costs, low (or no) discount points, and low interest rates. Avoid any loans that have early-payment penalties.

IN THIS CHAPTER

» **Generating quality leads through networking**

» **Making yourself the go-to person**

» **Marketing yourself as a foreclosure investor**

» **Optimizing the storage and retrieval of good contacts**

» **Taking care of the people who take care of you**

Chapter **6**

Networking Your Way to Foreclosure Success

As a real estate investor, you can't climb very far up the ladder of success on your own. You need access to cash, leads on potentially profitable properties, information about those properties, guidance from more experienced investors, legal and financial advice, referrals to affordable contractors and handymen, and much more. You need assistance, and the best way to get that assistance is through networking.

In this chapter, I unveil the power of networking and reveal techniques and tips that can transform a lone wolf into a well-connected real estate investor. By mastering the techniques in this chapter, you can reduce your workload and streamline the process of buying, renovating, and selling foreclosure properties.

Grasping the Power of Networking

I owe much of my success as a real estate investor to the advice, assistance, and resources of thousands of people. These people generously donate their time and expertise to provide me the financing and high-quality leads I need to succeed at investing in foreclosures and other real estate. Without the guidance and support of thousands of people, I'd never have experienced the level of success I now enjoy.

I strongly encourage you to take the same approach when you're starting out and for however long you continue to invest in real estate. In the following sections, I reveal the benefits of networking in all aspects of foreclosure investing.

REMEMBER

Today, right now, start building a strong network. Every business day, I make 100 phone calls and send another 150 email messages to keep in touch with clients, colleagues, distressed homeowners, and a host of others who need my assistance and who assist me. I'm not saying you need to make 100 calls per day. Start slowly, with three to five new contacts a day; then work your way up. Every person you contact probably knows about 250 other people, many of whom may eventually need your help or who can help you. Over a short period of time, your network begins to grow exponentially and almost effortlessly. Think of it this way: If business is slow, turn *not*working into *net*working, and you'll have more business than you can handle.

Generating leads on profitable pre-auction properties

The earlier you step into the foreclosure process, the greater your chances are of eventually taking possession of a property, and the earliest you can find out about a foreclosure is through word-of-mouth leads. Distressed homeowners, knowing that you buy foreclosures and have a reputation for being fair, may call you out of the blue to buy their property. Maybe someone you know knows someone who knows someone who's currently facing a financial crisis. Or perhaps another investor you know is too busy or doesn't have the funds available to follow up on a golden opportunity.

TIP

Networking delivers people and property to you, saving you from having to do the legwork to track down potentially profitable properties. Everyone you meet is a potential lead generator: attorneys, real estate agents, mortgage brokers, title-company staff, loan officers, contractors, even the person who delivers your mail or your pepperoni pizza. Let everyone know that you can help homeowners who are facing financial crises. You may have secrets, but what you do and what you want to do shouldn't be one of them. Tell everyone what you do!

DISCOVERING OPPORTUNITIES IN DIVORCE

Divorce frequently orphans properties. A couple splits up, neither partner can afford the monthly mortgage payments on their own, and they're forced to sell their home.

When a divorce attorney gets involved, the couple has even less money to pay the mortgage. In many cases, one party or both parties use the home as collateral to pay their attorneys out of the proceeds from the property settlement. The attorney often works unpaid until the property sells, so the attorney places a lien on the property to secure payment. Many divorce attorneys have liens on several properties, and they don't get paid until those properties sell.

You can profit from these situations in two ways:

- By networking with divorce attorneys, you may find attorneys with clients who are seeking to sell their homes before losing them in foreclosure.

- You can negotiate a short sale with the divorce attorney. Suppose that the wife receives the home as part of the divorce settlement and starts missing mortgage payments, so the bank initiates foreclosure proceedings and posts a foreclosure notice. You're trying to buy the property from the wife, but if you paid what she's asking, you wouldn't profit. The house has a lien on it for $8,000 from the husband's attorney, because the husband used the house as collateral to pay his attorney. You could show the foreclosure notice to the husband's attorney, explain that his $8,000 lien is going to be wiped out by the foreclosure, and ask whether he'd be willing to take $1,500. That way, the attorney gets something out of the deal, you save $6,500 on the purchase, and you can afford to offer the wife a little more for the house.

For details on how to network effectively to find foreclosure properties, see Chapter 7, for a list of the top people to contact for leads.

Securing your financing

Need money? Maybe all you need to do is ask for it. Securing financing may not be quite that easy all the time, but it can be some of the time. If people who have plenty of money lying around know that you have a proven track record for making money, they might prefer to invest in you than to bet their money on stocks and bonds or entrust it to a financial adviser.

Network with lenders in your area, such as local banks, mortgage companies, and private investors. You may make these contacts through real estate investment clubs, while you're doing your personal banking, through your mortgage broker, or as you network with other real estate professionals and investors.

When you borrow money from private lenders, be careful not to present the transaction as something other than a personal loan. If you pitch the deal as an investment opportunity, the loan may fall under U.S. Securities and Exchange Commission (SEC) guidelines for investors. You can borrow money from family and friends as a personal loan, but if you plan to establish a relationship with the lender as an investor, work through a mortgage broker. Consult your attorney to make sure that you're doing everything legally and aboveboard.

Tracking down reliable, affordable professionals

Without networking, you're working in a vacuum whenever you hire an attorney, accountant, agent, title company, inspector, or contractor. Other people in your area are fishing the same pool, and they've already scoped out the best fishing holes. Don't waste your time searching online for top-notch professionals. Word-of-mouth referrals are the way to go.

Real estate agents are in the business of assisting people with all issues related to buying, owning, and selling homes. They often have a large database packed with valuable contacts: other agents, attorneys, title companies, home inspectors, accountants, and contractors. They know the power of networking and typically are more than willing to recommend people, especially if you tell the people you call who recommended them.

Selling your house for more money in less time

When real estate agents place a house on the market, they essentially network to find interested buyers. Sure, they may create full-color flyers and brochures and plant a For Sale sign on the front lawn, but they connect to most prospective buyers by using a networking tool called the Multiple Listing Service (MLS). When a seller works through an agent, the agent posts the listing on one or more MLSes. Buyers' agents can pull up these listings to find houses for their clients. The top agents also network with large companies that have relocation divisions.

In Chapter 18, I strongly recommend that if you decide to sell your foreclosure property, you work through an agent who has access to all the multiple listing services in your area. Using the MLS enables you to tap the power of the most powerful networking tool for selling properties quickly and for top dollar.

TIP

You can generate additional interest in your property through your own network. Before you list the property, start talking about it. Inform everyone you know in the area that you have a property you're fixing up that promises to be spectacular. Everyone you tell potentially knows a friend, relative, or colleague who's thinking of moving to the area. The person you tell may be just the one who delivers a buyer right to your front door! Consider creating a business card specifically for a single house you're selling and passing it out to everyone. You can get a box of 1,000 cards very reasonably, and this strategy works.

Realizing the Importance of Being Good

As the old saying goes, "News travels fast. Bad news travels faster." You can take months building a support network, but if you start doing shoddy work, stealing houses from financially strapped seniors, or transforming neighborhoods into slums, your support network is likely to turn into an angry mob that would just as soon see you tarred, feathered, and run out of town.

REMEMBER

Every foreclosure property you buy, renovate, and sell is a reflection of you and how you do business. Build a strong reputation by treating everyone you meet fairly and with respect. When you renovate a property, make the house a home you'd be proud to put your name on. Work to improve the housing in the community where you do business. I usually have more opportunities to acquire properties than I can reasonably follow up on, so I have to rule out some prospects. I ask myself, "After I get the place all fixed up, could I envision myself living here?" If the answer is "No," I cross it off the list.

Acting with integrity — always

People are generally willing to trust others. Only after they're disappointed do they form a negative opinion. In short, your good reputation is yours to lose or improve.

REMEMBER

You wouldn't recommend a restaurant to a friend if the food was bad, the service was lousy, and everything on the menu was overpriced. The same is true in real estate. By building a reputation as a straight shooter who plays by the rules, you become the person to whom others steer their business. This doesn't mean that you need to be kind to the point of giving away all your profits; it simply means telling the truth, fully disclosing your intentions, following through on promises, and doing high-quality work.

Investing in quality craftsmanship

Homeowners as well as real estate investors often try to boost their bottom line by hiding defects in a property. Instead of repairing a leaky foundation, they install wood paneling over the weeping walls and run a humidifier to take out the dampness. Rather than repair the termite damage in the floorboards, they lay wall-to-wall carpeting. They try to hide the foul odors by creating an aromatic cloud of potpourri.

When repairing and renovating a home, your goal should be to bring the home up to market standards. I'm not saying that you need to transform a Quonset hut into the Taj Mahal. If you're renovating a foreclosure property in a low-rent district, using builder's-grade materials instead of top-of-the-line stuff may be sufficient. Hiding defects in a property, however, can come back to bite you in the seat of your pants. When the homeowners discover the defect, they're liable to come back to you, and if you don't rectify the situation immediately, you may be dragged into court, or worse: They may start telling all their friends, family, and neighbors that you ripped them off!

TIP

For details and pointers on renovating a home affordably without cutting too many corners, see Chapter 17.

Building thriving communities

Neighborhoods, especially the most profitable neighborhoods, like to see investors come in and clean things up. When you transform the neighborhood eyesore into an attractive abode, you not only make the neighbors feel better about where they live but also improve their homes' values. You gain your own personal sales force of enthusiastic supporters who spread the good word about the new house on the block that's up for sale.

Some investors who are just out for the quick buck buy a property, cash out the equity, and quickly lose interest in it. Con artists may even use the house for some illegal flipping scheme, paying an appraiser to inflate the home's value, cashing out the inflated equity, and then abandoning the property altogether. Don't join the ranks of these real estate leeches.

WARNING

Don't get seduced by quick-cash opportunities. In the long run, you stand to make much more money investing in foreclosures by being sincerely interested in the neighborhoods you're investing in. When con artists descend on a neighborhood like a swarm of locusts and leave it devastated, they earn a quick profit, but they also earn the loathing of the neighborhood. When you work to improve a neighborhood, you build a neighborhood that's ready and willing to support you.

Marketing Yourself

Productive networking requires some proactive efforts on your part, especially when you're starting out. People are often ready, willing, and able to assist an honest and competent investor if they know that such a person exists. By marketing yourself, what you have to offer, and what you need to do your job, you soon discover that your name, face, and reputation are recognized throughout the neighborhood.

To market yourself effectively, assemble your marketing tool kit and then get busy talking, calling, emailing, and mailing out notices to let everyone know what you do, what you offer, and what you need. In the following sections, I show you how to market yourself effectively as a foreclosure investor.

Gathering your marketing tools

You don't need to hire a public relations firm to market yourself as a foreclosure investor. All you have to do is gather a few basic tools and get to work. You probably already have most of the marketing tools you need, as described in the following sections.

TIP

Field research I've performed (by attending weddings and funerals) reveals that every person knows about 250 other people. When you impress one person, you have the opportunity to impress at least 250 others. Word of mouth is the most powerful networking tool.

Designing and printing business cards

Even in this high-tech age of computers, websites, and mobile phones, the lowly business card is your key marketing tool. If you have a computer and a decent printer, you can design your own business card and print it on card stock that you can pick up at any office-supply store in your area. If you don't have a computer and printer, head down to the local print shop or to a website like Vistaprint (www. vistaprint.com) to have your cards printed for you. Include the following on your cards:

» A cameo shot of yourself, so that people know your face.

» Your name and business name, if you have a business.

» Your mailing address. Don't use a post office box number; it's too impersonal, and nobody will trust you. People trust bricks-and-mortar establishments.

» Your phone number.

>> Your email address and website address, if you have one.

>> A statement about what you do (such as "I buy houses for cash").

TIP

Pass your card out to everybody you meet, and I mean *everybody*. You'd be amazed by how many people know a homeowner who's embroiled in a financial crisis.

Carrying your phone at all times and answering it

Homeowners facing foreclosure are usually in desperate situations, and they need help yesterday. You want to be the person they can contact in their hour of need, so carry your mobile phone 24/7, and answer when it rings or buzzes. Every missed call is a missed opportunity.

Equipping yourself with a computer

Nowadays, a computer is a necessity in all areas of real estate. Before you venture out into the world of foreclosures, equip yourself with a decent computer, an Internet connection with email, and a printer. Your computer is an essential tool for performing the following foreclosure–investing tasks:

>> Researching state and county foreclosure laws and regulations

>> Finding and researching foreclosure properties

>> Keeping in touch with contacts

>> Designing and printing your own marketing materials

>> Establishing a web presence for additional leads

>> Shopping and applying for loans

>> Managing your finances, if you choose to do your own accounting

Creating ads

I recommend against advertising yourself in the local newspaper as a foreclosure investor until you're well established and have a strong enough financial base to buy and hold multiple foreclosure properties.

TIP

After you're well established, however, you can generate additional leads on pre-auction properties by placing a small ad in the classifieds that says something like "I Buy Homes for Cash," followed by your phone number. For details about advertising for leads, see Chapter 7.

Starting with your inner circle

The most challenging step in networking is often the first step. You may simply not know where to start. The best place to begin is your inner circle: family, friends, and co-workers. Tell them your plans, brainstorm for additional ideas, and try to find out whether they know anyone who may be able to assist you — real estate agents, attorneys, loan officers, bankers, local officials, private investors, and so on.

Whenever you work with a mortgage broker, title-company representative, or other real estate professional, ask whether they know anyone else who may be able to help. Take names and phone numbers, even if you don't need a certain person's expertise right now. You may find that the person can help somewhere down the line.

When networking with your inner circle, avoid the dream-killers, especially family members who don't believe in you. These confidence-busters can often convince you to give up long before you buy your first foreclosure property. Only you know what you're capable of accomplishing, and often, *you* don't even know until you've accomplished your goal.

TIP

Start at the top. Referrals tend to work from management to employees rather than up the chain of command. If you have a friend who sells cars, for example, they can refer you to their employees, to the porter, to the clerical staff, and so on.

Keeping in touch: A daily chore

When's the last time you called your best friend from grade school? If it was more than about a year ago, chances are good that you'll never touch base with that person again. The same is true in business, but the time is shorter. If you lose touch with a valuable contact for more than a month or two, that person is going to quickly forget that you ever existed.

I have a database of more than 6,000 people (and growing) whom I assist and who assist me in my various business dealings. Every day, I personally contact nearly 250 people over the phone and by email, which keeps my name and face in the minds of the people I rely on.

TIP

Harvey Mackay, motivational speaker and author of *Swim with the Sharks,* taught me some of the most valuable lessons I've learned about sales. Harvey said he made sure that he knew at least 66 things about every one of his customers. This sales tactic applies to networking as well. Try to find out 66 things about every person you contact: their birthday, anniversary, spouse's name, kids' names and ages, hobbies, interests, and so on. You don't have to find out everything at once; slowly gather details over time. The more you know about a person, the more you can become genuinely interested in their life, and the stronger the bond you can establish with that person.

Managing Contact Information

Don't rely on memory alone or a purse stuffed with scraps of paper to keep track of all the people in your network. Use a contact management program or database to record all the pertinent and not-so-pertinent information about each person.

TIP

I use Microsoft Outlook because it enables me to enter the names, addresses, phone numbers, and email addresses of everyone I know. Outlook's robust features allows me to do several additional things:

>> Record the person's birthday, anniversary, and spouse's name.

>> Type additional notes about the person's family, interests, and specialties.

>> Remind myself of important dates and activities so I can contact the person on key dates.

>> Send multiple people a single email message.

>> Synchronize contact information between my computer and smartphone so that I always have access to my contacts.

Rewarding Good Deeds and Good Leads

When you're asking for guidance, assistance, and good leads, be prepared to reward the helping hands who assist you. People quickly forget or become resentful when others keep asking for assistance and forget to demonstrate their appreciation in some tangible way. To expand your network, show your appreciation. Here are some suggestions on what you can do to keep the people in your network happy and reaching out to others:

>> Refer other people to your agent, attorney, mortgage broker, title company, contractor, handyman, and other professionals who've provided excellent service. Ask for extra cards, carry them with you, and pass them out. A referral is the highest form of flattery.

>> When you contact someone you've been referred to, let the person know who referred you.

>> Treat everyone you encounter — from your real estate attorney to the person who's repairing the leaky faucet in the home you just bought — with sincere respect. If you value others, they value you.

>> When someone helps you, show your appreciation by sending them a quick handwritten note. People have different needs, but everyone needs to be thanked.

>> Keep an ear to the ground for people in your network who need your assistance. If they're in trouble, a random act of kindness with no thought of what you'll eventually receive in return demonstrates that you're genuinely interested in their success.

TIP

Give back to the community. Think of networking as a ladder, and you're standing on one of the middle rungs. Above you are more-experienced people who can reach down and pull you up. Below you are less-experienced people you need to reach down to. You never stop learning, and when you learn, you have an obligation to teach.

3
Creating Win–Win Situations in Pre-Foreclosure (Before Auction)

Scoop up the best opportunities in pre-foreclosure, before other investors find out about them and have a chance to bid up the price.

Scope out the best sources for pre-foreclosure properties, including referrals, probate and divorce attorneys, For Sale by Owner (FSBO) opportunities, and dontwanners — rundown or vacant properties that the owners obviously "don't want."

Perform your due diligence so that you know what you're getting (and what you can sell it for) before you bid on it. In other words, avoid getting burned by unpleasant surprises.

Get in touch with homeowners and lenders in pre-foreclosure so that you can negotiate win–win–win solutions — good for you, for the lenders, and for the homeowners.

Analyze a deal in pre-foreclosure and put it in writing, in the form of a purchase agreement, so that the price and terms are clear and legally binding.

IN THIS CHAPTER

» Plugging your ear into the neighborhood grapevine

» Advertising for additional leads

» Cruising the neighborhood for disheveled or abandoned properties

» Checking out properties for sale by owner

» Finding and deciphering foreclosure notices

Chapter **7**

Discovering Homeowners Facing Foreclosure

The earlier in the foreclosure process you contact distressed homeowners, the better chance you have of helping them claim some of the equity they've built up in a property while snagging a property that's worth your time and effort.

But how do you track down distressed homeowners early in the process? You can take any of several approaches. My personal favorite is through word-of-mouth networking because it often delivers the timeliest information. But you can also discover opportunities by cruising the neighborhood for unkempt homes or homes that are for sale by owner (FSBO); searching and advertising for properties online; perusing the county legal news for foreclosure notices; and discovering how to acquire houses being sold as part of divorce, bankruptcy, or probate proceedings.

In this chapter, I explain how to locate distressed properties and homeowners as early as possible in the process to beat out other investors while providing distressed homeowners additional options for solving their legal and financial problems.

TIP

In Chapter 8, I explain how to gather the information about the property and the homeowners that you need to provide the homeowners the assistance they need, and in Chapter 9, I reveal tips and strategies for personally contacting homeowners so that you can discuss their situation and their options.

Networking Your Way to Promising Properties

Before the foreclosure notice is posted and the foreclosure becomes public knowledge, you have only two ways of finding out that the homeowners are in a jam and need to sell their home in a hurry:

>> **Word-of-mouth networking:** You hear of someone who needs your assistance, or a distressed homeowner hears of you.

>> **Must-sell ads:** You notice an ad in the classified section of the local newspaper that conveys a sense of duress. Look for ads that say, "Must Sell" or "Relocating." These ads often clue you into the fact that the owners must sell in a hurry and are possibly in jeopardy of losing their home.

In Chapter 6, I reveal some basic networking strategies to obtain the assistance you need and get the word out about what you do. In the following sections, I list the people who are often the best sources for leads on foreclosure and pre-foreclosure properties.

Identifying your personal lead generators

A *lead generator* is anyone or anything that can refer distressed homeowners to you or point you in their direction — a banker, real estate broker, loan officer, divorce attorney, the minister of your church, a casual acquaintance, a classified ad, a website, or an Internet bulletin board on which you post a notice and others respond to it.

In the following sections, I list the human lead generators you can often rely on to identify foreclosure opportunities in your market.

DEALING WITH AN EMBARRASSING SITUATION

When homeowners are in a dire financial situation, they often stop talking, telling nobody, not even their family or closest friends, what's going on. In some cases, they contact a lawyer or tell the minister at their church, a counselor or therapist, or even a complete stranger. If they know that you assist homeowners who are financially strapped, they may tell you.

If the distressed homeowners remain uncommunicative, you have no chance of finding out about the situation until the foreclosure notice is posted. If they tell someone, your chances of hearing about it increase in direct proportion to the number of people who know that you assist distressed homeowners.

As a professional and someone who's not intimately involved in the situation, the homeowners may be more willing to talk with you, especially if you act professionally and have the confidence that you can help them out of a very challenging and uncomfortable situation.

REMEMBER

People who know you personally are the best lead generators because they act as mutual friends, referring and recommending you to homeowners they know. Keep in mind that when people refer you to their friends or acquaintances, that referral reflects on the person who gave it. Earn that person's trust by treating the homeowners with respect and doing everything possible to assist them in their time of need.

Creating your A-list

Real estate professionals and attorneys who specialize in certain areas can feed you some of the most productive leads. These are your A–listers:

>> **Foreclosure attorneys:** Foreclosure attorneys post the foreclosure notices and handle the liquidation of properties. You should know all the foreclosure attorneys in your market by name and have their phone numbers and email addresses at the top of your A-list.

>> **Real estate attorneys:** The real estate attorneys in your area know the market and the foreclosure rules and regulations and are often in contact with distressed homeowners. In addition to providing you with leads, real estate attorneys often provide some excellent advice. Pick their brains for additional information.

>> **Divorce attorneys:** Often when couples divorce, they can no longer afford the house they purchased together. In many cases, the divorce settlement requires them to sell the house and split the proceeds, and divorce attorneys often want this to happen as quickly as possible so that they can get paid.

>> **Bankruptcy attorneys:** Bankruptcy often requires the homeowners to sell their real estate to restructure their debt. Bankruptcy attorneys frequently need to work with investors who can close on the deal in a hurry. Few, if any, of the bankruptcy attorneys I know buy real estate; they do their thing and would love to have an investor in their network to purchase properties.

>> **Probate attorneys:** When a homeowner dies leaving behind a home or other real estate, it must be liquidated and the proceeds divided among the heirs. When settling an estate, probate attorneys often rely on investors who can pay cash for properties to expedite the process.

>> **Loan officers:** Loan officers specialize in working with people who have bruised credit and refinancing homeowners out of foreclosure or bankruptcy. In many cases, the loan officer can't help the homeowners and needs an investor to step in and purchase the property. By networking with loan officers, you can become their go-to investor.

>> **Real estate brokers who specialize in selling bank-owned properties**: Some real estate brokers specialize in selling bank-owned properties. In most cases, the foreclosing banks don't allow their real estate brokers to buy the properties the bank forecloses on. Some people might see these brokers as competitors, but they aren't. Their job is to sell the properties as quickly as possible. Fewer than 10 percent of real estate brokers invest in real estate, and those who do invest rarely do so in the markets they serve.

A friend who's a real estate broker owns a bunch of offices. During dinner with this couple one night, I asked, "Out of all your agents, how many can retire and live off their investments?" Of 200, only one — a couple who work as a team — can retire and live comfortably off the real estate they've invested in.

Contacting friends, family, and neighbors

When you're shopping for a car, you ask a dealer or a mechanic for advice. When you're in the market for a diamond ring, you ask a jeweler. In the same way, when you're looking for foreclosure properties, your best leads often come from real estate professionals, because they specialize in the housing market where you invest.

In the case of foreclosures, however, real estate professionals aren't your only lead generators. Family members, friends, and neighbors often know about homeowners who are having financial problems long before word reaches the real estate community. Tell family members, friends, and neighbors that you provide assistance to distressed homeowners. If the people closest to you don't know that you provide services to help homeowners in crises, they won't even think of telling you or referring their friends or relatives to you.

Building on your church affiliations

Churches exist primarily to meet the spiritual needs of their congregations, but they also function as community centers to assist members with relationships, raising children, and financial matters. Some homeowners feel more comfortable telling their ministers or other church members about their financial woes than they are breaking the bad news to their spouses.

I'm not telling you to join a church solely to tap its membership for leads, but if you already belong to a church or are thinking of joining one, the church can be an additional lead generator, and you can often assist members when they don't know where else to turn for help.

TIP

When an entire area suffers a serious financial blow, such as mass layoffs or a major employer's move out of the area, consider holding a meeting at the church to inform homeowners in the congregation of their options and foreclosure rights. You may do more good than you could ever imagine.

Networking through clubs and other organizations

Do you belong to any clubs in your area — the Rotary Club, Kiwanis, the Elks, the Moose, the American Legion, the Lions Club, or the Purple Hatters? If so, don't forget to mention to your fellow members that you assist distressed homeowners.

You never know when a fellow member may be facing a financial hardship or knows a homeowner who's in a financial pickle. By letting others know what you do, you give them someone they can approach to ask questions or seek assistance. Don't forget to hand out your business cards, as explained in Chapter 6, assuming that sharing business cards is part of the culture.

TIP

Close your eyes and try to picture your spouse, your child, your favorite pet, or the first president of the United States. Chances are good that you have a pretty clear image of that person . . . or dog, or cat, or hamster in your mind. By telling everyone that you assist distressed homeowners and buy properties, you begin to create an image in their minds that you're the go-to person whenever they or someone they know is about to lose their home.

Getting the word out on the streets

Unless you wear blinders while driving around or flipping through the local newspaper, you've probably noticed signs (often referred to as *bandit signs*), billboards, or ads that say stuff like "We Buy Ugly Houses" or "Need Cash? We Buy Houses!" or "Foreclosure? We Can Help."

The people who post these ads are investors, just like you, fishing for early leads on pre-auction properties. They're usually pretty well-established investors who have plenty of money and resources on hand to field all the calls they get.

WARNING

Don't post an ad or paint your name and phone number on a billboard until you're capable of handling numerous phone calls. Advertising before you're prepared can backfire on you and ruin your reputation in the community as the resident champion for the distressed homeowner. When you're starting out, focus on fewer properties so that you can devote all your energy, expertise, and resources to doing an outstanding job. Later, you can think about advertising and expanding your operations.

TIP

You can also advertise on sites such as Craigslist (www.craigslist.org) or create your own website, blog, or social media accounts to spread the word online. Some real estate investment groups also have their own bulletin boards on which you can post messages asking for financing or for leads on investment properties. Just don't forget to do your due diligence; con artists often prowl websites to look for suckers.

Scoping Out the Neighborhood for Dontwanners

In *Flipping Houses For Dummies*, 4th Edition (John Wiley & Sons, Inc.), I encourage real estate investors to cruise their neighborhoods looking for *dontwanners* — properties that the owners so much don't want that they're willing to do anything to get rid of them, including offering their homes for sale at a deep discount.

Dontwanners are especially relevant when you're investing in foreclosures, because homeowners who are strapped for cash typically don't have a budget for home maintenance. Some homeowners even pack up and move out, abandoning the house altogether. By knocking on the door and talking to the homeowners or their neighbors, you may just stumble on a property with residents who are in the very early stages of foreclosure.

Although word-of-mouth networking is often the best way to track down pre-auction properties, don't focus so much on networking that you overlook some prime real estate opportunities that you may be driving past daily. Keep your eyes peeled for the dontwanners in your market. Here are the common signs of a dontwanner:

>> Newspapers stacked on the front step

>> Neglected lawn

>> Vacant-looking house (lack of furniture inside, no window blinds or curtains)

If you spot a dontwanner, talk to the neighbors to find out who owns the house; then try to contact the owners to see whether they want to sell it. Sometimes, the owners are so fed up with a property that they're not even willing to take the time and trouble to place it on the market.

TIP

To gather inside information about the property, contact the owners. If you can't find out who owns the property, head to your county's Register of Deeds office, and ask to see the title. For more about researching a property, check out Chapter 8.

Searching for FSBO Properties

One of the smartest actions homeowners can take when they find themselves in a financial hole they can't dig themselves out of is to sell their home and move into more affordable accommodations. To save money, they may try the for sale by owner (FSBO) route so that they don't have to pay the standard 6–8 percent real estate commission. This approach, however, often backfires, because selling a home without the assistance of a real estate agent isn't easy. The homeowners may find that nobody's interested, or they don't have the money to fix up the house to make it marketable, and the house lingers on the market while their financial hole deepens.

FSBO sellers aren't always experiencing financial hardship, of course, but you never know until you knock on the door, take a look around, and talk with the homeowners.

You can locate FSBOs by driving around the neighborhood and looking for "For Sale" or "For Sale by Owner" signs — usually, cheap-looking signs that you can pick up at your local hardware store, write your phone number on with a permanent marker, and plant on your front lawn.

Another way to locate FSBOs is to check any of the many FSBO websites. One of the most popular sites is cleverly called ForSaleByOwner.com (`www.forsalebyowner.com`). You can find additional sites by pulling up your favorite Internet search tool and searching for "for sale by owner." Look for keywords in the listing such as "fixer-upper," "needs work," "foreclosure," and "must sell." I mention FSBO sites only because they may lead you to opportunities.

Finding Foreclosure Notices

I take a foreclosure notice as being somewhat of a personal failure. I wonder, "Why didn't this homeowner come to me first?" The foreclosure notice marks the beginning of the end — the day when the lender first publicly announces that the homeowners haven't been making their payments. It's also the day when foreclosure investors ramp up their efforts to contact the homeowners and when con artists begin crawling out from under rocks (or wherever they were hiding).

Even though the foreclosure notice marks the beginning of the end for most distressed homeowners, it usually appears several weeks before the auction, so you still have time to assist the homeowners. Also, if the house does end up on the auction block, the foreclosure notice provides you additional information you can use to start tracking the foreclosure so that if the opportunity arises for you to purchase the property later, you can be well prepared with the information you need to enter competitive bids without overbidding.

Tracking down local publications

When lenders initiate foreclosure proceedings, they post a foreclosure notice or Notice of Default (NOD) in the county's legal newspaper or a local newspaper. Contact your county's Register of Deeds office and ask where foreclosure notices are posted. Some jurisdictions have privatized everything; they've outsourced the entire foreclosure process to private practices that handle all the cases and manage their own legal publications.

Get to know the staff at your county's Register of Deeds office. While you're there, see whether they have an extra copy of this week's county legal news. A rack of copies may be sitting near a desk or just outside the office. Pick one up, head to your local coffee shop, and read it from cover to cover.

If you live in a county that sees a fair share of foreclosures, the foreclosure listings can seem overwhelming at first. You skim page after page of listings written in legalistic gobbledygook. The trick to making the listings less cumbersome is knowing what you're looking for and then weeding out any listings that raise red flags. If you find a property on Main Street with a mortgage of $500,000, and you know of no property on Main Street that you'd pay more than $250,000 for, you know that property isn't for you. If the same property is listed for $100,000, however, it may be worth investigating.

Getting on the mailing list

Whoever publishes your county's legal news is likely to have a subscription service, so you can have the publication delivered to your door or sent to you electronically via email. In some counties, you can view foreclosure notices on the Register of Deeds website for free.

Ask one of the staff members at the Register of Deeds office about your options or search the current edition of the county legal news for information about subscribing.

REMEMBER

Your county's legal news isn't recommended reading; it's *required* reading. Carefully read the foreclosure listings every single week and keep track of every property that catches your eye. You may see that a notice for a property one week doesn't appear the following week, indicating that the owners may have worked out a forbearance with the lender or received an adjournment. Keep following the property to see whether it appears again. Properties often disappear from the radar only to reappear weeks or months later. In Chapter 8, I explain how to create a database for tracking properties.

Subscribing to commercial foreclosure information services . . . or not

You can find plenty of commercial services that deliver foreclosure notices via email, snail mail, or member-only websites. Some of these services charge reasonable fees, and you may be able to buy notices by city, county, or zip code to keep costs down. Other services may charge $3,000 a year to mail you notices that are out of date by the time the mail carrier delivers them.

WARNING

Don't waste your money on high-cost foreclosure subscription services, and never rely solely on a commercial subscription service for leads. These services are no replacement for reading the weekly county legal news. Why pay more for a commercial service when your county provides the same or better information for free or for a modest subscription fee? If you decide to subscribe to a service, sign up for your own zip code first, and test it. Compare the results with your own research to see whether the information is timely and accurate. Most of these services offer dated material, but sometimes they provide valuable leads.

Deciphering a foreclosure notice

Attorneys write foreclosure notices so you can expect them to be written in cryptic legalese that seems to discourage the average person from thinking about buying the property. In Chapter 8, I present a sample foreclosure notice that shows just how cryptic they can be, and I highlight the important pieces of information the foreclosure notice contains:

>> File number

>> Foreclosure attorney's name and contact information

>> Liber (the legal book in which the deed is recorded at the county courthouse) and page number of the mortgage

>> Mortgagors' (usually the homeowners') names

>> Lender's name (bank or mortgage company)

>> The amount that remains to be paid on the loan

>> The interest rate

>> Legal description of the property

>> Length of the redemption period, if any

>> Whether this is the first, second, third, or fourth posting of the foreclosure notice

Hurry. The clock's ticking. You have about 30 to 90 days from the time the foreclosure notice appears in the paper before the property goes on the auction block. You also have more competition now that the foreclosure is public knowledge. Head to Chapter 8 and start gathering information about the property pronto!

TIP

After you find a property in which you're interested, double-check to make sure that it's going to be sold. Sometimes, after the foreclosure notice is posted, the homeowner files for bankruptcy or takes some other action to cancel or postpone the sale. Call the attorney listed in the foreclosure notice, introduce yourself, and find out everything you can about the property. You may be able to obtain additional information from the attorney, such as the opening bid and when it's scheduled for sale, but don't count on it; the attorney is acting as a debt collector on behalf of the lender.

Teaming Up with Attorneys to Help Distressed Clients Sell Their Homes

As a result of life-changing events, people may inherit property they don't want or are forced to sell property they own. The transactions are usually part of a complicated and often unpleasant legal process: probate, divorce, or bankruptcy. If you know how to find these properties and are willing to accept additional complexities and delays, these legal processes can be an excellent source of deeply discounted properties.

In the following sections, I explain the pros and cons and ins and outs of buying properties that become available through various types of legal proceedings.

Acquiring properties in probate

When someone dies without bequeathing their property to an heir, that property ends up in probate. At this point, the state probate court works with the executor named in the deceased's will or with the person's closest living relative to determine how the property is distributed among the heirs. Usually, the heirs want to sell the property quickly without putting a lot of work into it, so they're willing to accept a price well below market value.

REMEMBER

Heirs are thinking about the money they can put back in their pockets, and they want the money in their pockets as quickly and with as little hassle as possible, giving you an easy opportunity to strike a deal in which everyone wins. If five heirs inherited a $250,000 home, for example, you may be able to get it for $200,000, with each heir pocketing $40,000 and having to give up only $10,000 each in exchange for a hassle-free sale.

Finding properties in probate

To find properties in probate, check out the following sources:

>> **Real estate agents:** Real estate agents, especially those who focus on selling probate properties, can provide some of the best leads. As you become more experienced with the probate system in your area, you'll notice which agents and attorneys are most involved in probate.

>> **Probate attorneys:** Probate attorneys work with the heirs to help them navigate and manage the probate process. They may contact one or more real estate investors when they need to sell a property quickly.

>> **The local probate court:** Visit your local probate court to look at all the new filings. When someone passes away, the court must advertise the death, giving the heirs an opportunity to claim the deceased's property. Thanks to freedom-of-information laws, you can examine the inventory of the deceased's property for any real estate. The deceased's probate documentation will list all the known heirs and any of their personal reps or attorneys. You can use this information to track down and contact the heirs or their legal counsel to discuss the possibility of buying the property. In some cases, heirs choose to navigate the probate system themselves without legal counsel.

REMEMBER

Contacting the heirs or their legal representatives directly gives you an inside track on acquiring properties in probate. Doing the research and legwork yourself is one of the most effective ways to acquire these properties.

>> **Local newspapers:** Real estate that's in probate may be listed in local newspapers or their online equivalents.

Buying properties in probate: Navigating the process

Probate cases typically run about six months but can take up to three years to resolve, so be prepared for the long haul. During the process, take the following steps:

1. **Inspect the property as thoroughly as possible.**

   You may not be able to have a formal inspection, but you should at least visit the property and inspect all four sides. Contact the executor to see whether you can get a look inside, too. (See Chapter 8 for guidance on performing an initial inspection.)

2. **Make an offer and pay 10 percent down if your offer is accepted.**

   If the executor counteroffers and you accept, you'll need to pay 10 percent down on the agreed-upon price.

WARNING

   You're not permitted to include contingency clauses in the purchase agreement, so be sure that you really want the property at that price.

3. **Follow the lead of the executor or the judge:**

   - In some cases, the executor has the right to sell everything with no contingencies, as is the case with most probate cases.

   - In other cases, if the judge determines that disagreements exist among the heirs, the judge will require that all offers be approved by the court, in which case other offers on the property may need to be considered (or reconsidered).

4. **If your offer is accepted, pay whatever's required to bring your initial down payment up to 10 percent of the adjusted price.**

5. **Close on the property as you normally would close on any real estate purchase.**

Adopting homes orphaned by divorce

When couples divorce, they often sell the property and split the proceeds, or one of them gets the house and doesn't want it or can't afford it. You may be able to purchase a property for well below market value at different stages of the divorce process: predivorce, during divorce proceedings, or after the divorce.

I once bought a home at a deep discount from a woman who was awarded the home as part of the divorce settlement and was ordered to spit the proceeds 50/50 with her ex if she ever sold the home. After the divorce, she married an affluent man, so selling the home for top dollar wasn't important to her. Sticking it to her less–fortunate ex was far more important, so she sold the home to me for significantly less than market value.

Finding properties orphaned by divorce

You can find properties being orphaned by divorce through many of the same sources where you can find probate properties (as discussed in the preceding section):

>> **Real estate agents:** To drum up additional business, some real estate agents focus their marketing on one or more niche markets — divorcing homeowners being one of them. As you research divorce cases, you'll start to notice which real estate agents in your area are most active in listing properties for couples who are getting divorced.

>> **Divorce attorneys:** Although divorcé(e)s typically are motivated sellers, so are divorce attorneys, who often don't get paid until the couple's assets are sold. Get to know at least a few divorce attorneys in your area. If you're fair, reasonable, and have a good reputation, you have an excellent chance of being contacted by them when they need to dispose of a property quickly.

>> **The local divorce court:** Contact your county's clerk to request a list of divorce cases that have been filed. Review the list for active cases, which will include the names of the spouses. The clerk's office might not give you this information over the phone; you may have to go in and have someone show you how to access that info yourself. If the first person you meet isn't helpful, go back another time. If this process were easy, everybody would do it.

TIP

Visit your county's circuit court, where all divorces in your county are filed. There, you can look at new filings, the names and ages of the plaintiffs, the names of their kids (if applicable), whether either party owns real estate, and so on. Divorces aren't private. The divorce decree, which finalizes the divorce, shows all the terms, including who gets the house or whether it needs to be sold. If neither party owns real estate, move on. But if one party or both parties own real estate, the divorce decree will contain valuable information to help you contact the owners or their legal representatives to find out more about the property.

>> **Local newspapers:** When a couple files for divorce, the local newspapers may include the filing in a list of public records, usually online, not necessarily in the print version.

Buying properties from divorcees

Buying properties that are part of divorce proceedings generally involves the typical process for buying properties: You present your offer, negotiate the price and terms, and (if the offer is accepted) proceed to the closing. Access to the property may be more limited, however, and you may not know who's controlling or in charge of selling the property. The owner may be the husband, wife, or both and may be selling the property through a real estate agent or one of their lawyers.

The first two steps are to inspect the property as carefully as possible so you'll know what you're getting before presenting your offer, as well as to find out who owns the property and who's in charge of selling it. A good way to start is to contact one of the divorce party's attorneys. Then have your real estate agent write up and present your offer to the person who's selling it.

Teaming up with bankruptcy attorneys

Homeowners who file for bankruptcy rarely get to keep their house, and even if they do, they may not want it. As an investor, you may have an opportunity to purchase the property at any stage in the bankruptcy process:

>> Before the homeowners file for bankruptcy, you can purchase the home directly from them as you normally would.

>> After the homeowners file for bankruptcy, you can purchase the home from them, but the creditors must approve the sale.

>> When the trustee is liquidating the property, you can buy the home from the trustee with the creditors' approval.

>> If liquidation results in one of the creditors buying the property, you can buy the home from that creditor.

By becoming familiar with the bankruptcy process and getting to know bankruptcy attorneys in your area, you can often get early leads on discounted properties. Bankruptcy attorneys appreciate having multiple solutions to present to their clients, and as a real estate investor, you expand the clients' options.

See Chapter 14 for more about buying properties that need to be sold due to bankruptcy.

» **Gathering legal documents at the Register of Deeds office**

» **Inspecting the property from the street**

» **Checking your list to be sure you have everything you need**

Chapter **8**

Performing Your Due Diligence

A large part of foreclosure *invest*ing consists of *invest*igating — knowing what you're about to buy before you lay your cash on the line. You need to know how much the property is worth, how much is owed on it, whether it has any additional liens or encumbrances, whether the property is in violation of any building codes, and whether the person selling the house is really the legal owner.

TIP

For each property you consider buying, create a separate folder (paper or digital) with a photo of the property, its address, and all publicly accessible information available for it. This chapter shows you the type of information you need and provides instructions on how to dig it up and organize it to create your very own custom property dossier.

In addition to helping you determine whether the property is worth your time pursuing, this information is critical for assisting homeowners, negotiating with homeowners and lenders, and bidding on a property at auction.

Collecting Essential Information about the Property

Every property has some vital statistics that must find their way into your property dossier. You can collect most of the data you need through the Notice of Default (NOD) or foreclosure notice (if one has been posted) and from your county's courthouse and city or town offices. Chapters 7 and 9 point you in the direction of foreclosure notices. Later in this chapter, I show you how to get essential details from the foreclosure notice and dig up additional information at the county courthouse.

If you're working with the homeowners in pre-foreclosure, gather as much information as you can from them first, as explained in Chapter 9. You need to know as much as possible about their situation to be of assistance and minimize your risk as an investor.

In the following sections, I point you to the sources of key information and provide a couple of forms for recording the essential data in a format you can quickly reference later.

Honing your title acquisition and reading skills

TIP

To hone your skills at gathering data related to foreclosure properties, consider practicing on your own home first. Unless you're currently in foreclosure, of course, you won't have access to a foreclosure notice (lucky you), but you can practice researching your title, mortgage, and other documentation relating to your property. You may have several of the documents you need to practice on in the closing packet you received when you purchased your home, but don't cheat by referring to those documents. Go out in the field to see what sorts of publicly accessible data you can gather on your own:

1. **Head down to your local title company.**

   You can find a list of title companies in your phone book.

2. **Meet with one of the representatives.**

   Explain that you're reading this book called *Foreclosure Investing For Dummies,* and you want to know everything they can teach you about titles.

3. **Request a title commitment on your own property.**

   The title company may take a couple of days to prepare the title commitment. Offer to pick it up when it's ready so that the company won't have to pay postage.

4. **Visit your county courthouse and track down the Register of Deeds office.**

5. **Ask nicely to see everything recorded against your house in the past 24 months.**

   In some cases, the records may not go that far back, but you should be able to obtain the last two recorded documents — perhaps the deed and the mortgage showing when you purchased the property.

6. **Compare the title commitment you received from the title company with the documents you picked up through your own detective work.**

You should notice a big difference in the documents. The title commitment won't include all the information from the documents you picked up at the county courthouse. Instead, it extracts the essential details and presents them in a more easily accessible format, showing the following:

>> Homeowners' names

>> First mortgage

>> Any second mortgage or other liens against the property

>> Property taxes paid or due

>> Delinquent water bills or bills for other services supplied by the municipality

Picking up details from the foreclosure notice

When a NOD or foreclosure notice is published, like the one shown in Figure 8-1, you have a wealth of information at your fingertips. The NOD or foreclosure notice presents the following details, which you can record on your foreclosure information sheet, like the one shown in Figure 8-2:

>> **Case or reference number[1]:** Some attorneys include a case or reference number in the foreclosure notice to simplify the process of searching for information in their database.

>> **Insertion date[2]:** The date may appear in the notice itself, but if it doesn't, use the date of the publication in which the notice is posted. In the legal news, the advertisements are listed under subtitles to indicate the order of the posting: first, second, third, and so on.

GETTING BURNED BY BAD DECISIONS

Dr. Beecher, highly educated and very successful in her field, attended a seminar on foreclosure investing. She purchased the books and CDs for sale at the seminar, studied them carefully, and decided to begin purchasing foreclosure properties.

The system seemed straightforward enough, so she began attending auctions and purchasing properties right out of the chute. Well, she *thought* she was purchasing properties. At foreclosure auctions, you actually purchase foreclosed-on mortgages. If you buy a first mortgage, you're likely to take possession of the property after the redemption period. Second mortgages and other liens against the property are usually wiped out by the foreclosure process; in most cases, they're worthless.

The doctor bought about seven or eight second mortgages thinking that she would own the properties when the redemption periods expired.

Paul, my buyer at foreclosure auctions, observed the doctor over the course of a couple of weeks. One week, he approached her and asked whether she understood what she was doing. During the conversation, Paul realized that the doctor was following some bad advice. He brought her back to the office to meet me.

We researched the properties for her and helped her understand what she'd done. She had purchased several second mortgages that were destined to become worthless pieces of paper because the foreclosure would wipe them off the books. She had invested about $100,000 and was going to lose all of it. That lesson was a tough one to learn, but with her newfound understanding, the doctor went on to become a successful real estate investor.

The moral of the story is this: Do your homework before you start investing. Know what you're buying before you put your money on the line.

» **County[3]:** The county in which the property is located is your key to unlocking other details about the property. Using this bit of information, you know which county's Register of Deeds office to visit to research the title and mortgage and find the property's address. (Start with your county.) This issue may not arise if the paper you're using is county-specific, in which case pay attention to the city with a special focus on the city where you live or the cities that are most familiar.

» **Legal lot, subdivision, and city[4]:** The legal description of the property doesn't provide the property's mailing address, but from the legal description, you can find the mailing address. See "Finding the property" later in this chapter for details.

» **Name of the mortgagor[5]:** The *mortgagor* is the borrower, typically the homeowners — the person or people who owe the money, even if they're not in possession of the property.

» **Name of the mortgagee[6]:** The *mortgagee* is the lender that is foreclosing on the property.

» **Amount owed on the mortgage[7]:** The NOD or foreclosure notice always states the exact amount the homeowners currently owe on this mortgage. They may owe additional sums on other loans. The amount owed changes between the times when the notice is published and the sale occurs, so call the foreclosing attorney closer to the date of sale to determine the actual opening bid amount.

» **Interest rate of loan[8]:** The longer the amount owed on the mortgage remains unpaid, the more it increases by the specified interest rate. You can use the interest rate to monitor the amount owed as it increases over time. In addition, you earn this interest rate if you purchase the mortgage and someone buys it back from you during the redemption period.

» **The mortgage company's attorney[9]:** The mortgage company attorney's name and contact information are useful for double-checking the sale date and the opening bid and then contacting the mortgage company to work out a deal.

» **Mortgage sale date[10]:** This date is when the attorney for the lender expects the mortgage to be auctioned. The date can change, but jot it down so that you can keep track of it.

» **Length of the property's redemption period, if applicable[11]:** If your area has a mandatory redemption period, it should appear in the NOD or foreclosure notice. Using the date of sale and redemption period, you can determine the last day the homeowners can redeem the property. Verify the redemption period with your own research; occasionally, the wrong redemption period is published.

» **Liber (the legal book in which the deed is recorded at the county courthouse) and page number of the recorded mortgage that is in foreclosure[12]:** This information tells you where to find the mortgage document and which mortgage is being foreclosed on if the homeowners have more than one mortgage on the property.

If you're buying properties directly from homeowners who contacted you before the beginning of foreclosure proceedings, you can gather most of the information you need to complete the foreclosure information sheet from the homeowners, as explained in Chapter 9. Just be sure to verify the information by inspecting the title and other records, as explained in the following sections.

ROBERTS & KRAYNAK, P.C.
Attorneys and Counselors
1313 Mockingbird Ln., Ste. 200
Dellingham Farms, MI 48025

THIS FIRM IS A DEBT COLLECTOR ATTEMPTING TO COLLECT A DEBT. ANY INFORMATION
WE OBTAIN WILL BE USED FOR THAT PURPOSE.

ATTN PURCHASERS: This sale may be rescinded by the foreclosing mortgagee. In that event,
your damages, if any, shall be limited solely to the return of the bid amount tendered at sale,
plus interest.

MORTGAGE SALE - Default has been made in the conditions of a mortgage made by
JOHN Q PUBLIC and **JANE Q PUBLIC**[5], husband and wife, original mortgagor(s), to Federal
City Mortgage Co D/B/A Commonwealth United Mortgage Company[6], Mortgagee, dated
March 4, 2017, and recorded on April 10, 2017 in Liber 55555 on Page 617[12], in Oakland county[3]
records, Michigan, on which mortgage there is claimed to be due at the date hereof the sum
of Four Hundred Seventy-Two Thousand Seven Hundred Fifty-Eight And 23/100 Dollars
($472,758.23)[7], including interest at 5.625% per annum[8].

Under the power of sale contained in said mortgage and the statute in such case made and
provided, notice is hereby given that said mortgage will be foreclosed by a sale of the
mortgaged premises, or some part of them, at public venue, at the Main entrance to the Court
House in Pontiac at 10:00 AM, on **JANUARY 31, 2023**[10].

Said premises are situated in Charter Township of West Bloomfield, Oakland County,
Michigan, and are described as:

Homesite No. 55, Amberleigh Condominium, according to the Master Deed recorded in Liber
55555, Pages 665 through 730, Oakland County Records, as amended, and designated as
Oakland County Subdivision Plan No. 1555[4] together with rights in the general common
elements and the limited common elements as shown on the Master Deed and as described
in Act 59 of the Public Acts of 1978, as amended

The redemption period shall be 6 months from the date of such sale[11], unless determined
abandoned in accordance with MCLA 600.3241a, in which case the redemption period shall
be 30 days from the date of such sale.

Dated: December 30, 2022[2]
For more information, please call:
FC F 555.555.5555
Roberts & Kraynak, P.C.[9]
Attorneys For Servicer
1313 Mockingbird Ln., Ste. 200
Dellingham Farms, MI 48025
File #055000F05[1]

FIGURE 8-1:
Collect important
details about the
foreclosure
property from the
NOD or foreclo-
sure notice.

Foreclosure Information Sheet

Date: _____

Foreclosure Notice

Case or Reference Number: _____

Insertion Date: _____ Thru: _____

County: _____

Legal Lot: _____

Subdivision: _____

City: _____

Mortgagor (Homeowners): _____

Mortgagee (Lender): _____

Mortgage Amount: _____

Interest Rate: _____

Mortgage Company's Attorney: _____

Mortgage Company's Attorney Phone Number: _____

Mortgage Sale Date: _____

Redemption Period: _____

Last Day to Redeem: _____

Register of Deeds (Title)

Property Address (Ask Clerk): _____

Mortgagor Names: _____

Price Paid for Property: _____

Deed Warranty Names: _____

Previous Mortgagor (Previous Title): _____

Price Paid for Property (Previous Title): _____

Current 1st Mortgage Mortgagee (Lender): _____

Original Mortgagee (Lender): _____

Register of Deeds (1st Mortgage and Note)

1st Mortgage Loan Amount: _____

Interest Rate: _____

Date Recorded: _____ Liber: _____ Page: _____

Mortgagee (Lender): _____

Address: _____

FIGURE 8-2: Record information from the foreclosure notice and public records on your foreclosure information sheet.

Mortgage Assumable? ☐ Yes ☐ No

Register of Deeds (Second Mortgage and Note)

2nd Mortgage Loan Amount: _____

Interest Rate: _____

Date Recorded: _____ Liber: _____ Page: _____

Mortgagee (Lender): _____

Address: _____

Mortgage Assumable? ☐ Yes ☐ No

Register of Deeds (Additional Mortgages or Liens)

Junior Lien Holder 1: _____

Address: _____

Junior Lien Holder 2: _____

Address: _____

Tax Lien: _____

Address: _____

County Tax Assessor

Sidwell (Tax ID #): _____

Taxable Value (SEV): _____

Property Tax Formula: _____

Unpaid Property Taxes: _____

Property Tax Lien? ☐ Yes, Amount: _____ ☐ No

State, County, City or Town Property Worksheet

Building Permits: _____

Code Violations: _____

Other: _____

Other Information

Opening Bid: _____

Homeowner's Phone: _____

Estimated Property Value: _____

Total Owed on Property: _____

FIGURE 8-2: (continued) Estimated Equity in Property: _____

Digging up details at the Register of Deeds office

Whether you're planning to bid on a property at auction or purchase the property directly from homeowners, a trip to your county's Register of Deeds office is a necessity. The Register of Deeds or county clerk is the one who records most of the legal paperwork for a property, including the title work, deed, and mortgage. In the following sections, I point out the essential information you need to scrounge up from this most important source.

The records you need to research can be recorded on any of several types of media. You may be pulling out folders, flipping through pages in a book, or looking for records on microfilm.

Finding the property

The NOD or foreclosure notice describes the location of the property through a legal description rather than simply providing a mailing address. Isn't that just like lawyers? Fortunately, you can use the property description to track down the mailing address by employing one of the following strategies:

>> Ask the clerk at your county's Register of Deeds office.

>> Ask your real estate attorney.

>> Contact your title company. If you have a good relationship with the company, someone there may be willing to look up the address for you.

>> Use a land data software program to search a database of property information. These programs are available in some areas and on the web.

THE CHICKEN MAN

One of the most successful foreclosure investors in our area is dubbed "The Chicken Man" because he delivers buckets of chicken to the staff members in the Register of Deeds office. By catering lunch on a regular basis, The Chicken Man has established an outstanding relationship with the clerks. He can walk in through the back door of the Register of Deeds office and help himself to the records. When he can't find a record he needs, the clerks are more than willing to lend a hand. You might say that The Chicken Man has a leg up (and a wing and a thigh and a breast) on the competition.

Before you step into the Register of Deeds or county clerk's office, turn on your charm, and brush up on your manners. Ask politely for assistance and say "Thank you" when the people behind the desk provide that assistance. The office staff stands between you and the information you need, and they're usually as helpful as you are polite.

Some companies, such as HomeInfoMax (`www.homeinfomax.com`), provide online search tools that can help you find a property's address based on its legal description. Most online tools don't cover all counties, however, and typically charge per search. You can get the information for free by doing a little legwork or contacting the Register of Deeds office.

When you have the address, plug it into an online mapping program you use, and print a map of the property's location. I also use Google Earth to print a satellite image of the property. Keep in mind, however, that satellite images are often months or even years old; they're no substitute for driving to the property and inspecting it with your own two eyes. See "Doing Your Fieldwork: Inspecting the Property" later in this chapter.

Obtaining the property's title and other key documents

When most homeowners buy a property, they agree to buy it from the seller before any mention of the title occurs. Before closing on the transaction, they hire a title company that inspects and insures the title to protect the buyer from any messy legal battles over who owns the property.

When buying foreclosure properties, however, inspect the title *before* you decide to pursue a property. If anything about the title smells fishy, you may want to do a little extra research or simply cross the property off your list.

You can do your preliminary title research yourself by heading down to your county's Register of Deeds office and asking the clerk to provide you the information of what's recorded on title for a particular property. At the bare minimum, obtain a copy of the deed and any other recorded documents for the current and previous owner. If possible, obtain copies of all documents recorded in the past 24 months.

Although you can do this research yourself (and you really should do it yourself to learn about title research), when you're starting out, I recommend that you consult your title company for a second opinion and order a title commitment. When you feel comfortable doing your own research, you can take on more of the burden. For more about title commitments, see Chapter 4.

Researching the property's title

Inspect the title work and deed for the following critical pieces of data, and record them in the corresponding spaces of the foreclosure information sheet (refer to Figure 8-2):

- » **Mortgagor (homeowners') names:** Note whether the mortgagor's name matches the name of the property's title holder. Differing names raise a red flag; make a note of any.

- » **Price paid for the property:** Depending on how long ago the current homeowners purchased the property, this information can provide some indication of the property's current value.

- » **Deed warranty names:** The names on the deed should match the homeowners' names on the title. If they don't match, the difference raises a red flag; again, make a note of it.

- » **Previous mortgagor:** Check the previous title, and jot down the names on it. Note any chinks in the chain of ownership. If the title work shows that Johnson sold the property to Davis and then Howard sold it to Pinkerton, who did Davis sell the house to? This gap indicates a problem in the chain of ownership. Consult with your title company whenever you notice any irregularities in the chain of title. Take note of maiden-name changes (changes in names after divorce). A name change may result in what only appears to be a gap in the chain of ownership.

- » **Previous price paid for the property:** This piece of data isn't crucial, but it can point to a pattern of an increasing or decreasing property value.

- » **Current first mortgage mortgagee (lender):** The *first mortgage mortgagee* is the bank or other lending institution that holds the first (senior) lien on the property. By obtaining the lender's name from the title, you can begin the process of tracking down the lender. Their information should be on the actual mortgage document, a copy of which you can obtain at the Register of Deeds office. For more about liens, including which liens take precedence, see "Uncovering facts about any additional liens" later in this chapter; also check out Chapter 15.

- » **Original first mortgage mortgagee (lender):** In many cases, a lending institution loans the homeowners money to buy the property and then sells the mortgage to another lending institution almost immediately. The title typically includes the name of the original lender. When you start making calls, having this information at your fingertips helps convince the person you contact that you know what you're talking about.

If the property has a second mortgage on it, record the same information for the second mortgage. You may be able to work with the second-mortgage lender to shore up your position. See Chapter 9 for additional details on collaborating with lenders.

PROTECTING YOURSELF AGAINST MORTGAGE FRAUD

By carefully researching the properties that interest you — particularly the legal documents associated with them — you protect yourself not only from inadvertent errors, but also from con artists who are trying to fleece you. Con artists often manipulate the legal documents and file false documents as part of their scams. Sometimes, they can even sell a house they don't own or sell a house several times to different buyers. To protect yourself from falling victim to a real estate scam, take the following precautions:

- Check the records to see whether the mortgage on the property was paid off recently. Sellers rarely pay off mortgages right before they sell, so any document that shows the mortgage as having been recently paid off is likely to be phony.

- Be wary of an investor who's pitching you a great deal on a property. Con artists often target novice investors in double-sales scams.

- Analyze the title commitment for suspicious transactions.

- Ask your title company for a 24-month property history, including mortgages.

- Purchase title insurance as soon as possible, and pay for it upfront. Sometimes, this insurance is your only protection.

Gathering information from the mortgage and note

The mortgage and note are recorded along with the title when someone purchases a property. These documents include important details about the senior lien, so be sure to record these details on your foreclosure information sheet:

» **First-mortgage loan amount:** How much did the homeowners borrow to finance the purchase of the property?

» **Interest rate:** Knowing the interest rate on the first mortgage helps you calculate the homeowners' current monthly payments and provide them refinance options.

» **Date recorded, liber, and page number:** With the date recorded, liber, and page number, you can access the information much more quickly.

» **Mortgagee (lender):** You may have already obtained the mortgagee's name from the title, but check the mortgage for any discrepancies. Also, jot down the mortgagee's address for future reference.

Uncovering facts about any additional liens

Although the first (senior) lien is the most important, the property may have other liens from second or third mortgages or construction liens that you should know about. Unless the homeowners very recently took out another loan using the property as collateral, or the Register of Deeds is way behind in recording documents, records of these liens should be accessible.

REMEMBER

Some liens take precedence over others. Buying liens with a higher precedence gives you more power. Property tax liens almost always take precedence over other liens. Then the pecking order usually follows the dates on which the loan agreements were executed and recorded, typically giving the first mortgage the most power. If you order a title commitment, it lists the liens in order of precedence. For more about the lien pecking order, see Chapter 15.

On your foreclosure information sheet, record the names and addresses of any additional lien holders. The date on which a lien was recorded should alert you to the fact that a particular lien is a junior lien. The liber and page number on which the junior lien was recorded should also be higher than that of the senior lien, because the junior lien was recorded later.

Uncovering unpaid property taxes and other tax liens

When homeowners get behind on their taxes, government agencies at the federal, state, or county level can place additional liens on the property. While researching the title, inspect it for any of the following additional liens:

>> Internal Revenue Service federal income tax liens

>> State income tax liens

>> Property tax liens

>> Record of deceased owner (if the death certificate is on the title)

  If you see a death certificate, and the property is in foreclosure, try to locate the probate attorney who's in charge of liquidating the property. To locate the attorney, head down to the county building, visit the probate office, and ask whether anyone has opened a probate case in the name of the deceased party. If the case is in probate, ask to see the file, which will contain the name and contact information of the person who's handling the case.

TIP

Additional liens — most important, liens for overdue property taxes and IRS tax liens — are a good sign that the homeowners will be unable to redeem the property. They're probably too deeply in debt to catch up on their payments.

Gathering tax information at the assessor's office

In addition to checking the title for any property tax liens, visit the county treasurer's or assessor's office, and ask for the following:

» **The property's tax ID number (often called a *property identification number,* or PIN):** The city or county taxing authority assigns this number to the property for reference and tracking. Some cities, such as Detroit, have ward numbers that serve the same function. Regardless of what the number is called, it identifies a specific parcel of land. As soon as you have a feel for the identification system, you can almost tell just by the number where the property is located.

» **The taxable value of the property:** You may have to visit the county assessor's office for this tidbit. Knowing the taxable value of a property may assist you in guesstimating the property's market value, but it's no substitute for an accurate current appraisal or your own research on market values of comparable properties. In some cases, the taxable value may be expressed as state equalized value (SEV). SEV may represent a fraction of the actual assessed value of the property; in some areas, for example, the SEV is calculated as half the previous sales price.

» **The property tax formula:** Currently in Michigan, a house is generally worth 2 to 2.2 times the SEV, so a house with an SEV of $200,000 is worth $400,000 to $440,000. Ask the assessor what formula your area uses. This information can often give you a rough estimate of the property's market value.

» **Property tax status:** Find out whether property taxes are currently paid up and whether the assessor's office has a property tax lien on the property.

Getting your hands on the property worksheet

Every town, city, or county in the United States keeps a worksheet on every property, showing when it was built, any building permits issued on the property, code violations, inspection reports, and so on. Find out who keeps the property worksheets and obtain a copy of the worksheet for any home you're considering buying. On your foreclosure information sheet, record the following data from the property worksheet:

» **Building permits:** Building permits provide a record of all approved property improvements. If you inspect the property later and discover an improvement that was performed without a permit, this information may be a warning that the improvement doesn't conform to building codes.

» **Code violations:** If the property has any code violations recorded against it that haven't been resolved, you want to know so that you don't unknowingly take possession of a property that you'll be responsible for bringing up to code later.

» **Other interesting tidbits:** The property worksheet may include additional information about health code violations that warn you to inspect the property more closely before purchasing it. For tips on physically inspecting a foreclosure property, see "Doing Your Fieldwork: Inspecting the Property" later in this chapter.

WARNING

A permit showing that the work passed final inspection is best. That permit shows that no matter who pulled (obtained) the permit (the homeowner or a licensed contractor), the work was completed and was at least up to code. Open permits — those that don't indicate that the work passed final inspection — may indicate that the work was completed to code or that you're going to be in for some costly repairs. In any event, knowing what's been recorded with the city concerning work begun or completed on the property is beneficial.

Gathering additional information

To complete the foreclosure information sheet, do a little extra detective work to gather the following additional details:

» **Opening bid:** If you found out about the property through a NOD or foreclosure notice, call the attorney listed in the notice to find out the opening bid.

» **Homeowner's telephone number:** Finding the homeowners' phone number can be challenging, especially if their account has been canceled or the number is unlisted. Using the homeowner's name and the property address, try looking up the phone number on a site such as www.whitepages.com. If you can't get the phone number, don't worry. In Chapter 9, I provide some additional tips for finding homeowners.

» **Estimated property value:** The property's current value is how much the homeowners could get for the property if they sold it today. You can obtain a ballpark estimate by checking the prices of comparable homes that have sold in the past month or so. A real estate agent can come in handy here. See Chapter 10 for details.

» **Total owed on the property:** Add up the balance on all liens against the property. You can come up with a pretty accurate figure by adding the original balances and deducting estimated payments. If the loans are less than 10 years old, chances are pretty good that the balances haven't been paid down very much, because a good chunk of each payment in the early years is applied to interest, not principal.

Doing Your Fieldwork: Inspecting the Property

An investment property may seem like a steal on paper when it's actually a gutted shell of a home in the center of the low-rent district. Until you see the property for yourself, you have no idea what it is, what kind of homes surround it, or what condition it's in.

REMEMBER

Before you plop down your money or borrowed money on a property, always inspect it as closely as possible with your own two eyes, carefully record your observations, and add the details you gather to your growing property dossier. In the following sections, I provide an exterior home inspection form to complete, and I lead you through the process of performing your due diligence in the field.

Doing a drive-by, walk-around inspection

The least you should do (and the most you can do in some situations) to inspect a property is to drive over and walk around the property — at a safe distance, of course; I'm not suggesting that you trespass. Even if you can't get inside to take a closer peek, the drive-by, walk-around inspection provides you enough preliminary information to develop a ballpark estimate of the property's value and rule out any really bad properties.

WARNING

Whenever you visit a property in person, you're at some risk. The homeowners, and sometimes their dog, may not appreciate uninvited guests, especially if you trespass. Keep your distance. Knocking on the front door is usually okay, but if the homeowners ask you to leave, respect their wishes and follow up with a letter, as explained in Chapter 9.

As you perform your drive-by, walk-around inspection, complete the exterior inspection form provided in Figure 8-3. I use my iPhone to take photos and video clips and to record notes. If you decide to use your smartphone, refer to Figure 8-3 as a checklist for the information you need to gather on your phone. You may be unable to collect all the information listed on the form, but collect as much information as possible without becoming too pushy if the homeowners confront you.

Exterior Property Evaluation

Owner: _____

Home Phone: _____ Work Phone: _____ Pager/Mobile: _____

Address: _____

Distinguishing Feature of Property: _____

Property is: ❑ Vacant ❑ Owner Occupied ❑ Tenant Occupied

Tenant Info: How Long at Home? _____ Monthly Rent: _____

Neighborhood Details: ❑ Brick ❑ Frame ❑ Mix

Block Club? ❑ Yes ❑ No

# of burn-outs: ____ #of board-ups: ____ #of vacant lots: ____ %ownership: _____

Neighborhood Rating: ❑ Poor ❑ Fair ❑ Good ❑ Excellent

Neighborhood Listings:

    Address: _____ Phone: _____ Asking Price: _____

    Address: _____ Phone: _____ Asking Price: _____

    Address: _____ Phone: _____ Asking Price: _____

House Details:

Garage: ❑ Yes ❑ No # of Cars: ____ Condition: ❑ Poor ❑ Fair ❑ Good

Driveway: ❑ None ❑ Solid ❑ Ribbon ❑ Asphalt ❑ Alley

    Condition: ❑ Poor ❑ Fair ❑ Good

Roof Type: _____ Age: _____ Condition: ❑ Poor ❑ Fair ❑ Good

Type of Construction: ❑ Brick ❑ Frame ❑ Aluminum ❑ Block

    ❑ Asbestos ❑ Vinyl ❑ Brickote ❑ Stucco

    Condition: ❑ Poor ❑ Fair ❑ Good

Year Built: _____ Square Footage: _____ Number of Bedrooms: ___

House Style: ❑ Tudor ❑ Bungalow ❑ Ranch ❑ Split-Level

    ❑ Colonial ❑ Cape Cod ❑ Multi-Family: _____

Foundation: ❑ Basement ❑ Slab ❑ Crawl ❑ Piers

Storm Doors/Storm Windows/Screens Condition: ❑ Poor ❑ Fair ❑ Good

Window Condition: ❑ Poor ❑ Fair ❑ Good Lot Size: _____

Fence: ❑ Chain ❑ Wood ❑ Wire Landscape: ❑ Poor ❑ Fair ❑ Good

Porch: ❑ Cement ❑ Wood ❑ Brick Condition: ❑ Poor ❑ Fair ❑ Good

Steps: ❑ Cement ❑ Wood ❑ Brick Condition: ❑ Poor ❑ Fair ❑ Good

Door: ❑ Wood ❑ Steel Condition: ❑ Poor ❑ Fair ❑ Good

Recommendation: ❑ Cash Buy ❑ Re-Fi ❑ Listing ❑ Short Sale ❑ Pass

    ❑ Other: _____

Reasoning/Notes: _____

_____

_____

FIGURE 8-3: Personally inspect the neighborhood and the exterior of the property and record your observations.

TIP

If the home is currently listed for sale, call the agent, and take a tour of the inside of the house. You don't need to tell the agent that you know the homeowners are facing foreclosure. In Chapter 9, I provide an inspection form for the interior of the property; take the form with you and fill it out.

TIP

Never pass up the opportunity to talk to a neighbor. If a neighbor wanders out to ask what you're doing, strike up a conversation, and try to find out more about the homeowners and the condition of the property. Aren't the neighbors nosy? Then consider becoming a little nosy yourself and knocking on doors. A neighbor may have been inside the house recently. If you can't get in to inspect the property, a secondhand report from a neighbor is the next-best thing. In some cases, you may even stumble across a neighbor whom the homeowner has anointed to be caretaker; if they have keys or are willing to show you around, you've struck gold! For tips on how to get inside a house to do an interior inspection, see Chapter 9.

Snapping some photos

As you walk around the property, take a couple of photos of every side of the house, the landscape, and surrounding houses. The photo documentary you create is priceless. If you inspect dozens of properties, you're not likely to remember a specific house. A few photos can take you right back to the day when you inspected the property.

TIP

If possible, take your photos in late morning or early afternoon, when the homeowners are more likely to be at work and the kids to be in school, to avoid any confrontation with the homeowners and keep the kids from asking their parents embarrassing questions like "Why is that person taking pictures of our house?" You can also keep a low profile by snapping photos from inside your car. Whatever you do, just make sure you're on public property — the sidewalk or street rather than in someone's yard.

In addition to photographing the property itself, photograph the neighborhood:

>> Take a photo of the street view (both ways).

>> Take a picture of the houses across the street.

>> Photograph any eyesores.

If you're using old-school folders for your property dossiers, as soon as possible after snapping the photos, print them or upload them to your favorite photo processing service to have them printed. Stick the photos in your property dossier for later reference. If you prefer a more modern approach, upload all your data to the cloud so that you can access it from anywhere with any digital device. Create a separate folder for each property.

Assembling Your Property Dossier: A Checklist

For every property I investigate, I create a separate folder for all the documents pertaining to that property. I use different-colored folders to keep data for my top prospects separate. I recommend using a similar strategy, but feel free to be creative;

just make sure that your system keeps all the data on each house separate and easily accessible. You can even store the information in separate folders on your computer or in the cloud.

However you choose to organize your property information, make sure that each folder contains the following items:

>> An 8-by-10-inch photograph of the property. I tape this photo to the front of the folder for quick reference.

>> The foreclosure notice.

>> The foreclosure information sheet you completed.

>> The exterior inspection form you completed.

>> Neighborhood inspection, complete with photos.

>> Information on any other properties that are listed for sale in the area so you can track their sale prices and how long they took to sell.

>> A map showing the location of the property.

>> The title commitment and 24-month history in the chain of title or (at minimum) the last two recorded documents.

>> The last recorded first mortgage, so that you know how much the homeowners currently owe on the property.

>> Records of other liens on the property, such as second mortgages, construction liens, and tax liens. Property tax liens are especially important, because if you buy the property, you're responsible for paying any back property taxes.

>> A copy of the deed with the current homeowners' names. These names should match the names on the title.

>> The city worksheet on the property showing its history.

>> The SEV.

>> Multiple Listing Service (MLS) listings of comparable properties that have recently sold or are currently for sale.

TIP

If you gathered information to bid for properties at an auction, bring all your folders with you. You may have researched 20 properties and narrowed your prospects to the top 3, but take all 20 folders with you, because you never know what will happen come auction day. You may have ruled out a $250,000 house that had a $260,000 mortgage on it, but when the auction rolls around, it may open with a bid for $170,000. By referencing your property dossier and doing some basic math, you realize that you can pick up $80,000 in equity. Because you've done your homework and have your property dossier with you, you may be the only person in the room who knows what that house is worth. When that happens, you're like a fox in the henhouse.

Recognizing the Most Common and Serious Red Flags and Big Mistakes

Part of performing your due diligence involves spotting red flags and avoiding big mistakes. Here are a few of the most common and serious red flags and big mistakes to avoid:

>> **Right address, wrong street:** When inspecting a property, be sure that you're at the right address on the right street, not one or two streets over. Take a photo of the address from the front of the property or its mailbox; then go to the corner and take a photo of the street signs at the nearest intersection. Check the address in your research notes to be sure you're inspecting the right property. (This issue is less common in newer neighborhoods.)

>> **Overlooked lien:** If a property has a tax lien against it and the foreclosing bank or its attorney failed to give proper notice to the IRS, the state, or the county, the lien may not get wiped out in the foreclosure process. You're not legally liable to pay other people's income taxes, but the taxing authorities could make your life uncomfortable.

>> **Condemned home:** If you're looking at an older home that needs work, check with the municipality to ensure that it's not condemned and subject to being torn down.

TIP

When you're buying a bank-owned property or a property at a foreclosure sale, using the title company that's owned by the law firm representing the bank can save you a lot of time. Large law firms across the country that represent banks frequently own their own title company, which provides them another revenue source.

» **Establishing a solid relationship with distressed homeowners**

» **Gathering key information from the homeowners**

» **Explaining the homeowners' options**

» **Inspecting the property's interior**

» **Negotiating deals with lenders**

Chapter **9**

Contacting the Homeowners and Lenders

When you choose to deal directly with homeowners facing foreclosure, you become the resident rescue worker in a burning building. Your job is to assess the situation, point out the exits, and do everything in your power to assist the homeowners in extinguishing the flames or safely retreating from the building.

As a foreclosure rescue worker, you must first contact the homeowners and obtain detailed information about their situation. This contact requires an empathetic ear and the ability to jot down the most important details. With this information and the details about the property (see Chapter 8), you can assess the situation and lay the homeowners' options on the table. Perform your job well, and you'll earn the homeowners' trust and place yourself in a better position to obtain the property should they choose to sell it.

In this chapter, I lead you through the process of contacting the homeowners, gathering information about their situation, and presenting their options to them. I also show you how to deal effectively with lenders to negotiate a solution that's less painful for all involved.

Scheduling Your Foreclosure Activities

Having a game plan for researching the property and contacting the homeowners and lenders is always a good idea. By planning your activities, you create a schedule that keeps you on track and in touch with the homeowners and lenders.

Your schedule is generally dictated by the period between the posting of the foreclosure notice and the sale and on the redemption period if you have one in your area. If your area has a redemption period, you can continue to educate and work with the homeowners even after their home has been sold at auction.

REMEMBER

Planning is important, but be flexible. The foreclosure process is predictable, but the homeowners and their situations are often very unpredictable. Be prepared to ride some serious waves.

In Michigan, the foreclosure notice is published four to six consecutive weeks before the sale and is typically subject to a redemption period of six months or more. My plan kicks into action as soon as I spot an interesting foreclosure notice and continues for four consecutive weeks. Start with the following plan, and tweak it to conform to the foreclosure schedule in your area:

Week 1:

1. **Find the foreclosure notice or Notice of Default (NOD).**

2. **Do some preliminary research on the property, as explained in Chapter 8:**

- Find the property's address.

- Visit the property to see whether it's something you'd be interested in purchasing.

- Take photos of the property if you're interested.

REMEMBER

Don't waste time or resources ordering a title commitment or heavily researching a property that you have no intention of buying. At this point, you're just trying to spot the best prospects. When you have a short list, you can do more research.

3. **Send your first foreclosure letter introducing yourself to the homeowners.**

   See "Delivering a letter of introduction" later in this chapter.

Week 2:

1. **Find the second foreclosure notice.**
2. **If the notice doesn't appear, send a congratulations letter to the homeowners.**
3. **Review the title work.**
4. **Attempt to contact the homeowners by phone.**
5. **Knock on their door to attempt a face-to-face meeting.**
6. **Send your second foreclosure letter.**

Week 3:

1. **Find the third foreclosure notice.**
2. **If a third notice doesn't appear, send a congratulations letter to the homeowners.**
3. **Attempt to contact the homeowners by phone.**
4. **Research the property more thoroughly if it appears to be a hot prospect:**
   - Research comparable sales.
   - Order a title commitment, or obtain the title work yourself.
5. **Contact the junior lienholders.**

   See "Contacting the Lenders" later in this chapter.
6. **Contact the mortgagee's (lender's) attorney and find out the following:**
   - Whether the property is still going to auction.
   - Whether there's an opening bid and what that amount is.
   - Whether the lender is considering an adjournment (postponing the sale), which is usually a sign that the homeowners and lender are negotiating a possible solution.
   - Any other background information. Contact the lienholders for possible short sale opportunities. Chapter 15 provides additional information about negotiating short sales.
7. **Send your third foreclosure letter.**

Week 4:

1. Find the fourth (probably final) foreclosure notice.

2. If a fourth notice doesn't appear, send a congratulations letter to the homeowners.

3. Drive by the house you're interested in bidding on at auction, and take new photos if the condition of the property has changed significantly.

4. Attempt to contact the homeowners by phone.

5. Send your fourth foreclosure letter.

6. Organize your property dossier for the auction (see Chapter 8).

REMEMBER

If your state has no redemption period, stress to the homeowners that they're very likely to lose their house and all its equity unless they take action *before* the mortgage sale. In areas with redemption periods, homeowners still have time after the sale to take action, but the longer they wait, the less attractive their options are.

If your area uses NODs, begin by contacting bank Real Estate Owned (REO) departments as soon as the NOD is filed. See Chapter 12 for details.

AVOIDING LEGAL BROUHAHAS: IGNORANCE IS NO EXCUSE

Before contacting the homeowners directly, brush up on the legal and ethical rules of the foreclosure game so that you don't get slapped with a lawsuit and so you can look yourself in the mirror every morning knowing that you're not ripping off distressed homeowners. Here are the do's and don'ts you must follow to work foreclosures ethically and legally:

- Never do anything to mislead homeowners into thinking you're someone or something you're not, such as an attorney, accountant, or financial adviser. Let homeowners know upfront that you're an investor who purchases properties. If you're a real estate agent, you must disclose the fact that you act in both capacities.

- Always let the homeowners decide what's best for them. You can present their options, but this is their home and their debt. Don't steer them into selling the property to you simply because it's in *your* best interest.

- Always recommend that the homeowners contact their lenders directly or consult an attorney or accountant if that would be in their best interest. If they're hesitant or afraid to call their lender, you can have them sign an authorization form and call the lender with them. Unfortunately, con artists often use authorization forms to collect personal information that enables them to rip off distressed homeowners.

- Present all the homeowners' options to them, including the option to file for bankruptcy, even if that means that you lose out on the deal.

- Don't befriend the homeowners for the sole purpose of persuading them to sell the house to you below market value.

- If you decide to purchase the property from the homeowners, put your offer in writing in the form of a purchase agreement. In real estate, only agreements in writing stand up in court.

- Avoid any contact with the homeowners during the last month of the redemption period. At this point, homeowners may become very desperate and accuse you of making promises you never made. The unfortunate reality is that this time is exactly when they'll contact you, usually from one of the letters you sent that they've been holding on to. If you do talk with them, record the conversations as protection, provided that you have the legal right to record conversations.

- Audiotape your conversations with homeowners, whether you meet with them in person or talk on the phone. Bring a recorder and ask permission to record the conversation for their protection and yours. This way, no one can conveniently forget what was said.

Anyone with a chip on their shoulder and a hundred bucks can file a lawsuit. My company was dealing with a couple who were facing foreclosure. The wife never told the husband that she hadn't made the payments until they lost the house. We told her that she needed to come to the office to find out more about their options. The last week of the redemption period was the beginning of hunting season, and the husband was out of town, so the couple never showed up for the scheduled meeting. They retained an attorney who sued us. Their claim was that we had promised they could stay in the home. They lost the case and then hired another attorney.

I strongly encourage you to consult a real estate attorney who's familiar with foreclosure laws in your market before working foreclosures in your area. Also find out about your legal rights for taping conversations. In Michigan, you can legally tape a phone conversation as long as you're participating in the conversation.

Contacting the Homeowners Directly

To purchase properties directly from homeowners before auction, you have two big challenges ahead of you: tracking down the homeowners and getting them to sit down with you at the kitchen table to discuss their situation. Rarely do homeowners who are facing foreclosure seek help. Most often, they do everything they can to avoid lenders, collectors, attorneys, and investors — yeah, people like you.

In the following sections, I reveal strategies and tips that I use to track down homeowners and make a good first impression when I contact them.

TIP

Many real estate investors avoid foreclosures because the homeowners can be so difficult to track down and deal with, which reduces some of the competition for foreclosure properties. With stamina, determination, people skills, and this book, you have everything you need to tap into this open market.

Tracking down the homeowners

When people can't pay their bills, the repo company is trying to take their car, bill collectors are harassing them, and the phone company has disconnected their service, they can be a little tough to get hold of. Many distressed homeowners even go into hiding. They refuse to answer the door or the phone, avoid the neighbors, and sometimes even up and leave, vacating the premises.

To contact homeowners, you often need to do some detective work to find out where they're living and to obtain a phone number, in case they're answering the phone. Here are some tips that have worked well for me in tracking down homeowners:

>> **Contact the county's tax assessor's or treasurer's office (whichever sends out the tax bills).** The address where the tax bills are sent is public information, and the bills go to the homeowner. If the homeowner isn't residing at the property, the tax bill may be going to a different address.

>> **Send a letter to the property's address with a return receipt request attached to it.** There are sample letters later in this chapter. If the person is no longer at the address you used, you get the letter back with the person's forwarding address on it. The postal service charges about a buck for the return receipt request.

>> **Contact the neighbors.** Knocking on doors is often the most effective approach.

- **Search for the homeowners by name online.** Social media such as Facebook is often a good place to start, especially if the homeowners have a unique last name. USA People Search at `https://www.usa-people-search.com` is also very useful, enabling you to search by address for a property to find out the names and contact information for people who live there.

- **Flip through the phone book and call everyone who has the same last name as the person you're trying to contact.** Start with the people who live in the area near the property and fan out. If the homeowners have a common last name, of course, this approach isn't practical.

- **In cases of divorce, you may need to go down to the county courthouse and look up the marriage certificate to find out the wife's maiden name.**

REMEMBER

The more difficult a homeowner is to contact, the better the opportunity is for you. Most foreclosure investors give up when their first few attempts to contact the homeowner fail, leaving you with less competition. With persistence, you may be the lone investor who succeeds in contacting the homeowner.

Kicking off your mail campaign

Contacting homeowners before the auction isn't a one-time event. Like a doctor who's treating a patient in recovery, remain in constant contact with the homeowners up until the time they decide how they want to resolve the situation. Your goal should be to contact the homeowners at least once a week via phone, mail, personal visits, email, or a combination of methods. Success in pre-foreclosures hinges on your ability to continually let the homeowners know how you can assist them.

Your primary medium for contacting distressed homeowners is the letter — either mailed to the homeowners' address or hand-delivered. In the following sections, I supply samples of letters I use, but in most cases, you should edit the letter to give it a more personal touch.

Delivering a letter of introduction

In your first letter, let the homeowners know that you know they're facing foreclosure, that they have options, and that you can provide some guidance. Include your phone number so they can contact you for additional information and to set up an appointment. Figure 9-1 shows a sample letter of introduction.

TIP

You can type the letter, but hand-address the envelope. If you use your printer to print the mailing address, the letter may appear to be too official, and the homeowners may not even open it. For your return address, use the address of your business or personal residence; a PO box number is too impersonal.

<Your Address>
<City>, <State> <Zip>
<Date>

<Homeowner's Names>
<Address>
<City>, <State> <Zip>

Dear Friend,

Sometimes bad things happen to good people. I am sorry to learn that the lender who holds your mortgage has begun foreclosing on your home. Despite what you may be hearing from other people trying to make a quick buck at your expense, you may have other options other than losing your home.

I am dedicated to helping people in this area achieve the American dream of homeownership. I am also dedicated to helping people hold onto that dream when they are facing hard times. I am committed to making sure that people in foreclosure know all of the options available to them when facing this situation.

You are not alone. Hundreds of thousands of homeowners in the United States face similar situations every year. Foreclosure is almost epidemic. Most of the people in these situations are just like you—hardworking people who have had a few bad breaks.

I have studied the foreclosure process in our area and can explain your options to you in detail. Some of these options may enable you to retain possession of your house or at least delay the process, so you have more time to seek better solutions and preserve your credit rating. The sooner you take action, the better your options.

Don't lose your home and the equity you've worked so hard to build up just because you're too embarrassed to get advice. I have helped many people in your situation and I can help you too. Please call me at <Your Phone Number>, so we can discuss your options and start putting this nightmare behind you.

The worst thing you can do now is nothing! I can't be forceful enough on this point. If you ignore this problem, you will lose your home. Please call me today.

FIGURE 9-1:
Write a letter of
introduction,
letting the
homeowners
know how you
can assist them.

Sincerely,

<Your Signature>

<Your Name>

Foreclosure Specialist

Delivering follow-up letters

Read the foreclosure notices every week, as explained in Chapter 7. If a foreclosure notice is posted for the property in this week's legal news or local paper, send a follow-up letter to the homeowners. You should send a follow-up letter every week leading up to the week of the foreclosure sale.

TIP

With each letter, add a touch more urgency in your call to action. Always emphasize that doing nothing is the worst thing anyone in foreclosure can do. Time is of the essence! Figures 9-2, 9-3, and 9-4 provide sample letters that you can send to homeowners at the beginning of weeks 2, 3, and 4. Note that each letter increases the sense of urgency.

<Your Address>
<City>, <State> <Zip>
<Date>

<Homeowner's Names>
<Address>
<City>, <State> <Zip>

Dear Friend,
You are receiving this letter because, incredibly, your financial difficulty is now a matter of public record.

I say, "Dear Friend," because I have a good idea what you're going through. My mentor, Ralph Roberts, was in your shoes when he lost his own home back in 1979. He knows what it's like to be angry, frustrated, and hounded by creditors. You wonder if you'll ever get ahead. Ralph hated the ring of the phone, but he hated it even more when they shut off his phone.

Today, 20 years after his ordeal, Ralph will tell you that he lost his home because he was too embarrassed to ask for help. He lost his home because he did nothing and allowed it to be taken from him without even putting up a fight. Fortunately for you, however, that horrible experience motivated Ralph to do everything he could to make sure other people—good people like you—don't have to go through the same thing he did.

That is why Ralph began training investors all over the country to help people in foreclosure. He studied foreclosures throughout North America to learn about every possible option available to people facing this nightmare. With Ralph's training and consultation, I have developed a system—a step-by-step strategy –for helping people like you to escape the trap of foreclosure.

This system has worked for countless others across the country. I'm sure it can work for you if you'll just give me the chance to help you out.

With my assistance, you can successfully navigate the foreclosure process. I'm sure you don't realize the many options you do have available to you. In many cases, if you act quickly, you can keep your home. If that's not possible, you can at least receive fair market value for the property, protect your credit rating, and avoid seeing your house sold to the highest bidder at a Sheriff's Sale.

I am here—ready, willing and able to help. But YOU have to make the first move and give me a call. Please call me directly at <Your Phone Number>, so we get started putting this nightmare behind you.

Sincerely,

<Your Signature>

<Your Name>

Foreclosure Specialist

FIGURE 9-2:
Write a follow-up letter for the second week.

P.S. As I mentioned above, you do have many options available to you. But, the longer you wait, the fewer options you will have. And, if you sit and do nothing, you will lose your home. Please do something to help yourself and call me today.

<Your Address>
<City>, <State> <Zip>
<Date>

<Homeowner's Names>
<Address>
<City>, <State> <Zip>

Dear Friend,

The Sheriff's Sale on <Mortgage Sale Date> is fast approaching.

I am extremely concerned!

This is the third letter I've sent you—yet I still haven't heard back from you. Just so that you are completely aware of what's going on here, I believe that it is very important that you fully understand what will happen if your house goes to that Sheriff's Sale.

At the Sheriff's Sale, your property will be sold to the highest bidder. If no investor comes forward to bid on your property, it will be turned over to the bank that holds your mortgage. Either way, you will have no right to reinstate your existing mortgage once the sale takes place.

If you continue to do nothing, you WILL lose your home. That is a harsh statement, but I want to be perfectly clear so that I know you are completely aware of your situation and the consequences of your actions—or inaction.

Please, call me directly at <Your Phone Number> to let me know that you do indeed understand what is going to happen. If you call me right away, you still have options available to you. But realize that your time is quickly running out.

Sincerely,

<Your Signature>

<Your Name>

Foreclosure Specialist

FIGURE 9-3:
Write a follow-up letter for the third week.

P.S. If you want to save what equity you have in your home—not to mention your credit rating—doing nothing is NOT an option. Please call me TODAY before it's too late. Don't let embarrassment about your situation cause you to lose your home; I've helped many good people, just like you, turn things around.

TIP

Consider sending a letter the day of the sale, informing the homeowners that the house went to sale and that you have the amount it sold for, the name of the person who bought the property, and the amount of the overbid (if an overbid occurred). An *overbid* occurs if someone bids more for the property than the amount owed on it; homeowners can claim the overbid money. Let them know how to contact you so that you have another opportunity to talk with them, set up a face-to-face meeting, supply them this valuable information, and explain what it means.

<Your Address>
<City>, <State> <Zip>
<Date>

<Homeowner's Names>
<Address>
<City>, <State> <Zip>

Dear Friend,

You are almost out of time.

You have only a few days until your home will be sold to the highest bidder at the Sheriff's Sale. Unless you do something immediately, someone else will own your home within the week.

Believe it or not, you still have options available to you. If you'll just take the first step and give me a call, I have all the knowledge, resources, and expertise available to help you escape your foreclosure nightmare and get your life back on track. But, unfortunately, I am powerless to help you—UNLESS you call me RIGHT NOW!

If you do nothing, you WILL lose your home. The sad part is that you don't have to.

Right now you probably feel totally alone, as if you don't have a friend in the world. But, in reality, you have a friend right here who is ready, willing, and able to help. I know what you're going through.

My mentor, the best-selling Realtor in America, Ralph Roberts himself lost his own home to foreclosure back in 1979. That is why he has taught me all about foreclosures so I can help people like you—good people who have had some bad breaks. I have helped many people facing the same situation as you. I CAN help you, too.

Please call me NOW at <Your Phone Number>.

Sincerely,

<Your Signature>

<Your Name>

Foreclosure Specialist

FIGURE 9-4: Write a follow-up letter for the fourth week.

P.S. People facing foreclosure commonly remain in denial about this horrible thing that is happening to them. But, unfortunately, time is working against you. If you continue to do nothing, IN A FEW DAYS SOMEONE ELSE WILL OWN YOUR HOME. Please, please call me NOW so I can help!

Congratulating the homeowners

As you're checking the weekly foreclosure notices, you may find that a foreclosure notice doesn't appear for a property you're tracking. In some cases, the homeowners have negotiated a solution with the lender. When this occurs, don't assume that your relationship with the homeowners has ended. Send them a letter of congratulations, as shown in Figure 9-5.

```
<Your Address>
<City>, <State> <Zip>
<Date>

<Homeowner's Names>
<Address>
<City>, <State> <Zip>

Dear <Homeowners' First Names>,

I was happy to see that you were able to reinstate your loan with <Lender's Name>. I know
that the past few months have been terribly stressful for you and your family. I hope the
information outlining the options available to people facing foreclosure that I've sent to you
over the past few weeks has been helpful.

If you, or anyone you know, ever faces a similar situation, please don't hesitate to call me. I
am happy to help in any way I can. I've enclosed a few of my business cards just in case you
meet someone who needs my assistance. I wish you the best!

Sincerely,

<Your Signature>

<Your Name>

Foreclosure Specialist
```

FIGURE 9-5:
Congratulate the
homeowners if
they work out a
solution with
their lenders.

REMEMBER

Many homeowners who survive the current financial crisis end up in the same position later. If you've been helpful and supportive, they're likely to contact you the next time they experience difficulties. Even if they don't have future problems, they may recommend you to friends or relatives who find themselves in a similar situation.

Getting in touch over the phone

As a result of your letter campaign, the homeowners may call you, but if they haven't called by the second week, try giving them a ring. When you eventually do get in touch with them, your goal is to set up an initial face-to-face meeting at their kitchen table. Be prepared to listen closely to what they say and take notes. Figure 9-6 provides a sample phone script you can use as a guide through your initial conversation with the homeowners.

Be prepared to field calls at any time of the day or night from people who are afraid. You should have a cellphone and be very accessible. I've received phone calls well into the wee hours of the morning. Distressed homeowners seem to gain courage as the sun sets. Many people call when their spouse is at work or sleeping. Keep in mind that these callers don't know what to do, and they may be dealing with other tragic situations, so expect an atmosphere of uneasiness.

You say: Hello, my name is <Your Name>. I'm a real estate investor who helps homeowners just like you escape the foreclosure trap. I have been trying to reach you for some time now. As crazy as it sounds, the fact that you're facing foreclosure is now a matter of public record.

Despite what others who have already contacted you may have told you, you do have rights and options available to you to save your home.

I would like to get together with you as soon as possible to discuss your options. Can we meet at your house or at my office sometime this week?

Homeowner says: Yes.

You say: Fantastic, let me know what's best for you. (Set up an appointment.)

Homeowner says: No.

You say: I think you owe it to yourself to at least find out how the foreclosure process works and what rights you have so people don't try to take advantage of you. Will you at least take a few minutes right now to let me tell you about your rights?

> **Homeowner says:** Yes.
>
> **You say:** Believe me, you are doing the right thing. I've helped a lot of people save their homes and credit ratings. How many months are you behind on your mortgage? Tell me a little about how you got into this situation. (Ask questions from the homeowner information sheet shown in Figure 10-6.)
>
> **Homeowner says:** No.
>
> **You say:** If you change your mind—and I really hope you do—give me a call. I would definitely be willing to give you a second opinion on any deals that someone else offers you. My name and number are <Your Name> <Your Phone Number>.

FIGURE 9-6:
This phone script can guide you through your first conversation with the homeowners.

WARNING

Don't forget to include the spouse if a couple owns the home. Early in your conversation, ask whether the spouse knows about the situation. Eventually, the spouse needs to be brought into the discussion, but you want to make sure that it's done properly. I've had spouses ask me to be the bearer of bad news, but the partner should have the option of breaking the bad news. When both homeowners are apprised of what's going on, both of them need be included in the decision process and the signing of any agreements.

Before you call, brush up on the options available to the homeowners, just in case they ask about them. Ideally, your phone call results in a face-to-face meeting with the homeowners, but if they ask about their options, be prepared to provide some general information. For details about homeowners' options, see "Presenting All Available Options" later in this chapter.

As you converse, keep the following in mind:

>> Realize that the homeowners may have already been contacted by others.

>> Listen more than you talk, and show compassion for their situation. The homeowners can really use a sympathetic ear, and hearing their story provides you valuable background information about their situation and mindset. This conversation is your opportunity to establish a bond of trust.

>> Let the homeowners know that you want to assist them and are an expert in foreclosure options.

>> Emphasize that the worst action they can take is to do nothing.

>> Ask lots of questions but don't interrupt. They need to know that you care before they'll care what you know. Interrupting someone who's pouring their heart out is potentially devastating to your relationship. Keep in mind that something you feel is important can seem completely unimportant to someone whose emotions are ruling their thoughts.

Your initial conversation is a success if you achieve the following goals:

>> Obtain the homeowners' complete contact information.

>> Establish yourself as an expert in foreclosure matters.

>> Let the homeowners know that they have options and that you can explain their options when you meet for the first time.

>> Assist the homeowners in understanding their rights and the foreclosure process. In Michigan, for example, few homeowners realize that they control the home through the redemption period.

>> Inform the homeowners that they need to be very careful, because unsavory characters may mislead them to take advantage of them.

>> Schedule a face-to-face meeting.

>> Instruct the homeowners to gather all the paperwork related to the property, including the closing package they received when they purchased the property, correspondence from the lender and the foreclosing attorney, and (if available) any notices posted on the property by the sheriff.

TIP

After you've set up a meeting, ask the homeowners why they called you instead of talking with another investor, and ask to see any correspondence they received from other investors. Get to know the people you're competing against, and what you're doing that works and doesn't work.

Adding the Homeowners' Profile to Your Property Dossier

To assess the homeowners' current foreclosure situation, you need to gather some essential details. When you meet with the homeowners for the first time, explain the foreclosure process, and ask the following questions:

>> How did the situation escalate to this point?

>> Have you discussed your situation with any other professionals, such as agents, lawyers, accountants, or lenders?

>> If you discussed the situation with others, what did they suggest?

>> What do you want to do? Save your house? Cash out your equity and move? File for bankruptcy? (When mentioning bankruptcy, stress that you're not an attorney and can't provide legal advice or representation but you can share general information about the different types of bankruptcy.)

>> Can I take some time to explain your options? (Options vary depending on the amount of time the homeowners have to act; the amount of equity they've built up in the property; and the resources they have at their disposal, such as friends or family members who may be willing to help financially.)

>> Do you have any questions about your rights and options?

When you've gained the homeowners' trust, explain that to help them, you need more-detailed information. Work with the homeowners to complete the home-owner information sheet shown in Figure 9-7.

Name: _____

Address:_____

Home Phone:_____ Work Phone:_____ Pager/Mobile: _____

How long have you lived in the house?_____

Marital Status: ☐ Single ☐ Married ☐ Divorced

Is your spouse aware of this situation? ☐ Yes ☐ No

Number of Children: _____ Ages of Children: _____

Occupation: _____ Employer: _____

What made you decide to contact me? _____

Why are you in foreclosure? _____

_____

Gross Income: _____

Foreclosure Sale Date: _____ Redemption Period: _____

Type of loan: ☐ Conventional ☐ FHA ☐ VA ☐ Other: _____

Loan Balance: _____ Interest Rate: _____

Monthly house payment: _____ No. of months behind: _____

How much are you comfortable paying each month? _____

How much do you have in available cash or liquid assets? _____

Can you borrow from family or friends? ☐ No ☐ Yes, how much? _____

Owner's estimated value of home: _____

Do you have any: ☐ Second mortgages ☐ Tax liens ☐ Mechanic's liens

Been in foreclosure before? ☐ Yes ☐ No

Now in or ever filed for bankruptcy before? ☐ No ☐ Yes

If yes, what type? ☐ Chapter 7 ☐ Chapter 13

Bankruptcy details: ☐ Currently in ☐ Completed on: _____

Others consulted: ☐ Bank/Mortgage Co. ☐ Attorney ☐ Realtor

☐ Accountant ☐ Others: _____

What advice did they give you?_____

_____

What would you like to see happen to your home? _____

_____

When can I come to see the property? _____

What Owner Wants: ☐ Cash Buy ☐ Re-Fi ☐ List ☐ Short Sale ☐ Other

Reasoning/Notes: _____

_____

_____

FIGURE 9-7:
Gather information from the homeowners.

Presenting All Available Options

After you've completed the foreclosure information sheet (in Chapter 8) and the homeowner information sheet (refer to Figure 9-7), and have a firsthand account of the situation, the homeowners' situation becomes much clearer. You begin to get a sense of what the owners want to do; what realistic options are available to them; and which is the best course of action for them to take, whether it's refinancing, selling, downsizing, renting or (worst case) filing for bankruptcy.

CONVINCING THE HOMEOWNERS TO SEEK HELP

Convincing distressed homeowners to seek assistance from family members is a challenge. You can often succeed by asking the homeowners what they would do if they were in a position to help someone in their family who was experiencing financial problems.

My office once assisted a young couple who had three small children. Initially, I met with the wife at the home. When she felt comfortable, she and her husband came to the office. As I began laying out their options, the first option I presented was to ask friends and relatives to help. I explained that homeowners in similar situations often have people in their lives who can help but because of shame or embarrassment, most of them won't ask for help. I asked whether they had anyone they could go to for some financial assistance. They explained that they didn't want to ask for help.

Then I asked them how they would feel if a loved one needed help and they had the means to help that person, but weren't asked. The couple continued to refuse to ask for help.

I proceeded to explain their remaining options. After each option, I asked them whether the option was something they thought would fit their situation better. The husband became a bit uneasy and said that they actually did have someone they could go to but his wife was unwilling.

After some discussion, I learned that the wife's parents were very wealthy and owned a thriving business on the East Coast. She didn't want to call because she was afraid that her father would be angry. I told her that her father would probably be angry because she hadn't called him earlier and that he'd probably be more upset to know that his grandchildren were needlessly evicted. I also asked, "If one of your children needed help, wouldn't you want to be called immediately?"

The answer, of course, was "yes." We called the wife's parents right then from our conference room. All the emotions that you would expect poured out during that phone conversation, and the couple worked through a very painful experience, but the call resulted in saving their home.

In the following sections, I describe the various options available so that you can understand them and present them to the homeowners. I also show you how to rule out unrealistic options based on the homeowners' situation.

Reinstating the loan

If the homeowners can come up with enough cash to bring their mortgage payments up to date and to pay any back taxes and penalties, they may be able to reinstate the mortgage. In most cases, the homeowners are required to sell other assets or obtain financial assistance from family members or friends.

REMEMBER

Most homeowners in foreclosure are too embarrassed to ask family and friends for help, but this is often the best solution. Encourage the homeowners to contact any family members who may be able to give or loan them the money to pay off the lender that's foreclosing on the property. In many cases, I meet with family members personally to help the homeowner tell family members about their situation.

Negotiating with the lenders for a forbearance

If the homeowners have experienced a temporary financial setback, they may be able to work out a solution with the lender to restructure their payments and get back on track. If they've fallen way behind in their payments, however, and their prospects of getting back on track look bleak, the lender is unlikely to agree to a forbearance.

TIP

With the homeowners' approval and a signed release form like the one shown in Figure 9-8, you can negotiate with the lender on the homeowners' behalf to agree to a forbearance. Remember, however, that you won't be the one sending the check to the lender each week, so the homeowners must be on board and be able to perform; otherwise, you'll lose credibility with that lender.

Refinancing the mortgage

For homeowners with solid, stable incomes and assets other than their home who are experiencing a temporary financial setback, refinancing to a nonconforming loan may be an option. A *nonconforming loan* is a mortgage that typically charges 2–3 percent interest above conventional rates plus additional points at closing. In some cases, if the homeowners can make their payments on time for a year, they qualify for refinancing back to a conforming mortgage.

WARNING

Refinancing is usually a poor choice for people with lower incomes, because even if they qualify for a nonconforming loan, they may end up having higher monthly mortgage payments than they previously had. Refinancing simply sets them up for another round of foreclosure.

<Your Address>
<City. State, Zip>

Borrower Certification &
Authorization to Release Information

1. I/We authorize you to provide <Your Name or Business Name> its representatives, successors, and/or assignees, any and all information and/or documentation that they might reasonably request. Such information includes, but is not limited to employment history and income; bank, money market, and similar account balances; credit history; and copies of income tax returns.

2. I/We further authorize <Your Name or Business Name> its representatives, successors, and/or assignees to request a credit report and all credit information required by <Your Name or Business Name>.

3. A copy of this authorization, including a facsimile transmission, may be accepted as an original.

X_____   _____   _____
     Borrower   Date   Social Security Number

X_____   _____   _____
     Borrower   Date   Social Security Number

FIGURE 9-8:
Ask the homeowners to sign a statement giving you permission to discuss the situation with lenders.

If the homeowners' gross income is sufficient to cover their monthly bills in addition to a higher monthly mortgage payment, offer to set up a meeting with your loan officer to discuss their options. But hurry; the clock is ticking!

Listing the property

Homeowners who have several thousands of dollars' worth of equity built up in their homes are often best served by placing the house on the market, selling it, and moving to more affordable accommodations. This option enables the homeowners to keep much or all of the equity they've accumulated in their home. Unfortunately, this option is usually the last one they're willing to consider.

When presenting this option to homeowners, highlight the following key points:

>> If the homeowners have little, no, or negative equity in the property, this option is off the table.

>> If the auction is scheduled to occur in the next few weeks, the homeowners may not be able to sell it in time. If your area has a lengthy redemption period, however, they do have time to sell.

>> If the homeowners are already in their redemption period, remind them that interest is accruing on the amount the bank or investor paid for the mortgage at the auction. The sooner they sell, the less interest they pay.

>> To sell the home faster, recommend that the homeowners sell through a qualified real estate agent, and make sure that the agent they pick understands foreclosure and that time is of the essence.

>> If the homeowners are reluctant to sell just because it's their home, remind them that it's only a house and that the next house they move into will provide the same opportunities to create wonderful memories. (This obstacle is harder to overcome when the house has been in the family for many years or generations.)

TIP

Sometimes, you can persuade the homeowners to list their house right away by explaining that having more time to market the home gives them a better chance of selling it for full market value. Waiting to list could back the owners into a corner, forcing them to accept less than market value or lose their home outright. Keep in mind that they may need time following the offer for a buyer to get financing and for the closing packages to be put together.

Selling short

When the homeowners owe more on a home than they can sell it for, you can sometimes work a short sale with the lending institution. In a *short sale*, the bank may accept less money than it is owed for the purpose of getting the bad loan off its books. Then the homeowners can afford to sell their home below market value for the amount that the bank agreed to accept. For details on short sales, consult Chapter 15. (*Note:* Negotiating a short sale takes time and patience.)

Accepting your cash offer

When homeowners want to sell their home but don't have sufficient time to sell it for market value or aren't interested in going through the hassle of selling their home, selling the house to you for cash is often a very attractive option. The more equity the homeowners have in the house, the more cash you can offer them for the property. If the foreclosure is a result of divorce or the death of one of the homeowners, cash is often even more appealing.

To decide how much to offer for a property, check out Chapter 10.

Refinancing through you

In some situations, refinancing the mortgage through you is the best option for the homeowners, which is often the case when homeowners lose the property in foreclosure but still have an opportunity to redeem it. Because they now have a foreclosure on their credit history, they may not qualify for a loan or the interest rates may be cost-prohibitive, even if they can afford the monthly payments now.

Consider this somewhat common scenario: The homeowners suffer a financial setback (such as a job loss), causing them to lose the property at the foreclosure sale; then, they recover from the setback, which enables them to start making payments again. They can't get loan approval because of the foreclosure. Here's where you step in. You buy the property and sell it back to the owners on a land contract, trust deed, or some other form of seller financing.

By offering an interest rate several percentage points below what they would probably pay on a nonconforming loan from an equity lender (assuming that they could even quality for such a loan), they could keep their monthly payment near their current level or even lower it and stay in their home. Over time, they may even be able to rebuild their credit history and qualify for a conventional loan at a lower interest rate. Using the proceeds from the conventional loan, they could pay off the balance they owe you and start making monthly mortgage payments to the bank.

Your state probably has a cap on the interest you can charge on land contracts. Make sure that you know the rules. You don't want to be in violation of any usury laws prohibiting unfair lending practices.

For additional information and advice on selling a home back to the homeowners, check out Chapter 19.

Selling the home and leasing it with an option to buy it back later

Homeowners who are high credit risks — those who have bad credit history, low income, questionable job security, and little or no assets — may be able to afford to buy back the home through a rent-to-own arrangement known as a lease-option deal.

In a *lease-option deal*, you purchase the property and lease it back to the former owners, providing them the option of buying it later if they meet the criteria outlined in the agreement. You may want to apply all or a portion of the lease payments toward the purchase price if your customers exercise their option. See Chapter 18 for more information about lease-option deals.

Selling the home and leasing it without an option to buy

When homeowners can no longer afford their monthly mortgage payments and refuse any option that requires them to vacate the premises, you might consider buying the property and leasing it back to them. After some time, you can present your tenants a couple of other options:

>> Purchase a less-expensive house from you in the same area.

>> Purchase the house back from you or sign a lease-option agreement that enables them to rent to own, as explained in the preceding section.

WARNING

Establish rental relationships only with homeowners who've shown that they've been taking good care of the property and can afford to pay enough rent to make the relationship profitable for you. You don't want to put yourself in the position of having to evict your tenants two months down the road. For more about leasing the property back to the homeowners, see Chapter 18.

Giving a deed in lieu of foreclosure

When homeowners owe more on a property than it's worth and the lender refuses to agree to a short sale, the best option for the homeowners may be to offer the lender the deed in lieu of foreclosure. When homeowners give a deed in lieu fore-closure, they relinquish ownership of the home and walk away.

Offering a deed in lieu of foreclosure is better than foreclosure. It's the right thing to do if no other options make sense and the lender agrees to go along with it. The lender may even report the mortgage as paid as agreed but there's no guarantee. In some cases, the lender refuses to accept the deed, such as if the property is condemned or has some sort of environmental problems, or if the owners have other assets that the lender wants to go after.

WARNING

If the homeowners have little, no, or negative equity in the property, they may be willing to deed the property to you in exchange for your paying off the balance of the mortgage. They do this by signing a quitclaim deed. If you accept a quitclaim deed, pay off the mortgage immediately. Real estate con artists often persuade homeowners to sign a quitclaim deed, promise to pay off the mortgage, and never do.

REMEMBER

Giving the deed in lieu of foreclosure makes sense only if the homeowners have negative equity in the home and are near the end of the foreclosure process. If the homeowners have time before the auction or during the redemption period, they should seek other options first, such as negotiating a short sale or selling the property themselves. Some mortgage companies will pay for a deed in lieu of fore-closure, which may make the option more appealing to the homeowners.

Filing for bankruptcy

Bankruptcy is the option of last resort. Usually, it's just a quick-fix solution that only temporarily prevents the mortgage sale. When someone files for bankruptcy, the court issues a stay that stops all actions. Many lending institutions simply adjourn the foreclosure proceedings until the owner is out of bankruptcy or until they can persuade the court to lift the stay. The owners end up with the same problems that drove them into bankruptcy, and now they also have attorney and trustee fees to pay.

Bankruptcy, however, can be an effective tool for wiping out junior liens on a property. In this situation, your relationships with bankruptcy attorneys can be helpful to distressed homeowners. If homeowners start talking about bankruptcy, clearly state that you're not an attorney (unless you actually are one) and that you believe they should talk about that option with a lawyer.

WARNING

If the homeowners decide to file for bankruptcy, make sure that they see a repu-table attorney. Cheap, fly-by-night legal services, commonly referred to as *mills*, can churn out the necessary paperwork, but they don't provide the appropriate personal advice. Encourage the homeowners to seek out a bankruptcy trustee or at least have consultations with several attorneys.

Waiting (and saving) during redemption

If you're working the foreclosure circuit in an area with a somewhat-generous redemption period (at least three months), the homeowners have the option to continue living in the house for the duration of the redemption period without having to pay their monthly mortgage.

In addition to buying some time to explore options, if the homeowners can set aside the money they'd normally be paying on the mortgage, they could sock away enough cash to pay a security deposit on a lease or to cover an option fee to purchase a more affordable property on a lease-option contract, as explained in Chapter 19. The problem with this option is that homeowners whose finances are already strained may not be able to set the money aside. I've seen situations in which homeowners were very successful with this strategy, so be sure to present it as an option.

Doing nothing

Although doing nothing isn't really an option, unfortunately, it's what most people in foreclosure do, and it's the worst possible thing to do. Doing nothing ultimately leads to the homeowners losing their home, any equity they've built up in it, and their ability to qualify for future financing.

REMEMBER

Constantly remind homeowners who are facing foreclosure that doing nothing is absolutely the worst choice. After they lose their house, they have no option but to move and are in a terrible position to do even that effectively.

Getting Inside to Take a Look Around

At some point in your dealings with the homeowners, try to get inside the home to inspect it. If you do end up trying to buy the property from the homeowners or later at auction, you should know the condition of what you're buying. If possible, inspect the home, and complete the home-interior inspection form shown in Figure 9-9.

WARNING

If you're a real estate agent purchasing the home at a price below market value, you're probably required by the laws in your state to inform the homeowners of this fact. Have the homeowners sign a statement that you informed them that you're purchasing the house below market value and that the deal is advantageous to them because you could cash them out quickly without any of the hassles associated with listing and selling.

Interior Property Evaluation

Owner: _____

Home Phone: _____ Work Phone: _____ Pager/Mobile: _____

Address: _____

Cross Streets: _____

Occupant reported problems:

❑ Electrical ❑ Plumbing ❑ Heating ❑ Leaks ❑ Others: _____

Details: _____

KITCHEN

Check: ❑ Water Pressure ❑ Lights ❑ Floor ❑ Cabinets ❑ Counter Tops ❑ Sink

Overall Condition: ❑ Poor ❑ Fair ❑ Good ❑ Excellent

Kitchen Notes: _____

_____

BATHROOM

Check: ❑ Water Pressure ❑ Lights ❑ Floor ❑ Sink ❑ Tub/Shower
        ❑ Mirror ❑ Vanity

Overall Condition: ❑ Poor ❑ Fair ❑ Good ❑ Excellent

Bathroom Notes: _____

_____

OTHER ROOMS (Living Room / Bedrooms / Family Room / Den / Library / etc.)

Check: ❑ Floor Covering ❑ Paint/Wallpaper ❑ Ceiling

Overall Condition: ❑ Poor ❑ Fair ❑ Good ❑ Excellent

Other Rooms Notes: _____

_____

Interior Extras: _____

BASEMENT

Check: ❑ Cracks in Walls & Floor ❑ Windows ❑ Watertight? ❑ Stairs/Handrail
        ❑ Lights

Overall Condition: ❑ Poor ❑ Fair ❑ Good ❑ Excellent

Basement Notes: _____

_____

Recommendation: ❑ Cash Buy ❑ Re-Fi ❑ Listing ❑ Short Sale ❑ Pass
                 ❑ Other: _____

Reasoning/Notes: _____

_____

FIGURE 9-9:
Inspect the
home's interior if
possible.

Contacting the Lenders

When homeowners take out loans, they enter into legal contracts that are similar to wedding vows in some ways. As a foreclosure specialist, you might take on the role of mediator when the marriage takes a turn for the worse. As mediator, your job is to establish some sort of communication among the parties to resolve their current dispute.

REMEMBER

You can call lenders to inform them that you're interested in the property and willing to make deals with them during the foreclosure process, but to mediate effectively between the homeowners and lenders, you must have written permission from the homeowners. Figure 9-8 earlier in this chapter provides a permission form for the homeowners to sign.

Contacting the senior lienholder

The senior lienholder (who holds the first mortgage) has the strongest position, because they stand to take possession of the property if the homeowners don't act and nobody buys the property at auction. Most lenders don't want to take possession of a property, so they're often very motivated to resolve the situation before the sale.

You can get in touch with the lenders either through the foreclosing attorney (listed on the foreclosure notice) or by obtaining the lender's phone number from the homeowners, if you're working with them directly. In some cases, the bank that made the loan has a loan servicer who processes the payments. You may need to call the loan servicer to obtain the lender's phone number.

TIP

Negotiating with big-time national lenders usually isn't an option. This strategy is better if you're dealing with local lenders or credit unions, especially if you've established a relationship with them.

Ask the lender or attorney whether the homeowners have the following options:

>> **Reinstatement:** How much would the homeowners have to pay, and on what date, to have the loan reinstated?

>> **Forbearance:** Is the lender willing to work with the homeowners to restructure the payments and perhaps delay payment for a period to enable the homeowners to establish their financial footing? What can they offer?

>> **Short sale:** Is the lender willing to accept something less than the full mortgage amount currently due?

TIP

When negotiating a short sale, you usually need to make an offer: how much the homeowners or you are willing to pay. Work the numbers as explained in Chapter 10. Often, you can strengthen your position by having an appraisal or an offer to purchase the property that shows the lender that what you're offering is more than the lender is likely to get by following through with the foreclosure. When submitting an offer, send it to both the lender and the foreclosing attorney so that all interested parties are aware of your offer.

Contacting the junior lienholders

Any lienholder can lay claim to a property for payment of an unpaid debt. Even if you purchase the senior lien, a junior lienholder may choose to redeem your lien to avoid a total loss. The more effectively you can negotiate with junior lienholders from your position of power as senior lienholder, the more likely you are to ultimately take possession of the property uncontested.

Because junior lienholders are likely to have their liens wiped out at the foreclosure sale, they're usually much more willing to negotiate. When you call junior lienholders, let them know the following:

» Their claim may be wiped out during foreclosure proceedings.

» You're willing to make deals with them.

» You'll let them know in the future if you ever come across a property where their interests are at risk.

» You'd like the opportunity to list any properties they plan to sell.

Junior lienholders are often willing to accept payments of 50–80 percent less than they're owed, but your strategy may vary depending on whether your state has a redemption period:

» In states with no redemption period, you have more power to negotiate in the days leading up to the auction, because if the property ends up selling at auction, any junior liens are wiped out and the junior lienholders often stand to get nothing.

» In states with a redemption period, you gain bargaining power the closer you get to the last day of the redemption period, because if the junior lienholder has only two options — accept a payout from you or redeem your position and end up with a house — they may not want the hassle of fixing up and selling.

For details about junior liens and information on negotiating short sales, see Chapter 15.

Chapter **10**

Analyzing the Deal and Presenting Your Offer

A t least three parties share an interest in the outcome of the pre-auction foreclosure: the homeowners, the lenders, and you. As a foreclosure investor, your mission is to craft a deal that satisfies all three parties. The homeowners may salvage their credit and cash out some or all of the equity in the property, the lenders trim their losses to a satisfactory amount and remove the bad loan from their books, and you walk away with the property or a consulting fee and the satisfaction of having done a good deed.

In this chapter, I show you how to take the information you gathered in Chapters 8 and 9 and any additional information you may have collected on your own and complete a deal analysis worksheet. With this worksheet in hand, you can determine which options are best for the homeowner, for the lenders, and for yourself.

If the homeowners decide to accept a cash offer from you, I show you the basics of drawing up a purchase agreement to make the transaction official and close on the deal.

Completing the Deal Analysis Worksheet

With the foreclosure information sheet and exterior inspection report from Chapter 8 and the homeowner information sheet and interior inspection report from Chapter 9, you have the details you need to analyze the deal and determine which options are best for the homeowners, the lienholders, and yourself.

The deal analysis worksheet, shown in Figure 10-1, assists you in consolidating the information you gathered and analyzing that information. In the following sections, I lead you through the worksheet and explain the significance of each of its sections. For now, complete the first three lines of the worksheet to record the homeowners' names; the property address; and the homeowners' home, work, and mobile phone numbers.

Calculating the homeowners' equity in the property

As a property increases in value and homeowners pay down the principal on the mortgage, they build equity in the property. *Equity* is the amount of money homeowners would receive after selling the property and paying off the total amount borrowed against it.

By knowing ahead of time exactly how much a property is worth and how much the homeowners owe on it, you can estimate the equity they have in the property and be in a better position to assess their situation and present viable options to them.

TIP

The less equity homeowners have in a property, the less attractive their options are. With little, no, or negative equity, the homeowners are likely to lose the property and walk away with nothing. Homeowners facing foreclosure often are unaware of the power of the equity they have in their homes. You may have to explain what equity is and how it can expand their options. But if they wait too long, and the property is auctioned off, they can end up losing all their hard-earned equity.

Deal Analysis Worksheet

Homeowner Name: _____

Property Address: _____

Home Phone: _____ Work: _____ Mobile: _____

Market Value As Is: $ _____ Total Liens: $ _____

Homeowners' Equity: $ _____

Improved Market Value: $ _____ Repairs/Renovations: $ _____

Purchase Costs: $ _____ Holding Costs: $ _____

Sales Costs: $ _____ Top Cash Offer: $ _____

Loan Status

❏ Delinquent—Foreclosure – Sale Date: _____

❏ REJ—Redemption Date: _____

❏ Terminal—Cash buy only safe option

LTV

❏ Low – Options:	❏ Cash Buy	❏ Re-Fi	❏ List
❏ Marginal – Options:	❏ Re-Fi	❏ List	❏ Pass
❏ High – Options:	❏ List	❏ Short Sale Negotiation	

Homeowner Credit

Does homeowner make payments in a timely manner?	❏ YES	❏ NO
Does homeowner have some bad credit?	❏ YES	❏ NO
Any judgments, collections, tax liens on credit report?	❏ YES	❏ NO
Any bankruptcy?	❏ YES	❏ NO
Was bad credit a one-time problem?	❏ YES	❏ NO

Homeowner Mentality

❏ Wants to keep home   ❏ Wants to get rid of home   ❏ Relocating

❏ CANNOT afford payments   ❏ CAN afford payments up to: $ _____

Homeowner Status

❏ Employed   Gross Income: $ _____

❏ Unemployed   ❏ Going through divorce

Course of Action

❏ Reinstate	❏ Forbearance	❏ Refinance	❏ List	❏ Sell Short
❏ Cash Offer	❏ Lease-option	❏ Sell-and-Rent	❏ 2nd Mortgage	
❏ Deed in Lieu of Foreclosure		❏ Bankruptcy	❏ Nothing/Pass	
❏ Track through Foreclosure Sale		❏ Other: _____		

Reasoning/Notes: _____

_____

_____

_____

I/We, the homeowners have read and understand the options described above.

X _____   _____

    Homeowner   Date

X _____   _____

    Homeowner   Date

FIGURE 10-1:
Complete the
deal analysis
worksheet.

Guesstimating the "as is" market value

The market value of a property is always a best-guess estimate. As most real estate agents can tell you, a property's value is whatever a buyer is willing to pay for it and a seller is willing to sell it for. To evaluate the market and estimate a realistic resale value, research the following and add the results of your research to your property dossier:

>> Actual sale prices of comparable homes that have recently sold in the same area.

>> Asking prices of comparable homes currently for sale in the same area.

TIP

While checking the recent sales prices of comparable homes, check the health of the market too. Look at the number of sales per month and the sales values of comparable homes over the past 6 months, 3 months, and 30 days. A steady increase in sales volume and prices is a great sign. If the numbers are flat, the market is in decent shape. If you see a large volume of sales 6 months ago but few over the past 30 to 60 days, that trend may indicate a slowing market you should either avoid (until it bottoms out) or account for when you purchase properties.

If you're uncertain about your ability to assess a property's market value, consult a real estate agent in the area. Recent Multiple Listing Service (MLS) listings from a real estate agent in the area typically provide you the most recent and accurate sales figures for comparable properties. Another option is to hire an appraiser, but if your appraiser can't get inside to inspect the property's condition, the appraisal probably won't be any more accurate than your own best guess.

REMEMBER

Real estate agents work on commission. Don't waste their time by having them run *comps* (information about recently listed and sold properties that are similar to the property you're interested in) without giving them some paying work. Consider promising to list the property with the agent when you're ready to sell it.

Calculating the amount owed on the property

Calculating the amount that the homeowners currently owe on their home is fairly easy, assuming that you know about all the liens on the property. With the assistance and permission of the homeowners, you can call the lienholders and find out how much the homeowners currently owe on each loan. For tips on how to obtain the homeowners' permission to contact their lenders, see Chapter 9.

If you can't get permission, you can still come close by adding up all the liens and subtracting any principal the homeowners are likely to have paid down on them. When in doubt, default to the face value of the liens (that is, assume that no payments were made). Your estimate is likely to be high, but it gives you a number to work with.

Tally the numbers to figure out how much the homeowners owe. Then subtract the total from the home's estimated market value and you will have the amount of equity built up in the property.

Calculating your top cash offer

Your goal in any real estate investment property should be to earn no less than 20 percent on your total investment. In other words, you should be fairly certain that you can sell the property for 20 percent more than the entire amount of money you've invested in it, including

» Amount paid for the property

» Payments to lienholders to pay off loans and back taxes

» Cost of repairs and renovations

» Holding costs (monthly loan interest, taxes, insurance, utilities, and any homeowners' association fees) to cover the time between when you buy the property and when you sell it

» Costs of buying and selling the property

TIP

Don't be blind to opportunities just because they don't ring the magical 20 percent bell. You need a tighter budget to profit on low-priced properties, but when you're dealing with million-dollar properties, a 15 percent return may be worth exploring. When investing in these ritzy neighborhoods, however, keep in mind that putting all your eggs in one basket may be risky and often ties up a lot of cash. Know what you're getting into before you get into it.

Take the following steps to calculate your top cash offer:

1. **Guesstimate how much you can sell the house for after repairs and renovations.**

    Base your guess on the recent sales prices of comparable homes in the same area. Guess low on price and high on costs.

2. **Multiply the amount from step 1 by one of the following:**

    - 0.80 in a market where homes values are rising
    - 0.70 to 0.75 in a market where home values are steady
    - 0.65 to 0.75 in a market where home values are declining
    - 0.50 to 0.65 depending on the percentage of profit you want to make

3. **Subtract the amount of money required to pay off back taxes and other liens.**

4. **Subtract the closing costs for purchasing the property.**

5. **Subtract renovation expenses × 1.2 (to add 20 percent for unexpected cost overruns).**

6. **Subtract monthly holding costs (interest, insurance, property taxes, utilities, any homeowners' association fees) × the number of months you plan on owning the house.**

   Figure on at least three months.

7. **Subtract agent commissions and/or marketing and advertising costs.**

8. **Subtract closing costs for selling the property.**

The resulting dollar figure is the maximum amount of cash you can pay for the property to be fairly certain of earning a 20 percent profit.

Logging the loan status

In the Loan Status section of the deal analysis worksheet (refer to Figure 10-1), check the box next to the option that represents the current status of the mortgage that's in foreclosure:

>> **Delinquent:** The payment is delinquent, the lender is foreclosing, and a date has been set for the sale.

>> **REJ — Redemption:** REJ stands for Real Estate in Judgment. The foreclosure sale has already occurred, and the homeowners are currently in the redemption period.

>> **Terminal:** The homeowners have run out of options, and the only option left is for them to sell the property to an investor.

Determining options based on LTV

To evaluate the risk level of a loan, lenders often evaluate the loan to value (LTV): the amount of the loan compared with the value of the property. The lower the LTV, the less the risk. An LTV of 40 percent on a $200,000 property, for example, means that the owners owe only $80,000. If they default on the loan, the bank has a pretty good chance of recouping the full $80,000. With an LTV of 90 percent, however, the owners would owe $180,000 on the property, making the risk much higher.

One of the best ways to determine which options are viable for distressed home-owners is to examine their LTV. The lower the LTV, the more attractive the options:

» **Low:** With a low LTV, homeowners have substantial equity in the property and have three attractive options: cash buy (sell the house to you), refinance, or list the property and sell it to cash out their equity.

» **Marginal:** With an LTV in the middle range, refinancing or listing the property are the two best options for the homeowners in most cases. If you can work a short sale with one or more lenders, a cash buy may be feasible.

» **High:** A high LTV indicates that the homeowners have little, no, or negative equity in the property and few attractive options. In such cases, a deed in lieu of foreclosure, a short sale, or selling the house at a loss may be the only options.

Assessing the homeowners' credit health

You may decide to give some homeowners a break if they have a strong credit his-tory leading up to this financial fiasco and if their financial future looks fairly solid. To take the homeowners' credit pulse, answer the Yes/No questions in the Homeowner Credit section of the deal analysis worksheet (refer to Figure 10-1):

» **Does homeowner make payments in a timely manner?** Before defaulting on the current loan, did the homeowners generally make their pay-ments on time?

» **Does homeowner have some bad credit?** If the homeowners are in foreclosure, they have some bad credit, but you can order a credit report to see details. Sometimes, homeowners have bad credit due to a temporary job loss but they have a new job now that makes them a low-risk borrower, although their improved credit status doesn't say so on paper.

» **Any judgments, collections, tax liens on credit report?** Help the homeown-ers obtain their free credit reports, as explained in Chapter 5, and inspect the reports for any warning signs.

» **Any bankruptcy?** Bankruptcy filings in the past are often an indication of future problems.

» **Was bad credit a one-time problem?** If this bad credit was a one-time problem, and the homeowners have stable income that's sufficient for covering their monthly expenses and debt payments, they may represent a fairly low credit risk.

The answers to these questions help you paint a financial portrait of the homeowners to assist you in determining the types of options you want to offer them. If the homeowners have a terrible credit history and not much promise of future income, you probably don't want to set them up with a lease-option contract or rental agreement, which is likely to set them *and* you up for future failure. If, however, the homeowners have experienced a temporary financial setback and have sufficient financial resources, you may want to help them regain their footing.

Gauging the homeowners' wants

The homeowners own the property and the problem, so the decision about what to do is ultimately theirs to make. Always ask the homeowners what they want to do. Do they want to keep the home, sell it, or relocate? Can they afford the current payments if the lender would be willing to make some arrangements on paying back the past-due amounts? Could they afford a lower payment?

Although what the homeowners want is often unrealistic, ask the questions, and jot down the answers. You may not be able to deliver what they want, but with a little creativity, you may be able to get close.

Determining the homeowners' gross monthly income

One last key piece of information you need to complete the homeowners' financial portrait is homeowner status, which consists of three pieces of information:

» **Employment:** Is at least one homeowner employed?

» **Gross monthly income:** What's the total gross monthly income of the homeowners? (Include side jobs if they regularly make extra money working on the side.)

» **Marriage/divorce status:** If the homeowners are currently married, are they going through a divorce?

You don't want to get into a situation with the homeowners in which you're offering them a lease-option agreement or renting them the house if they have no income to pay you or if they're going through a messy divorce that's almost certain to wreck their finances.

Assessing the Homeowners' Options

Based on the information in the deal analysis worksheet, you can develop a pretty clear idea of which options are available to the homeowners. In Chapter 9, I describe these options in detail. Here, I list the options again and provide guidelines on which options are best based on the homeowners' situation and resources:

>> **Reinstating the loan:** For homeowners who owe relatively little and can obtain financial help from family members and friends, this option is best. The homeowners don't have to move and can usually retain the same mortgage with the same interest rate, although they may have to pay some late fees and attorney fees. Homeowners are often reluctant to seek assistance from even very close friends and relatives; in Chapter 9, I offer some tips on how to encourage them to ask for help.

>> **Negotiating with the lender for a forbearance:** Again, if the homeowners have a fairly solid financial future, the lender may agree to a forbearance and provide a payment schedule that's suitable for the homeowners. Make sure that the homeowners agree to a payment schedule they can afford because they won't get a second chance. Also, everything needs to be in writing, and the homeowners must understand everything they're agreeing to.

>> **Listing the property:** When the homeowners can't afford the mortgage payments and probably won't be able to afford the mortgage payments in the near future, selling the property is usually the most prudent option. This option is available only if the homeowners have sufficient time to list, sell, and close. If they run out of time, they may lose a pending sale, their house, and any equity they've built up. Time is of the essence.

>> **Refinancing the mortgage:** Homeowners who have substantial equity built up in their property may be able to refinance their way out of foreclosure by taking out a mortgage to consolidate their outstanding debt. Calculate the homeowners' total monthly payments. If they can pay off all their debt with a new mortgage that requires a lower total monthly payment, they may be able to keep their home. The problem with this option is that, usually, by the time homeowners try to initiate something, their payment history is downgraded to "slow pay" at best, and they may have other issues with their credit history, so they can almost count on a higher interest rate. Make sure that the homeowners can afford the higher payment; most can't.

>> **Selling short:** When homeowners have insufficient equity built up in a property, they probably face a situation in which they simply lose the home and have no money to move on. If you can negotiate a short sale by persuading the lenders to accept less than full payment, you may be able to work a deal in which you can pay the homeowners a little extra for the house and save enough money by paying off the reduced loan amounts to make the deal profitable for you.

- » **Accepting your cash offer:** Cash offers are often best if the LTV is low, the homeowners have little time to market and sell the property, and the home requires some major repairs or renovations to make it marketable.

- » **Opting for a lease-option agreement:** The homeowners sell you the house, and you sell the house back to them on a rent-to-own basis. A lease-option agreement may be feasible for homeowners who've experienced a temporary setback, can't work out a deal with their current lender, but can now make rental payments to you and possibly be in a position to secure financing to buy the property from you a few years down the road. See Chapter 19 for details.

- » **Selling the home and renting it back:** If the homeowners have sufficient income to pay rent, you might consider renting the home to them after you buy it. Chapter 19 covers this option in more detail.

- » **Giving a deed in lieu of foreclosure:** Negative equity is a pretty good sign that the homeowners may benefit by offering the lender a deed in lieu of foreclosure. The lender may refuse the offer, however.

- » **Filing for bankruptcy:** Bankruptcy is rarely a good option; it ruins the homeowners' credit and simply delays the inevitable. But if the homeowners choose this option, check the Bankruptcy box in the Course of Action section of the deal analysis worksheet, recommend a good bankruptcy attorney, thank the homeowners for their time, and let them know that you're interested in purchasing the property if they decide to sell it later. Keep in touch with the bankruptcy attorney; you may be able to purchase the property later.

- » **Nothing/pass:** If the homeowners choose to do nothing, or if you can't come up with a creative way to assist them, check the Nothing/Pass box in the Course of Action section of the deal analysis worksheet, and move on. Keep tracking the property just in case anything changes or the home goes to auction.

Have the homeowners sign and date the deal analysis worksheet at the bottom stating that they've read and understand the options described. Give them a copy of the signed worksheet.

Consider creating an audio recording of your conversation. Ask the homeowners whether recording the conversation would be okay to protect their interests and yours from any future confusion about who said what. Make sure to list the names of all those present and state that they're aware the conversation is being recorded. Finally, state the date and time of the recording. Then set the recorder on the table and converse naturally.

Presenting Your Offer: The Purchase Agreement

Whenever you buy a home directly from the homeowners, you must present your offer in the form of a *purchase agreement:* a legal document that spells out the terms and conditions of the sale and transfer of the property from the seller to the buyer.

Purchase agreements are fairly standard documents, but they vary from one area to another. Ask your real estate agent or attorney for a copy of the purchase agreement used in your area.

With the assistance of your real estate attorney, prepare and present the purchase agreement to the homeowners. Your area may have special laws governing the sale of property during the foreclosure process, so be sure that your attorney checks the agreement and reviews any special issues you need to be aware of.

Your purchase agreement should including the following details:

» Purchase price you're offering.

» Statement that the homeowners are aware that they're agreeing to sell the property below market value.

» Conditional clause (commonly referred to as a *weasel clause*) that gives you an exit if something goes wrong. A good condition to add is "Sale is conditional upon review and approval of my attorney." (Most purchase agreements have conditions built into them, such as "Sale is conditional upon home passing inspection.")

» Date of possession — the date when the current residents and their possessions are to move out and you can start working on the property.

» A list of anything in the home that isn't not nailed down that's to stay with the property, such as appliances, furniture, and furnishings.

» The agreed-upon condition of the property when it's transferred to you. You might indicate "current condition or better" or "broom-clean."

» A statement that the buyer (you) is responsible for all closing costs.

» A statement that the seller will deed the property to the buyer.

» A statement that the buyer may resell the property.

>> Amount of earnest-money deposit (EMD), if any. To prove that you're serious about the purchase, provide an EMD to be held by your attorney or the title company and to be released on condition of a successful closing. (Sometimes, you need to give some cash to the homeowners because they're really strapped for cash. Keep that amount as small as possible, because any money you give the homeowners is at risk.)

TIP

Normally, I recommend making a fairly substantial EMD when you present your offer. A substantial EMD shows the sellers that you're serious and have the money to close the deal — something that other buyers may not have. In the case of buying foreclosure properties directly from homeowners, the EMD doesn't carry much weight if nobody else is presenting an offer; $1,000 is usually sufficient. If an agent is representing the homeowners, the EMD can range from 3–10 percent.

Consider adding a penalty or bonus to the purchase agreement to encourage the current owners to move out on time and leave the property in excellent condition. You might stipulate, for example, that $1,000 is to be withheld and paid when the property is vacated in reasonable condition, or an extra $500 is to be paid if the homeowners vacate on time and leave the premises broom-clean. Be candid; tell them that you'll pay the extra money but only if they do what you both agree on. If they perform, you'll perform. You may even make a check out to them in advance and show it to them; tell them that when they fulfill their end of the bargain, you'll hand over the check. That way, they'll see that you're not stringing them along.

REMEMBER

All owners listed on the mortgage must sign the purchase agreement. If a couple owns the property, both partners must sign the purchase agreement.

TIP

If the auction date is fast approaching, you may be able to secure an adjournment by giving a signed purchase agreement to the attorney who's representing the lender. This agreement gives the lender some assurance that the mortgage will be paid in full at closing. During the closing, funds are distributed to the lenders to pay off the loans, and the lenders provide payoff letters — written proof that the loans have been satisfied. Don't be shocked if the attorney still wants to proceed to sale, especially in states with redemption periods. The lender doesn't want to lose time in case your deal doesn't close.

Even if you do have a legally binding purchase agreement with the homeowners, other investors may step in and offer the homeowners a little more money or do something else to make them want to back out of the deal. You can certainly make your case to the homeowners, but if they decide that they want to sell to another investor, I recommend that you let them. Trying to legally enforce your purchase agreement against homeowners in foreclosure who have a better deal on the table doesn't look good in court, even if you've acted on the level.

Closing Time

As soon as you and the homeowners agree on the price, terms, and conditions stated on the purchase agreement, contact your attorney or title company to arrange the closing and set a closing date. Your attorney or closing agent can provide the paperwork to you and the homeowners so that you can review it ahead of time.

On the day of the closing, the property is deeded over to you. You pay the sellers the agreed-on price (typically, in the form of an electronic transfer to the title company). The title company pays off the loans (liens) on the property, pays any remaining proceeds to the sellers, and records the deed in your name.

WARNING

Always purchase title insurance and hire a title company to handle the closing. This practice ensures that everyone who is owed money is paid, that you're insured if anyone lays claim to the property after closing, and that the paperwork is recorded properly. If you close without a title company (against my recommendation), don't allow the seller to be the one who pays off the loans after closing.

Don't forget to obtain the keys from the sellers. Also, before leaving the closing table, call the utility companies to have the water, electricity, and gas service transferred to your name. Many buyers overlook this important step.

TIP

Changing the locks immediately isn't a bad idea. You never expect to have a problem, but if you get into some disagreement with the homeowners near the end of the deal, an extra key in their possession can cause a problem. Protect your investment. Change the locks but keep the old ones (especially if they're in good shape); you may be able use them on the next house. I tape the keys to the lockset and put the whole cluster in a safe place — ideally, one that I'll remember. If the lockset will work at the next house I buy, I'm ready to go.

4

Finding and Buying Foreclosure and Bankruptcy Properties

Find out where foreclosure auctions are held in your county and get up to speed on the rules and process your county follows.

Buy Real Estate Owned (REO) properties from lenders after they foreclose and nobody else buys them at auction.

Find and buy government-owned properties from the U.S. Department of Housing and Urban Development (HUD), the Department of Veterans Affairs (VA), Fannie Mae, Freddie Mac, and other government agencies and programs.

Acquire real estate lost in bankruptcy.

Explore other foreclosure investment strategies, including short sales, wholesaling, and property tax sales.

IN THIS CHAPTER

» **Finding foreclosure auctions**

» **Calculating your maximum bid amount**

» **Bidding at open- and sealed-bid auctions**

» **Tying up the loose ends after the auction**

Chapter **11**

Bidding for Properties at a Foreclosure Sale

When most people think "foreclosure investing," they think "auction" — a bidding free-for-all where you can purchase properties at bargain-basement prices simply by showing up with a wad of cash. Unfortunately, this kind of thinking gets novice investors into trouble. Without the proper know-how, knowledge of what you're bidding on, and some self-restraint, you can really get burned at an auction.

In this chapter, I steer you clear of the most common pitfalls and toward the most promising prospects. I show you how to prepare properly for a foreclosure sale so that you don't get sucked into a bidding war that you're destined to lose. I show you how to calculate and stick to your maximum bid, assist you in packing for auction day, reveal some bidding strategies from a seasoned veteran, and lead you through the process of paying for and holding a property through the redemption period (if your area has a redemption period).

REMEMBER

When bidding at a foreclosure sale, keep in mind that you're bidding on mortgages, loans, or tax deeds, not properties. As a beginner, bid only on first mortgages or tax liens, which are less-risky investments. When you're more experienced, you can enter into the complex areas of investing in second mortgages and construction liens. Whatever lien position you're bidding on, you should know all the positions and what owning/holding those positions means so that you don't run into problems later.

Tracking Down Auction Dates, Times, and Places

When a lender posts a foreclosure notice or Notice of Default (NOD), the notice typically specifies the auction date, time, and place. Chapter 8 shows a typical foreclosure notice and highlights the important bits of information it contains. If the auction's location isn't specified, contact the county's Register of Deeds office, and ask where the auctions are typically held. In most areas, auctions are held at the courthouse. In some counties, auctions may be held at the property's location.

REMEMBER

A couple of days before the scheduled sale date, call the attorney who's handling the sale, and ask the following questions:

>> **Is the mortgage going to be auctioned at the advertised date and time?** The sale may be canceled or adjourned if the homeowners filed for bankruptcy or worked out a deal with the lender.

>> **What's the opening bid?** The opening bid is the balance of the loan that's in foreclosure plus any interest and penalties. The day before the sale, the attorney should be able to supply you a fairly accurate amount for the opening bid.

Write this information in the folder you created for the property in Chapter 8.

If the attorney seems reluctant to tell you the opening bid amount, say that you intend to bid and that your bank needs time to issue a check for the certified funds. Most attorneys will cooperate with serious bidders; after all, their clients (the mortgage companies) need investors to bid on properties. If you win the bid, the next time you call, mention that you bought a property that their firm represented before. This information is a huge boost to your credibility. Next time, you won't face such a hassle.

TIP

Several days before attending your first auction, contact the sheriff's office or whoever's in charge of handling the auction in your county, and find out what you need to bring to the auction and how the bidding works. The following list gets you up to speed on the basics of what you can expect:

- >> In some areas, you may need to register ahead of time.

- >> You need some form of identification — typically, a driver's license, but find out for sure.

- >> The day before the auction, call the foreclosing attorney for any of the properties you intend to bid on, find out the opening bid amount, and head down to your bank to obtain a cashier's check for an amount that matches the opening bid amount.

  You need a cashier's check for every property you intend to bid on. If your check is off by a small amount, the sheriff may allow you to make up the difference in cash but won't accept large amounts of cash. If you're the successful bidder with an overbid amount of more than $1, you usually have a period ranging from one hour to the end of the day to get that amount in. If you win the bid for "plus a dollar," which is $1 more than opening bid and means that nobody bid against you, have small bills on you so you can pay that amount immediately.

- >> Some counties require you to show proof of certified funds before the sale, at the time you bid, or immediately after the sale.

WARNING

  Don't bid if you don't have the required certified funds. You not only risk losing the property and perhaps getting into some legal mess with the lender and the court, but also could be banned from future auctions.

- >> Some counties have minimum bid raises to speed the process of bidding. After someone bids $1 over the opening bid, for example, subsequent bids may need to be in increments of $100 or $500 higher, or the auctioneer may specify the incremental raise on the fly.

REMEMBER

Know exactly what to expect on sale day so you can remain calm during the bidding process. Some veteran bidders may try to fluster you by asking the auctioneer to verify your funds or ensure that you meet some other requirement. This procedure may seem to be silly, but if bidders have the auctioneer question you about something you know nothing about, you may begin to wonder whether you're in way over your head, and you may not bid, thereby losing out on a potentially profitable property.

Preparing Your Maximum Bid

One of the biggest mistakes you can make at an auction is to start bidding without a concrete ceiling defining just how high you can afford to bid. Set your maximum bid to ensure a profit of 20 percent or more, then stick to it. (That figure means 20 percent profit on your total investment. It doesn't mean that you can bid up to 80 percent of the property's value.) In the following sections, I lead you through the process of determining your maximum bid.

Record your maximum bid in the folder you created for the property (see Chapter 8) and recommit yourself to that amount before bidding begins. If you think you may be tempted to bid in excess of your upper limit, take someone along with you to act as your conscience and rein you in if your exuberance seems to be overstepping your logic.

Guesstimating the property's improved value

To calculate the maximum amount to bid on a property, start from the end and work back. First, estimate the price you can sell the property for after repairs and renovations. Your real estate agent can provide you the recent sales prices of comparable homes in the same area. Chapter 10 also offers a discussion of how to estimate the "as is" value of a property and provides useful tips that apply to estimating the improved value of a property as well.

When comparing property values, compare apples and apples. Look for homes that recently sold in the same area that are comparable in lot size, square footage, house style, number of bedrooms and bathrooms, and so on. Don't go out of your way to find comparables that justify a higher bid, which only increases your risk of paying too much for a property.

Estimating repair and renovation costs

From your preliminary inspection of the property, you should have some idea of how much you can expect to pay for repairs and renovations. If you haven't been able to fully inspect the interior of the property, use 10 percent as a ballpark estimate. If, for example, you're buying a property that you're confident you can sell for $150,000 after repairs and renovations, figure in at least $15,000 for repairs and renovations.

When you're purchasing a property at auction, you buy the property in "as is" condition, so you own it no matter how much the repairs and renovations cost. The safest route is to have the house thoroughly inspected, but that's not always possible, so overestimate costs to give yourself a little buffer.

Figuring in holding costs

Holding costs consist of expenses that you incur between the time you purchase the property and the time you sell it. Holding costs include the following:

- » Property taxes
- » Homeowner's insurance
- » Interest on any loan you took out to buy the property
- » Any utilities you pay
- » Recording fee and transfer tax

REMEMBER

Water bills, at least in some states, stay with the house. In other words, during the redemption period, while the occupants are running the water, they're also running up a bill that you're likely to get stuck with. If the pipes leak, you pay. Figure this cost into your holding costs.

Add up the monthly amount for each item in the list, and multiply by the number of months you plan on holding the property. In an area with a six-month redemption period, calculate holding costs for the duration of the redemption period plus the number of months you plan to spend on renovations and selling the property.

When I flip properties, I use $100 per day as the average holding cost but that figure includes utilities. During the redemption period, you pay only property taxes, homeowner's insurance, and interest if you took out a loan to pay for the property, so your holding costs may be less than $100 per day. In some markets, the average daily holding costs may be considerably higher.

WARNING

Make sure that you know your state's tax foreclosure process and the total taxes owed on the property before you bid. If the tax redemption period runs out during your redemption period, and you didn't pay the taxes to protect your investment, the foreclosing bank or mortgage company thanks you for your donation, and you lose your collateral. Property tax liens trump almost every other type of lien, so be aware of any unpaid property taxes.

Subtracting agent commissions and closing costs

I strongly recommend that after you fix up your fixer-upper, you list it with one of the top seller's agents in your market. On average, an agent can sell a home in half the time and for more money than you can sell it for on your own, which not only increases the sale price, but also reduces your holding costs. In most areas, the standard real estate commission is 6–8 percent of the sales price, but you may be able to negotiate commissions if you give the agent lots of work.

You're also likely to pay closing costs at the time of the sale. Consult your attorney or title company for an estimate of closing costs.

Arriving at your maximum bid amount

Estimating the future sales price of the property and all expenses related to buying, fixing up, and selling the property is the tough part. When you have the required numbers, calculating your maximum bid amount comes down to performing some basic math:

1. **Start with the future sale price of the home after improvements.**

2. **For an estimated profit of at least 20 percent, divide the amount from step 1 by one of the following:**

   - 1.20 in a market where homes values are rising (to shoot for a 20 percent return on your investment)

   - 1.25 in a market where home values are steady (to shoot for a 25 percent return)

   - 1.30 in a market where home values are declining (to shoot for a 30 percent return)

   - 1.35 to 1.50, depending on the percentage of profit you want to make (to shoot for a 35–50 percent return)

REMEMBER

The resulting number shows you how much you can afford to invest in the property to earn the desired 20 percent return. In a hot market, you shoot for a 20 percent return. In a slower market, you have to aim for a higher return (say, 25 percent) to hit the goal of making 20 percent.

3. **Subtract any back taxes you'll be responsible for paying when you purchase the property.**

4. **Subtract estimated costs of repairs and renovations.**

5. **Subtract monthly holding costs.**

6. **Subtract agent commissions and/or marketing and advertising costs.**

7. **Subtract closing costs for selling the property.**

The result gives you a general idea of how much to offer for the property to be fairly certain you can profit at least 20 percent from the transaction.

REMEMBER

Be realistic. Your chances of earning a 40–50 percent profit on a property are very low. You'd have to buy the property for less than 50 cents on the dollar at sale. It's possible. I've done it a couple of times. But it's the exception to the rule.

The following example shows the maximum bid amount for a $150,000 property in a stable market with $5,000 in unpaid taxes, assuming a 10 percent allowance for repairs and renovations and a three-month holding period:

Final improved sale price	$150,000.00
Increasing market	÷ 1.20
Total	$125,000.00
Unpaid property taxes	– $5,000.00
Repairs and renovations	– $15,000.00
Holding costs	– $9,000.00
Agent commission (6%)	– $9,000.00
Closing costs	– $1,500.00
Maximum bid	**$85,500.00**

The opening bid may exceed your maximum bid, in which case you sit on your hands and either let the bank buy back the mortgage or let some less-informed bidder buy the property and try to wring a profit out of it. If the opening bid is lower than your maximum bid, you have some room to dive in and start bidding.

REMEMBER

This example simply demonstrates how to crunch numbers on a sample property. Not all $150,000 houses are going to fit this model. A house in pristine condition, for example, won't require $15,000 in repairs, and if the taxes have been paid up, you may save a little there as well, and be able to bid a little higher at auction.

WARNING

Make sure that you're bidding on a first mortgage, not a second mortgage or some other lien. Many beginners get burned by purchasing a junior lien, thinking that they're getting a great deal when in fact, they're paying tens of thousands of dollars for a piece of paper that's likely to be worthless after the first mortgage is foreclosed on. You can buy a junior lien to control the senior lien, but that advanced move is one for experienced investors. See Chapter 15 for details.

SNAGGING A DIAMOND IN THE ROUGH

Your best chance of bagging a deal that gives you a profit of 50 percent or better is to do great research and track adjournments. By "track adjournments," I mean keep track of properties that were scheduled to go to sale but had their sales adjourned for one reason or another. Most investors lose interest after the adjournment, leaving some low-hanging fruit that's easy pickings.

Once, I researched a house that sat on a 2.8-acre lot in a very prestigious and highly sought-after area in Oakland County. The house wasn't much to speak of — a small ranch-style home — but the land was a gold mine. The neighborhood was dotted with multimillion-dollar homes designed by famous architects. Nestled among these valuable gems was that little old ranch house — the diamond in the rough. Because of my experience, I knew that developers would be knocking my door down to get their hands on such a valuable parcel.

I expected very stiff competition at the sale, so I did my homework. When I called the attorney, he informed me that the home wouldn't be going to sale that week. Still, an extraordinarily large crowd showed up at the sale that week, all waiting for the bidding on this property to start. When it didn't come up for auction, they muttered under their breath and wondered what had happened.

Fortunately, I knew what had happened and what to do about it. I continued to track that property for the better part of six months, calling every week to see whether it was going to come up for sale that week. Then one week, I heard what I'd been waiting for: "Yes, this will be up for sale, and here is the opening bid." When the woman at the attorney's office gave me that opening bid, my heart started to flutter, which doesn't happen very often anymore. The reason: I knew that anyone who had been interested in that property had long since given up and forgotten about it.

That morning at sale, I quietly bid the opening bid plus $1 and picked up the diamond in the rough I'd been waiting for. Those in the audience were stunned. Some thought that I'd lost my mind and bid on something that I shouldn't have, but I overheard one person say to their neighbor, "I've been coming here for a while. That was no mistake. He knows something we don't." He was right. My hard work and diligence paid off. Did they ever!

Within a week of the property's not being redeemed, I had a rock-solid cash offer for $350,000 from a developer who was going to tear down the house and build another one that would "better fit in with the neighbors." I probably could have held out for more, but you strike while the iron is hot . . . or so I've been told. Oh, by the way, I paid just over $150,000 for the property at sale.

Keep tracking the properties after adjournment and continue to bring the property dossier (see Chapter 8) to the auctions with you, so that you'll be prepared if the property becomes available. You may be carrying 10, 20, or 100 property dossiers to the auction with you, depending on the size of your market, but at least you won't miss out because you weren't prepared.

Bidding at a Foreclosure Auction

You've done your homework. You inspected the property's title and other paperwork. You visited the property to see it with your own two eyes. Perhaps you even talked with the homeowners and lienholders. Now you have a property dossier packed with the information that you need to make a well-educated investment decision.

Now it's showtime! Time to pack your briefcase full of your property research and head out to the foreclosure auction for an afternoon of bidding. If you store all your property dossiers electronically, on a computer or in the cloud, be sure that you have the means to access them quickly and reliably.

THE BIDDER AND THE GOVERNOR

When you decide to start bidding at auctions, consider teaming up with your spouse or someone else you trust. One of you can act as the bidder, and the more restrained member of the team acts as the governor. Over the years, I've noticed several couples employing this very strategy.

So what's a governor? A *governor* regulates the flow of gas or fuel to an engine, primarily so that the engine doesn't get too much gas all at once. During an auction, the governor plays a similar role, restraining the bidder from overbidding. The bidder remains ready to bid the instant the governor gives the go-ahead.

I've seen this technique used as a method to win bids as well. The governor plays up the role as restrainer, acting as though every bid is inflicting pain, while the bidder is champing at the bit, eager to beat any bid offered by the competition. Just when the competition thinks they've won the bid, the governor gives the nod to bid just one more time. This approach can be quite a show. The point is that at least one member of the dynamic duo has a maximum bid, and when that person pulls the plug, it's over.

Always be ready to accept losing a bid. At foreclosure auctions, entering a winning bid that's too high can make you a big loser months later.

Packing for an auction

A couple of days before auction day, start packing so that if you don't have everything you need, you have time to get it. Here's a list of everything you should bring with you on auction day:

>> The foreclosure property dossiers you assembled in Chapter 8. (Bring *all* of them, not just those for the properties you plan to bid on.) If you created digital property dossiers, bring the computer they're stored on, or if they're stored in the cloud, bring a portable Internet-enabled computer.

>> Paper and two pens or pencils so you can take notes.

>> A calculator.

>> A cashier's check for sufficient funds to cover a purchase, if you plan to bid. Have the check made out to yourself in the amount necessary to cover the opening bid. If you win the bid, you can endorse the check. (In the following sections, I suggest that you sit in on a few auctions as an observer before you start bidding on properties.)

Sitting in on a few auctions

For your first three or four auctions, I suggest that you observe and take notes that answer key questions such as these:

>> Who's running the sale?

>> Who's bidding?

>> Who's just watching?

>> What are the winning bids on the properties you researched? Jot down the winning bid in the property's dossier.

If someone shows up at one auction and bids on a single property, that person may be an attorney representing the bank. The people who show up every week and bid on properties consistently are foreclosure investors. They're the real deal. These are the people you want to watch, talk with, and learn from.

WARNING

Sit in on at least four auctions before you start interacting with anybody. You can say "Hi" and exchange the usual pleasantries, but avoid getting into any deep conversations about real estate investing. People who often appear to be know-it-alls and don't actually buy and sell properties can fill your head with all sorts of confusing misinformation.

Crafting a winning bidding strategy

Foreclosure auctions are serious business in which the high bidder stands to acquire a valuable property at well below market value or pay way too much for a worthless piece of paper. Bidding is no board game, and the money's real, so developing an effective bidding strategy is key.

Every bidder has a unique strategy and various techniques for psyching out the competition. Here are some common strategies you may want to try:

» **Bore 'em into submission.** Keep outbidding the highest bidder by the minimum incremental amount. If the minimum increment is $100, whenever someone makes a bid, bid $100 more. Just don't exceed your maximum.

» **Go all in.** Open with an outrageously high bid (but below your maximum bid) to shock the competition into silence. This tactic is usually a very bad idea, because it can result in paying thousands of dollars more than necessary. If you're trying to scare off a novice, and you know that the property is going to sell for thousands more than the opening bid, you may want to make a dramatic leap, but avoid starting with your maximum bid.

» **Speak softly and carry a big wad of cash.** Quiet bidding often conveys confidence and can undercut the high-energy, emotional tone of the auction. It forces other bidders to ask "What did they bid?", which can be a little unsettling and give you the edge you need.

» **Crank the volume.** Bark your bids as though you're a mad dog in control of the room. If you've ever had your parents yell at you, you know the effect this technique can have. It can rattle your opponent just enough to make the person back off or think that you've lost your mind. Either way, you're in control.

» **Mix it up.** Go erratic. Be random. Don't follow a pattern. As long as your bids make sense to you without exceeding your maximum bid, experiment to see what works best.

Submitting sealed bids

Some auctions require buyers to submit their bids in writing in sealed envelopes. As soon as all the bids are in, they're opened, and the property goes to the highest bidder. If you're buying foreclosures in an area that uses sealed bids, you won't be able to use the clever techniques described in the preceding section.

TOYING WITH THE COMPETITION

I attended an auction where I got into a bidding war with a "bore 'em into submission" bidder and decided to have a little fun with him. The minimum incremental increase was $10. Every time I bid, my nemesis would bid $10 more. The bidding proceeded like this:

I opened with a bid of $120,000.

Bore 'em countered with $120,010.

I bid $130,000.

Bore 'em bid $130,010.

I bid $135,000.

Bore 'em bid $135,010.

That's when the fun began.

I bid $139,990.

Bore 'em fidgeted during an awkward moment of silence. The audience caught on to what was happening, and a few people started to laugh. Even the sheriff chuckled a little.

It took Bore 'em about a minute to calculate his next bid: $140,000. He spent another couple of minutes trying to figure out what was happening.

At this point, I strayed from the script. With a big smile on my face, I announced, "Ah ha, so you can bid in big round numbers after all!" and then proceeded to bid $140,010, much to the pleasure of the crowd.

Bore 'em was too flustered at this point to continue bidding. I acquired the property in addition to my own personal following. For several weeks after that, the crowd returned just to watch the show.

— Anonymous bidder

Winning a sealed bid hinges on your ability to size up the competition and on how confident you are in your maximum bid. If you think the property is going to draw a lot of competition, you may need to submit your maximum bid. If you're fairly certain that nobody else is going to bid against you, you may want to submit $1 more than the opening bid amount.

TIP

If you're constantly losing, you're probably bidding too low. When your bid loses, ask the sheriff or check the public records to find out how much the winner bid. Compare that amount with your bid and make the necessary adjustments. Keep in mind, however, that a winning bid doesn't always mean that the winner bid the right amount. They may have bid too much and will suffer later when the property isn't as profitable as expected.

Playing the Role of Backup Buyer

A *backup buyer* is one who keeps an offer on the table even after another offer or bid has been accepted. If the other offer falls through, the backup buyer is in an ideal position to get the property — usually for less than the winning bid.

A seller (which may be the bank in the case of a foreclosure) often becomes even more motivated to sell after a deal falls through. Suppose that the sellers have an offer of $200,000 with no backup offer. If that offer falls through, they're facing the prospect of having to put the property back on the market and probably listing it for significantly less — maybe as low as $190,000. Also, they're looking at having to pay holding costs until the property sells and they close on it. And if the purchase of their new home is conditional upon the sale of this property, they're under even more pressure to sell quickly. If those same sellers had a backup offer of $195,000 or even $190,000, they might just snap it up.

Some people are trained to follow scripts and checklists, so when they're accepting offers, they don't think about a Plan B. They may not even imagine the possibility of the buyer's offer falling through. When that first offer falls through, they're back to square one. By positioning yourself as a backup buyer, you're giving them a Plan B. And if that "winning" offer falls apart before closing, your second-place offer could be the only one to cross the finish line.

SCORING A BACKUP-BID WIN

I recently helped a high school friend's son buy a foreclosure property. I told him to make sure that his ducks were in a row before moving forward: getting preapproved, providing the verification of funds, performing his due diligence, and so on. When he had his finances in place, after he found a property he was interested in and performed his due diligence, he was ready to go. The property was a U.S. Department of Housing and Urban Development (HUD) foreclosure, and the opening bid was set at $110,000. My friend's son submitted a bid of $115,000.

This particular auction, via the HUD bid site (www.hudhomestore.gov), allowed backup offers to be considered even if they weren't the first ones to be accepted. Another investor entered the winning bid, but following my advice, my protégé agreed to have his bid serve as a backup offer.

Ten days later, he received an email message through the automated system. (By the way, buyers, banks, loan officers, and everybody else gets notified at the same time, which is how the third-party administrators handle these auctions now.) The message informed him that if he still wanted the property, HUD would move forward with his offer. He got the house.

Following Up After the Auction

You submitted the winning bid. Congratulations, but you're not quite finished. Now you have to take several steps to pay for the property and protect your interest in it. Proceed through the following checklist to make sure that you've attended to all the details:

>> **Follow through on the conditions of the sale.** Ask the Register of Deeds office or whoever is holding the auction to supply you a list of conditions to finalize the sale. Read the conditions and draw up a list of what you have to do. Consult your attorney if you find anything confusing. As soon as you know what to do, do it.

>> **Pay any remaining balance.** If you didn't have to pay the full price that you bid immediately following the auction, you have a limited time to pay off the balance — typically, fewer than 30 days, but in some cases only a couple of days or even hours. Be sure to pay the full amount on time; otherwise, you may end up losing the property.

>> **Record the deed.** Upon payment or after some period of delay, you receive the deed to the property. As soon as possible, take the deed to the county clerk's or Register of Deeds office (or in some counties, the sheriff's office) and have it recorded to protect your legal claim to the property. Recording the deed in your name provides extra insurance against someone who files another deed and claims to have purchased the property. Some states are "race to record" states, meaning that the first person to file the deed obtains the strongest position. Putting off this important step could jeopardize your position.

WARNING

Ask the Register of Deeds office or your real estate attorney to explain the recording requirements in your area. You usually have a grace period from the time you receive the deed to the date on which you must record it, but the recording date could affect the redemption period. In Michigan, you have 21 days to record the deed to have the redemption period start from the date of sale. If you miss the deadline, the redemption period may commence sometime after the sale date.

>> **Obtain title insurance.** Visit your title company to obtain title insurance for the property. Using a title company that's familiar with the foreclosure process is best. Check any restrictions (or exceptions) on the title insurance carefully, ask the title company representative to explain any you don't understand, and see whether you can have them removed. If your area has a redemption period, the title company may offer a title commitment that takes effect only after the redemption period expires, but this delay is usually not a problem. Assuming that you hold the first lien position and taxes are paid up, when the redemption period expires, other liens will be wiped out, and you'll have full title.

>> **Obtain property insurance.** If any major damage occurs to the property during the redemption period, you want to have insurance to pay for it. Contact your insurance agent as soon as possible to obtain a policy for the home.

>> **Notify any taxing authorities that have liens on the property.** If the Internal Revenue Service (IRS) or the state has an income tax lien on the property, the foreclosing attorney usually notifies the IRS before the sale. Make sure that the IRS notice accompanies the bidding paperwork. If the foreclosing attorney didn't notify a taxing authority that has a lien on the property, consult the foreclosing attorney and your own attorney, if necessary.

>> **Return any overbid money to the homeowners.** An *overbid* situation occurs if you bid more than is required to cover any liens on the property. When a buyer submits an overbid, the homeowners have the right to claim the overbid amount. All they need to do is go down to the courthouse and file a claim for the money, and it's theirs.

If someone outbids you at the auction, your area has a redemption period, and you're still interested in buying the property, consider writing a letter to the homeowners to inform them of their redemption rights. Figure 11-1 shows a sample letter.

<Your Address>
<City>, <State> <Zip>
<Date>

<Homeowner's Names>
<Address>
<City>, <State> <Zip>

Dear <Homeowner's First Names>:

I've sent you many letters in the past about the foreclosure process. Unfortunately, those letters went unanswered. This letter is to inform you that your mortgage to <Bank's Name> was sold to <Winning Bidder's Name> at mortgage sale on <Date of Sale>, for <Sale Price>.

By law you have <Number of> months to redeem your property, which means you have until <Redemption Date> to pay off <Winning Bidder's Name> the <Sales Price> plus interest, at <Interest percentage>. At the Sheriff's Department there is an over bid of <Overbid Amount> waiting to be claimed. However, if you choose to pick up this money, you will have a much more difficult time redeeming the property, should you choose to do so. Either way, you may contact <Sheriff Department Contact Person's Name> at the Sheriff's Department at <Sheriff Department's Phone Number> for more information.

The purpose of my letter is to help you either save your home or sell it so you do not lose it in foreclosure. You still have time to act, but time is running out. I may be able to assist you. Please contact me as soon as you receive this letter so I can help you get out of this situation. My number is <Your Phone Number>.

Sincerely,

FIGURE 11-1:
Inform the
homeowners
what happened
at the sale and
where they stand.

<Your Signature>

<Your Name>

Foreclosure Specialist

REMEMBER

If you're buying foreclosure properties in an area that has a redemption period, you're not out of the woods yet. Check out Chapter 16 for suggestions and tips on surviving the redemption period and helping the homeowners move out of the house and on with their lives.

FRUITLESS LABOR FROM A FAILURE TO FOLLOW THROUGH

I purchased the senior lien on a property at an auction and received a sheriff's deed that allowed me to take possession of the property at the end of the six-month redemption period, assuming that nobody redeemed my sheriff's deed. I later learned that another investor had stepped in and bought the property directly from the homeowners for about $10,000 to $15,000 cash. Typically when this happens, the investor who purchased from the homeowners redeems the sheriff's deed. In other words, this other investor needed to pay me off before the redemption period expired.

As time passed, I watched the investor as she slowly transformed the house from a run-down shack into a very respectable-looking home. I was a little surprised, however, that nobody had contacted me about redeeming my sheriff's deed.

About five months into the redemption period, the house was completed, and a "For Sale" sign went up in the yard, but I still hadn't been contacted about a payoff. I got a little nervous and decided to check the title. My sheriff's deed was there, plain as day, right where it should be. No superior liens had been placed on the property.

The day after the redemption period expired, I took my usual steps and filed for possession. A couple of days later, I got a call from a very distraught woman. She explained to me that this house was her first investment house and that she had learned how to "flip houses" from a late-night real estate guru but didn't realize that the deed she obtained was subject to the sheriff's deed, which I held. I told her that she had lost everything. The phone went silent, and then, under a muffled cry she asked, "What do you mean I lost everything?"

"Well," I said, "I now own the house legally per my sheriff's deed, and you have to take down the 'For Sale' sign and stop trying to sell my house." (I was being particularly blunt so that she would grasp the importance of the situation.) Again, she explained that she had intended to redeem the property but failed to do so, that she had put money into rehab, yada yada yada. I felt really bad for her and the position she was in, so I asked her, "What would you do if you were me?"

She said, "I guess you could say 'Thank you very much for a lovely new house, and then sell it for a profit,' but I would like to see us be able to work something out." And that's what we did. I told her that she was definitely going to lose money, and probably a lot of it, and that I would soften the blow by giving her a portion of what she spent on rehab, but she wouldn't be getting the profits. We agreed to a dollar amount, and after selling the property, I paid her that amount. She lost all the money she paid the homeowners and much of what she put into rehabbing the property, plus any profits she expected to see.

(continued)

(continued)

Before you write me off as a total jerk, I should explain why I acted like such a heartless beast. When talking with this particular investor, I learned that her secret to buying properties was to watch me at the sheriff's sale and then approach the owners of the properties that I'd bid on at auction. She told me that she was so confident in my research that she seldom if ever researched the properties herself; she just piggybacked on my hard work and efforts.

Well, that explanation didn't sit well with me. I don't mind some honest competition, but when you try to take the easy way out, sometimes justice has a funny way of catching up with you. It certainly caught up with her. I consider myself to be a fairly nice guy because I turned what could have been a third-degree burn into a harsh and painful sunburn — painful, but not lethal. I heard later through a mutual investor that she had gotten out of the flipping game, because when she started doing all the research herself, it didn't seem worthwhile to her.

This story has two morals: Do your own research, and pay attention to details.

IN THIS CHAPTER

» Getting the lowdown on the REO process

» Networking with REO managers to find the best deals

» Contacting REO brokers for additional leads

» Scheduling your offer for optimum results

» Presenting an attractive offer to the bank's REO manager

Chapter **12**

Buying Repos: Bank Foreclosures and REO Properties

When you sit in on a few auctions, you may notice that the opening bid is the final bid. A lucky investor may scoop up a deal uncontested simply by bidding the opening amount plus $1. More likely, however, the lender's representative, seeing that no investor is willing to submit the opening bid, buys back the mortgage on behalf of the lender. Then the lender can sell the property to try to recoup some of its losses or even turn a profit.

After the lender takes possession of the property, it turns the property over to its Real Estate Owned (REO) division or to an REO broker, who prepares it for resale. (The broker is a real estate agent hired by the REO manager to list the property; the broker isn't a bank employee.) As an investor, you get another buying opportunity from this process.

This chapter shows you how to approach the lender's REO manager or broker and present an offer that enables the bank to cut its losses while providing you a valuable investment property.

Acknowledging the Drawbacks of REO Opportunities

You won't always find the best deals in REO properties. Lenders aren't willing to give away properties simply so they won't have to deal with them. Each case is different, and you may discover that REOs aren't the best deals in town for any of several reasons, including the following:

>> Before auction, lenders often ask their local REO broker to provide a broker's price opinion (BPO) or comparative market analysis to determine the current value of the property. Using this information, the lender knows the market value of the property and is unlikely to want to sell significantly below market value.

>> The bank may have already written off the debt and may not have to cut its losses. To the bank, the house may represent a windfall profit, not a burden that it needs to unload.

>> Some banks — especially smaller, smarter banks — are developing REO departments that are quite capable of rehabbing and selling properties. I've even seen cases in which the bank offers the foreclosed-on homeowner cash to move out, just as an investor would do.

WARNING

>> Banks are highly motivated to turn a nonperforming loan into a profit, and they don't mind unloading their loss on an investor. Be careful. Don't take on the bank's burden if you're not fairly certain that you can profit from the property.

>> Banks often prefer working with several well-established investors. REO departments are often overwhelmed by calls from novice investors making all sorts of promises. They don't have the time to sort through all the calls and determine who's a real investor and who's a wannabe, so they either list with a broker or sell to someone they know and trust.

Although banks and other lending institutions are often in a position of power when dealing with investors, that position can be weakened by pressures from bank regulators. If a bank has too many bad loans on its books, bank regulators begin cranking up the heat, and the bank becomes much more motivated to make deals and cut its losses. You have no way of knowing when regulators are pressuring a specific bank, but if you have your financing in place and continue to pursue opportunities, eventually, you're more likely to find yourself in the right place at the right time.

REMEMBER

Badgering the loss mitigation or REO department rarely leads to success. In many cases, you won't even get to talk to a person. An automated system plays a recording that states the bank's policy and provides a fax number. One thing is for sure: If you get a break and have the chance to place an offer on a property, you'd better be able to follow through on it. If you waffle, your first opportunity will be your last.

Getting Up to Speed on the REO Process

Banks and other lending institutions (credit unions, mortgage companies, finance companies, and others) like to lend money and collect the interest on loans. They don't like to own property. When homeowners default on a loan, however, and no investor steps in to pay the balance, the lender has no option but to purchase the home, place it back on the market, and try to sell it. Here's how the REO process works:

1. When homeowners miss a payment or two, the nonpayment is transferred to the lender's collections department.

2. Over the course of 6–8 months, the collections department tries to contact the homeowners to negotiate a payment plan.

3. If the collections department is unable to resolve the issue, it transfers the matter to the loss-mitigation department, which deals with the problem (and the property) through the foreclosure process. During this time, the lender seeks the assistance of a title company and attorney, and the cost of hiring these professionals is added to the *payoff amount:* the total amount required to redeem the property.

REMEMBER

   When you hear that the house sold for $1 at auction, the house actually sold for the payoff amount plus $1. Late-night TV real estate investment gurus spin this fact into a pumped-up promise of buying houses for a buck. Don't fall for it.

4. At the foreclosure auction, if no investor purchases the mortgage, the lender buys it and transfers it to its REO department.

5. In an area with a mandatory redemption period, the lender's REO department waits for the redemption period to expire, evicts the previous homeowners (if necessary), and sells the property to recover any losses.

6. In some cases, especially when the lender is out of state, the lender hires an REO broker to prepare the property for resale and place it back on the market. The REO broker typically gets involved just before the end of the redemption period or shortly thereafter; they may play a role in evicting the homeowners or offering cash for keys to encourage the homeowners to move out voluntarily.

At the foreclosure sale, the lender can set an opening bid high enough to cover only the balance of the mortgage and any costs incurred trying to collect that amount before the auction. In other words, the lender can't profit from the sale of the property at auction. When the bank takes possession of the property, however, it becomes the owner and can sell the property for more than is owed on it. In other words, the bank may not be all that eager to unload the property.

Shaking the Bushes for REO Properties

If I haven't yet been able to talk you out of trying to pursue REO properties, you obviously have the determination required to get through to the gatekeepers: the lender's REO people or the broker who's listing the property. Now you need to find these people and present yourself as a reliable investor who can help them remove a nonperforming loan from their books.

In the following sections, I show you how to position yourself properly as a reliable, trustworthy investor and reveal some strategies for getting yourself connected with the "in" crowd.

Positioning yourself as an attractive investor

Banks and other lending institutions field many calls from would-be investors inquiring about REO properties. A good majority of these investor wannabes have no money. They expect the lender not only to hand them a prime piece of real estate for a bargain price, but also to finance the purchase and the cost of repairs and renovations. Although some small banks and credit unions may be willing to sell you a bargain property *and* finance your purchase, most larger banks won't even consider it.

REMEMBER

Don't be a time-waster. Call an REO manager or broker only if you have sufficient funds to buy, hold, renovate, and sell the property. The best way to succeed at investing in REO properties is to prove yourself: Have cash on hand, and do what you say you're going to do.

Connecting with REO brokers

A good way to find REO properties that a bank is willing to sell is to call on listings with REO brokers — real estate agents who sell properties on behalf of lenders. A good way to track down REO brokers is to network at foreclosure auctions. Start talking with the people who attend these auctions (the *gallery*). They can steer you in the direction of brokers who list REO properties. If that approach doesn't lead you to REO brokers, respond to that list properties with words and phrases like "REO," "Foreclosure," "Seller Willing To Look At All Offers," and "Bank Owned," or simply call local banks and brokers to ask.

REMEMBER

REO brokers are in the business of getting the bank top dollar for the properties they sell, so do your homework. The sheriff's deed filed at the county courthouse after the sale shows what the bank paid for the property. Compare that amount with the listing price to determine whether you have room to negotiate. The broker may not cut you a sweet deal, but with proof that you have the financing in place to close the deal quickly and hassle-free, the broker and the bank may be willing to negotiate the price.

Getting connected with REO A-listers

When you're dealing with banks, try to contact the person who's in charge of making the decisions, who may be the bank president, vice president, or someone high up in the REO department. This person can put you in contact with the lender's REO manager so that when you contact the REO manager, you're making a warm call instead of a cold call. Establishing relationships with bankers requires some people skills and determination that no book can help you develop. Learn by doing and by talking with people.

Consider contacting the banks in your area that have REO properties and letting them know what you do. Figure 12-1 provides a sample letter of introduction that you can customize to fit your needs.

<Your Name>
<Your Address>
<City>, <State> <Zip>
<Date>

<REO Manager's Name>
<Company>
<Address>
<City>, <State> <Zip>

Dear Mr./Ms. <Last Name>:

You know better than anyone that the primary business of <Bank's Name> is lending money, not owning property. That is why I want to propose a partnership that I believe will create a win-win situation for both of us.

I'm sure your REO list is full of properties that gobble up your department's valuable time and resources. I'm also sure that you and your staff have more important things to do than worry about property taxes, maintenance expenses, mandatory waiting periods, and all of the myriad other headaches that come with bank-owned real estate.

On the other hand, buying, selling, and owning property is my business. I have the resources to pay cash for properties and the know-how to make them profitable for everyone. Each piece of real estate <Bank's Name> owns represents valuable resources that could be better spent elsewhere in your institution's operations. I would like to help free up that money so you can put it back to work for you.

Let's meet face-to-face to discuss how we can work together in a mutually beneficial relationship. I will call you soon to select a time and date that fits into your schedule. Thank you for your time and interest.

Sincerely,

FIGURE 12-1:
Introduce
yourself to the
bank's REO
manager via a
letter.

<Your Signature>

<Your Name>

Foreclosure Specialist

TIP

Developing positive rapport with local bankers and REO personnel is a good move regardless of the stage of the foreclosure process in which you decide to invest. In many cases, you can establish these contacts when working with homeowners before auction. If bankers know that you're working in the area to help homeowners catch up on their mortgage payments, they're more likely to respond to you when you approach them about REO properties. In addition, knowing the bankers and other lenders in the area can help you negotiate better deals for distressed homeowners. Get to know the key personnel:

>> Bankers, including the president and vice president of the bank

>> The manager in charge of collecting late mortgage payments

>> The manager of the loss-mitigation or Real Estate in Judgment (REJ) department, who handles the property during the foreclosure process

>> The REO manager

>> The REO brokers in your area

If you're interested in a particular property that the lender is foreclosing on, consider sending the letter shown in Figure 12-2 instead. This letter has a more targeted appeal. In addition, it lets the lender know that you may be able to help distressed homeowners work out a payment solution — something that lenders like to hear. If the lender has already turned the matter over to an attorney, you may not get a response, so try sending a copy of the letter to the attorney as well.

TIP

Create a database or address book for the REO managers and brokers in your area and maintain contact with them. This task is an important part of networking your way to foreclosure success, as discussed in Chapter 6.

<Your Name>
<Your Address>
<City>, <State> <Zip>
<Date>

<REO Manager's Name>
<Company>
<Address>
<City>, <State> <Zip>

Dear Mr./Ms. <Last Name>:

I noticed that you had a property go to mortgage sale in <County Name>. This is an area in which I specialize. I would like to see if you have a list of properties that I could purchase in this area.

I also encourage and assist homeowners who are facing foreclosure work with their lenders to develop solutions that are mutually beneficial for the homeowners and their lenders. If one of your customers is behind on mortgage payments, feel free to pass along my name and contact information to the homeowner. I may be able to help.

Please contact me on my direct line <Your Phone Number>.

Sincerely,

<Your Signature>

<Your Name>

Foreclosure Specialist

FIGURE 12-2:
Send a letter to the REO manager to inquire about a particular property.

Tracking the property through the REO stage

In Chapter 8, I suggest that you track a property from the time the foreclosure notice or Notice of Default (NOD) appears until the time somebody purchases the property. If you followed my advice, you know from sitting in on the auction whether somebody purchased the property, but you may not know who purchased it. In many cases, the purchaser is the lender who foreclosed on the property.

To find out who purchased the property, head back to the Register of Deeds or county clerk's office to check out the deed. Whenever someone buys a mortgage at auction, the first thing the buyer does is record the sheriff's deed. That deed tells you who bought the property. If the lender bought it, you now know that you have an opportunity to purchase the property from the lender.

Some third-party purchasers intentionally wait to record the deed so that another investor doesn't poach their purchase, as discussed in Chapter 11. If you know that somebody purchased the property but you can't find the sheriff's deed with the buyer's name on it, this is probably what's going on. Ask the Register of Deeds office whether it has a statutory recording period or deadline for when the deed must be recorded. In some jurisdictions, the buyer must record an *affidavit of designee* or a *buyer's affidavit* — a separate sheet that must be attached to or recorded at the same time as the deed, which tells you when the sale took place; who foreclosed; and (more important) who purchased the property or who needs to be paid off to redeem the property, including their contact information.

Working your way to the better deals

People who work in the REO departments tend to give the best deals to investors whom they trust most and who offer the best service to the bank. By doing what you say you're going to do, closing on deals, and relieving the bank of its burden, you become an attractive investor. When a property becomes available, the REO manager is more likely to contact you than a less-qualified or unproven investor.

You can make yourself even more valuable to the REO department by putting the following tips into practice:

>> **Be courteous.** Act like a partner. The bank doesn't owe you anything. Be polite and treat everyone from the bank president down to the secretaries with respect.

>> **Solve problems.** When a bank takes possession of a property, it has a problem that you can solve by buying the property. Don't create more problems or offer a litany of complaints. Solve the bank's problem.

>> **Take the bad with the good.** REO departments often have some highly profitable properties and some not-so-profitable properties. Offer to buy one property that has a low potential profit along with a property that has a higher potential profit. In other words, bundle your purchases.

When you're getting started, avoid bundle purchases. I strongly recommend that you purchase properties that are almost certain to deliver a profit. When you become more experienced and have a reliable team that can renovate several properties at the same time quickly and affordably, bundling may be a good strategy. So long as your overall profit on the bundle is sufficient, you can afford to buy a few mediocre properties along with those that have a higher profit potential.

Following up with homeowners during redemption

In areas with a redemption period, you can continue to work with the homeowners during redemption, even if the bank's REO department bought back the mortgage. Use this opportunity to inform the homeowners that they can still redeem the property.

At this point, the bank isn't likely to reinstate the loan or agree to a forbearance, but it may agree to a *short sale* (accepting less than full payment of the loan's balance). The redemption period also gives the homeowners extra time to find a less-painful exit, such as selling the house to you, borrowing from friends or relatives, refinancing, and so on. See Chapter 9 for a complete list of options that may be available to the homeowners.

Inspecting the Property

Even when you're buying bank-owned properties, you need to inspect the property with your own two eyes, as discussed in Chapter 8. Getting inside to take a look around, however, can be a monumental challenge. Here are a few suggestions to assist you in inspecting the property as closely as possible:

>> **If the homeowners are residing in the home, knock on the door.** They may not let you in, but try to engage them in conversation long enough to look past them into the house. This approach doesn't provide a thorough inspection, but it can give you a general idea of how well the current residents have been caring for the home.

>> **Look through the windows if the house is vacant.**

>> **Contact the bank's REO department and explain that you're seriously interested in buying the property but can't place an offer until you can get inside the house to look around.** Explain that you want to be fair, but you also need to know what you're getting into.

TIP

>> **Offer to visit the house and change the locks for the bank.** Here's a chance for you to problem-solve for the bank. If you have some old locks left over from a previous property you purchased, you can change the locks at no cost and seize the opportunity to inspect the home at the same time. Ask where you can drop off the keys (giving yourself another chance to meet a contact person with some authority).

> » **If you can't get inside to look around and still want to make an offer on the property, consider adding a contingency clause to the purchase agreement, stating that the purchase is conditional upon the house passing inspection.** Contingency clauses make your offer less attractive, but unless the bank flat-out refuses to consider an offer with a contingency clause, it's worth a try.

REMEMBER

After you inspect the property, follow up with the bank, even if the house is a total wreck. If you like what you saw, place an offer within a reasonable time.

Timing Your Offer for Optimum Results

In real estate investing, being in the right place at the right time often brings you the best properties. This is even more true with REO properties, because banks and other lending institutions are highly motivated to get the bad loans off their books.

As an investor, you have four excellent opportunities to scoop up REO properties:

» Right after the auction, if your area has no redemption period

» Right after the redemption period expires, if your area has a redemption period

» At the end of the month or quarter, when lenders are often in a hurry to clear bad loans off their books

» When the REO broker first lists the property

REMEMBER

Banks and other lending institutions often receive funds to lend based on their ratio of good to bad loans. The more bad loans they can clear off the books, the more money they can borrow from the government to invest in loans with profit potential. In addition, bank managers often receive bonuses and promotions based on their performance numbers, so they're highly motivated, particularly at the end of the month or quarter, to clear those bad loans off the books.

In the following sections, I explore these opportunities in greater detail.

Acting quickly after the auction

If your area has no redemption period, and you've been tracking a property that you're interested in buying, contact the REO broker who's in charge of the property just before the auction. (The REO broker is usually an independent agent, not an employee of the bank.) Tell the broker that if nobody purchases the property at the auction, you're interested in it. If the property has some equity in it, of course, the broker isn't likely to offer you a clear shot at it after the sale. You're more likely to be told that if you're interested, you should show at the sale and bid.

Tell the manager of the bank's REO department that in exchange for negotiating the price you need to make the deal worthwhile to you, you're willing to take on the burdens of helping the previous owners move on with their lives and of renovating and selling the property.

Timing your move with the redemption period

In areas with a redemption period, the bank isn't going to move on the property until the homeowners have exhausted their final opportunity to redeem the property. Contacting the REO department during the redemption period is always a good idea, however, just to let the REO manager know that you're interested in the property.

Soon after the REO department assigns the property to a broker, the property is typically listed on the open market and your competition for that property heats up. By telling the REO manager that you're interested in the property, you improve your chance of getting the property before it's listed. The manager may tell the broker something like this: "Hey, so-and-so really wants this house. I'd like you to contact this investor and get an offer." Letting the manager know about your interest gives you the opportunity to be the first person to place an offer on the property, assuming that the REO manager or the broker doesn't already have someone lined up.

Tuning in to the lender's fiscal calendar

Banks often set end-of-month and end-of-quarter dates for their REO personnel. Often, bonuses are tied to an REO manager's ability to unload a certain number of properties in a given time period, and when the end of the month or quarter rolls around, the REO manager is highly motivated to make a deal.

A bank's fiscal and calendar years may differ, so coordinate your activities with each bank's fiscal calendar. Keep a record of each bank's fiscal year so that you have a better idea of how to time your offers for optimum success.

THE CROOKED BROKER

In the sidebar earlier in this chapter called "The exclusive REO insiders club," I reveal that the REO circuit is often shady. REO brokers are often in a position of power, and as Lord Acton once said, power corrupts, and absolute power corrupts absolutely.

I once had lunch with an REO broker I'd known for years who wanted to sell me his business. I asked him what I would have to do to guarantee my continued success with his business, and he replied that every once in a while he sells a house to the asset manager at a different bank at a good price. He sold properties that guaranteed a $30,000 profit per property, which is (obviously) an illegal kickback.

This same REO broker sold houses to his girlfriend. She bought properties well below market value and then sold them at market value to earn what's called a *pass-through profit.* My staff and private investigating team discovered that the girlfriend had "earned" more than $90,000 in pass-through profits. That money really belonged to the lender whom the REO broker represented.

Another REO broker (scoundrel) I know lists only half the properties he sells. Instead of listing all the properties on the MLS, as he should, he lists the worst half of them and then sells the listings with the greatest profit potential to his buddies. We call these listings *pocket listings,* because the broker puts the listing in his pocket and then transfers it to a friend's pocket. In a matter of days, the listing is sold and closed, and the seller scores a huge profit for doing nothing.

I tell these stories for two reasons:

- Don't get involved in these scams.
- Realize that as an investor, these sorts of underhanded deals seriously jeopardize your access to the best deals. REO investing isn't easy, and these types of scams make it even more difficult.

Waiting for the broker to list the house

Waiting for the REO broker to list the house is rarely the best move, because the broker's commission is calculated on the sale price of the property. The broker isn't likely to sell you the property at a bargain-basement price. Keep in mind, however, that both time and money contribute to making an offer appealing. The broker may be willing to accept a lower price in exchange for the time savings.

TIP

Consider submitting a copy of your offer to the broker and the bank. This approach isn't necessarily the best way to buddy up with a broker, but it does let the bank know who you are and what you do. In the future, the bank may decide to deal with you directly rather than through a broker.

Pitching an Attractive Offer

When you're buying a property from a bank or other lending institution, you take the same steps that you'd take if you were buying the property from a homeowner. You complete a purchase agreement stating the price and terms you're offering. The bank or other lending institution can, and usually does, present a counteroffer that you can accept or counter.

In the following sections, I provide some guidance on determining how much to offer for the property and what you can expect when the lender makes a counteroffer.

TIP

Banks often require you to sign documents in addition to the purchase agreement that slap more restrictions on the deal. These documents aren't deal-killers, but you should have your attorney look them over before signing them.

Sizing up the lender's needs

When pitching an offer to a seller, knowing what the seller needs can always help. In most cases, the REO manager or broker who's selling the property estimates a target price by totaling the following amounts:

>> Unpaid balance on the loan

>> Collection fees

>> Legal fees and other expenses related to the foreclosure

>> Property taxes the bank paid

>> Repair and maintenance expenses

>> Other expenses

If the home is obviously worth much more than the unpaid balance on the loan, the bank usually takes this fact into consideration and seeks to profit from the sale beyond simply recovering the unpaid loan balance and expenses.

Reevaluating your needs

Knowing how the lender calculates the asking price is valuable information to have when preparing your offer, but it's more important to know the maximum price you can pay for the property to be fairly certain that you can resell it for 20 percent more than you invest in it.

In Chapter 11, I provide detailed instructions on gathering the numbers and plugging them into a formula to determine your maximum bid. The formula is the same for determining your top offer on an REO property:

1. **Start with the future sale price of the home after improvements.**

2. **For an estimated profit of at least 20 percent, divide the amount from step 1 by one of the following:**

   - 1.20 in a market where home values are rising (to shoot for a 20 percent return on your investment)

   - 1.25 in a market where home values are steady (to shoot for a 25 percent return

   - 1.30 in a market where home values are declining (to shoot for a 30 percent return)

   - 1.35 to 1.50, depending on the percentage of profit you want to make (to shoot for a 35–50 percent return)

3. **Subtract any back taxes you'll be responsible for paying when you purchase the property.**

4. **Subtract estimated costs of repairs and renovations.**

5. **Subtract monthly holding costs.**

6. **Subtract agent commissions and/or marketing and advertising costs.**

7. **Subtract closing costs for selling the property.**

The result gives you a general idea of how much to offer for the property to be fairly certain that you can profit at least 20 percent from the transaction.

REMEMBER

Don't make your first offer your best offer. REO managers are trained to haggle, and they always counteroffer. If you want a property for $200,000, and you offer $200,000, the REO manager is going to counter with $220,000 or $225,000. To get the property for $200,000, you'd better start with a lower offer of $175,000 or $180,000. This rule is pretty much hard-and-fast, but be prepared to take a different strategy if the situation warrants doing so, as I demonstrate in the nearby sidebar "Haggling with REO managers."

HAGGLING WITH REO MANAGERS

After you've established a close relationship with an REO manager, you can get away with making your first offer your best offer — so long as the REO manager knows that you've done your homework, you can close the deal, and this offer is truly your best one. The worst that can happen is that the REO broker rejects your offer.

The worst thing you can do is pitch $200,000 as your best offer and then increase that offer when the broker counters it. I once tried to sell a house to a couple with whom I was unwilling to haggle (not in the mood, I guess). I needed to sell the property for at least $150,000 to make the deal work for me. I told the buyers, "Give me your best offer. If it works, we'll go with it. If not, I'll tell you that upfront." They offered $135,000, and I said, "No, that won't work." They immediately upped their offer to $145,000, and I said, "I thought $135,000 was your best offer. Didn't I tell you that I would be willing to deal with you if you gave me your best offer?" The buyers replied, "Well, yes, but . . ."

At this point, the buyers' credibility was in shreds. I offered to sell them the house for $157,000, saying, "And this *is* my final offer." The couple bought the house.

The take-home message is this: If you don't want to haggle, don't haggle. If you have a relationship with a REO manager who says, "All right, let's just cut to the chase. You tell me what you want to pay, and if it works, we're a go . . .," and then you deliver a lowball offer, you've lost your credibility.

Putting your offer in writing

Whether you're buying a property from homeowners or from a lender, your offer must be in writing in the form of a purchase agreement. In real estate, verbal agreements and handshakes aren't enforceable and won't hold up in court. Everything must be in writing. Your attorney can assist you in drawing up and presenting the purchase agreement. Even if an REO manager tells you a price that the bank is willing to accept, get it in writing. Follow the rules to meet the statute of frauds, and your offer will go from an unenforceable oral offer to a rock-solid, legally enforceable one.

TIP

When you're pitching an offer to a bank, you typically have to offer a few more concessions than you do when you're buying a property from a homeowner. Following are some guidelines to assist you in drawing up an attractive offer:

>> **Available cash:** Having the cash available enables you to close on the deal without having to wait for loan approval. This situation gives the bank confidence that you won't back out on the deal at the last minute, and it gives

your offer an edge over any other offers that the bank may receive. Gather proof that you have the cash — copies of bank statements (with account numbers blacked out) and other financial statements.

>> **Proof of financing:** If you don't have cash, you need proof that you're preapproved for a loan. Contact your lender to obtain the required documentation.

>> **Large down payment:** If you can't come up with all the cash, offering a large down payment is the next-best thing. A down payment of 20 percent or more, along with a preapproval letter from the bank or investor who's lending you the money, usually carries sufficient weight.

>> **Bank's purchase agreement:** You may be required to use the bank's purchase agreement to present your offer. Banks often do this so that their employees can easily locate the necessary information on a standard form rather than having to learn how to read various purchase agreements.

>> **No conditions:** When buying a property from a homeowner, you often make your offer conditional on the house passing inspection. When you're buying from a bank's REO department, any conditions weaken your offer, and the bank is likely to reject the offer outright.

>> **Bank's addendum:** The bank typically counters with an addendum of its own, stating that the purchase is unconditional, that the bank provides no warranty for the property, and so on. These addendums basically state that you're agreeing to buy the property "as is," which can be a little intimidating, but that's part of doing business with the bank's REO department.

TIP

Prepare all the documentation well in advance and have your attorney review it before signing. Your attorney can do little to help you after you've signed.

After you and the lender agree on a price and terms, have the lender work with your attorney to set a closing date, and review any documents before closing. At this point, the closing arrangements are pretty much in the hands of the bank and your attorney. The closing is typically held within 10 to 14 days, provided that no other timing issues need to be met.

REMEMBER

During negotiations, never counter yourself. After making an offer, wait for the bank to accept your offer or counter back. If you offer $160,000 and later begin to think that your offer is too low and then boost your offer to $170,000 before the bank has responded, you end up bidding against yourself. On the other hand, if you have reliable information and know that the bank has multiple offers, you may want to increase your bid.

Closing on the deal

Even when you're buying a property from the bank, always purchase title insurance. You can get seriously burned if you missed something on the title work or a lien wasn't properly recorded against the property and you don't have title insurance.

During one transaction, I entertained the idea of forgoing title insurance and saving a little money. The deal seemed to be pretty straightforward, and I'd done my research, so I figured that I'd covered all the bases. But I decided to live by my rule and scheduled the closing with a title company. It's a good thing I did.

The closing went smoothly enough, with no problems. Weeks after the closing, however, I started receiving notices about taxes and fees I supposedly owed on the property. First, I received a notice from the county treasurer that I owed a substantial amount in back taxes. Then one of the condominium association's board members stopped me to say that I owed some back dues. The board had just voted to file a lien against my property. In both cases, I thought there'd been some kind of mistake, because I'd just closed and everything was paid at that closing — or so I thought.

Had I not purchased title insurance, and had the title company not handled the closing, I'd have had to pony up thousands of dollars extra to keep my property. As it turned out, the title company was responsible for paying because it made the mistake. The moral of the story: Always use a title company to insure the transaction.

IN THIS CHAPTER

» **Finding and buying HUD homes**

» **Tracking down VA properties**

» **Buying a bank's assets when it goes belly up**

» **Finding and buying government-owned and -seized properties**

» **Qualifying for government financing**

Chapter **13**

Finding and Buying Government Repos

The government often plays a supporting role in the real estate business. It insures or secures loans, and when homeowners default on those loans, the government has to step in, foreclose on the property and then sell it to recover some or all of its loss. When citizens fail to pay their taxes, the government may seize their real estate to cover the bill. Law enforcement agencies often get in on the act by seizing the homes of convicted drug dealers and other criminals.

Nobody likes to think of the government kicking people out of their homes, but that's the tragic reality that some homeowners face when they experience a significant financial setback, commit a serious crime, or make some poor financial decisions.

Anyone with enough money or financing can purchase these homes, either from designated real estate agents or by bidding on the properties at auction. In this chapter, I discuss the pros and cons of buying government-owned properties and show you how to track them down, online and off.

REMEMBER

Strictly speaking, the properties I cover in this chapter aren't your average foreclosure properties, but because they're properties that are taken away from the owners and then placed on the market, I lump them in with foreclosures.

WHY IS THE GOVERNMENT IN THE REAL ESTATE BUSINESS, ANYWAY?

Home ownership is one of the major forces that drives local, state, national, and even global economies. In addition to providing people a roof over their heads, a home is one of the best and most accessible investment vehicles for the average citizen. It's no wonder, then, that the federal government goes out of its way to facilitate the purchase of homes by making home loans more affordable, especially for first-time buyers.

For decades, people have relied on loans insured by the Federal Housing Authority (FHA) to finance the purchase of their first homes. Likewise, veterans of the armed forces have used federally guaranteed Veterans Affairs (VA) loans to purchase homes. Most government-secured loans are originated by mortgage brokers. At closing or shortly thereafter, the loans are assigned to lenders that service the loans.

Lenders love these loans because the government takes most of their risk out of the equation by insuring the loans. If a homeowner defaults on the loan, the lender has a relatively safe exit; the government pays the balance and takes possession of the home. These government-owned properties fall into the following two categories:

- **HUD homes:** FHA loans are insured by the federal government program through the U.S. Department of Housing and Urban Development (HUD). The lender forecloses on the property and then has two options: keep the property or turn it over to HUD and be fully reimbursed for all costs, including principal, interest, late fees, and court and attorney fees. Then HUD sells the house.

- **VA homes:** The VA underwrites the loan, and because the loan is being offered to military veterans, loan qualifications are more lenient. But lenders aren't lenient; when veterans default on a VA loan, the lender forecloses on the property and evicts them. Then the lender assigns the property back to the VA and is reimbursed for all costs.

When a homeowner defaults on one of those loans, the government usually ends up with the property but has neither the means nor the motivation to fix up the home and sell it. These government properties go back on the market where investors can often pick them up for prices below market value.

Bargain Hunting for HUD Homes

First-time buyers often finance their homes through the federal government, primarily by way of FHA-insured loans. When the property owner fails to make mortgage payments on the property, the FHA initiates a foreclosure, which commonly results in the agency's taking possession of the house and reselling it through a HUD-registered real estate agent.

In the following sections, I discuss the pros and cons of investing in HUD homes, encourage you to team up with a HUD-registered real estate agent in your area, and show you how to research HUD homes online.

WARNING

HUD sells homes "owner-occupied." If you purchase a HUD home, you must sign a document stating that you'll live in the home for at least 12 months before selling it. You may be tempted to stretch the truth a bit and sign the document even though you have no intention of living in the house, but you'd be committing fraud. If you're caught and convicted, you may face a hefty fine and some jail time. Do the right thing. If you don't plan on living in the house for at least a year, don't buy it. You can find plenty of good deals on investment properties without committing a felony.

Note that HUD does make exceptions. Although first-time home buyers get first crack at buying foreclosures, investors just need to be patient. If a first-time-buyer-to-be's loan application is declined for any reason, the property is made available to all bidders when it goes back on the market.

Weighing the pros and cons of HUD homes

Because HUD homes are sold owner-occupied, they're not candidates for a quick flip, but for an investor who needs a place to live while investing in other properties, a HUD home may be a good long-term investment. Before becoming involved with HUD homes, however, be aware of the following potential drawbacks:

>> HUD homes are often sold at or just below market value, so they're not always the best deals available. You need to assess the potential profitability of these properties just as carefully as you would that of any property you consider buying.

>> The homes that HUD owns are typically low- to midmarket homes repossessed from first-time homeowners. They're rarely located in the ritziest neighborhoods.

>> You need to purchase the home through a HUD-registered real estate agent and pay a sales commission.

>> HUD homes are sold as-is, so inspect a home as closely as possible before making your offer. After you buy it, you own it, my friend . . . and all the defects that come with it.

One of the big benefits of purchasing HUD homes is that you may qualify for FHA financing. The agency often offers special interest rates for loans used to purchase and rehab run-down properties.

WARNING

Don't assume that because the government is selling the home, you're getting a great deal on a great property. Do your homework. Research the value of comparable properties in the area, and inspect the home before you hand over your money.

Hooking up with a HUD-approved agent

If you're interested in investing in HUD homes, hook up with a real estate agent who specializes in these properties. The right real estate agent can supply you a steady stream of leads along with tips on how to profit most from your investment properties.

You can find HUD-approved agents by networking or by checking out HUD homes for sale online, as discussed in the following section. Online listings typically display contact information for the agent who's listing the home. When you contact the HUD-approved agent, tell the agent if you're already working through your own agent (assuming you have one); otherwise, you could end up in the middle of a messy legal battle.

TIP

Sales of owner-occupied houses fall through more often than investor deals do, so don't give up just because someone bought the property you wanted. Keep an eye on the pending sale and be prepared to pounce if the sale falls through. At that point, most of your competition for the property has lost interest and dropped out.

Finding HUD homes online

HUD Homes at `https://www.hudhomestore.gov` enables you to search by state, county, city, or zip code for homes made available through HUD. Most listings provide a complete description of the property along with a photo and links to additional information, including disclosures, environmental compliance, and condition of the property. See Figure 13-1.

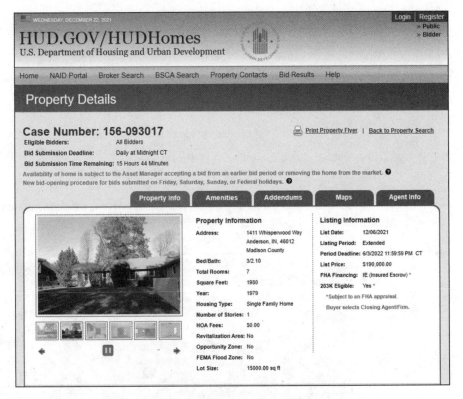

FIGURE 13-1:
Go online to find HUD home listings in your state.

After you find a home, you can place a bid online or click a link to obtain contact information for a HUD-registered broker in your area. In most cases, you have to make an offer through a registered broker.

WARNING

If someone tries to sell you some HUD Homes Investor program for $1,500 or so, don't fall for it. That person can't tell you any more than I reveal here. HUD and VA home opportunities are available to anyone who has the financing and energy to pursue them. Don't assume that you need some special high-priced program.

Finding and Buying VA Repos

To make homeownership more affordable to military veterans, the U.S. Department of Veterans Affairs (VA) offers VA loans. You can find VA listings in either of the following ways:

>> Contact a VA-registered real estate agent in your area.

>> Visit Vendor Resource Management (VRM) at www.vrmproperties.com, and register as a buyer to create an account. Then take the following steps to search for properties:

1. Log in at https://www.vrmproperties.com.

2. Type your city, state, or zip code in the search box near the top of the page and press Enter.

3. Use the filters near the top of the page to narrow your search, if desired.

4. Click a listing that interests you.

   Figure 13-2 shows a sample listing.

5. If you're interested, complete and submit the contact listing agent for details.

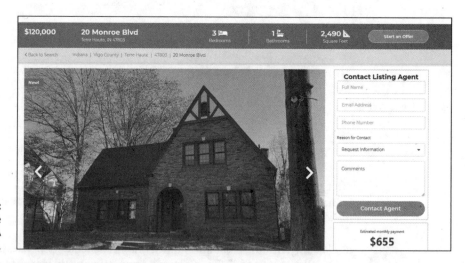

FIGURE 13-2: Visit VRM online to view VA listings.

WARNING

If you're already working with an agent you like, mention this point when you speak with the agent assigned to sell the VA property. Otherwise, you may inadvertently cause some conflict between the two agents, both of whom want the sales commission, and you don't want to get caught in the middle of a legal battle.

VRM is a financial corporation that the VA has contracted to manage its properties. New listings may not yet be assigned to real estate brokers, in which case the listing will be labeled "Coming Soon," and you'll need to revisit the site regularly until the property becomes active.

REMEMBER

You don't have to be a military veteran to buy a home from the VA, but you may need to sign a statement that you intend to live in the house, just as though you were purchasing a HUD home. (Some exceptions may apply, but if the property is being sold owner-occupied, don't bid on it unless you plan to live there for at least 12 months.)

TIP

While you're at the VRM site, open the menu in the top-right corner of any page and click the About the Vendee Program link. This program offers VA financing to veterans and nonveterans alike. When making your offer, structure it in a way that makes it as easy as possible for the listing agent to say yes. Offering a 20 percent down payment streamlines the processing, which almost guarantees instant approval. If you find a really good deal for $100,000, for example, and you offer a down payment of $20,000, you're almost assured of getting the property. The Vendee Loan Program page has current information about required down payments and fees.

Profiting from Fannie Mae and Freddie Mac Properties

One way that the federal government promotes homeownership is providing financing through Fannie Mae (a nickname for the Federal National Mortgage Association [FNMA]), Ginnie Mae (Government National Mortgage Association [GNMA]), and Freddie Mac (Federal Home Loan Mortgage Corporation [FHLMC]).

All these organizations do pretty much the same thing: purchase residential mortgages and then convert the mortgages to securities for sale to investors, indirectly financing the purchase of homes. Because Fannie Mae and Freddie Mac are such integral parts of home financing, they end up with a huge number of foreclosure properties that they must sell, particularly in large markets, and many of these properties aren't HUD or VA homes.

WARNING

If you stumble upon what looks like a great deal, make your offer subject to a satisfactory home inspection. Delaying your offer until you can have the home inspected opens the possibility that another buyer will swoop in and buy the property. By making your offer subject to a satisfactory home inspection, you can get your offer in and then back out if the property needs a lot of work. Present your offer, but make sure that it has a good contingency clause you can use for an emergency exit.

Tapping into Freddie Mac's home clearinghouse

Freddie Mac has a website devoted exclusively to promoting the sales of the homes it owns: HomeSteps, at www.homesteps.com. This site features a searchable online database, primarily Real Estate Owned (REO) properties, across the nation. Freddie Mac lists most of the homes with brokers, but it also holds online auctions, so you can bid on properties from the comfort of your home or office.

To search for homes for sale, type your state, county, city, or zip code in the Find a Home box on the opening page, and click Search. If HomeSteps has any homes for sale in the area you searched, a map showing their locations appears along with a list of the properties. You can click a marker on the map and then click Details, or click the address of a property in the list to view the property's listing. Figure 13-3 shows a sample listing, which provides photos of the property, details about the property (scroll down to see them), and the name and phone number of the real estate agent to call. When you find a home that interests you, call the agent to schedule a tour.

FIGURE 13-3:
HomeSteps can assist you in finding Freddie Mac homes in your area.

TIP

Click Resources on the menu bar near the top of the page for additional goodies, including a link to sign up for a HomeSteps.com Home Search account, which notifies you weekly about any new homes that match your search criteria; information about getting the HomeSteps app for your smartphone; and a link to useful calculators and other tools.

Shopping for Fannie Mae properties

Freddie Mac's older sister, Fannie Mae, has her own website for home buyers: HomePath, at www.homepath.fanniemae.com. Click the search box near the middle of the page; type the state, city, or zip code you want to search; and click the Search button. If HomePath has any homes for sale in the area you searched, a list of properties appears on the left side of the page, and a map on the right side of the page shows their locations (see Figure 13-4).

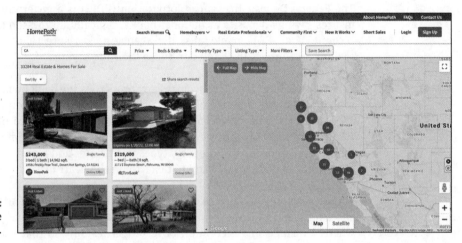

FIGURE 13-4:
Fannie Mae homes for sale.

Click a listing to obtain additional information, including contact information for the listing agent. Figure 13-5 shows a sample listing of a Fannie Mae-owned property. You can also get a map that shows exactly where the property is located.

FIGURE 13-5:
Sample listing for a Fannie Mae home.

While you're at the Fannie Mae site, open the Home Buyers menu near the top of the page, and click Resource for Investors for additional information. If you're an investor who's having trouble finding financing for an investment property, you may be able to finance the purchase through a local lender that's connected with Fannie Mae.

Buying FDIC properties

The Federal Deposit Insurance Corporation (FDIC) is a government agency that insures savings deposits at member banks, typically up to $100,000 per savings account. If an FDIC bank fails, the agency makes sure that people who have savings accounts at the bank don't lose their life savings.

When a bank fails, the FDIC acquires any properties the bank owns and lists those properties for sale. It's sort of like foreclosing on the bank. Then these properties are offered for sale. You can check out what the FDIC has to offer by visiting www.fdicrealestatelistings.com, but I wouldn't waste my time. When I visited the site, I searched for all property types in all states and found three lousy properties for sale in Texas . . . and not exactly in the heart of Texas.

When a rash of bank failures occurs, you may be able to find plenty of FDIC properties for sale. In the meantime, you can find a wider selection of properties elsewhere. I include this section on FDIC properties only so that you won't think I omitted something by mistake.

Finding and Buying Government-Seized Properties

Various government agencies at all levels often seize or purchase properties. These agencies aren't interested in the properties themselves; they generally want to unload them quickly for whatever they can get. In other words, the government is the ultimate motivated seller.

You can track down government-seized properties by contacting law-enforcement and government agencies directly, especially at the state or local level. The following sections describe various agencies — local, state, and federal — that commonly have properties for sale.

Buying properties at tax sales

Taxing authorities don't mess around when citizens don't pay their taxes. They simply send a few notices, and if the homeowners don't come up with the cash or work out a payment plan, the taxing authority seizes the property, puts it up for auction, and attempts to collect the taxes from the sales proceeds. Taxing authorities show little leniency, and the homeowners rarely dodge the bullet by claiming bankruptcy.

Tax sales, like foreclosures, are typically processed through the county sheriff's office, as explained in the following section, but the state may hold its own tax sales. Your real estate attorney can fill you in on the details and tell you where to go for additional information related to your state and county.

HOUSEJACKING IN WAYNE COUNTY

Wayne County announced that it was holding the equivalent of the county fair of tax sales. My investment team spent months preparing for it, and I brought my banker along to the auction. I had the funds on hand to purchase $1 million worth of real estate.

I ended up buying only two properties that day. One property was a lot without a house, and the other was what I considered to be a good rental property, perfect for use as a long-term investment. Well, my long-term investment didn't turn out quite as I planned. I rented it, only to discover later that some sinister con artist had stolen the property from me. I'd been victimized by a housejacker!

That experience was a little discouraging. After all, I'm a renowned expert on real estate fraud, and I often warn people about real estate con artists. I felt like a police officer who'd just fallen victim to a carjacking. The perpetrator used the information from the tax sale with the original homeowner's name on it and recorded the deed in his name before I had a chance to record the deed in my name!

Needless to say, I was able to track down the con artist with the help of my friendly neighborhood law enforcement agency and make him pay for his crime.

The moral of this story: Remain vigilant for real estate con artists, file your deed as soon as possible after the sale, and take out title insurance to cover your back.

Avoiding the tax lien sales gurus

WARNING

Most of the tax sales you hear about in real estate investment books and articles and on late-night TV programs are property tax sales. Your average investment guru typically overhypes the available opportunities of this type. They lead would-be investors to believe that they can pay $4,000 in back taxes at a tax sale and scoop up a $200,000 property. In theory, you may be able to take ownership of a property by paying the back taxes, but in practice, that situation rarely happens. This area has become so competitive that bidding quickly drives up the price of the property. You'd be very lucky to get a $200,000 property for $120,000 at auction.

If you decide to search for "tax sales" or "tax liens" online, even if you look for tax sales specifically in your state or county, you're very unlikely to discover any useful information. You'll find thousands of sites that attempt to sell you on get-rich-quick schemes related to tax sales and purchasing tax liens, and very little information directly from official state or county websites . . . unless your state or county posts some good information. (Most states and counties don't.) Don't waste your money on whatever program and services a particular commercial site is peddling. You'll get more valuable information by calling or visiting your county sheriff's or treasurer's office.

Buying properties from the IRS

In most foreclosure situations, the Internal Revenue Service (IRS) releases any lien it has on the property soon after it changes hands. The investor who buys the senior lien must give the IRS 30 days' notice, just in case the agency decides that it wants to redeem the property and try to sell it to recover lost tax revenue, but the IRS usually passes on such deals. Sometimes, however, the IRS takes possession of the property and sells it at auction.

To find out about properties that the IRS has for sale and obtain more information about upcoming auctions, visit www.treas.gov/auctions/irs, click the IRS Auction Home link, and then click All Real Estate or Real Estate – Seeking Guaranteed Bids (near the bottom of the page). If you see a property that looks interesting, click its link to view a description of it, along with the date, time, and location of the sale; encumbrances against the property; contact information for the person who's in charge of disbursing the property; and a link to a form for mailing in your bid.

If you submit the winning bid, you're typically required to come up with 20 percent of the opening bid immediately for a down payment; the remainder is due within 30 days of purchase. If the opening bid is $300,000, for example, you'll need to make a $60,000 deposit. The homeowners may have up to 120 days to redeem the property, but check to make sure.

Before placing a bid, inspect the property with your own two eyes and research the title, just as you'd do before making an offer on any other home. The IRS site lists encumbrances against the property, but it may have additional liens that the IRS doesn't know about.

Contacting your county treasurer's office

Your county treasurer's office or property tax division is the best place to start your search for information about tax sales, particularly property tax sales. Visit the treasurer's office or whichever county office handles the tax sales, and try to obtain the following information:

>> **Bidder's packet:** Many counties put together a bidder's packet with general information for investors. For a small fee, you can obtain most of the basic information you need about tax sales in your county.

>> **Property list:** As the date nears for the property tax sale, the county treasurer may offer a list of all the properties that will be auctioned. The problem with such a list is that it's generally subject to change until the date of the sale.

>> **Regulations:** If your bidder's packet contains no information about how redemptions are handled for property tax sales, ask. Different states and counties may handle tax sales differently. During the writing of this book, Michigan's tax sales gave homeowners no redemption rights, for example. After you purchase a property at a tax sale, the homeowners have no chance to redeem it. Find out the rules that govern tax sales in your county.

REMEMBER

The rules and regulations regarding tax sales are very complex and vary from state to state. The entire delinquent-tax foreclosure process can take anywhere from three to seven years from the time a homeowner stops paying taxes until the time the government takes possession of the property and puts it up for sale. In that time, the taxing authority attempts to contact the homeowners and anyone else who has a lien on the property, giving them the opportunity to pay the back taxes. In most cases, someone who has an interest in the property ponies up the money and takes controlling interest in the property. Contact your real estate attorney to find out more about how tax sales are handled in your area.

Taking a trip to the state department of transportation

A state department of transportation (DOT) commonly purchases real estate before building or widening roads or making other improvements to the infra-structure. If the property isn't destroyed during the construction project, the DOT lists it for sale. Often, you can buy property directly from the DOT or through an auction at a deep discount.

Contact your state DOT for leads on properties that the agency may have for sale. The agency may list properties with a particular broker or post notices in specific legal publications. Find out who's in charge, call and introduce yourself as an investor, and ask whether the department has any properties for sale. In many cases, the properties consist only of land, but occasionally, you'll find a property that has a house on it.

TIP

Some DOT websites list properties for sale. Oregon's DOT has a special section on its website for property management (www.oregon.gov/odot/row/pages/property-sales.aspx). Michigan's DOT also provides information about excess properties at www.michigan.gov/mdot. On most DOT websites, however, you won't find much about properties for sale, so you have to make phone contact. The U. S. Department of Transportation also ends up owning property after completing construction projects. To track down properties owned by the feds, you'll have better luck visiting the sites listed in the next section than trying to wade through the federal DOT site.

Finding government-seized property online

TIP

You can poke around on the web to find various federal, state, and local agencies that seize and dispose of real estate. Use your favorite search tool to look for "government seized property," "government-seized properties," or "government-seized real estate." Use your imagination to come up with other search phrases, such as your county or state followed by "seized property." Be sure to check out the following sites:

>> **General Services Administration (GSA) Auctions** (https://realestatesales.gov): GSA Auctions features links to various categories of government-owned properties, including Residential, Commercial, Industrial, Land, Agriculture, Lighthouse, and Multiple Use. A link is active and has a number next to it in parentheses if properties are available in that category. You can click the link to view a list of those properties and then click a property in the list for a more detailed description.

>> **Real Property Utilization & Disposal** (https://disposal.gsa.gov/s): This GSA site enables you to search for government-owned properties. Select a state and property type (such as Residential or Commercial) and then click Find Properties to access a list of properties or click a pin on a map of the United States and then click More to see a detailed listing for a specific property.

>> **U.S. Treasury Real Property Auctions** (`www.treasury.gov/auctions/treasury/rp`): This site features a list of properties that the U.S. government has seized and put up for auction. In most cases, these properties were seized because they were purchased with drug money or other funds from criminal activity. Click Upcoming Auctions on the home page to view properties scheduled for sale (see Figure 13-6).

>> **U.S. Department of Agriculture (USDA) Real Estate for Sale** (`https://properties.sc.egov.usda.gov`): This site displays links to single-family housing, multifamily housing, and farm and ranch properties. Simply click the link and follow the trail of maps to your state and county to find out whether any USDA properties are for sale in your neighborhood.

JANUARY 2022 AUCTIONS

NEW TO TREASURY AUCTIONS? View the "how to register" guide for online bidding.

OFFICE CONDO UNIT: 4524 Gun Club Road, Unit 103, West Palm Beach, Florida 33415
ONLINE AUCTION DATE: Friday, January 14, 2022

425 ± sq. ft. commercial condo with shared restrooms and parking. 1st floor unit includes reception area, work space, and break room. Sale # 22-66-106.

For complete details on this property click on the photo or CLICK HERE

SINGLE FAMILY HOME: 2141 Thorndike Avenue, Casper, Wyoming 82601
ONLINE AUCTION DATE: Thursday, January 20, 2022

1,100 ± sq. ft. home with 3 bedrooms, 1 bath, laundry, and attached 1-car garage. The finished basement includes a family room and full bath. Sale # 22-66-818.

For complete details on this property click on the photo or CLICK HERE

SINGLE FAMILY HOME: 1615 SE 159th Avenue, Portland, Oregon 97233
ONLINE AUCTION DATE: Wednesday, January 26, 2022

1,560 ± sq. ft. home with 3 bedrooms, 1 bath, covered patio, and attached 2-car garage. The home includes a bonus room over the garage. Sale # 22-66-124.

For complete details on this property click on the photo or CLICK HERE

SINGLE FAMILY HOME: 621 Hudson Road, West Palm Beach, Florida 33405
ONLINE AUCTION DATE: Thursday, January 27, 2022

1,138 ± sq. ft. home with 3 bedrooms, 2 baths, covered patio, shed, and driveway. Located in the Fairfax Park neighborhood. Sale # 22-66-126.

For complete details on this property click on the photo or CLICK HERE

FIGURE 13-6: Check out the latest properties seized and being auctioned by the U.S. Treasury Department.

REMEMBER

If you're looking for properties that have been seized from drug dealers, racketeers, and other criminals, you may not have much luck contacting the law enforcement agencies. The agencies usually prefer to place a lien on the property and collect some money later — when the property is sold or the mortgage is refinanced. Sometimes, the mortgage company offers to pay the lien to protect its interest. In the rare case in which law enforcement does take possession of a property, the agency typically sells it through an auction house or real estate broker.

IN THIS CHAPTER

» **Getting up to speed on bankruptcy laws**

» **Picking a strategy that works for you**

» **Gaining an edge on the competition**

» **Getting leads on properties in bankruptcy**

» **Maneuvering when a foreclosure you bought ends up in bankruptcy**

Chapter **14**

Banking on Bankruptcies

When you're focused on foreclosures, you may overlook another type of foreclosure-related opportunity: bankruptcies. If financially strapped homeowners file for bankruptcy, they shut down the foreclosure process, buy themselves some time to restructure their finances, and buy you some additional time to work your magic.

Dealing in bankruptcies can be even more complicated than trying to acquire a foreclosure property. In most cases, you can't simply deal with the homeowner or bid at an auction. You have to work with the homeowners' attorney or the court-appointed trustee, who is committed to selling the property for fair market value or at least a fairly decent price. Even if you obtain the attorney's or trustee's approval, creditors may oppose the sale of the property in court. To turn a profit with bankruptcies, you really need to know your stuff.

This chapter delivers tips and tricks to improve your odds of success and shows you what to do when a property you purchased in foreclosure ends up in bankruptcy court.

Acquiring bankruptcy properties can be a royal pain, which is exactly why most real estate investors avoid them like the plague. If you're a novice investor, I suggest that you do the same. Because so many investors steer clear of properties in bankruptcy, however, the opportunities are more plentiful for anyone who can learn the ropes. Just make sure that you have an attorney who specializes in bankruptcy in your corner.

Brushing Up on Bankruptcy Laws

Filing for bankruptcy is like pressing the pause button on your DVD player: It stops everything . . . or, in legal parlance, *stays* everything. It stops foreclosure (only temporarily). It freezes the bill collectors. It transforms the bankruptcy filer's loose collection of assets into an estate, from which nothing can move until the bankruptcy courts and trustee can resolve disputes.

As an investor, you're frozen too. You can no longer negotiate with the homeowners. The home becomes part of the estate, which may need to be sold to pay outstanding debts. If you're already in the midst of negotiations, you must include in your offer a statement that it's subject to the bankruptcy court's or trustee's approval. Small-claims court (a district court) has the most power in bankruptcy.

In the following sections, I explain the differences between the two main types of bankruptcy you're likely to encounter: Chapter 7 and Chapter 13. Consult an attorney who specializes in bankruptcy for specific rules that apply to bankruptcies in your area. Pay close attention to any rules governing what you're permitted and prohibited from doing as an investor.

Selling assets through Chapter 7 bankruptcy

Homeowners filing for Chapter 7 bankruptcy hand over control of all their assets to a court-appointed trustee. The court empowers the trustee to liquidate the assets to pay any claims against the estate, including back taxes, unpaid mortgages, and credit card debt.

When you're negotiating for the purchase of a home that's part of a Chapter 7 bankruptcy, you deal with a court-appointed trustee. You may present your offer to the homeowners, but that offer must state that it's subject to the trustee's approval.

Restructuring debt through Chapter 13 bankruptcy

In Chapter 13 bankruptcy, people seek to *restructure* their debt — a fancy way of saying that they work out some sort of deal with the people to whom they owe money (the *creditors*). Restructuring may include selling some assets, including the bankruptcy filer's home, assuming they own a home.

REMEMBER

When you're negotiating for the purchase of a home that's part of a Chapter 13 bankruptcy, you deal with the homeowner's attorney and must present your offer to the attorney.

THE VALUE OF A GOOD ATTORNEY

After I purchased a foreclosure property at auction, the homeowner filed for bankruptcy. She had a great attorney. I didn't.

Two courts became involved in the proceedings; the bankruptcy court was dealing with the bankruptcy, while the district court was handling the foreclosure proceedings. Despite the fact that the homeowner had filed for bankruptcy, the district court gave us permission to proceed with the eviction. Shortly after the court-appointed officers showed up at the house to evict the homeowner, the homeowner showed up with her attorney and then proceeded to attack and bite one of the police officers. She was escorted to jail. After her release, she sued everyone involved. The police dropped all charges.

My attorney did a little more research on bankruptcy law and discovered a few additional items that he'd overlooked. We moved the homeowner's possessions back into her house, and the bankruptcy court called an emergency hearing. The bankruptcy judge ordered the district court judge and the court officer who'd been bitten to testify and requested that I testify as well.

After gathering testimony, the judge handed down his verdict. The homeowner was allowed to live in the house for another six months for free, and I was ordered to pay her $20,000.

I had all the right paperwork and all the right judgments but the wrong attorney. He wasn't well versed in bankruptcy. The homeowner, however, had chosen the right attorney, and it made all the difference.

Shop for an attorney the same way you shop for a doctor. A general practitioner is okay for general legal issues, but when you're dealing with bankruptcy, hire a bankruptcy specialist.

Knowing When to Purchase

Acquiring bankruptcy properties requires a great deal of patience. Normally when people buy a house, they present an offer, the seller responds in a day or two, negotiations proceed for a few days, and then the buyer and seller meet at closing and seal the deal. When you make an offer on a property in bankruptcy, the seller may still be able to negotiate with you, but the sale must be approved by the trustee or the courts. In addition, the trustee must notify all creditors of your offer, and they must sign off on it. In many cases, the creditors object to the sale.

Knowing when to purchase a property is often the key to acquiring it. Following are the various stages of the bankruptcy process, along with some tips on how to position yourself effectively at each stage:

>> **Before the bankruptcy filing:** At this stage, you can present your purchase agreement to the homeowners and deal with them as you would if you were following the standard operating procedure of buying a home. Unfortunately, at this stage homeowners who are planning to file for bankruptcy are often reluctant to accept anything less than full market value.

>> **Debtor in possession stage:** Upon filing for bankruptcy, the homeowners remain in possession of the property and can accept offers and negotiate the sale. The bankruptcy attorney or court-appointed trustee, however, is legally obligated to notify the creditors, and they must approve the sale. At this stage, you're even more unlikely to obtain the property for a price significantly below market value.

TIP

>> **Liquidation stage:** At the liquidation stage, control of the property is transferred to the trustee. Unless the judge objects, the trustee is in control of the property and chooses the most attractive offer. This stage is usually the best time to make your move. Although a creditor can object at this point, the trustee has the power to overrule the objection. The trustee also has the power to reject your offer, of course, and hand the property over to one of the creditors. Dealing with the creditors is often your key to acquiring the property at this stage.

>> **Post-liquidation:** If one of the creditors buys or is given the property during the liquidation stage, you may be able to purchase the property from the creditor. This stage is another excellent opportunity to purchase the property, especially if you've established a solid relationship with the creditor.

What happens if the homeowners file for bankruptcy after you've purchased the property at auction? The bankruptcy court may now consider you to be a claimant or creditor, and contacting the homeowners at this point may violate the bankruptcy code. Consult a qualified bankruptcy attorney if you find yourself in such a situation. If you're able to work out a deal with the homeowners, and you manage to structure the deal in a way that gets you more money than you'd otherwise be entitled to, the court may decide that you received a *preference,* which means that you may be required to *disgorge* (pay back) the excess and then some.

WARNING

Never contact the homeowners before consulting an attorney who's well versed in bankruptcy law in your area. In some cases, you may be able to work out a deal that's acceptable to both the homeowners and their creditors, but being in this situation is like tiptoeing through a minefield. If the homeowners perceive you as working on behalf of the lenders to circumvent their bankruptcy protection, they can have you hauled into court, and you're likely to find yourself paying a hefty penalty.

Tracking Down Houses in Bankruptcy

Bankruptcy isn't a private affair. As soon as someone files for bankruptcy, the attorney handling the case records the bankruptcy filing and posts a notice in the local paper or legal publication. This requirement gives you several ways to find out about potentially available properties:

>> Local paper

>> County legal news

>> Bankruptcy filings at the county courthouse

>> Court-appointed bankruptcy trustees

>> Personal bankruptcy attorneys

In the following sections, I show you how to tap these resources for leads on prospective investment properties.

You often obtain some of your best leads on bankruptcy properties by being involved with homeowners during the foreclosure process. Your previous dealings with the homeowners and their lenders give you a significant advantage in the bankruptcy arena, because you know what's going on and already have established relationships with most of the parties who are involved.

As mentioned in "Knowing When to Purchase" earlier in this chapter, when dealing with homeowners who've filed for bankruptcy, be particularly careful. Don't represent yourself as something you're not. If you're not an attorney, let the homeowners know upfront. Tell them that you're an investor who may be able to assist them in working out a win–win transaction. If the homeowners even mention bankruptcy, suggest that they seek independent counsel or ask them to sign a waiver that you offered this suggestion and they decided not to pursue this option. If the relationship sours later, and the homeowners claim that you advised them against seeking counsel, a signed waiver provides you some valuable legal protection.

Skimming publications for bankruptcy notices

In Chapter 7, I direct your attention to foreclosure listings or Notices of Default (NODs) that appear in local papers or your county's legal news publications. You can find bankruptcy notices in these same publications.

Check the Public Notices section of your local newspaper's classifieds to find listings of bankruptcies that have been filed in your area. Your county's legal news publication should also have a section devoted exclusively to bankruptcy filings.

The bankruptcy notice contains the information you need to get started, including the homeowners' names and the attorney's or trustee's name and contact information.

Researching bankruptcy filings

Whether you're looking for leads on properties in bankruptcy or have found a lead and want more information, head down to the bankruptcy court at your county courthouse and ask to see the recent bankruptcy filings. Examine the documents for the following bits of information:

>> Names of the people filing for bankruptcy

>> Whether the couple filed jointly

>> Whether bankruptcy was filed under Chapter 7 or Chapter 13

>> The name of the trustee (if one was appointed)

>> Whether the house is included in the bankruptcy

>> The home's stated value (if included in the filing)

>> How much of the equity can be protected

>> The names of any creditors who've been contacted and whether any of the creditors filed an objection at the confirmation hearing

>> The acting attorney's name and contact information

>> The schedule for proceedings

>> When the property will be placed back on the foreclosure docket (if the bankruptcy hasn't been confirmed)

>> Whether any creditor has moved to lift the stay

TIP

You can subscribe to an online service for access to bankruptcy filings. I use a service called Pacer, which you can find at https://pacer.uscourts.gov.

Networking with the gatekeepers

Personal bankruptcy attorneys and court-appointed trustees are the gatekeepers who protect those who file for bankruptcy from bill collectors and from anyone who's seeking to benefit from their misfortune of having to file for bankruptcy — which includes you.

Although these attorneys may function as speed bumps in your pursuit of investment properties, they can also be valuable assets. They're typically less involved emotionally, making them easier to deal with, and if you show up with the cash necessary to purchase a home and expedite the liquidation process, an attorney may regard you as an ally.

TIP

Get to know the personal bankruptcy attorneys and trustees in your area. Consider sending a letter of introduction to these attorneys, informing them of what you do and explaining your desire to create a mutually beneficial long-term relationship. Figure 14-1 shows a sample letter.

<Your Name>

<Your Address>

<City>, <State> <Zip>

<Date>

<Bankruptcy Attorney's Name>

<Company>

<Address>

<City>, <State> <Zip>

Dear <First Name> <Last Name>:

My name is <Your Name>. I am a real estate investor who regularly works with individuals who are facing foreclosure. They often need information about bankruptcy laws and regulations and legal advice about the proper course of action to take.

I believe we can create a win-win situation by working together to help my clients. You would win from the business I could refer to you. I would win because I believe that once you completely understand what I do, you will send referrals to me. And we both win by being kept fully informed about the progress of clients we refer to each other.

For your review, I have enclosed a few letters from people I have helped in the past. Once you have had a chance to look over these materials, I will give you a call to discuss the possibility of building a mutually beneficial relationship.

In the meantime, please give me a call at <Your Phone Number> or email me at <Your Email Address> if you have any questions. I look forward to speaking with you soon.

FIGURE 14-1:
Introduce
yourself to the
attorneys in your
area who deal
with
bankruptcies.

Sincerely,

<Your Signature>

<Your Name>

Foreclosure Specialist

Dealing with the Gatekeepers

To acquire a property that ends up in bankruptcy court, you need to serve two masters: the bankruptcy attorney or trustee and the homeowners. In bankruptcy, the legal people are your main contacts at this point, but if you were working with the homeowners before the date on which they filed for bankruptcy, you can use your relationship with them to influence the decisions.

In the following sections, I provide some tips on how to team up effectively with court-appointed trustees, personal bankruptcy attorneys, and homeowners to liquidate assets and perhaps purchase the home.

WARNING

Don't toss around terms when you're unsure of their meaning. Terms that have an everyday meaning to us common folk may have an entirely different meaning to an attorney. If an attorney thinks that you're both using the term the same way, the two of you create a disconnect that may lead to a costly miscommunication. This miscommunication can compromise your credibility if the attorney realizes that you don't know what you're talking about and are simply blowing smoke.

Cooperating with bankruptcy trustees

In deed-of-trust states, the court appoints a trustee to carry out the liquidation of property, maximize the amount that goes to the creditors, and dismiss as many claims from creditors as possible. In other words, the court passes control of the situation to the trustee and essentially says, "You sort out this mess in a way that's fairly equitable for all parties involved."

REMEMBER

When dealing with a trustee, realize that this person has a court mandate to sell the property for as much money as possible in a relatively short period of time. As an investor, the best approach is to present a fair offer that gives you a sufficient profit and doesn't turn the trustee against you. If your offer is laughable, you not only risk losing this property, but also jeopardize any future relationship with the trustee.

Teaming up with bankruptcy attorneys

Bankruptcy attorneys serve both their clients and themselves. Most of their clients don't have deep pockets, so the longer the proceedings drag on, the less they earn per hour. This fact gives you some room to haggle. Realize, however, that your haggle room varies greatly, depending on the attorney's motivation and skill. The attorney may be more self-centered or client-centered:

>> **Self-interested attorney:** Self-interested attorneys are more motivated to serve themselves. These attorneys typically file bankruptcy for anyone who's interested in filing, regardless of whether the homeowners qualify or will benefit from it. These attorneys simply want to make money and may pressure the homeowner to sell the property quickly. These situations are often attractive to investors like you.

>> **Homeowner-centered attorney:** Homeowner-centered attorneys truly represent the homeowner's best interests. They won't file for bankruptcy if the homeowner is unlikely to qualify, and they won't let an investor push the homeowner around. These attorneys know how to play the legal system and can make your life a living hell if you're not pitching what the attorney considers to be a fair offer.

Getting the homeowners on your side

Bankruptcy protects homeowners from bill collectors and anyone else who may be perceived as pressuring the homeowners for money or property, including you. If you try to skirt the law and strike a deal with the homeowners, you could find yourself in front of a judge and facing a stiff penalty. Before contacting the homeowners, take the following precautions:

>> **Contact your attorney.** Hire an attorney who specializes in bankruptcy, and obtain advice on whether you have the legal right to contact the homeowners directly. Also ask for advice and guidelines on how to approach the homeowners and ask what you're permitted and prohibited from doing as an investor when homeowners have bankruptcy protection.

>> **Contact the trustee or homeowner's attorney.** Always keep the trustee or homeowners' attorney in the loop. Present any offer to the trustee or attorney to obtain court approval for the sale.

By establishing a strong relationship with the homeowners, as discussed in Chapter 9, you place yourself in a great position to purchase the property eventually, should the homeowners choose to sell it. But don't compromise your good position by trying to work around the bankruptcy attorney or trustee.

Getting the creditors on your side

Homeowners often file for bankruptcy in response to a lender (creditor) that initiates the foreclosure process. The homeowners are rarely looking for a way to restructure their payments, and the finance-restructuring plans they and their attorneys submit are usually flawed. They're often designed not to enable the homeowner to pay the creditors, but to keep the house without paying.

Needless to say, most lenders aren't content to patiently watch the bankruptcy proceedings run their course. The lender often challenges the bankruptcy claim and seeks to have the stay lifted so that it can proceed with the foreclosure process. In many cases, the lender succeeds.

TIP

When a lender is successful in lifting a stay, the bankruptcy is simply a speed bump on your path to obtaining the property. You may be able to use this speed bump to your advantage. As soon as the homeowners file for bankruptcy and the auctioning of that property is adjourned, many investors lose interest and drop out. If the stay is lifted and the foreclosure proceeds, you may be the only one bidding on the property at auction, and you can buy the property without the worry of a bankruptcy stay. Keep tracking properties, especially when an auction is adjourned, so that you're prepared to bid in the event that the property pops back up on the auction block.

Dealing with Bankruptcy Delays on a House You Bought

Although you can work the bankruptcy system to your advantage by purchasing properties through the trustee or the homeowners' attorney, bankruptcy can often delay your ability to take possession of a house that you bought at auction. If the bankruptcy court grants a stay, you may be stuck holding a house and paying the bills while the homeowners remain in possession well past the expiration of the redemption period.

In the worst-case scenario, your profit is limited to the interest you charge the homeowners on the purchase price you paid. If the homeowners manage to redeem the property, they must pay you the purchase price plus interest and reimburse you for any property taxes and homeowner's insurance you paid out of pocket.

To sweeten the deal and increase your profit on the property, the best approach is to pitch a deal to the homeowners' attorney or the bankruptcy trustee. Following are a couple of suggested deals that the homeowners and the court/trustee may find appealing:

>> **Offer to lease the property to the homeowners.** The homeowners and the courts typically want to avoid a situation in which the homeowners are evicted and have no place to live. By offering to lease the property to the homeowners for a fixed period, you demonstrate your sensitivity to their needs and give them a little extra time to find new living arrangements.

>> **Structure a buy-back deal.** To avoid a long bankruptcy delay, consider selling the property back to the homeowners at a profit that's perhaps less than what you had hoped for. Why would the homeowners be willing to buy back the house? Challenging the sale can be costly both in time and money. If the attorney involved can see the benefit of a sure deal that will cost less in the long run and ensures payment of all legal fees, the attorney may be willing to accept it. A sure deal looks pretty good next to the alternative: a lengthy and expensive courtroom battle with little to no compensation for the attorney.

When you meet up with a determined and well-qualified bankruptcy attorney, be prepared to negotiate. I've had to deal with these attorneys, and you can benefit from my experience, as related in the nearby sidebar "Playing nice with the sharks."

REMEMBER

As a general rule, I don't like to be involved in bankruptcy buys, not because there isn't money to be made, but because I find that other investment opportunities are much more attractive and give me fewer headaches. Many real estate investors like me also shy away from bankruptcy properties, and that's exactly the reason why some investors are so successful in this area: They have less competition. If you do decide to work in the bankruptcy arena, develop a strong knowledge of how bankruptcy works in your area, and don't go it alone; hire an experienced bankruptcy attorney to serve as your Sherpa.

PLAYING NICE WITH THE SHARKS

When you're dealing with a knowledgeable, skilled bankruptcy attorney who's sincerely representing the best the clients' best interests, you'd better learn to play nice. I learned my lesson the hard way. I hope that you'll learn the easy way, by heeding my warning and reading my story.

I bought a house at auction and got a pretty good deal on it. About a week before the expiration of the redemption period, I received notice that the homeowners had filed for bankruptcy. "No biggie," I thought. I'd seen this situation before. It simply meant that I'd have to wait a little longer to take possession of the property. At least, that's what I thought.

To my dismay, the homeowners had found an attorney who really knew how bankruptcy worked and how to use it to his clients' advantage. Looking back, I commend the attorney for fighting so strongly and so wisely, but at the time, he was a pain in my shorts and my wallet. He managed to drag out the case for weeks on end. While his clients remained firmly planted in the house, I was footing the bill.

Just when I thought we'd be wrapping up the whole thing, I was told that the homeowners would be seeking a jury trial. Now, I'm no attorney, and I don't know what entitles you to a jury trial, but I knew that a jury would quickly see me as the big bad investor preying on the helpless insolvent homeowners, even though the homeowners got themselves into this mess and I did everything by the book. To add insult to injury, the attorney whispered to me at the preliminary hearing that the judge scheduled to hear the case was heading to China for a three-week vacation.

I almost popped a gasket. I'd done everything right, I had to defend myself in court, and now I was going to have to wait for Marco Polo to return from China to hear my case! That night, I stewed the defensiveness right out of me and decided to stop fighting the system. The next time the attorney contacted me, I asked him, "Do your clients want to just buy back the house so we can put this behind us?" The attorney responded, "I thought you'd never ask! We can probably wrap this all up before Her Honor goes on holiday."

The attorney was able to structure a deal for his clients that allowed them to keep their house, and I was able to make a fair profit on the buy-back price. We obtained court approval, and the whole fiasco disappeared as quickly as it surfaced. The attorney and I have since developed a relationship, and he explains to me that he could easily have kept that property tied up in the courts for two years, and maybe I wouldn't have gotten the house.

The moral of the story is that when you encounter a stubborn attorney who knows the law, don't dig in your heels and flex your muscles. You may need to take a different approach. Keep your eyes on the prize — in this case, the profit — and don't let anger or self-righteousness drive you into taking a no-win stance. Remain flexible and look for win–win solutions.

Chapter **15**

Sampling Some Other Foreclosure Strategies

Throughout most of this book, I encourage you to purchase properties directly from homeowners before auction or to bid on properties at auction — to purchase senior liens. You can also make money in foreclosures and improve your position as an investor by

» **Negotiating short sales:** Persuading lenders to accept a payoff of less than the full amount owed

» **Purchasing junior liens:** Acquiring second mortgages and other claims against the property

» **Acquiring tax deeds or liens:** Paying back taxes to obtain a tax deed or lien against the property

These strategies may even enable you to earn a profit without ever taking possession of the property and having to deal with the hassles of owning, selling, or leasing the property. They can also strengthen your position in acquiring the senior lien and eventually taking possession of the property.

Buying junior liens without buying the senior lien is risky. If another investor buys the senior lien, and foreclosure wipes out the junior liens, you can end up owning a worthless piece of paper. Don't buy junior liens until you've read the following section and have some experience buying senior liens.

Negotiating Short Sales

Your parents probably told you "never to sell yourself short," meaning that you shouldn't accept less than you're worth. When you're investing in foreclosures, however, you want the lienholders to sell themselves short by agreeing to negotiate *short sales* — transactions in which they accept less than the amount of money they're owed.

Lienholders who stand to lose something if a property goes into foreclosure are often willing to accept less money than they're owed. After all, less is better than nothing, and it's better than continuing to throw good money after bad.

In the following sections, I reveal the hierarchy of lienholders so that you know which liens hold the most weight in foreclosure. I show you how to recognize situations that are ideal short-sales opportunities. Then I guide you through the process of collaborating with the homeowners and lienholders to structure a deal that meets the needs of everyone involved, including you.

Don't start negotiating short sales until you've done your research on the property, as discussed in Chapter 8, and you've carefully researched the title. If you overlook a single lien on a property, that omission can come back to bite you — or at least bite a big chunk out of your profit.

Knowing the lienholder pecking order

Lienholders all lay claim to a property, but all liens are not created equal. Here's how the process works. Suppose that a property has a market value of $300,000. The owners owe $230,000 on the first mortgage, $20,000 on a second mortgage, $15,000 in property taxes, and $10,000 in federal taxes. At auction, the winning bid is $250,000. The property taxes are paid first (in full), leaving $235,000. The holder of the first mortgage receives payment in full of $230,000. That leaves only $5,000. Assuming that the holder of the second mortgage applies for their lien, they get the remaining $5,000 but not the other $15,000 they're owed. Nothing is left for the feds, and they typically drop their claim after the property changes hands, or it drops off automatically 10 to 15 years after the date when it was placed on the property.

Note that if any money remains after all lienholders who claim what they're owed are paid, that remaining money is considered to be an *overbid*. The foreclosed-on homeowners are entitled to that money, but they must contact the county clerk's office and file a claim for it.

Think of lienholder positions as the values of cards in a deck of playing cards:

>> **Ace:** The property tax collector generally holds the ace, because foreclosure can wipe out all liens except the property tax lien. If you can purchase the tax lien, you almost always hold controlling interest in the property. The tax lienholder, however, must adhere to some strict regulations regarding the notification of other lienholders.

>> **King:** The lender with the first mortgage holds the king. The first-mortgage holder can always pay any property taxes that are due, purchase the property at auction if nobody bids on it, wait for the redemption period to expire (to wipe out the junior liens), and then sell the property.

>> **Ten:** The lender who owns the second mortgage (if a second mortgage is in place) holds a ten but is in a very weak position and will receive payment only if money remains after the property taxes and the first mortgage are paid in full, and they claim the remaining money (which they don't always do). If you buy a second mortgage at auction, you're likely to lose your entire investment unless you also buy the first mortgage at auction or redeem the property from the first-mortgage holder after the auction. Some states have no redemption period. (See Chapter 2 for more about the foreclosure process and redemption, and turn to the appendix for specifics about the foreclosure process in your state.)

When you're starting out, buy only first mortgages (senior liens). If you buy junior liens (commonly referred to as *seconds*), you have a very strong chance of losing your entire investment. As you gain experience, you can buy a second mortgage — but only if it gives you great leverage to control the first mortgage.

>> **Three:** Construction (mechanic's) lienholders typically are the big losers in foreclosure. Because foreclosure wipes out their position, they become more and more motivated to negotiate a short sale as the foreclosure sale or the end of the redemption period looms. If the homeowners agreed to put up the construction asset as collateral for the loan, however, the lienholder may qualify for a step up in position. Suppose that the homeowners took out a loan to build a new room on the house. That new room may be what's called a *purchase-money security interest* (PMSI), and the construction lienholder can lay claim to it. This situation is very complicated, so if you encounter it, consult your attorney.

>> **Two:** Legally speaking, the Internal Revenue Service (IRS) may have a stronger position than the second-mortgage or construction lienholders, but they rarely step in and buy the property, so they hold the weakest card in the deck. The IRS must be notified and offered the chance to purchase the property, but that's not likely to stop an auction from going forward.

The IRS can't force you to pay someone else's taxes and can't seize your property in lieu of those taxes. If you buy a property that has a federal tax lien against it, just make sure that the IRS has been notified of the change in ownership. If the IRS doesn't remove its lien, the lien will fall off 10 to 15 years from the date when it was attached to the property.

The lien hierarchy is determined primarily by the dates on which loans are recorded against a property. The property tax lien is the strongest position, typically followed by a first mortgage (because that's the loan the homeowners took out to buy the property) and then other loans in order of the dates on which the loans ere recorded. In other words, if the homeowners took out a first mortgage to buy the house, then financed new windows, and then took out a second mortgage, you'd probably be looking at the following hierarchy (listed from strongest to weakest):

>> Property tax lien (strongest)

>> First mortgage

>> Construction loan (new windows)

>> Second mortgage (weakest)

Exceptions can always exist, of course. The window company, for example, may have subordinated its position to the second-mortgage holder (as often happens), or the holder of the second mortgage may pay the window company to step up into its position. Check the dates of recording on the mortgages and look for any wording that specifically states whether one mortgage is subordinate to another.

Don't confuse the date when the mortgage was taken out with the date when it was recorded. If a mortgage is taken out in June 2005 and isn't recorded until June 2006, and in between those two dates, another mortgage is taken out and recorded, the mortgage taken out in June 2005 loses its priority position. Other conditions and exceptions may come into play, so when you're starting out, consult a real estate attorney who has plenty of experience deciphering titles and mortgages.

The lienholder pecking order is important because it determines the winners and losers after the auction — who gets paid and who doesn't. Suppose that a $200,000 property has a $6,000 tax lien against it, a $140,000 first mortgage, a $20,000 second mortgage, and a construction lien of $10,000. At the tax sale, an investor may bid $160,000 for the $6,000 tax lien. The tax collector gets the first $6,000, the first-mortgage lender gets $140,000, the second-mortgage lender gets $14,000, and the holder of the construction lien walks away with nothing.

This example is a little odd, because the first-mortgage holder probably would pay the $6,000 in back taxes to protect its position rather than let an investor buy the tax lien. I provide the example only to illustrate who ends up with money and who doesn't, based on the strength of their claims to the property.

REMEMBER

Tax sale rules vary from state to state. In some states, the tax sale wipes out all other liens, so if you buy the property at a tax sale, anything you pay in excess of the taxes owed on the property goes to the state, and the other lienholders receive nothing. Before the tax sale, of course, the other lienholders must be notified that their claims to the property will be wiped out by the tax sale, so any lienholder with a major interest in the property is likely to pony up the unpaid taxes. Consult your real estate attorney to find out more about how tax sales are handled in your area.

Wheeling and dealing with lienholders

The lienholder pecking order is also very important to know when you're dealing with multiple lienholders, all of whom are trying to protect their positions. Keep in mind that any lienholder who's lower in the pecking order has the right to buy out the positions of the other lienholders simply by paying off the balance of the money owed them, along with any interest and associated costs.

Suppose that three lienholders — A, B, and C — have a stake in a property, with A holding the highest position and C holding the lowest. Depending on how much equity is built up in the property, any of several scenarios can develop, including the following:

>> You buy A's position (either at auction or directly from A) and wait for the redemption period to expire. B and C take no action, and their positions are wiped out.

>> You buy A's position. B buys you out to protect its position and waits for redemption period to expire to wipe out C's position. You have to sell, but you don't have to discount, so you should at least get your money back.

>> You buy A's position. C buys out both you and B to protect its position.

>> Another investor buys A's position. You buy B's position, giving you the right to buy A's position from the other investor, which you do, forcing C to either buy you out or lose out entirely.

>> You buy A's position and then buy B's and C's positions (typically by paying them less than the total of what they're owed via a short-sale agreement). Why buy out B and C? If the property has a lot of equity in it, buying out B and C prevents them from buying your position; it also prevents other investors from buying B's or C's position and then attempting to buy you out.

>> You buy A's position. Then, during the redemption period, the homeowner redeems the property (buys you out).

As you can see, the wheeling and dealing can get pretty complicated. Later in this chapter, in "Negotiating with the lienholders," I show you how a typical negotiation is likely to play out.

Recognizing a short-sale opportunity

Some scenarios are more conducive to short sales than others. If the property has little equity in it and is unlikely to draw bids at auction, the senior lienholder is looking at getting stuck with the hassle and cost of preparing the property for market and selling it. That lienholder may prefer to accept less than the full amount owed just to cut its losses.

If the senior lienholder has no reason to bargain, you may be able to strengthen your negotiating position by working out short-sale agreements with junior lienholders. If a bank holds the senior lien on a very valuable piece of property, for example, the bank probably won't accept less than the full amount owed on the property. By persuading junior lienholders to accept less than the full amount owed on their loans, you may place yourself in a position in which you can afford to buy out the senior lienholder's position. Following are descriptions of situations that are excellent opportunities for negotiating short sales with junior lienholders:

>> **The property has two or more liens on it, and the senior lienholder is foreclosing.** This process starts the clock ticking for the junior lienholders. Unless they purchase the senior lienholder's position, they stand to lose everything. An offer from an investor like you to a junior lienholder, even if that offer is for 30 or 40 cents on the dollar, is better than nothing.

>> **Unpaid taxes have driven the homeowners into foreclosure.** Again, the junior lienholders are in the unsavory position of having their interests wiped off the books.

>> **The senior lien is larger than any of the junior liens.** If a junior lienholder has more to lose than the senior lienholder, the junior lienholder is likely to buy the senior lienholder's position rather than negotiate with you for pennies on the dollar. When the senior lien is much larger, however, the junior lienholder rarely ties up more of its money by buying the senior lien position and is more likely to negotiate with you.

>> **Multiple junior lienholders lay claim to the property, but the senior lien isn't worth more than 75 percent of the property's market value.** All the liens can total more than the house is worth, but if the senior lien position gives you at least a 25 percent profit margin to negotiate, the lienholders should be willing to work with you.

Teaming up with the homeowners

You can't negotiate short sales without the homeowners' cooperation. They must sign a release (provided in Chapter 9) giving you permission to discuss their finances with the lienholders and negotiate short sales on their behalf. Let the homeowners know that by empowering you to negotiate the short sales, they retain more control of the situation and may be able to avoid foreclosure, and if they eventually decide to sell the property to you, they stand to earn more money from the transaction.

REMEMBER

You may be able to purchase a lienholder's position directly from the lienholder without the consent or cooperation of the homeowners. But if you're working on behalf of the homeowners, most lienholders can't and won't discuss the situation with you until they have a signed authorization from the homeowners. If you happen upon a lender that's willing to sell you seconds (second lienholder positions), keep the information under lock and key; buying seconds can be an effective strategy for gaining control of a property. See "Buying and Selling Junior Liens" later in this chapter.

Before you start calling lienholders, consider how you're going to profit from the short sales. You can profit in any of the following three ways:

>> **Buy the house.** Present the homeowners your offer to purchase the property, conditioned on your ability to negotiate the short sale successfully. See Chapter 10 for details on presenting your purchase agreement.

>> **Charge the homeowners for your services.** Contract with the homeowners to negotiate the short sales for a fee. Consult your real estate attorney to draw up a suitable contract.

>> **Foreclose on the house yourself.** If the homeowners aren't willing to work with you, you can still negotiate with the lenders and perhaps purchase the first-position, giving you the right to foreclose and ultimately take possession of the property. You can even buy a junior lien and foreclose on the house, but be careful: Check out "Buying and Selling Junior Liens" later in this chapter before attempting this strategy.

WARNING

Without a purchase agreement in place, you may negotiate the short sales and save the homeowners from foreclosure only to have them say thanks and cut you out of the deal. Unless you own the property tax lien or the first-mortgage lien, always have a signed purchase agreement with the homeowner or a signed contract stating how the homeowners will pay you if you're successful in negotiating a short sale that saves them from foreclosure.

Gathering payoff amounts

The first step in negotiating short sales consists of gathering some basic information: the amount required to pay off each loan in full by a specific date. Call each lienholder and ask for an explanation of the procedure for requesting payoff amounts.

In most cases, you'll be asked to fax or mail a letter to the lienholder. In your letter, provide the following information:

>> Borrowers' names

>> Account number

>> Property address

>> Payoff date

>> Your contact information

>> The signed release from the homeowners giving the lender permission to share the information with you

>> A request that the payoff letter be faxed or mailed to you

WARNING

Specify a payoff date that's at least one month away or a day or two before the homeowners are due to lose their home in foreclosure, so that you have time to negotiate with other lienholders. All your negotiations should be wrapped up before the payoff date; otherwise, a lienholder may retract its offer. Give yourself plenty of time to negotiate.

Crunching the numbers

When you receive the payoff letters from the lienholders, you know exactly how much the homeowners will owe on the payoff date. With this information in hand, you're ready to calculate the total amount required to pay off all balances in full. Use the form in Figure 15-1 to perform your calculations. Figure 15-2 shows a completed form.

Property Owner Names: _____

Property Location: _____

Foreclosure Sale/Redemption Date: _____

Payoff Date: _____

Property Value: _____

Lienholder Name	Payoff Amount
_____	_____
_____	_____
_____	_____
_____	_____
_____	_____
Total	

FIGURE 15-1: Calculate the total payoff amount.

Property Owner Names: <u>Liz and Peter Henderson</u>

Property Location: <u>1313 Mockingbird Lane</u>

Foreclosure Sale/Redemption Date: <u>May 31</u>

Payoff Date: <u>May 20</u>

Property Value: <u>$300,000</u>

Lienholder Name	Payoff Amount
City Mortgage (first mortgage)	$168,698.84
Capital Source (second mortgage)	$78,416.32
Jackson Heating & Cooling	$21,360.00
Internal Revenue Service	$33,606.86
Total	**$302,082.02**

FIGURE 15-2: Calculate the total payoff amount.

If you don't know how much you're prepared to pay for the property, see Chapter 10 to find out how to project your profit and determine the maximum amount you're willing to pay. Then you can work backward to adjust the short-sale payoff amounts.

TIP

As a general rule, the lower the lienholder's position in the pecking order, the bigger the discount it's likely to accept.

Suppose that you use the deal analysis worksheet in Chapter 10 to perform your calculations and decide that your top offer for the property will be $223,200. Using the information shown in Figure 15-2, you can work backward to identify opportunities for short sales:

>> The balance on the first mortgage from City Mortgage is $168,698.84. Because the estimated property value is $300,000, City Mortgage is highly unlikely to agree to a short sale; it would be better off owning the property. You're going to have to pay the full $168,698.84. That leaves you about $54,501.16 for paying off the other lienholders without exceeding your top offer of $223,200.

>> Capital Source holds the second mortgage of $78,416.32 — a perfect opportunity for a short sale. Capital Source stands to lose the entire amount of the foreclosure proceeds to conclusion and the homeowners fail to redeem the property. Capital Source may be willing to accept $48,000 to assign the lien to you, in which case the homeowners owe you the $78,416.32, which places you in a prime position to buy the first mortgage at auction. See the following section, "Negotiating with the lienholders," for details.

>> Jackson Heating & Cooling holds a construction lien of $21,360.00. It's in a very weak position and is unlikely to buy the first mortgage of $168,698.84 to protect its position, so it would be very likely to sell you its position for $4,000 to $6,000.

>> The IRS is also unlikely to invest $168,698.84 to protect its $33,606.86 position. The IRS can't force you to pay someone else's taxes or seize your property in lieu of payment. If you acquire the property at auction, let the IRS know about it. The agency will either remove its lien or the lien will fall off automatically 10 to 15 years after the date on which it was placed on the property.

Assuming that your negotiations unfold according to plan, you pay City Mortgage $168,698.84, Capital Source $48,000, and Jackson Heating & Cooling a cool $6,000 (at most), for a grand total of $222,698.84, slightly below your target of $223,200.

Negotiating with the lienholders

When you know where all the lienholders stand, you can begin calling them and negotiating your short sales. You can't negotiate the property tax lien, but you can negotiate short sales on the other liens. The following sections provide guidance on how to proceed, but every situation is different, so use your noodle and plan the strategy that you think is likely to be most effective.

TIP

If you have a purchase agreement signed by the homeowners stipulating that the sale of the property hinges on your ability to negotiate a short sale successfully, present copies to the lienholders. Explain that you're structuring a deal to minimize the lienholders' losses and that all lienholders must agree to the deal for it to succeed — and for them to receive payment.

If the property has a property tax lien against it, use that fact to your negotiating advantage. Tell the lenders that if they don't work with you, they can expect to incur another expense of $10,000 (or however much the tax lien is), which subtly informs the lenders that they can automatically offer you a $10,000 discount without losing anything. To make the process worth your while, request a discount in excess of what's owed in property taxes. If the lender discounts from $50,000 down to $40,000, and you have to pay $10,000 in taxes, you're not getting anything. If the lender discounts down to $34,000 or $36,000, you immediately increase your profit margin. Crunch the numbers, stick to your guns, and remember that the closer you get to the date on which the junior lienholder is scheduled to lose everything, the more negotiating power you have. Just be sure that you'll be able to act quickly and buy the first mortgage to protect your position; otherwise, you'll lose everything.

When you're buying liens, request an assignment of interest or assignment of lien or mortgage from the lienholder, and have your attorney look it over and approve it before you proceed (and before you hand over the check). After obtaining the assignment, run it down to the Register of Deeds or county clerk's office to have it recorded.

Notifying the IRS first

The IRS is often willing to release its lien on the property, simply because it's not all that interested in buying the first lien to protect its position. In addition, the IRS may be able to pursue the homeowners for unpaid taxes even if its lien is wiped out by the foreclosure.

Call your local IRS field office and request the name and contact information for the person who's in charge of real estate liens. Call that person, and ask whether the IRS would release its lien if the property changes hands. Unless the amount owed to the IRS is huge and the property is worth enough to justify the IRS's paying off the first lien, the agency is likely to agree to release its lien. Just make sure to get the release in writing.

REMEMBER

The IRS is likely to release its lien and usually takes the longest to get back with you, so contact the IRS first. While you're waiting to hear from the IRS, continue negotiating with the other lienholders.

Dealing with first-mortgage lenders

Because the first-mortgage holder is near the top of the lienholder pecking order (just below the property tax lien), it acts as puppet master, pulling the strings that control the entire outcome. In some cases, however, even the first lienholder's position can be weakened, such as in the following scenarios:

>> **The property isn't worth significantly more than the first-mortgage payoff.** If the property is worth $200,00, and the loan balance is only $175,000, the bank is unlikely to profit much by taking possession of the property and selling it. The repairs and holding costs alone are likely to gobble up that $25,000, and the bank won't want the hassle.

>> **The unpaid property taxes are high.** Remember that the property tax collector gets paid first. If the homeowners owe $60,000 in property taxes on a house that's worth $300,000, and the first-mortgage balance is $210,000, the bank would have to pay $270,000 to acquire the property and would stand to gain a maximum of $30,000 minus the costs to repair and sell the property.

If you crunch the numbers, and the result shows that first lienholder has something to lose or at least nothing to gain from the foreclosure, contact that lienholder, lay out the numbers, and consider offering to buy its position for less than the full payoff amount. As soon as you take possession of the first lien and pay the back taxes, you have control of the property. If the homeowners refuse to sell the property to you, you can foreclose on them. Even if they redeem the property, you earn a profit, because you purchased the note for less than the full payoff amount, and they're on the hook for that full amount.

WARNING

Don't overlook the tax lien. If you purchase the first mortgage and forget to pay any property taxes that are due, another investor can buy the tax lien and cut you out of the deal. Make sure that nobody has purchased the tax lien, and calculate the back taxes into the equation. You want to make sure that if the homeowners do redeem the property, you're still in a position to profit from the deal.

Contacting construction lienholders

Construction lienholders, such as Jackson Heating & Cooling (refer to Figure 15-2), are often difficult to deal with. They've been stiffed by the homeowners, and their emotions run high. They may not understand the foreclosure process and are often reluctant to deal with an investor who's offering pennies on the dollar.

The most effective way to negotiate a short sale with a lienholder who's in a weak position is to let the facts speak for themselves. With Jackson Heating & Cooling, for example, you could say something like this: "I'm negotiating with the senior lienholder. If they agree to sell to me, I won't need to buy your position at all. If you decide to sell to me before I work out a deal with the senior lienholder, I'll honor that deal. You could pay off the first and second mortgages to the tune of $247,115.16, foreclose on the property, and hope to recover your loss by selling it, but that's a costly proposition both in time and money. You could do nothing, and I can almost guarantee that you'll lose your entire $21,360 at the foreclosure sale. Or you can accept my offer of $6,000. I'm not trying to play hardball, but I want to give you the option to make an informed decision. I understand the position you're in with not being paid for the quality work you've done."

Any reasonable person would take the $6,000.

Contacting other major lenders

Lenders who hold second- or third-lien positions on the house (second or third mortgages) are next in line to get paid. The first challenge you face in dealing with these lienholders is tracking down the decision-maker. At a larger bank, ask to speak with the manager of the foreclosures or loss mitigation department. At smaller banks, ask to speak with the person in charge of buying and selling mortgages.

Dealing with major lenders is often easier than dealing with small businesses, such as those that may be holding construction liens, because major lenders know how the game is played and are often less emotionally involved. They take a rational look at the numbers, know what they have to lose in foreclosure, and understand what they have to gain by working with you. Major lenders are often willing to sell you the mortgage note (promise to pay) at a discount to cut their losses and pass the problem along to you.

Take a look at the numbers in Figure 15-2. Capital Source holds the second mortgage of $78,416.32, which it stands to lose in foreclosure. It's going to be highly motivated to agree to a short sale so that it walks away with something.

Suppose that the IRS releases its lien of $33,606.86, and Jackson Heating & Cooling sells its position to you for $6,000. Now you have $48,501.16 remaining to buy

Capital Source's position and hit your target of paying $223,200 for the house. Sure, your offer is $30,000 short of the second-mortgage payoff amount, but Capital Source gets a sure thing — more than $48,000 — and doesn't have to worry about losing everything in foreclosure.

Capital Source can respond to your generous offer in any of several ways:

>> **Reject it outright.** This outcome isn't likely, because you showed the lender the numbers, and this offer is the most it can hope to get out of the deal.

>> **Release the lien.** The lender agrees to accept your offer as full payment. You pay off City Mortgage. You pay Jackson Heating & Cooling its $6,000, and the IRS releases its lien. You close on the house and are now the proud owner of an investment property.

>> **Assign the mortgage note to you.** Assigning the mortgage note consists of passing the ownership of the debt to you, which places you in an excellent position to buy the first mortgage at auction. You don't even have to pay Jackson Heating & Cooling the $6,000, because now you hold a higher lien position. That extra money can come in handy when auction day rolls around.

The concept of assigning a mortgage note is a little complicated, so here's an example of how it could play out in our example:

>> You buy the mortgage assignment for $48,000.

>> When the first mortgage goes up for auction, bidding is likely to start at about $168,698.84 — the full payoff amount to City Mortgage.

>> You bid $247,000, because you own the $78,416.32 debt assigned to you by Capital Source. (The $168,698.84 first mortgage plus the $78,416.32 debt assignment equals $247,115.16.) Why bid so high? See the next bullet item.

>> Nobody is likely to outbid you because the profit margin just isn't there, but if someone does outbid you, you still profit. Here's how: By bidding $247,000, you guarantee yourself an overbid of about $78,000. If nobody outbids you, you own the house and then can apply for the $78,000 in overbid money, which you're eligible for as the second lienholder. You end up paying about $216,000 for the house ($168,000 plus the $48,000 you paid to Capital Source). If someone outbids you, you still collect the $78,000 overbid. Subtract the $48,000 you paid for the assignment of debt, and you earn a $30,000 profit free and clear.

How do you earn a $30,000 profit? Doesn't that overbid money go to the homeowner? Overbids are paid out first to the lienholders. The homeowner is the last in line to receive anything, assuming that any money is left over. When you negotiated with Capital Source to accept $48,000 in payment to assign its mortgage note of $78,000 to you, you set yourself up to earn $30,000 in the event that anyone bid at least $247,000 on the first mortgage.

So what happens to Jackson Heating & Cooling's lien? It's wiped off the books, because that lien is paid only if the overbid exceeds the amounts needed to pay off the first and second lienholders.

Buying and Selling Junior Liens

One of the most common and costly mistakes that novice investors make at auctions is buying a junior lien thinking that they're buying a property. Because junior liens are often wiped out by foreclosure, these uninformed investors often purchase a worthless piece of paper. If you know what you're doing, however, you can purchase seconds (junior liens) to gain control of a property or even earn a profit without taking possession of the property.

WARNING

Don't buy a junior lien without buying the senior lien and paying any overdue property taxes as well. If someone else buys a lien that's higher up in the pecking order, you stand to lose your entire investment if you don't buy them out before the end of the redemption period. If your area has no redemption period or the redemption period expires before you redeem the senior lienholder, you lose all your money. I strongly urge novice investors not to buy junior liens until they've gained some experience buying senior liens.

Buying junior liens to foreclose for a quick payday

Some investors like to roll the dice and gamble on buying *seconds* (junior liens) at a discount in the hope that the homeowners will redeem the liens to avoid losing their homes. This strategy offers several benefits:

>> Nobody else wants them.

>> They're affordable — typically, $4,000 to $30,000 instead of $200,000 or more.

>> Most of the time, the homeowners redeem the junior lien, which means that you earn the difference between what you paid for the lien and the foreclosed-on amount — usually, the face value of the lien plus interest. Because the interest rate on junior liens is typically higher than the interest rate on first mortgages, even if you earn only the interest, you'll usually get a better return on your money than you would if you'd invested it elsewhere.

>> If the homeowners don't redeem, the equity in the property may be sufficient to buy the first mortgage and recoup your investment plus a profit — definitely something you want to know before you buy.

>> You gain a controlling position in the property.

Buying junior liens, however, has several drawbacks, including these:

>> If most homeowners redeem, you rarely gain possession of the property.

>> If someone else buys a senior lien, you stand to lose your entire investment.

To take advantage of this strategy, search for junior liens that are in default already or that will soon be in default. If the homeowners continue to make payments on the loan, you can't foreclose. As you can see, this strategy is a bit of a gamble.

WITNESSING A TRAIN WRECK

At one auction I attended, I noticed a new buyer who seemed very interested in a property that I knew was a second mortgage. Out of love for my fellow man, I asked him whether he knew what he was buying. From his response, I could tell that he was a newbie. I told him that he was going to bid on a second and asked whether he knew what that meant. I wasn't able to persuade him that he was making a mistake, but it was his money.

I made one last attempt, I said, "Tell you what — you give me half of what you're going to bid today; I'll punch you in the gut as hard as I can; and in six months, you'll look back and thank me. Or you can buy that second, and in six months, when you're tens of thousands of dollars poorer, you can wish you'd listened to me." My attempt didn't work. I think he thought I was competing for the property and trying to persuade him to bow out.

I ran into the same guy about a year and a half later and asked him how his investment turned out. "Not well," he said.

"How much?" I asked.

"Around $18,000 and eight months of headaches," he replied, "I should have taken that punch in the gut. In fact, I'd take a kick a little lower if I could get that money back." I just laughed, but this situation is no laughing matter. Know what you're buying and avoid buying yourself in over your head.

WARNING

Never buy a second mortgage if you're not prepared to pay off the first mortgage or walk away from the deal, chalking up your investment as a loss.

Personally, I'm not fond of this strategy. For me, having controlling interest in the property is my prime motivation for buying a second. By purchasing the second, I force the senior lienholder to deal with me, and I can always pay them off and take them out, giving me the pole position. You have to know what you're doing, though; you can really get burned if someone swoops in and buys that first position.

Buying seconds to protect the first mortgage

If you buy a first mortgage and the property has enough equity in it even after accounting for the second mortgage, another investor can swoop in, buy the second, pay you off, and walk away with the property. You don't lose the money you paid for the first mortgage, but you do lose the property and the opportunity to earn a bigger profit. When you buy a first mortgage on a property that has sufficient equity to tempt another investor to buy the second, you can employ any of the following strategies to protect your investment:

>> **Pay off the second mortgage.** If the second mortgage is low enough, you may want to pay it off. I'm not saying that you should always pay off the second mortgage, but if you crunch the numbers and can still earn a tidy profit, it's an option.

>> **Buy the second mortgage at a discount.** You may be able to buy the second mortgage at a discount from the lienholder or if the lienholder forecloses on the property, you may be able to buy it at auction to protect your position. If the lienholder is unwilling to sell short, point out that you own the senior position and that if the homeowners don't redeem, it stands to lose everything.

>> **Persuade the owner of the second mortgage not to sell to another investor.** Contact the second lienholder to let it know that you purchased the first. Say that if nobody redeems your mortgage, and the second lienholder agrees not to sell or assign its position, you'll pay the second lienholder some fixed amount (as determined in your budget). If the lender agrees, have your attorney draw up an agreement.

This strategy prevents another investor from buying the second and then redeeming the first mortgage. It offers two benefits: You don't have to come up with the money upfront to buy the second mortgage, and the second lienholder doesn't have to give up its position. If the homeowners redeem your first mortgage, the second lienholder retains its position and can foreclose for full value rather than sell short to you.

>> **Overbid enough at the sale to satisfy the second mortgage.** You can essentially pay off the second mortgage by bidding enough to satisfy that debt or provide enough money to the second lienholder that redeeming you or selling its position to another investor wouldn't be worth the time and hassle.

Selling a junior lien for a profit

If the thought of taking possession of the property doesn't appeal to you, you can deal exclusively in paper by buying and selling junior liens. You may be able to negotiate a short sale with a junior lienholder, for example, persuading the lender to accept something like a $10,000 payment on a $25,000 lien. Then you can turn around and sell the junior lien to another investor for $15,000, earning a $5,000 profit without ever touching the property.

WARNING

Before venturing into the uncharted waters of buying and selling mortgages, consult your real estate attorney to make sure that you're set up to do it legally. Certain areas have restrictions on the number of mortgages a private individual can hold at one time.

Profiting from Property Tax Sales

When homeowners fail to pay property taxes, the taxing authority places a powerful lien against the property that almost always supersedes all other liens. Although other liens can get wiped out by foreclosure, the property tax lien can't be erased.

Unfortunately for you as an investor, a tax lien may never end up on the auction block. Another lienholder is highly unlikely to see its position wiped out because of a few measly dollars in unpaid taxes. If the lender with the first mortgage has a major stake in the property, the lender is usually going to pay the back taxes and then file an affidavit to add the taxes to the first-mortgage payoff amount — the amount the homeowners would have to pay to redeem the property.

To profit from tax sales, research the property carefully before the auction, as discussed in Chapter 8. Then do some additional homework, as explained in the following sections, to track down tax sales, find out the way tax sales are handled in your state or county, and locate tax sale opportunities.

WARNING

Although purchasing tax liens is a relatively low-risk way to acquire foreclosure properties and profit from foreclosures, you can still get burned when you purchase tax liens, especially if you don't know the rules, regulations, and deadlines that apply to tax sales in your area. The following section shows you how to find out much of the information you need, but you should also consult an attorney and gain a clear understanding of the process before buying tax liens.

Tracking down property tax sales

Delinquent property taxes are almost always processed at the county level, so your county offices are the most logical places to find information about tax sales. If your county has a website, that site should supply most of the information you need, so the clerks won't have to spend most of their days answering questions.

If no website is available, you can try contacting the tax assessor or commissioner, the delinquent-tax department, the treasurer, or the sheriff, but these offices generally shy away from providing details because they don't want to be accused of giving legal advice. Usually, your best bet is to consult your real estate attorney.

When you finally locate a quality information resource, gather information to answer the following questions:

>> Where and when are the tax sales?

>> Do you sell tax deeds or tax lien certificates? (See the following section for more about the difference between tax deeds and certificates.)

>> Does the tax lien hold priority over all other liens? If not, which liens can supersede it?

>> If I buy a tax lien, do I need to do anything to protect my position on the title? Do I have to record my interest? Do I have to buy future tax lien certificates as they go to sale?

>> How long is the redemption period on tax sales?

>> Can I do anything to shorten the redemption period, such as have the homeowners sign a non-redemption certificate?

>> What do I need to do to take possession of the property when the redemption period expires?

>> If I need to evict the homeowners, how much does eviction cost?

>> What percentage of homeowners redeem?

>> If the homeowners redeem, do they have to pay interest and penalties? If they do, what are the percentage and fees, and how much of those amounts do I receive upon redemption?

>> How can I obtain a list of properties scheduled for the tax sale?

>> What are the purchasing terms on tax liens at time of sale?

>> Do I have to register as a bidder in order to bid?

>> Does the county offer financing to purchase tax liens?

>> How does the bidding work? Is it a sealed bid or open auction?

>> Are any other costs added to the back taxes? If so, are those costs added to the total before bidding begins or when it's complete?

>> What happens to properties that don't sell at auction? Can I buy them directly from the county? If so, how do I go about placing an offer? Can I get a list of the properties?

TIP

Pick your real estate attorney's brain for additional information and advice concerning tax sales in your area. Because your attorney's job is to protect your interests, your attorney can highlight the pitfalls and perhaps offer tips to succeed that are specific to the tax sales in your area.

Finding golden tax sale opportunities

When most people buy a house, the lender requires the creation of an escrow account out of which property taxes and insurance are to be paid, because the lender knows that homeowners often forget to set aside enough money to pay their property taxes, or they simply forget to send in their payments.

When homeowners fall behind on their property taxes, unpaid taxes (along with penalties and interest) quickly add up, particularly if the homeowners are behind on their mortgage and other bills. In some cases, the homeowners may not even be receiving the notices that their property taxes are due. Perhaps the owner died, and the family is unaware that taxes are due, or the homeowners live out of state. In these situations, the tax lien may be the only lien on the property. This can be a perfect opportunity to acquire the tax lien and buy a property for much less than market value.

TIP

Pay particular attention to tax liens on properties that have no other liens against them, abandoned properties, properties with out-of-state owners, and properties that the owners use as their vacation home. In the case of a property used as a vacation home, the homeowners facing foreclosure may be using all their resources to save their primary residence, so they'll drop the ball on the vacation home.

Buying tax deeds and tax certificates

One of the most important differences in how tax sales are handled from state to state is whether the state sells tax deeds or tax certificates:

>> A *tax deed* is a document conveying ownership of the property to the high bidder. Before the tax deed sale, the county informs the homeowners and all lienholders that the property is going to be sold if nobody pays the back taxes. In most cases, a lienholder that has a large claim on the property pays the taxes. If nobody ponies up the money to pay the taxes, the county auctions off the tax deed.

>> A *tax certificate* or *tax lien* is a document giving the purchaser the right to collect the unpaid taxes. When you buy a tax certificate, you're essentially paying the taxing authority to take over its interest in the property, which gives you first-lien position on the title. Then you can foreclose on the property or place yourself in a better position with the homeowner and other interested parties to acquire the property.

Getting redeemed out of your position

When you buy a tax deed or lien, you may begin to feel as though you won the lottery. You control the property and can cut all junior lienholders out of the deal. You're on Easy Street, right? Not quite.

In a large percentage of cases, the homeowners redeem the tax deed. This situation isn't all bad. Worst-case scenario, you get your money back. In some areas, the homeowners may also have to pay penalties and interest, some of which you may be entitled to. In other words, you stand to profit even if you lose your interest in the property.

REMEMBER

To encourage investors to purchase them, tax liens typically carry a very high interest rate or are auctioned off for only a fraction of what's owed in back taxes, so investors can earn a worthwhile profit. If the homeowners or other lienholders don't redeem the tax lien, it may convert to a tax deed, allowing the holder to take action to gain possession of the property. Tax deeds may have no redemption period or a period that's shorter than that of tax liens.

Profiting from the tax lien or deed

When you own a tax deed or lien, how do you profit from it? The following are various strategies for profiting from a tax lien or deed:

>> Take possession of the property when the redemption period expires, and repair, renovate, and sell the property.

>> Sell the tax lien or deed to another investor or one of the other lienholders for a profit.

>> Sell the tax lien or deed to the homeowners for a profit.

5

Cashing Out Your Profit . . . After the Sale

Follow through on a property you purchased from the homeowners in pre-foreclosure or bought at an auction.

Protect your investment through the redemption period — the time in some states (up to a year) when the owners or other stakeholders can pay off the liens and accrued interest to regain possession of the property.

Repair and renovate your investment property to maximize your return on investment without overimproving yourself out of a profit.

Explore ways to cash out the equity in an investment property without necessarily selling it, including refinancing, selling the property back to the previous owners, or turning it into a rental.

Chapter **16**

Assisting the Previous Homeowners Out the Door

After working so hard to find a foreclosure property and negotiate with homeowners and lenders or submit the winning auction bid, you may think that you're home free. You're the proud owner of a valuable investment property that you can repair, renovate, and rent out or sell for a profit.

Whoa! Slow down. After purchasing a property, you need to tie up any loose ends to secure your purchase:

>> If the homeowners accepted the price and terms of your purchase agreement, you need to close on the home. See Chapter 18 for additional details on the closing process.

>> If you purchased the property at auction, you must satisfy the terms of the purchase, pay any back property taxes, and file some additional paperwork. See "Tying Up the Loose Ends after the Purchase" later in this chapter.

>> If your state has a redemption period, you must fulfill your responsibilities until the redemption period expires, as discussed in "Protecting Your Investment through Redemption" later in this chapter.

>> If the property is vacant, you need to make sure that it's safe, secure, and insured. See "Securing the property" later in this chapter.

Assuming you do all those things, then you face the often-painful task of evicting the residents. See "Evicting the Residents When Time Runs Out" later in this chapter for details.

Now's the time to work on your end game — to implement your exit strategy. Although you shouldn't start rehabbing the property until the redemption period expires, you can't just sit around twiddling your thumbs until it expires and the homeowners move out. You have work to do. This chapter covers the all-important follow-through that secures your ownership of the property and provides a smoother transition from the previous owners to you.

Tying Up the Loose Ends after the Purchase

You probably spent a great deal of time and effort finding a property, researching it, and bidding on it or negotiating with the homeowners. You already have a considerable amount of money tied up in the property as well, so you don't want to lose the property on some technicality or by overlooking a "minor" detail.

In the following sections, I show you what to do after you purchase a property to ensure that you've covered all your bases.

Closing on a pre-auction purchase

If you and the homeowners have a signed purchase agreement, the next step is to close on the property. At closing, you pay the homeowners, and they sign the title over to you. To make sure that you don't get burned on closing day, be prepared:

>> **Review the closing papers.** The title company should be able to provide you a copy of the closing packet a few days before closing.

>> **Call the utility companies.** To avoid getting socked with a high unpaid utility bill, call the utility companies and ask for any account balances on service provided to the home. Let the utility companies know the date on which you

plan to take possession of the house so you don't have to pay for utilities you didn't use, such as electricity and gas. The water bill usually stays with the house or is tacked onto the property tax bill. Make sure to have the seller pay the water bill at or just before closing so you don't get stuck with a huge bill.

>> **Inspect the property.** The day before closing or even the same day, drive by the property to make sure that the residents haven't trashed the place. If possible, knock on the door, and try to get a peek inside. If you can't get a peek inside, you may want to think twice about closing. You should have a relationship with the homeowners by this time.

>> **Verify title insurance.** Ask the title company for a letter verifying that the title is insured. Title insurance protects you from any unforeseen claims against the property.

>> **Obtain homeowner's insurance.** Call your insurance agent to obtain an insurance policy for the property. If you're financing the purchase through a mortgage company, the company will want an insurance policy up front before closing. Purchase a one-year policy and take a receipt for the purchase to closing.

TIP

To trim the cost of insurance, consider increasing the deductible or insuring it only for the amount you have invested in it rather than for its replacement value. If you purchased a property for $150,000, for example, and the house is worth $200,000, consider taking out a $150,000 policy. If you're paying cash for the house or buying it with a commercial line of credit, this strategy is one way to cut costs, but if you're financing through a mortgage company, you may be required to insure the property for its full replacement value.

At closing, you simply sign the necessary papers as the closing agent or attorney sets them in front of you. Inspect the paperwork to make sure that nothing has changed since you last reviewed it. As soon as you've wrapped up all the paper-work, attend to these details:

>> Obtain keys for the property.

>> Call the utility companies to have the services transferred into your name.

TIP

A few days after closing, make sure that the deed transferring ownership to your name has been recorded. If you're dealing with a title company, have it send or fax you a copy of the recorded deed. This copy will be date- and time-stamped and will bear the recoding information — the liber (book) and page number on which the deed was recorded — along with other information. If you're recording the deed yourself, ask the clerk for a copy that reflects the recording information. The office may take several weeks to record the deed officially, but the working copy is acceptable in the meantime. You may also be able to obtain a copy of the recorded document online.

Tying up the loose ends after the auction

When you purchase a property at auction, you escape the closing, but you may need to attend to other details, including fulfilling the conditions of the sale, obtaining title insurance, filing the deed, and insuring the property. Chapter 11 provides a complete checklist of everything you need to take care of after submitting the winning bid.

Protecting Your Investment through Redemption

In areas that have a mandatory redemption period, when you buy a property at auction, you become only sort of the owner. Your name is on the sheriff's deed, but depending on the rules and regulations that govern foreclosure in your area, the homeowners may have the right to redeem the property by paying back taxes and penalties and paying off all their loans in full, complete with interest and penalties. The homeowners aren't likely to redeem the property, but if their rich Aunt Millie lends a hand, it could happen.

Your job as sort of the owner consists primarily of waiting for the redemption period to expire. During this temporary lull, however, you must continue to attend to your responsibilities as prospective owner. The following sections show you how to fulfill your obligations and guard your investment.

REMEMBER

The homeowners aren't the only parties who can redeem the property. Other lienholders can redeem, and other investors may be able to work with the homeowner or buy out other lienholders and redeem your position. If you hold the senior lien, you can even sell your position to a junior lienholder, as explained in Chapter 15. Remain vigilant, and expect the unexpected.

Maintaining the property's status quo

Although the homeowners retain the right to live in the property until the redemption period expires, insuring the property and paying the property taxes to protect your investment are pretty good ideas, even though they're not technically required. Here's what you should do:

>> **Pay the property taxes.** The county treasurer sends you the tax bills. Simply pay them by the due date printed on them.

>> **Take out an insurance policy on the home.** Without insurance, your entire investment is at risk of going up in flames, blowing away in a tornado or hurricane, or washing downstream in a flood. Make sure your insurance agent knows that you purchased the property as an investment and won't be living in it.

REMEMBER

Finding an insurance agent who's willing to insure a foreclosure property is quite a challenge, but those agents are out there. The problems are that they usually can't get inside to take photos and you won't be living in the house. My insurance agent takes plenty of photos of the outside of the house and bases her quote on those photos and other details. You can expect to pay higher premiums (perhaps even double the cost of owner-occupied homeowner's insurance) because the risk for the insurance company is higher. Just make sure to file an affidavit showing how much you paid so that you stand to recover the expense if someone redeems the property.

>> **File an affidavit for all expenses.** If your area has a redemption period, file an affidavit showing all expenses you paid for back taxes and homeowner's insurance. Your attorney can help you draft the affidavit and file it for you. If the homeowners or another lienholder redeems the property, you may be able to get this money back, but only if you file the proper paperwork when you pay the bills. (The rights to seek reimbursement for costs vary from state to state, so consult your real estate attorney for clarification.) File your affidavit the same day you pay the taxes or the premiums; otherwise, you may be redeemed during the gap and lose your money.

Securing the property

If people are still living in the property, you have to rely on them (for the most part) to secure the property from theft and vandalism and to prevent someone from getting accidentally injured. As owner, however, keep an eye on the property and attend to the following tasks:

>> **Lock the doors if the property is vacant.** Make sure that the property is secure to prevent theft and vandalism and to discourage neighborhood kids from entering the house or garage and possibly suffering some injury.

TIP

Consider giving the neighbors your card and asking them to keep an eye on the house for you. Ask them to call you if they notice anything out of the ordinary. If the house is vacant, you may want to hire one of the neighbors' kids to mow the lawn each week and pick up any newspapers or advertising handouts that end up on the front porch. Try to make the house look as occupied as possible.

>> **Attend to any safety or health issues.** If the property has been cited for unsafe wiring, hire an electrician to inspect and correct the problem. Repair any broken windows or board them up. Invest a minimal amount of money to make the property safe. You're highly unlikely to be reimbursed for these expenses in the event that someone redeems the property, but you should still file an affidavit to maintain an official record of all your expenses.

>> **Perform any repairs that may lead to additional damage.** Spend only enough on repairs to prevent further damage. If the roof leaks, for example, instead of replacing the roof, have the leaks fixed to prevent further water damage.

WARNING

Don't invest a great deal of money or time in expensive repairs. If someone redeems your lien, any money you spend now becomes a housewarming present to the new owners.

Keeping hungry investors at bay

A major threat to your investment property during the redemption period is other investors who may try to persuade the homeowners that you're ripping them off. Another investor can step in, assist the homeowners with redeeming the property, and then buy it from them, cutting you out of the deal. Whatever you paid for the house at auction, along with property taxes and insurance premiums you paid (and filed an affidavit as having paid), plus interest, are refunded to you upon redemption, but you lose the house.

You can't prevent the homeowners or someone else from redeeming the property, and you certainly can't prevent another investor from swooping in and bumping you out of a deal, but you can make that scenario less likely. In the following sections, I provide tips for encouraging the homeowners to work with you toward a mutually beneficial conclusion.

Contacting the homeowners after the sale

As soon as possible after the auction, call the homeowners to let them know that you purchased their property. Tell them that other investors are likely to come knocking on their door or calling them to say that "So-and-so just bought your house and is going to kick you out." Explain that some of these other "investors" may try to persuade (or con) them to do something that's not in their best interest and that if they have any questions or concerns, they can call you.

Follow up with a letter containing all your contact information. I like to send one letter in standard mail and one as a certified letter. Let the homeowners know that you're an investor, not a house–stealer, and that you're willing to work with them if possible. For best results, send a letter immediately after the sale and then every six weeks or so until the redemption period expires.

ACTING WITH INTEGRITY

Some foreclosure investors pay no attention to the homeowners' redemption rights. We had an investor in Oakland County, Michigan, who was infamous for walking all over distressed homeowners. He'd buy a property at the sheriff's sale; then he immediately called the homeowners or knocked on their door to tell them that he had purchased the property and they needed to vacate the premises immediately. He knew full well that the homeowners had six months to redeem, but he flat-out lied to them. More often than not, his tactic worked: The homeowners immediately packed up and moved out.

I often use the dishonesty of other investors as a tool to bump them out of their deals. Knowing that a dishonest investor purchased a property at auction, I show up at the homeowners' door and say something like "I noticed that so-and-so purchased your property at the sheriff's auction the other day. Did he inform you that you have six months to redeem the property before you have to move?" They say "No," of course, and then I can present them a better offer.

I also do this when I see a property with an overbid — a bid amount in excess of what's owed on the property. The overbid money rightfully belongs to the homeowners. I'll say something like "I noticed that so-and-so purchased your property at the sheriff's sale the other day. Did he tell you that the property drew an overbid and you're entitled to some of the money from the sale?" This provides me another opportunity to work out a deal with the homeowners.

Some con artists make a living off overbids. They attend auctions, note the properties that draw overbids, and then contact the homeowners and charge them 50 percent of the overbid to "help" them recover the money. All they're doing is stealing 50 percent of the money that rightfully belongs to the homeowners.

You may choose not to bump other investors from deals, but whatever you do, don't try to con the homeowners out of what is rightfully theirs. Let them know about any redemption rights they have or overbid money that's theirs. Give the homeowners a hand, and you'll quickly find that the homeowners become much more cooperative and may even recommend you in the future to people they know who are in similar situations.

Offering cash for keys . . . and a non-redemption certificate

One of the best ways to keep other investors at bay is to visit the homeowners and offer them cash for keys and a signed non-redemption certificate. A non-redemption certificate isn't a deed — you don't get the official deed until the redemption period expires — but it provides you some additional assurance that you'll eventually get the property.

Consider giving only a small portion of the cash upfront, with the balance due after redemption and transfer of possession, so that you're not out too much if something goes wrong, and the homeowners have an incentive to honor the agreement.

WARNING

Don't offer cash for keys and a signed non-redemption certificate if other lien-holders have a claim to the property during redemption. You may end up handing the homeowners a thousand bucks only to have another lienholder redeem you the following day. Anything you give the homeowner is at risk, so don't offer a whole lot.

Before contacting the homeowners and offering cash for keys and a non-redemption certificate, consult your attorney. In some areas, having the home-owners sign a non-redemption certificate relinquishing their rights is considered to be unethical.

When you have a non-redemption certificate in hand, avoid problems by main-taining a positive relationship with the occupants. You can enforce the non-redemption certificate in court, but more importantly this approach gives you some leverage if the homeowners have second thoughts or another investor approaches them claiming to offer a better deal. Simply reminding the home-owners that you paid them money (consideration) for the agreement is usually sufficient to rein them in.

If the house is truly a good deal and you want to enforce the contract, you can try, but judges often rule on emotion rather than law and side with the homeowners. You'll have to hire an attorney, file an appeal, and pay attorney fees and court costs. If you think it's worth the expense and hassle, go for it. If not, you may want to walk away.

I've run into problems with homeowners changing their minds only a couple of times. In one situation, another investor offered to give the homeowners $5,000 instead of the $2,000 I offered if they would sell to him and not honor my non-redemption certificate. I ended up giving them $4,000 and explaining that that guy was a bum and probably would have taken the deed and scammed them out of their house without any money. I explained that I'd already invested thousands of dollars by purchasing the property at auction, and this guy was only a cheap imitation without any real ability to deliver on his promises. After all, if he could, he would have bid against me at the auction. The extra $2,000 was still less than what I would have spent on attorney fees had I taken the homeowners to court.

WARNING

Be very cautious when working with the homeowners during the redemption period, especially the last 30 days. You don't want to be accused later of taking advantage of the homeowners while they were under duress. My rule of thumb is to have no contact with the homeowners during the final month of the redemption period.

Planning Repairs and Renovations

During the redemption period, you own a nonperforming asset — an investment property that's not earning you any money. You realize your profit only upon selling the property or leasing it out. To expedite repairs and renovations and realize your profit sooner, start planning renovations and lining up contractors now. In Chapter 17, I provide additional details on renovating your property.

REMEMBER

Never spend lots of money on a house you don't yet own or that doesn't have a clear title. If you invest a lot of money in renovations and the homeowners redeem the property, you can lose your entire investment. If the property requires some repair or preventive maintenance, to prevent costlier repairs later, go ahead and make the repair, assuming that the property is vacant or the homeowners give you permission.

Evicting the Residents When Time Runs Out

Eviction can be ugly, so my advice is to avoid it if possible. Make the process of moving out as easy as possible. The following are some suggestions for helping the homeowners move out:

>> **Give 'em time.** In extenuating circumstances such as the illness or death of a close family member, consider offering to extend the eviction deadline. Show the homeowners the court documents with the date on which they're required to move out. Ask them whether that date is acceptable. If it's not, work with them to agree on a new date and have them sign a commitment that they're going to move out on that date.

Don't let the homeowners take advantage of your kindness, however. I once had a couple blame their failure to move out on the death of a grandma. They used the same excuse about 17 times to string me along.

>> **Give 'em money.** Homeowners who have just experienced foreclosure are usually strapped for cash. Consider offering them $1,000, payable on the agreed-on moving date, on the condition that the property is in good condition and broom-clean on that date. *Broom-clean* means no junk is left behind; it doesn't mean shiny clean.

>> **Give 'em a dumpster.** To enable the homeowners to dejunk the place, consider offering them a free trash bin before moving day so they can toss their junk in it.

>> **Give 'em a moving truck.** If the homeowners don't have the means to move, take away the excuse by hiring a moving truck for them. Specify the time when the movers are going to show up, and have the homeowners commit to being prepared to load their stuff. Call the homeowners a couple of days before moving day to remind them.

>> **Give 'em free storage.** Contact a local ministorage complex and arrange to prepay the storage fee for a couple of months. The homeowners can move their belongings into storage and pick them up later, after they've settled into their new residence.

TIP

Arguing at this point is counterproductive. The homeowners' emotions are probably running a little high. Simply explain that you didn't create the problem and are willing to do anything reasonably possible to assist them in moving on with their lives and leaving this problem in the past.

Playing nice guy doesn't always work, in which case you need to proceed with Plan B: a formal eviction. Fortunately, the court can assist you to keep the eviction legal and to distance you from what may be an ugly scene.

To initiate the eviction, head down to the county courthouse to file a *trespassing action* with the court. The court assigns you a court date, which in my area is about two weeks from the date of filing. You meet the homeowners in court, and unless they have a good legal reason for not moving out, the judge gives them ten days or so to move out. If they need extra time, they can say so at the hearing, and if the extension is reasonable, you can agree to it. If the homeowners request 30 days, agree and sign without debate. I usually take the opportunity to offer an added incentive: "Move out by the agreed–on date, leave the property broom-clean, and I'll pay you an extra $1,000." Now you have something in writing.

I recommend that you always hire an attorney who's experienced in evictions to handle these matters for you. When I started out, I handled most of these jobs myself to save money, and I quickly learned that my approach was actually costing me more money.

If the homeowners fail to move out by the agreed-on date, you can call the sheriff and have the homeowners forcibly evicted. The bailiff shows up with the sheriff; the homeowners and all their stuff are moved out of the house, and the sheriff locks the homeowners out of the house.

When the homeowners receive an eviction notice, they often become enraged. They may beat the house up, steal the furnace, break windows, tear out the kitchen cabinets, or gut the place, stealing everything. Your homeowner's policy may cover the damage, but you still have the headache of trying to put the pieces back together. Work with the homeowners as closely as possible to keep their emotions in check.

TIP

Are you worried about homeowners trashing the house before eviction? Talk to your attorney about getting a temporary restraining order (TRO) or a preliminary injunction that bars the homeowners from "committing waste" on the property. A TRO or injunction may make them think twice about punishing you by vandalizing the property, because the TRO carries the weight of the court's contempt powers. You may not need to go to the trouble of obtaining a TRO, but if the homeowners make an offhand comment about trashing the joint, or if you suspect that they might take such action, look into getting such an order as a way to protect your investment. Homeowners who threaten vandalism are often homeowners you can't work with, so call your attorney immediately to see whether a TRO or injunction is appropriate.

Chapter **17**

Repairing and Renovating Your Investment Property

A cquiring a foreclosure property for a price significantly below market value is like taking the perfect backswing in golf: It's a necessary first step to ensuring a profitable investment, but it's not enough to land you on the green. After you acquire a property, work on your forward swing and follow-through. You need to renovate the property without blowing your budget, and you need to do it as quickly as possible so you can sell the house before holding costs bite a huge chunk out of your profit pie.

In this chapter, I reveal the overall strategy for repairing and renovating an investment property to get the most bang for your buck. I warn you against making the common mistake of over-improving the property and then present renovation strategies and tips for everything from quick cosmetic makeovers to major reconstruction projects.

TIP

All home buyers want a nice, clean house in the price range they can afford with as few mechanical problems (plumbing, gas, electricity, and heating) as possible. When buying and renovating houses, let these factors guide your renovation decisions.

Choosing a Renovation Strategy

Having a plan of attack in place when you purchase a property can significantly reduce your holding time (and costs), as well as provide the focus you need to score a quick profit. You have four strategies to choose from:

>> **No renovation:** Buy the property and then turn around and resell it to another investor. Many investors are quite successful in finding bargain properties and then reselling them for $15,000–$20,000 over all costs.

>> **White-box:** Take a good but ugly house, clean it inside and out, patch any holes, and paint over any stains with a sealant primer such as Kilz. Make sure that the mechanicals (heating, electricity, plumbing, and air conditioning) are in good working order and that the roof has several years of life left in it. Price the house slightly below market value and pass the savings on to the buyers so that they can decorate and perform cosmetic improvements to suit their tastes.

REMEMBER

By advising you to paint over stains, I'm not suggesting that you try to cover major defects. If you notice a leak or have problems with mold or mildew, deal with the cause, and proceed with essential repairs. Use Kilz and paint to freshen the appearance.

>> **Complete rehab:** Clean the house inside and out as you do with white-boxing, but perform the cosmetic renovations, too, including applying a fresh coat of paint, laying new carpet, and bringing the kitchen and bath up to market standards. See "Giving Your Property a Quick Makeover" later in this chapter for details.

>> **Value-add renovations:** Perform a complete rehab and then take it one step further by adding a valuable feature to the house, such as an extra bedroom or bath, a dormer, a deck, or maybe central air conditioning. See "Adding Valuable Features" later in this chapter for details.

Illegal house flipping has given flipping a bad name. Many lenders are now closely scrutinizing any sales in which the seller has owned the property for fewer than one or two years. Keep all your receipts and a detailed journal of your renovations to prove that you improved a property sufficiently to justify the selling price.

Planning Repairs and Renovations

The key to making money on an investment property is buying low and selling high. What trips up many novice investors is the mistaken notion that "selling high" means transforming a Quonset hut into the Taj Mahal. They take the right first step — buying the property below market value — but then they over-improve the property in an attempt to maximize their profit. They end up owning a property that's worth more than any reasonable buyer is willing to pay for it.

When you're budgeting for repairs and renovations, your goal is to spend enough to bring the property up to the market standard in your neighborhood. Nobody is going to pay $300,000 for a house in an area where the next-best house is selling for $200,000.

In the following sections, I focus your attention on the essential no-brainer repairs you must make, assist you in identifying the renovations that bring the highest return on investment (ROI), and show you how to estimate your return so that you don't renovate your way out of a profit.

Calculating the return on your investment

The producers of those house-flipping TV shows like to show the cost of a renovation followed by the amount it boosted the property value and the total return on the investment. On one show, a $5,000 landscape job supposedly boosted the value of a property by $20,000! In the real world, the ROI is rarely so cut-and-dried. I'm not about to tell you that a new $30,000 kitchen is going to increase the value of a property by $50,000 or that a $15,000 bathroom remodel will even pay for itself. Things just don't work that way.

The renovation isn't adding value to the house; it simply brings the property's value in line with that of other properties in the neighborhood. In the real world, you discount the purchase price by enough to cover the cost of the renovation and provide you a profit of at least 20 percent. If the kitchen needs a $20,000 update to bring the house up to snuff, for example, subtract at least $24,000 from your maximum purchase price. If the bathroom needs a $10,000 facelift, subtract at least $12,000 from your offer. In other words, you calculate the cost of renovations into your purchase price.

Some renovations do add real value to a property. Converting an attic to a third bedroom, for example, or adding a garage to a house that doesn't have one adds value to the property, boosting the property into a higher price bracket. Are value-added renovations worth the expense? The answer to that question depends on your market. To determine whether a particular feature is worth the expense, consider the following:

>> **Comparable properties:** Check the value of comparable properties that have the feature you plan to add. How much more are these properties selling for? If you plan to add a third bedroom, for example, check the recent sale prices of three-bedroom homes against the value of the average two-bedroom model.

>> **Market demand:** Visit open houses in your area to find out what buyers are looking for. You want to make your house competitive with comparable houses in the same neighborhood. Find out how much extra buyers are willing to spend for a house with an additional feature your house is missing.

>> **Cost:** Obtain estimates on how much you can expect to pay to add the feature to the property. Does the added feature boost the property value enough to justify the expense?

Search for properties that have a missing feature and then add the missing piece. Some investors specialize in adding a bedroom to two-bedroom houses or adding a bathroom or half-bath to houses that have only one bathroom. Others may add central air conditioning to houses that don't have it.

Roughing out your budget and schedule

How much you profit from the sale of the house often hinges on the cost of repairs and renovations. Overzealous flippers get burned when their visions for improving a house exceed their ability to pay for them. Whether you have $10,000 or $50,000 budgeted for repairs and renovations, decide early how much of that money to set aside for each project. To establish a budget, follow these steps:

1. **List the projects you plan to hire a professional to complete.**

2. **Obtain estimates for these jobs.**

   Estimates should break out the cost of materials and labor.

3. **Jot down the projects you plan to do yourself.**

4. **For each of these projects, list the required materials.**

   If you're remodeling a bathroom, for example, you may need a new toilet, sink, cabinet, tile (for the walls), flooring, paint, and caulk. Visit your local hardware store to research the cost of materials.

TIP

   Many hardware stores display two prices for materials: an uninstalled and an installed price. Use these comparisons to determine how much you'd save by doing the work yourself.

5. **Tally all the estimated costs and add 20 percent to cover sales tax and unexpected expenses.**

   The cost of most projects exceeds estimates.

Use the renovation planner shown in Figure 17-1 to estimate costs and keep all your notes in one place. The planner features space for listing each project, its start and completion dates, and costs of materials and labor.

The tentative budget provides you a clear idea of whether the total costs of your planned projects are on track. If you do your homework before purchasing the property, your costs should be right on target to ensure a profit when you sell. If costs are running over budget, consider scaling back on nonessential projects.

WARNING

Don't let some sweet-talking contractor charm you into taking on a project in which you're destined to overspend. When budgeting, make sure that you're the one making the decisions on how to spend your money.

Renovation Planner					
Project	Start Date	Completion Date	Materials Cost	Labor Cost	Total Cost
				Total Cost	

FIGURE 17-1:
A renovation planner is a handy tool for estimating costs and scheduling work.

Giving Your Property a Quick Makeover

You bought a good, solid home in a decent neighborhood for well below market value. The house needs no major renovations, but the previous owners failed to update and maintain the property properly. Now you're the proud owner of an ugly house — the perfect candidate for a quick and affordable makeover.

For a few thousand dollars over the course of a few days or weeks, you can polish that diamond in the rough into a jewel that's well worth full market value. In the following sections, I step you through the process of renovating a decent property on the cheap.

TIP

Your goal with most renovations is to fix anything that distracts from the rest of the house. You don't want prospective buyers to walk out because something doesn't look or smell right. You don't want them offering you $20,000 less than your asking price because the house needs a $10,000 repair job. If you can't picture your significant other happily living in the house, it probably needs something.

Freshen the exterior

Curb appeal is the number-one area of focus for home buyers. If the property is ugly on the outside, prospective buyers will never step through the front door to peek inside. To freshen the exterior of the property quickly, here's what you do:

>> Trim tree limbs and shrubs.

>> Mow and edge the lawn.

>> Replace dead or dying shrubs, and plant flowers (in season, of course), especially near the front.

>> Apply a fresh layer of mulch.

>> Remove clutter and eyesores.

>> Fill driveway and walkway cracks.

>> Power-wash the siding, tuck-point a brick home (add fresh mortar between the bricks), or paint a wood-sided home.

>> Remove any window air conditioning units.

>> Repair or replace windows and screens.

>> Add or replace shutters.

>> Paint the front door and trim.

- » Paint the garage door, the front door, and shutters the same color to match the house.

- » Replace the gutters. (Seamless gutters are best.)

- » Replace the front and rear storm doors.

- » Replace exterior light fixtures.

- » Replace the mailbox with something classy that matches the exterior style of the house.

Gussy up the interior

Foreclosure properties are usually neglected, particularly inside where the neighbors can't see. Every room in the house is likely to require a little tender loving care, which you can provide by doing the following:

- » Give the place a good scrubbing.

- » Wash the windows.

- » Install new window blinds.

- » Clean or replace any drapes or curtains.

- » Remove hooks or nails from all walls and patch the holes.

- » Apply a fresh coat of paint to all rooms, using flat, neutral colors and semi-gloss white for the trim.

- » Check and repair all doors and doorknobs. Doors should open and close effortlessly.

- » Install new light-switch and outlet-cover plates.

- » Install new smoke detectors.

- » Recarpet, refinish, or replace damaged or worn flooring.

- » Swap out the register covers.

- » Replace exhaust-fan covers and maybe the fans themselves.

Tidy up the kitchen

You don't have to gut the kitchen to make it look shiny and new. The following affordable solutions often do the trick:

>> Install a new stainless-steel sink.

>> Install a new faucet.

>> If the countertop looks old or crusty, have it replaced.

>> Refinish the cabinets, if necessary, and add new hardware (knobs and handles).

>> Put new liner paper in all cabinet shelves and drawers.

Scour the bathrooms

Bathrooms in foreclosure properties often look like the inside of a neglected fish tank. If a thorough scrubbing won't do the trick, consider making the following affordable renovations:

>> Install a new vanity.

>> Install all new fixtures.

>> Replace the toilet seat.

>> Replace old towel hangers.

>> Replace the shower curtains or install glass shower doors.

>> Apply a fresh bead of caulk around the edges and base of the tub or shower, around the sink, and around the base of the toilet.

>> Scrub the grout between any tile work thoroughly.

TIP

Some companies, often referred to as *grout doctors*, specialize in cleaning out the mold and mildew between tile or even regrouting it or reglazing it, making the tile look shiny new without replacing it. The investment is well worth the money, and it rarely costs as much as most people assume. If the bathtub looks bad, consider having it reglazed as well.

Spiff up the bedrooms

Assuming that you've already painted and recarpeted the entire house, you've done pretty much all you need to do to the bedrooms:

>> Paint.

>> Recarpet.

>> Replace light fixtures, cover plates, and register covers.

>> Install closet organizers, if necessary.

Make the basement tolerable

Converting the basement to an extra living room, bedroom, rec room, or personal gym is rarely a smart investment. Focus your efforts on making the basement a clean storage or utility area, as follows:

>> Sweep the cobwebs out of the rafters.

>> Dust any ductwork, pipes, or wiring (be careful around the wiring).

>> Tack up any dangling cables without shocking yourself.

>> Seal all cracks in the walls.

>> Whitewash concrete or cement-block walls with a sealing paint. (If the basement smells musty, scrub with a bleach solution before painting. You can also run a dehumidifier in the basement, but run the overflow hose to a floor drain so that you don't create the appearance of standing water in the basement.)

>> Paint the concrete floor, using gray enamel paint, or tile the floor.

>> Install new glass-block windows.

>> Buy a roll of insulation and stuff pieces of it between the joists where the joists meet the outside wall. Painting the joists a darker color often adds a nice clean touch.

TIP

Unless a basement has its own entryway to the great outdoors, you can't consider it to be official living space. Novice investors often try converting basements to living space, but when you list the house, it's officially a basement and doesn't figure into the square–footage calculations.

Attend to the mechanicals

Everything in the house should function properly and look its best, including the water heater, furnace, air conditioning unit, and plumbing. Make these repairs:

>> Change the furnace filters.

>> Clean or replace the hot-water tank.

>> Repair any leaky faucets.

>> Unclog any plugged or slow drains.

Investing in High-Profile Rooms: Kitchens and Baths

Kitchens and bathrooms sell houses, so don't overlook or underestimate the need to transform these high-profile living spaces into attractive and highly functional rooms. In the following sections, I suggest some kitchen and bathroom renovations that range from affordable updates to pricy upgrades.

Cooking up a remodeled kitchen

For an investment starting at about $20,000, you can gut an average kitchen and install new midlevel cabinets, countertop, sink, and dishwasher. For a few thousand dollars more, you can kick in a new range, stovetop, microwave oven, and refrigerator. You don't have to spend that kind of money updating the kitchen, or you can spend a lot more. In the following sections, I take you on a tour of kitchen upgrades, starting with cost-cutter rehabs and moving up the ladder.

Giving the kitchen an affordable facelift

You can give the kitchen a whole new look with a few very affordable updates:

>> **Refinish the cabinets.** Paint the cabinets white, strip and restain them, or reface the cabinets. Refacing consists of removing the doors and the fronts of the drawers and then applying wood or plastic laminate to all exterior surfaces. Refacing is much more expensive than a standard paint job, but it costs about a third less than installing new cabinets, and it usually looks just as good.

>> **Replace the cabinet doors.** If the cabinets are solid, refinishing the cabinets and replacing only the doors is always an option.

>> **Replace the drawer knobs and cabinet handles.** For a few bucks per drawer or door, you give the cabinets a whole new look.

>> **Polish or replace the countertop.** For a few hundred dollars, you can hire someone to polish a solid countertop (such as marble, granite, or a composite material) to buff out the dings and scratches. If the counter is laminate, replace it.

>> **Install a new sink and faucet.** For a couple hundred bucks, a new sink and faucet make the entire kitchen look cleaner and more modern.

>> **Lay new flooring.** In most older kitchens, the floor looks bad no matter how clean it is. To make it look brand-new, install new flooring — ceramic (high-end) or vinyl or linoleum (lower to midrange markets).

Gutting the kitchen

Some kitchens are hopeless. The cabinets are shot, the countertop is scratched, the sink is beyond salvation, or the kitchen is simply too dinky to accommodate the average family comfortably. When a kitchen sinks to this level, consider gutting it and starting over.

WARNING

I don't recommend that you redesign a kitchen on your own. Head down to the local cabinet or building-supply store and consult a professional kitchen designer. If you're planning to knock out a wall or two to expand the kitchen, you should also consult a builder or engineer so that you don't accidentally demolish a wall that's supporting the roof or the second story.

TIP

You can save yourself some money on a kitchen remodel by doing the tear-out yourself or hiring unskilled laborers to do the work for you. Even if you're very careful, you can complete the tear-out operation in less than a day. Then you'll be ready to call in the installation crew to mount the cabinets, install the countertop, lay new flooring, and fit the rest of the pieces into place.

Modernizing kitchen appliances

Chances are pretty good that the distressed homeowners took their kitchen appliances with them or that the ones they left behind are shabby. In a high-end market, buyers are likely to want to pick out their own appliances. In a low-end to midrange market, however, having clean, functional appliances in place is a big plus.

Before you shell out $10,000 or more for top-of-the-line appliances, take a deep breath, take a look around at the housing market in your area, and let your market guide your choices:

>> In low-end to midrange housing, supply the bare essentials: a dishwasher, garbage disposal, refrigerator/freezer, and free-standing range.

>> In midrange to upper-end housing, consider supplying the higher-end essentials along with a cabinet with warming drawers and a built-in wine cooler. Upgrade to a built-in refrigerator with an icemaker and water dispenser; consider upgrading the oven and cooking surfaces, and possibly adding a trash compactor.

>> In any market, replace the old microwave with a new, space-saving, over-the-counter model. Counter space is golden; free as much of it as possible.

TIP

If you purchased a house without a dishwasher, add one, even if it involves losing a little cabinet space. You can pick up a standard dishwasher for as little as $400. If the kitchen already has a dishwasher, installation runs about $100, and the installer usually hauls away the old unit for $25 or so. Expect a first-time installation (for a kitchen that doesn't have a dishwasher) to cost another $200 or more for the plumbing installation.

Updating the bathrooms

Modern and shiny clean — that's what most buyers want in a bathroom. If you already thoroughly cleaned the bathrooms thoroughly, as explained earlier in this chapter in the section "Scour the bathrooms," that may be sufficient. One step up would be to replace the plumbing fixtures and towel hangers.

For a more ambitious renovation, examine the bathrooms to see what you have to work with and then head to your local home improvement store to check out what's available. The latest offerings are mesmerizing — free-standing sinks, elegant fixtures, one-piece shower stalls, prefab vanities with single or double sinks, lighted medicine cabinets, and numerous collections of floor and wall tile — and they're all pretty affordable.

My son shared with me a story about his first home-flip. He and his business partner spent an hour at their local hardware superstore standing in shower stalls to get a good sense of the homeowner's shower mobility. At least they were sure they landed on the right one!

Adding Valuable Features

In most of the foreclosure properties I renovate, I rarely add value-boosters. I buy the house below market value, renovate as needed to bring the house in line with market value, and sell it. But I do stumble across the rare property that has the potential to jump from one price bracket to the next. A small home that's nestled in an area with much larger homes, for example, may be a prime candidate for expansion.

When you're planning renovations, look for any opportunity to boost the property into a higher price bracket by adding valuable features that other homes in the area already have. Following are some ideas to get your creative juices flowing:

>> Replace the windows.

>> Replace the doors.

>> Add central air conditioning, if it's missing.

>> Open the floor plan by knocking out nonsupporting, nonessential walls.

>> Raise the roof.

>> Add a deck or patio.

>> Convert underused spaces to living spaces.

>> Add a bathroom.

>> Add a bedroom.

>> Build a garage.

WARNING

Don't go too crazy modifying the floor plan or converting unused space to living quarters. I once purchased a house in which the previous owner had converted the garage to a den. The house had no garage, and the lot had no space for one, so the first thing I did was convert the den back to a garage. When you're renovating, follow the Hippocratic oath: First, do no harm. Sometimes the less you do, the better.

IN THIS CHAPTER

» **Selling quick and for top dollar through an agent**

» **Primping your property for a showing**

» **Marketing your property to spark interest**

» **Negotiating offers and closing the deal**

» **Leasing your property for steady cash flow**

Chapter **18**

Cashing Out: Selling or Leasing Your Property

M ost investors who deal in foreclosures flip properties; they buy the property at a bargain price, repair or renovate it if necessary to maximize their return on investment, and then turn around and place the property back on the market. Some investors, however, prefer the buy-and-hold strategy, leasing the property for a steady cash flow.

In this chapter, I cover both strategies. If you decide to sell, I steer you clear of the common mistake of trying to sell the home yourself to avoid paying a sales commission to an agent. I reveal strategies and tips for pricing the property to sell and sprucing it up so that it sells faster at a higher price. You also discover some high-power marketing strategies to generate interest in the property and savvy negotiating maneuvers to obtain the best price without haggling yourself out of a sale.

For those of you who are practicing the buy-and-hold strategy, I suggest some of the pros and cons of leasing the property and taking on the role of landlord, which many investors simply aren't cut out to do.

Selling Through a Qualified Real Estate Agent

You can boost your bottom line on a property in two ways: increase the price or cut expenses. Increasing the price, as discussed later in the section, is often counter-productive, as discussed in "Generating Interest Through Savvy Marketing" later in this chapter. Cutting expenses within reason may be a possibility, but steer clear of any temptation to cut costs by trying to sell the house yourself. Why? In the following sections, I answer that question and then provide tips on how to select an agent who's best qualified to sell your property.

Selling faster for a higher price

Sure, a 6–8 percent agent commission can take a sizable bite out of your net profit, but consider the advantages of having an agent:

>> On average, an agent sells a home in half the time it takes a homeowner working alone. If you ballpark your holding costs at $100 per day, you lose about $3,000 every month your property sits on the market.

SELL IT YOURSELF?

Sellers often try to sell their homes on their own to avoid paying an agent's commission, but doing so rarely saves them enough to justify the hassle. What usually happens is that when prospective buyers place an offer on the house, they know that the seller is saving about 6 percent by self-listing, so they deduct 6 percent from their offer. If the sellers accept that offer, they essentially give the buyer as much as they would have paid the agent, and they had to do all the work without the additional benefits of professional assistance and advice!

Most people choose to sell without a real estate agent because they had a bad experience with an agent or felt that the agent didn't do enough to justify their 6 percent commission. This point is very valid, but it simply means that the seller didn't pick the right agent.

When you're selling a house, don't look only at the cost of hiring an agent. Look also at the cost of *not* hiring an agent and consider the benefits an agent brings to the table — particularly the closing table.

>> According to the National Association of Realtors (NAR), the average home sells for 16 percent more when sold by a Realtor. (A Realtor is a real estate agent who's certified by the NAR and is required to receive additional training and adhere to a strict code of ethics.)

>> An agent can market to other agents through Multiple Listing Services (MLSes) and network with other agents, relocation firms, and other services to increase interest in your property, ideally triggering a bidding war that can boost the sale price.

>> An agent can prescreen buyers so that you don't waste time showing the home to people who don't have the cash and can't obtain the financing to buy it. You want qualified buyers not lookie-loos.

>> An agent takes on the burden of fielding phone calls from interested buyers, scheduling tours, showing the house, and handling the paperwork. That's time you can spend working on other investment properties.

>> Having an agent during negotiations is like putting on a poker face when playing cards. The agent can negotiate with a buyer without giving away any secrets concerning what you may be willing to accept.

TIP

I recommend that you sell the property yourself only if the conditions are right:

>> Someone walks through while you're rehabbing and is willing to sign a purchase agreement on the spot, and you completely understand the purchase agreement and are confident in executing the agreement without the assistance of a professional.

>> You're in a seller's market — an area where you have significantly more buyers than sellers. Try this approach for only a short period of time, however. If the house doesn't sell, call an agent.

>> The house is on a street that already has plenty of buyer traffic and you have the best house with the best price. (If you follow my guidance in Chapter 17, of course, you should always have the best house at the best price.)

>> You have the time and desire to show the house at any time of day or night when a buyer calls to see it.

>> You have the computer skills required to produce slick marketing materials and advertise on the Internet.

>> You're able to show the house without tipping your hand.

>> You intend to hire an attorney to approve all the documentation and attend the closing.

In the following sections, I offer guidance on finding an agent who's best qualified to sell the property.

TIP

If you're trying to sell the home yourself, plant a for sale by owner (FSBO) sign in the front yard along with a note saying something like "Buyer's Agents Welcome" or "Commission Paid to Broker." This message lets buyer's agents know that if they show the home to someone who purchases it, you're willing to pay them something, which may increase traffic.

Choosing a top-notch seller's agent

Real estate agents generally fall into two camps: buyer's agents and seller's agents (also called *listing agents*). Think of the difference in terms of prosecuting and defense attorneys. Each type of attorney specializes in serving a different type of client with very different needs.

In real estate, a buyer's agent is typically much more skilled at looking out for the interests of the buyer — finding the right house for the buyer at the right price and negotiating for a lower price and more attractive terms. A seller's agent has a skill set that leans more toward marketing and sales. (Some top-producing firms have both buyer's and seller's agents.) For a seller like you, a seller's agent offers the following unique benefits:

>> Prices your house to sell for top dollar without lingering on the market.

>> Markets your property more effectively. A buyer's agent may be less skilled at marketing.

>> Ensures that you properly disclose any defects in the property.

>> Passes along any information about the buyer that may assist you in negotiating for a higher price.

To choose a qualified real estate agent, make sure that the agent has the following:

>> **Credentials:** Designation or certification proving that the agent received proper training, such as Certified Residential Specialist (CRI), Graduate Realtor Institute (GRI), StarPower Star or member, or Golden R-Top 1% Club.

>> **Experience:** Ten years or more of experience. You may find an inexperienced agent who's very well qualified, but an experienced agent with a solid track record is more of a sure thing.

>> **Drive:** Choose an agent dedicated to research who can provide you market analysis and listings of comparable properties. The agent should be willing to hold open houses, show the house on a moment's notice, and be attentive to your questions and needs.

Staging Your House for a Successful Showing

Staging a property consists of making it look as pretty as possible. Studies by the staging industry (yes, it's an entire industry) prove that a properly staged home sells in half the time for 7–10 percent more than a comparable unstaged home. Given those numbers, a home that normally would take three months to sell at a price of $250,000 would sell in six weeks for $267,500–$275,000 with professional staging!

You're free to hire a professional stager, of course, but if your budget is already strained, you can probably do a pretty good job staging the home yourself. In *Flipping Houses For Dummies*, 4th Edition (Wiley), I devote an entire chapter to the basics. In the following sections, I provide a brief overview of the areas to focus on when you're staging the house you're selling.

Jazzing up the front entrance

During your renovations, you improve the appearance of the house so much that minor imperfections stick out. Carefully inspect the outside of the house for anything that sticks out and attend to it immediately. Here are some tips for perking up the curb appeal:

>> **Spruce up the landscaping.** Mow and edge the lawn, pull weeds, fix any cracks in the pavement, and sweep up after yourself. Lay fresh mulch, plant fresh flowers (in season), and keep the plantings watered. While you're at it, put the garden hose away and hide the garden gnomes.

>> **Freshen the entryways.** Sweep the porch and stairs, lay down an attractive new doormat, fix the screens, wash the windows, polish the doorknobs, and clear the clutter out of the entryways. Make sure that the doors open and close with ease.

>> **Check the outside lights.** Make sure that the porch and security lights are working.

Decluttering the joint

Clutter makes a house feel cramped and makes buyers nervous. Investment properties usually don't have a problem with clutter. You probably dejunked the place before you started repairs and renovations, but if you can't walk through the house without tripping over something, take the following steps to remove nonessential items:

>> **Dejunk the joint.** Remove all nonessential items. You can sell the stuff, dump it, or give it away. Just make sure that it doesn't appear on the premises.

>> **Clear the counters.** Counter space is pure gold. In the kitchen, remove everything from the counters, including coffeepots, electric can openers, blenders, toasters, flour tins, cookie jars, and especially knife racks and dish drainers. In the bathroom, hide the toothbrush holder, hairbrushes, lotions, creams, and other glamour paraphernalia.

>> **Empty the closets.** Storage space is prime real estate.

>> **Ditch politically incorrect décor.** A house showing is an emotional event. Any decor that may stir negative emotions in potential buyers has to go, including religious icons, political paraphernalia, and zodiac signs.

Adding a few tasteful furnishings

When showing a house, your goal is to create a blank canvas on which buyers can paint their dreams and visions. Less is more, but a vacant house can be just as unappealing. Homeowners want to be able to envision themselves living in the house, so make it look livable with a few tasteful furnishings:

>> A small kitchen or dining room table with matching chairs. Dress the table with an attractive tablecloth (not plastic), a bouquet of fresh-cut flowers, or some other attractive centerpiece. Better yet, opt for a table with a glass top; it can make the kitchen look a little roomier.

>> An attractive sofa and a coffee table in the living room or den. Accent the room with a few small lamps and a bit of greenery. Hanging one or more stylish mirrors that reflect the windows can also create the illusion of wide-open space.

>> A standard-size bed and small dresser in the master bedroom.

>> A few neutral paintings or other artwork on the walls.

Seasoned investors often have some surplus furniture left behind in other homes they've sold. To keep costs down, consider moving furniture from your permanent residence to the house you're selling or borrow surplus furniture from friends or family members.

To gather some ideas about how to stage a home professionally, visit a few model homes in newly constructed subdivisions. You'll quickly notice that these model homes are clean, tastefully furnished, and attractively decorated; they're never vacant. Also, check out the window dressings. In models, instead of heavy curtains or blinds, you typically see something more airy such as valances.

Appealing to the senses

When you go out to eat at a fine restaurant, the quality of your dining experience relies on much more than the quality of the food and service. The lighting, aromas, and background music all contribute to the ambience. When staging a home, you want to create a pleasant sensory experience for the buyer. The following are some tips to assist you:

>> **Light it up.** Turn on all the lights to make the house appear warmer and roomier and to prove that you're not trying to hide something.

>> **Bring the outside in.** If the weather's nice, open the house to air it out. Place fresh-cut flowers in the kitchen, living room, and den to add a fresh, natural aroma. Most professional stagers recommend against using potpourri, scented candles, and air fresheners. If the home has a fireplace, consider lighting it — only in season, of course. Another nice touch is to arrange cut and uncut citrus fruit in a glass bowl on the kitchen counter or dining room table; the natural aroma of fresh citrus is pleasant without being overpowering and the arrangement is both attractive and inexpensive.

>> **Play some relaxing background music.** Classical music is often a good choice. Rock, rap, and heavy metal are usually bad choices.

If you're living in the house you're selling, you may be tempted to hang out while your agent shows the prospective buyers around. Avoid the temptation. Your presence can make the buyers nervous and make the house feel crowded. Step out until everyone leaves. You can contact your agent after the showing to find out how it went.

Generating Interest Through Savvy Marketing

If you took my advice and hired a top-notch seller's agent to list your property, your agent can handle the marketing for you, primarily by creating an MLS listing. If you decide to sell the home on your own, the marketing job falls on your shoulders, and without access to the MLS, you need to ramp up your marketing efforts. Here are some ideas for creating your own effective marketing campaign:

>> **Set a competitive asking price.** Shoppers look for value. Set the right asking price and you attract more buyers. Set your asking price too high and the property is likely to linger on the market while holding costs chip away at your profit. Set the price too low and prospective buyers may think something is wrong with the house. Starting a little high is preferable to starting a little low; you can adjust down, but adjusting up can raise some eyebrows. Smart agents and buyers ask for a listing history.

>> **Plant a "For Sale" sign on the front lawn.** The sign taps into "the power of 20"; the 5 neighbors on either side of you and the 10 neighbors across the street notice the sign immediately and start telling people about it. Use a professional sign, not one of those cheap, wire-frame jobs you can buy at the local hardware store.

>> **List the property online.** Several companies list homes for sale by owner, and buyers can search for homes without going through an agent. Before you sign up with one of these services, make sure that it's legitimate, that it lists plenty of homes in your area, and that it's used by many buyers in your area.

>> **Advertise in the classifieds.** Post an ad in the classifieds section of your local newspaper and on any classifieds websites such as Craigslist (`https://craigslist.org`).

>> **Design, print, and distribute flashy flyers.** Include full-color photos of the property, highlighting its most attractive features. Also include the address of the property, the asking price, a description of the property, your name, and your phone number. Print the flyers on high-quality paper and post them wherever you can legally do so — grocery stores, gas stations, restaurants, and apartment complexes, to name a few.

>> **Design, print, and distribute business cards.** Create a business card for the house and pass it out to everyone you meet.

>> **Generate some word-of-mouth buzz.** Soon after placing the house on the market, host an open house and invite the neighbors. Post some "Open House" signs around the neighborhood and provide food and beverages. Sunday afternoons are usually the best times to schedule an open house because many people have nothing better to do.

To market any product effectively, determine who's likely to buy it. When you're marketing a house to a first-time homeowner, for example, you might highlight the affordability of the house and provide a lead on where to go for financing. When you're marketing to movin'-on-up buyers, you may want to pitch the house as being spacious beyond belief. Empty-nesters and downsizers are often looking for something smaller that's in move-in condition. Consider sending flyers to the residents of local apartment complexes. Modify your marketing materials to appeal to your target buyers.

Negotiating Offers and Counteroffers

When prospective buyers deem your house to be worthy of purchase, they present an offer in writing. The high-profile part of the offer is the purchase price, but savvy sellers don't focus on price alone; they also consider the price and terms of the offer. In many cases, a lower offer is superior if the buyer has the cash or financing in place and doesn't demand a lot of extras, such as closing costs and repairs.

In the following sections, I provide some guidance on how to pick the best offer when you have two or more competing offers and show you how to negotiate to get more of what you want.

Comparing offers

When you're buying and selling houses, you need to be able to evaluate offers based on the following factors:

>> **Price:** An obvious lowball offer may cause some concern, but if you set your asking price in line with comparable properties, the offer should include a price that's close to your asking price. I usually consider a cash offer of 5 percent below my asking price to be pretty good, and I expect a higher offer if the buyer needs to finance the purchase.

>> **Buyer's financing:** Cash is king, preapproved financing is queen, and prequalification is a jack. An offer that proves the ability of the buyer to close on the sale is much better than an offer from buyers who plan on applying for a loan after they find the house they want. If you have any doubts about a buyer's financing, ask them to contact your mortgage specialist (loan officer), who can advise you on their ability to qualify for financing.

>> **Earnest money:** The more earnest money a buyer includes with the purchase offer, the more likely they are to be willing and able to purchase the property. An earnest-money deposit of at least 1 percent of the purchase price shows a fairly strong buyer commitment.

>> **Conditional clauses:** Standard conditions include that the property must appraise at the sales price or higher, title must be clear, and the house must pass inspection. Watch out for anything that can undermine the closing, including conditions that the buyer's existing home must sell first. Contingencies that allow the buyer to back out of the deal without just cause (commonly called *weasel clauses*) also raise red flags, such as "Buyer's attorney must review and approve the offer."

>> **Closing date:** A faster closing reduces your holding costs, so if one buyer offers $2,000 less than another buyer but can close a month earlier, the lower offer may be the better offer.

Accept offers only from serious buyers who are at least prequalified for a loan that's sufficient for purchasing your house. Have your mortgage specialist on call to check up on a prospective buyer's qualifications before you sign the purchase agreement. Your mortgage specialist can contact the buyer's lender and perform background checks to ensure that the buyer has sufficient financing in place.

STEERING CLEAR OF "CASH BACK AT CLOSING" DEALS

More and more buyers are looking to get a little cash back at the closing table. They may even offer to pay more than your asking price with the agreement that you'll hand the excess cash back to them at closing. "Cash back at closing" deals are illegal, no matter what the buyer claims to need the money for — repairs, renovations, credit card or medical bills, or whatever.

Why are these deals illegal? Because the lender is never in the know. To obtain cash back at closing, the buyer must fool the lender into thinking that the house is worth as much as the buyer is asking to borrow. The lender approves the loan, thinking that the home's value is sufficient to cover the loan amount. If the borrower can't pay the mortgage, the bank can foreclose and sell the house to cover the loss. "Cash back at closing" deals trick lenders into approving riskier loans.

If someone approaches you with one of these deals, call the lender. The lender's phone number is usually listed on the mortgage note or the closing instruction letter included in the closing papers.

If you're not 100 percent confident in a buyer's offer, consider countering the offer with a 72-hour contingency that which allows you to accept the buyer's offer while continuing to market the property. Your agent should be well versed in this strategy.

Mastering the art of counteroffers

Some offers are so low that all you can do is laugh and shrug them off, but in most cases, no offer is too low to reject outright. When you receive an offer that appears to be irrational, don't take it personally. If you're not ready to say either yes or no, simply reply with your counteroffer.

To navigate counteroffer negotiations more effectively, employ the following strategies and tips:

» Pitch the counteroffer through your agent. Otherwise, you risk tipping your hand.

» Make yourself readily available to your agent during the negotiation process so that you can respond quickly to counteroffers.

» Don't bid against yourself. Wait for the buyer's counteroffer before offering any additional concessions.

» Don't give ultimatums. Ultimatums or take-it-or-leave-it offers shut down communications. Successful negotiations require an open forum.

» Don't let a personality clash get in the way of making the deal.

» Keep a lid on it. If you talk too much, you're liable to tip your hand or upset the buyer, neither of which is productive.

» Respond only in writing. If the buyers or their agent contact you over the phone with a proposed offer, request that they present it in writing to keep it legal. In real estate, everything has to be in writing to be legal.

If you receive an offer that's close to what you want, you don't have to counter. If you can live with the offer, countering a couple thousand dollars higher may be a bad idea (and generally is), because it lets the buyer off the hook and free to pursue the search for another house. If you're receiving lots of offers, you may want to counter, but in a buyer's market, an offer that's close to what you want with acceptable terms may be a great offer.

TIP

Consider countering a lowball offer with a highball offer. If the prospective buyers offer $100,000 on a house you listed for $143,000, consider countering with $142,500. This offer lets the buyers know that you'll deal, but they must be serious. Have your agent contact the buyers' agent and try to find out why the offer was so low. Have your agent play the game; your agent tells the buyers' agent that you have some wiggle room, but not much and that you were ready to walk away but after some convincing decided to try to work with the buyers. This approach may build some goodwill with the buyers that may result in a more reasonable offer. Your other option is to simply write *Rejected* across the offer and send it back.

Closing the Deal

After you and the buyers reach an agreement on price and terms, and assuming that nothing happens to sabotage the deal, the sale proceeds to the closing, at which you receive your money and sign over the deed to the buyer. At this point, you have two goals: to make the closing proceed as smoothly as possible and to ensure that your back end is covered.

REMEMBER

As soon as you and the buyer agree on price and terms, return the documents to the buyer's mortgage company and to your title company or real estate attorney and schedule a closing date. Closings typically occur 30 to 45 days from the day you sell the property, so you don't want to waste any time. As soon as you sell the property, you must order the title policy. Neither the buyer nor the seller needs to worry about this process; your real estate agent keeps it moving forward and can recommend a title company or attorney to handle the paperwork.

To ensure that the closing proceeds as smoothly as possible, supply your closing agent any documents necessary for preparing the closing packets. Documents typically include the following:

>> Termite inspection report. If the buyer is receiving Federal Housing Administration (FHA) financing to purchase the house, immediately schedule a termite inspection and send the report to the closing agent or attorney who's handling the closing.

>> Purchase agreement and any addendums.

>> Mortgage-payoff information and any second mortgages or other liens.

Even if you sell the house yourself, you should have professional representation at the closing — a qualified Realtor or a real estate attorney. Remember that Realtors aren't lawyers and can't give legal advice. Obtain the closing packet two or three days before closing, review the papers with the assistance of your attorney or Realtor, and clear up any issues and concerns before the scheduled closing. Get your attorney involved before you sign on the dotted line. After you sign, your attorney has much less power to protect you.

Becoming a Landlord

Most people who invest in real estate are looking for a quick score. They buy, sell, and then sit back and count the money. Others prefer the buy-and-hold strategy, leasing the property for some period before selling it. The buy-and hold strategy offers several valuable benefits:

>> By holding the property for one year and a day, you pay long-term rather than short-term capital gains on your profit. During the writing of this book, the feds were charging up to 37 percent in short-term capital gains and only up to 20 percent in long-term capital gains.

>> You can claim depreciation of the property as a tax deduction. This approach is a rare tax situation in which you can claim depreciation as the property appreciates.

>> You profit in three ways. You profit when you buy the property below market value, the property appreciates over time, and the rent from your tenants pays down the principal on the loan.

>> You can deduct any expenses that you incur for maintenance and management of the property.

These tips are simply suggestions on strategies to discuss with your accountant.

Keep in mind that not everyone is landlord material. You need to find renters, collect the rent, maintain the property, and be able to handle calls from tenants at any time of day or night. You may be able to hire a property management company to take care of all these tasks for you, but that expense cuts into your profits. If you're considering the leasing option, I strongly recommend that you read the latest edition of *Property Management For Dummies*, by Robert S. Griswold (Wiley).

IN THIS CHAPTER

» Cashing out the equity in your property

» Selling the house back to the previous owners

» Renting the property to the previous owners

» Offering a rent-to-own agreement

» Selling your senior lien to a junior lienholder

Chapter **19**

Checking Out Other Cash-Out Strategies

B uying a foreclosure property, fixing it up (or not), and then placing it back on the market is the most common way to profit from a foreclosure, but it's not the only way. You can profit from your property instantly by refinancing your loan for more than you invested in the property or you can sell or lease the property back to the previous owners or even sell the senior mortgage you bought at auction to another lienholder.

In this chapter, I reveal several strategies for pulling the equity out of an investment property, along with other novel ways to profit from your foreclosure investment.

Refinancing to Cash Out the Equity

Homeowners commonly refinance their homes to cash out equity. Refinancing consists of taking out a new mortgage for more than you currently owe on the property and paying off the old mortgage. Assuming that you purchased the property for significantly below market value and your credit is in pretty good shape, you may be able to turn right around after the purchase and refinance to cash out that equity.

I say "may" because some lenders won't refinance a mortgage until after you've owned a home for six months and a day or a year and a day. The reason is that a house is worth only what you actually paid for it or what it appraises for, whichever is lower. A home-equity loan to cover repairs and renovations, however, is often easier to obtain.

TIP

You don't have to cash out all the equity in a property. You can cash out a portion of it to cover repairs and renovations, and cash out the rest when you sell the property.

REMEMBER

When you're refinancing to cash out the equity in a home, be as careful shopping for mortgages as were when you borrowed the money to purchase the property. Avoid high-cost loans and any loans that have prepayment penalties, especially if you're planning to place the house back on the market soon. See Chapter 5 for guidance on shopping for low-cost loans.

Reselling the Property to the Previous Owners or Their Family

After you officially own a property it's yours to sell, and the previous homeowners must move out if they haven't moved out already. Sometimes after foreclosure, however, the homeowners break the news to other family members who are in a position to bail them out by loaning or giving them some money or buying the house and letting them live in it. In such cases, you may be able to sell the property back to the original owners or their relatives.

In the following sections, I reveal some do's and don'ts that apply to these situations, along with some of the positive aspects of selling a foreclosure back to the previous owners.

Reselling to the previous owners

The previous owners are likely to do whatever it takes to remain in their home. If their financial situation has improved since the foreclosure, or if friends and family members have offered them a good chunk of cash, they may be in a position to buy back the property. The opportunity, however, is not always available or attractive for you as an investor. Keep the following caveats in mind:

>> If the property has any liens against it that were wiped off the books by the foreclosure, those liens reattach themselves to the property if the previous homeowners buy it back. This situation can drive the homeowners back into foreclosure, which isn't something that you or they really want.

>> Legally, you're prohibited from stripping the homeowners of all the equity they have in the property. Suppose that you purchased a property worth $300,000 for $175,000. If you sell it back to the previous homeowners for $300,000, you've taken all the equity out of the house. You have two options: Sell the house to someone else for $300,000 or sell it back to the previous owners at a discount of, say, $225,000. Whatever you do, you don't want to be an equity-stripper. See the nearby sidebar "Equity stripping: Don't do it!" for details.

Why would you agree to accept less than full market value for the house? Whenever I can earn a quick, tidy profit on a house and do the right thing for the homeowners, I jump at the chance. Usually, I develop a close relationship with the homeowners during the foreclosure process and I don't want to destroy their trust by taking them to the cleaners. In addition, I don't want to ruin my reputation in the community; I'm in it for the long term. If I treat the homeowners fairly, they're likely to recommend me to others they know who find themselves in similar situations. If you can earn a fair profit while helping your fellow humans, I strongly encourage you to do so. Otherwise, simply have them move out and sell to someone who can afford to pay the full price.

EQUITY STRIPPING: DON'T DO IT!

Homeowners who are facing foreclosure are often unaware of their options and of just how much equity they've built up in their property. They may have been making their monthly mortgage payments for 10 or 15 years while housing values in their neighborhood have been rising at a rate of 5 to 10 percent annually. They're completely unaware that the house they bought for $100,000 ten years ago is now worth $150,000, and they've paid off about $14,000 of the principal, so they have $64,000 worth of equity. All they see are the monthly bills coming in that they can't pay.

The homeowners' ignorance of the amount of equity they have in their home can make them vulnerable to predatory lenders and other crooks who want to cash out that equity for themselves. These equity-strippers employ a variety of schemes to bleed this money out of the homeowners, including these:

- Mortgage brokers attempt to persuade the homeowners to refinance their way out of a financial setback by taking out a loan with higher monthly mortgage payments than the homeowners can afford. The mortgage broker rakes in the payments until the homeowners run out of money, then they foreclose on the property.

- Crooked investors persuade homeowners who have a substantial amount of equity built up in their property to sell the property to them for significantly less than the property is worth. The "investor" may promise the homeowners that they can continue living in the home indefinitely, and then, as soon as the homeowners sign the papers, the con artist evicts them.

- Con artists offer to save the homeowners from foreclosure. All the homeowners are required to do is sign a quitclaim deed over to the con artists, who promise to "take care of everything." The con artists slither over to the county courthouse and have the deed recorded in their names, making them the owners. Yes, it's that easy.

- A con artist may offer to buy the home from the homeowners and lease it back to them. The con artist collects the monthly rent and never pays off the underlying mortgage, so the homeowners lose their rent money and also lose the house in foreclosure.

If you buy a property directly from homeowners who are facing foreclosure or at auction for a bargain-basement price and then sell the property back to the homeowners at full market value, you're practicing yet another form of equity stripping, which the courts frown upon. Regardless of whether you get caught, it's still wrong, and if you do get caught, you can look forward to a hefty fine and perhaps some jail time. At the very least, you'll be ordered to undo the transaction and put the homeowners back in the position they were in before they met you.

Another reason why you may want to consider selling the property back to the previous owners comes down to simple economics. Suppose that you're facing the likelihood of holding the property for six months. If you're paying $100 per day in holding costs, you're looking at a total bill of $18,000. On top of that, figure closing costs of 7 percent on $200,000 (a total of $14,000), and your bill is up to $32,000. Now figure in your time and effort plus the costs of repairs and renovations. Sure, the homeowners get a break, but you also save yourself some money.

WARNING

If you took out a traditional loan to purchase the property, your mortgage probably has a due-on-sale clause, which means that you're prohibited from selling the property back to the previous homeowners without the lender's approval.

TIP

If selling the home back to the previous homeowners isn't an option due to the possibility of having other liens reattach to the property, you may be able to sell to a family member who agrees to let the homeowners remain in the house.

Financing the buyback through insurance-policy proceeds and other means

Homeowners are often unaware of assets and other collateral they have to secure financing, or they come into some quick money after the foreclosure is a done deal. In such cases, you may be able to help the homeowners obtain the funds needed to buy back the property simply by making them aware of their options. Following are two options that may be available:

>> **Life insurance policies:** If the home ended up in foreclosure because one of the homeowners passed away, and the deceased had a life insurance policy, cashing out that policy may provide sufficient funds for the surviving homeowner to repurchase the property. In some cases, a serious illness drives a couple into foreclosure, and then the spouse who was seriously ill passes away, leaving behind a life insurance policy that can cover the purchase price. See the nearby sidebar "Life-saving life insurance."

>> **Retirement savings:** You can borrow against some retirement plans for the purchase of a house. If the homeowners have sufficient retirement savings, they may be able to borrow against it to buy the house back from you.

LIFE-SAVING LIFE INSURANCE

I once had a very positive experience with a man who lost his wife and had substantial life insurance policy proceeds coming to him. He had suffered with his wife's illness on and off for the several years, struggling to keep things together both at home and at work.

I bought the house in foreclosure, not knowing the situation beforehand. The man's wife was still alive when the foreclosure happened. About a month or so before the end of the redemption period, she passed away. The man was now facing the loss of his home on top of everything else.

He told me that he wanted to buy the house back and that he would do so with cash from the life insurance, but the check wouldn't arrive until after the expiration of redemption. I spoke with him and his family quite extensively, and what he ultimately decided was to use the money to buy a different property. I think he made the right decision. The house he was losing needed some work, and he didn't feel that he was up to the challenge.

He decided to buy a condo, pay cash, and let someone else worry about the upkeep. I worked with him and gave him plenty of time — first to mourn and then to close on his new condo and move. He worked with me, and I with him, and he left the house he lost nearly spotless.

Sometimes, doing the right thing results in having to wait a little longer for your profits. I sold that house and made my money, he got a fresh start without the burden of the house, and I know that the time I waited will pay off tenfold with positive word of mouth. He and his family couldn't stop thanking me for what I had done.

Leasing the Property to the Foreclosed-on Homeowners

Families are often reluctant to move out of their home because they have kids in school. They really need to sell the house and find more-affordable accommodations, but they don't want to force their kids to change schools. In such cases, you may want to consider purchasing the property and then leasing it back to the family until the kids move out or the family has more time to plan.

WARNING

Don't jump into a lease agreement with the previous homeowners before you've performed some serious number-crunching. If the homeowners couldn't afford the monthly mortgage payments, don't sign them up for a lease that has them paying monthly rent they can't afford. You'll end up with deadbeat renters and set the family up for another failure. Before offering them the option to rent, make sure that they've resolved the issues that sent them into foreclosure and that they can afford the rent.

If you decide to lease the property to the previous homeowners, consult your real estate attorney to prepare a lease agreement for you. Keep in mind that not everyone is cut out to be a landlord. See Chapter 18 for details about leasing the property and for recommendations on additional resources that can assist you in managing a rental property effectively.

Offering a Lease-Option Agreement

When a buyer really wants to purchase a property but isn't currently in the financial position to do so (whether they're the previous owners or some other buyers), you may consider offering them a lease-option agreement, as discussed in Chapter 9. Perhaps the buyers need more time to secure financing or fix something on their credit report, or they're waiting for an insurance check or some other payment. With a lease option, the buyers agree to rent the property from you for a fixed period, with the option to purchase the property at the end of that period.

Lease options aren't always viable, but if the homeowners can come up with a down payment and provide some assurance that they'll be receiving money or be able to qualify for financing in the specified time, a lease option enables you to establish some revenue flow while you're waiting to sell the property. I usually structure lease-option deals as follows:

>> **Down payment:** Normally, I require 5–10 percent down. You may want more money down when dealing with buyers who've just been through foreclosure. You credit them for the down payment by taking it off the purchase price, but a substantial down payment assures you that they're serious. If they can't afford it, they can't afford it; let them move on.

>> **Rent:** I usually specify that rent is due on the first of the month and set the rent at about 1 percent of the purchase price or as close to that amount as is affordable. You don't want to be too flexible, but you don't want to break the bank, either. I offer a bonus for paying on time and add the monthly payments to the down payment.

>> **Terms and conditions:** The agreement should spell out the lease term and conditions. Your lease-option agreement should contain a forfeiture clause stating that nonpayment results in the forfeiture of the option and the down payment. The agreement should also contain a statement that the option is exercisable at any time, with no prepayment penalty or anything like that. What I tell them is that if they win the lottery and want to pay the balance owed on the house tomorrow, that's fine by me. I want them to succeed, and I want to realize my profit — the faster the better.

REPEATING THE SAME MISTAKE

Whenever you're working with homeowners who have a less-than-stellar track record, be careful. People tend to follow the same patterns and repeat the same mistakes.

I once purchased a foreclosure property at auction for $245,000. The house was worth about $550,000. The couple who owned the property were fairly affluent, but the wife, who was in charge of making the monthly mortgage payments, wasn't much of a money manager. She failed to make the payments and failed to tell her husband about it. The property ended up on the auction block and I bought it. I actually won the auction with an overbid of $50,000 — that is, I bid $50,000 more than what was owed on the mortgage. That $50,000 was placed in escrow. The couple was entitled to it.

I could have sold the property for $550,000 and walked away with nearly $300,000 in profit, but when I heard the husband tell the story, I figured that I'd give the couple a break and sell it back to them for about $300,000 — about $50,000 more than I paid for it. I knew that they had access to the $50,000 in overbid money, so that amount was a pretty good down payment, and the husband earned a good income, so the couple certainly had the means to regain their financial footing and could afford the house. The husband was going to take over the job of paying the bills. My attorney happened to be in my office that day and sat in on the interview. He advised me to have the couple move and sell the house at full value. I went against his advice because of the husband.

I offered the couple a lease-option agreement that gave them 12 months to buy back the house. They paid me the $50,000 down payment, and I gave them back $10,000 to help them cover their monthly bills. They managed to make their monthly payments for about five months. Then they stopped making payments. What happened? After about five months, the wife insisted on reassuming responsibility for paying the bills and the husband let her. As soon as he stopped managing the finances, the payments stopped. He didn't realize what was happening until I called and told him that they had forfeited the lease option.

During those first five months, they easily could have sold the house themselves for $550,000, paid me the balance of $250,000, and walked away with more than $200,000, but they chose to stiff me. I took possession of the property, and they lost everything — the $50,000 overbid, their house, and the opportunity to make $200,000 free and clear. I didn't feel any sympathy for them. I'd given them a break and they returned to the same old patterns that got them into trouble in the first place.

When you're working with distressed homeowners, be careful. People often develop expensive habits and destructive patterns that are tough to break.

Make sure the renters understand that they're renting with an option to buy. If they don't exercise their option during the option period, they may forfeit it. If they don't pay rent, they may forfeit it. Make the terms clear. Follow up with them throughout the lease-option period, ask how their mortgage hunt is coming along, and refer them to mortgage lenders you may know.

TIP

During the paper-signing stage, I open the recording app on my iPhone and ask permission to record the transaction from beginning to end. I tell my client that this recording is protection for all of us, ensuring that we all live up to our parts of the agreement. I make sure to be thorough and to allow them to ask questions, and I encourage them to seek legal counsel.

Assigning Your Position to a Junior Lienholder

Suppose that you buy the first mortgage. Do you have to take possession of the property to make a buck? Nope. You can sell your position to a junior lienholder and avoid the ugliness of eviction and the hassles of repairing and renovating the property. Here's how the process works, assuming that you're working in an area with a redemption period:

1. **Buy the first mortgage, either at auction or by negotiating a short sale with the lender.**

    Now you have controlling interest. Just make sure to pay any property taxes owed on the property.

2. **Wait out the redemption period.**

    If the property has other liens against it, and the lienholders decide to foreclose, another investor may buy one of the junior liens at a sheriff's sale. If another investor buys a junior lien on the property, the clock on that redemption period begins to start ticking while you're already partially through the redemption period on your investment.

3. **Approach the holder of the junior lien and say something like "Look, if you buy my interest, I'll sign over my position to you."**

    Make your offer worthwhile for the junior lienholder; otherwise, redeeming your lien and waiting a little longer may be the better option. One big advantage of buying your interest is that the junior lienholder then assumes your position in the redemption period instead of having to start from scratch.

TAKING ADVANTAGE OF YOUR POSITION

Knowing the lienholder positions, as discussed in Chapter 15, can often open your eyes to win–win situations with other parties who have a financial interest in the property.

I purchased a first mortgage on a property at auction. The house had a second mortgage on it — a lien by the local police department and our county prosecutor. The owner pleaded guilty to drug dealing and had to pay a fine of about $50,000, which was taken as a lien against the house. About one week remained in the redemption period, and the county was going to redeem my first mortgage, meaning that I stood to get my money back, and that was about all.

I knew from experience that the county didn't want to pay me off and then take possession of the property and have to sell it, so I called the prosecutor in charge of drug seizures in Macomb County and explained the situation to her. I told her that if she would agree not to redeem my first mortgage, I would split my profits with the county 50/50. It took me less than an hour to work out an agreement. She came back with a counteroffer. She wanted a guaranteed minimum of $20,000, which was a smart move on her part. I agreed.

I ended up taking possession of the property and selling it for a $37,000 profit. The county received the first $20,000, and I received $17,000. I sold the house pretty quickly and got what I wanted out of it, and the county was able to acquire $20,000 without the hassle of dealing with the property.

Had we not struck a deal, I would have walked away with next to nothing.

The take-home message is that you must remain vigilant throughout the process and be prepared to deal with the other lienholders. Remain flexible, and be on the lookout for win–win opportunities; otherwise, you may find yourself the big loser.

6

The Part of Tens

IN THIS PART . . .

Avoid some of the most common mistakes people make when they start to buy and sell foreclosure properties, such as not even looking at the property before bidding on it.

Build a referral business of profitable foreclosure properties by earning a solid reputation as a fair and reasonable real estate investor.

Take precautions to avoid ten of the most common pitfalls that undermine foreclosure investors.

IN THIS CHAPTER

» Avoiding the mistake of underestimating costs and overestimating profits

» Steering clear of overestimating a property's profit potential

» Stifling your desire to overbid on a property

» Suppressing the urge to skip research and make assumptions

» Avoiding the tendency to start renovations too soon

Chapter **20**

Ten Common Beginner Blunders

The difference between profiting in foreclosures and losing your shirt often hinges on your ability to avoid the most common mistakes. In this chapter, I point out the ten most common foreclosure investment blunders so that you don't have to experience them firsthand.

Having Insufficient Funds on Hand

Novice investors often underestimate costs and overestimate the future sales price of a property, or they take on too many projects and quickly find that they're in over their heads with maxed-out credit. To avoid these common pitfalls, I offer four suggestions:

> » **Play it safe.** Overestimate costs and underestimate profits. After doing your research and calculations, if you're not fairly certain that you can earn a profit of 20 percent or better on a property, don't buy it. Wait for the right opportunity.

>> **Start small.** Making mistakes on a half-million-dollar property generally costs more than making those same mistakes on a $200,000 property. Holding costs alone on a half-million-dollar property can sink a small-time novice investor. Start investing in more-affordable properties and work your way up slowly: Take the crawl–walk–run approach.

>> **Start slow.** Buy, renovate, and sell one foreclosure property at a time, and do each one right from start to finish. In your enthusiasm to become a wealthy real estate investor, you may be tempted to buy several properties at your first auction. Don't succumb to such temptation until you're well established.

>> **Don't rush a purchase.** Don't think you're failing because it has been three months and you haven't bought anything. Keep working on finding a property until the right opportunity comes along. Profits in real estate can be high, but mistakes are almost always costly.

TIP

By starting with one property at a time, you reduce your exposure to risk while learning from your mistakes. If you buy five properties at the same time, you're likely to make the same mistake on all five properties. Buy one, make your mistakes, learn from those mistakes, and then avoid making the same mistakes on your next property. After you've eliminated all your mistakes (something I'm still working on accomplishing in my 30 years of investing), consider taking on more projects.

Overestimating a Property's Value

Housing values don't exactly have a glass ceiling. The values of comparable homes in the same neighborhood set the upper limit on what you can expect. If you're thinking that you can break through the ceiling by transforming a shack into a showpiece, think again. You ultimately over–improve the house and end up giving away thousands of dollars in renovations as a housewarming gift to the buyers.

REMEMBER

You make your profit when you *buy* a house. Be sure to buy at a price that enables you to earn at least 20 percent on your total investment, which includes the purchase price, holding costs (monthly loan payments, property taxes, insurance, and utilities for the duration of the project), the cost of repairs and renovations, and the cost of selling the property.

Underestimating Your Holding Costs

Investors often take a hit on *holding costs:* property taxes, insurance, interest payments, and utilities paid between the time they purchase the property and the time they sell it. Holding costs can be particularly burdensome when you purchase properties in an up market and the market suddenly tanks. Anticipate holding costs to exceed $100 per day (more than $3,000 per month) when you're working with borrowed money, and carefully calculate your holding costs well in advance of any project. Sure, $100 per day in holding costs seems to be a little steep, but I've done the math. Trust me — you can expect to pay $100 or more per day in holding costs when you're financing the project with other people's money. See Chapter 11 for more about holding costs.

REMEMBER

Don't forget to account for holding costs through the duration of the redemption period, and whenever you pay property taxes and insurance premiums during this period, be sure to file an affidavit at the recorder's office so that if someone redeems the property you'll be reimbursed for these expenses.

Overbidding in the Heat of Battle

In Chapter 11, I cover the topic of bidding at foreclosure auctions in detail, and I warn you to set a maximum bid price and stick to it, but I can't emphasize this point enough: Bidding at auction is a very emotional experience that often drives up the price in a hurry. If you're anything like me, you hate to lose a property to another investor and are likely to bid yourself right out of a profit.

To avoid the temptation to overbid, write down your maximum bid amount before the auction and look at it before the bidding starts. Consider having someone who's less emotionally involved accompany you to the auction and prevent you from exceeding your maximum bid amount. When the bidding rises above your upper limit, drop out. You'll always have another opportunity.

Failing to Investigate the Title

The title is the single most important document attached to the property, containing the names of the legal owners of the property along with the names of any lienholders and the claims against the property. If you don't look at the title before you bid or make an offer on the house, you're flying totally blind with a completely disabled instrument panel. When you fail to inspect the title, you leave yourself wide open to the following risks:

>> **Buying a property that someone else already recently closed on:** Con artists may sell the same home to several buyers and let the buyers sort out who really owns it. Don't assume that this scam won't happen to you; it happens more often than you may think.

>> **Buying a junior lien thinking that you're buying the senior lien:** After the foreclosure process runs its course, your junior lien may be wiped out, leaving you with nothing.

>> **Buying the house from the owners when some other investor has purchased the senior lien without your knowledge:** When homeowners get desperate, they may try anything, even fraud. Even if you research the title on your own, when buying directly from homeowners, purchase title insurance and hire the title company to manage the closing.

REMEMBER

Always research the title before bidding on or purchasing a property from the homeowners. You can order a title commitment from your title company. In Chapter 8, I show you how to research a property thoroughly to avoid the common pitfall of buying a house without knowing what you're buying. If you do the research yourself, double- and triple-check your work before you bid.

Failing to Inspect the Property with Your Own Eyes

Just because a property looks like a great investment on paper doesn't mean that it's a great investment property. My crew came very close to purchasing a gutted shell of a home at auction, but fortunately, one of my colleagues prudently did a walk-around inspection and noticed that the back of the house was gutted by fire. The front and sides looked great!

Before you purchase a property, the least you should do is drive to the location, look around the neighborhood, and do a walk-around inspection of the property, taking several photos of every side. Knock on the front door and try to engage the homeowners in conversation. While conversing, try to look past them into the house. You may be able to persuade them to invite you in, but don't count on it. Stop short of hopping the fence so that you won't be charged with trespassing or find yourself staring down the barrel of a gun (which has happened to me).

Bidding on a Second Mortgage or Junior Lien

Shortly after some real estate investment guru comes to town and stages a "free" seminar on investing in foreclosures, my office receives a rash of calls from distressed investors who reportedly followed the guru's advice and stood to lose a lot of money. In most cases, the person failed to research the title and ended up purchasing one or more second mortgages or junior liens, which were likely to be wiped out by the foreclosure process. In one case, an intelligent professional purchased more than $100,000 in worthless paper during a single auction!

You can make money purchasing second mortgages or junior liens, but you really have to know what you're doing and remain constantly aware of the liens that hold precedence over yours. In Chapter 19, I introduce you to the strategy of buying and profiting from junior liens. But I always advise beginners to steer clear of junior liens until they've gained some experience buying senior liens.

WARNING

Never buy a junior lien unless you intend to purchase the senior lien at auction or redeem the property from the senior lienholder. Otherwise, you stand to lose your entire investment.

Renovating a Property before You Own It

In your enthusiasm to score a quick profit from your investment property, you may be eager to get inside and start renovating the property during the redemption period. Many investors have made this mistake and have paid dearly for it.

In areas that have a redemption period, the homeowners have the right to pay off the lien along with any penalties and interests at any time during the redemption period — up to the final day. If you invest time, money, and effort in repairing and renovating the property and the owners decide to redeem, you lose all the time, money, and effort you invested. You may even face legal claims.

REMEMBER

Some jurisdictions allow acceleration of redemption periods if the house is abandoned, but follow the required steps and have an attorney draft the paperwork and advise you on how to move forward legally.

Trusting What the Homeowners Tell You

Homeowners who are facing foreclosure are often willing to say anything to persuade you to let them remain in their home or pay them as close to full market value as they can get. They'll tell you that the house is in perfect condition, that they have money coming in, or that their grandmother just died for the third time this month, or they'll promise to move out as soon as they find a place (whenever that is). I've even had a couple tell me that their baby had died. Their baby hadn't died. Confirm anything that sounds fishy.

I can't blame people facing foreclosure for bending the truth. If I were in the same situation, I might be tempted to float a few white lies myself. As an investor, try to retain your compassion, but don't believe everything you hear. Offer a reasonable concession, have the homeowners agree to it (in writing), and then hold them to it. In Chapter 16, I offer some suggestions for perks to consider offering to encourage the homeowners to move on.

REMEMBER

The cleverest homeowners tell you that the house is in really bad shape and that you'll spend tons of money trying to fix it up, so why not let them stay for a "reasonable fee?" It may be that the house is in terrible shape, but if it's in bad shape now they probably made it that way, and now that you own it do you really trust the residents not to devalue your investment even more? Remain compassionate, but be firm.

Getting Greedy

For some investors, earning a fair profit isn't good enough. They drum up lies and deceptions to prevent distressed homeowners from understanding their rights and fully grasping the options at their disposal. Con artists will even steal homes from uninformed homeowners by befriending them and then persuading them to sign a quitclaim deed relinquishing all their rights to a property without paying the owners a fair amount.

WARNING

The minute that you see only $$$$ you're on the road to failure. Your name becomes mud, or at least dirty water, and you start losing out on deals. I have yet to meet someone who lost in the long run by taking the high road, but I know many who've lost in the very short run by associating with crooks or following unethical practices. Be fair, be honest, be brutally honest sometimes, negotiate hard, be firm, keep your ultimate goal (profits) in mind but never compromise yourself for a buck.

» Encouraging homeowners to get a handle on their finances

» Encouraging homeowners to seek assistance from family and friends

» Persuading homeowners to contact their lenders

» Hinting at the bankruptcy option

» Suggesting legal options homeowners can explore

Chapter **21**

Ten Ways to Maximize Future Leads by Acting with Integrity

Throughout the book, I discuss the need to be on the level with homeowners who are facing foreclosure. Acting with integrity distances you from the foreclosure predators who take undue advantage of distressed homeowners.

By remaining on the level, you can gain a competitive edge by building a reputation as the trustworthy go-to person for homeowners who are facing foreclosure. In other words, your integrity brings you more leads, which are the bread and butter and vegetables and meat of real estate investing.

In this chapter, I offer ten tips to use your integrity to maximize future leads — ten ways you can assist homeowners even if your assistance results in a missed opportunity to earn a profit.

Stopping the Bleeding: Providing Basic Financial Advice

Unless you're a certified public accountant or a financial adviser, you can't offer homeowners bona-fide financial advice. Many homeowners who are facing foreclosure, however, could benefit from such advice. They need to figure out a way to get a handle on their finances, perhaps consolidate their debt, and commit to an austerity program to avoid overspending. You may not be qualified to provide such advice, but you can highlight the possible benefits of a debt counselor or financial adviser, who can help consolidate debts, set budgets, negotiate with lenders, and so on.

TIP

Another way to network your way to future investment opportunities is to establish mutually beneficial relationships with debt counselors and financial advisers. Just make that sure you're not creating mutually beneficial relationships that compromise the homeowners' rights.

Assisting Homeowners in Their Job Search

A longtime friend of mine worked in a job placement agency. On several occasions, I found myself dealing with homeowners who had few options because they were out of work. I'd tell the homeowners, "I have one more trick up my sleeve. I'll place a call and see if my friend at the job placement agency can help you. Let me try, and I'll get back with you." When I called my friend, he asked me what field they were in before they were fired or laid off, and I told him. In almost every case, he was able to find the homeowners jobs.

If the homeowners need jobs and you know of any openings, give them a hand. You'll experience immediate gratification, and your good deed is likely to reward you somewhere down the line.

Suggesting That the Homeowners Seek Help from Family and Friends

When you're trying to acquire a foreclosure property, it may seem counterintuitive to recommend that the homeowners seek assistance from friends and family members, but this is exactly what you should be doing. I always ask, "Do you not want your relatives to know?" The answer is almost always, "Yes, we're embarrassed." "Well," I say, "do you think it will remain a secret or be any less embarrassing when the bailiff comes to put your stuff on the curb?" I know that question sounds harsh, but it often makes homeowners stop and really think. Often, this question has prompted homeowners to call a relative and get the help they need.

If the homeowners do ask for and receive sufficient assistance to enable them to dig themselves out of foreclosure, you lose an opportunity to acquire the property, but you gain a friend for life. Assuming that everything works out, the homeowners will sing your praises and refer you to the people they know who find themselves in similar predicaments. And even if they don't, you'll sleep better at night knowing that you did a good deed.

Encouraging the Homeowners to Contact Their Lenders . . . and Soon

When homeowners fall behind on their mortgage payments, they're likely to go into hiding, avoiding bill collectors, attorneys, and anyone else who's looking for a payment. They're taking things one day at a time, hoping to hold on to their home for as long as possible.

Although this approach is perfectly understandable, denial and avoidance are the worst actions (or, more appropriately, inactions) homeowners can take. Inaction almost always leads to the loss of the home and any equity in it. Encourage homeowners to contact their lenders and other creditors immediately, describe their situation, and explore their options. If the homeowners refuse to contact their lenders, at least you know that this option is off the table and you can move on to the next option. You may be able to act as the mediator between the homeowners and their lenders, but you'll need signed permission to do so. For details and a sample release you can ask the homeowners to sign, see Chapter 9.

WARNING

Don't cross the line by giving advice that you're not qualified to offer. Tell the homeowners — and repeat often — that you're not an attorney or an accountant.

Suggesting Short Sales and Other Debt Negotiations

Anxiety about debt, particularly large mortgage loans, can be so overwhelming to people that they lose perspective. Sure, "it's only money" to people who have enough money to pay their bills and to a few slackers out there who don't worry about paying their bills, but to responsible homeowners who can't afford their monthly mortgage payments, the problem appears to be insurmountable. Many people don't even realize that lenders and other creditors will often agree to accept less than full payment on a debt.

Inform the homeowners that creditors often negotiate with people who owe them money. Describe the situation that the lender is facing. If the lender forecloses on the property, it may receive no payment whatsoever and end up having to pay the costs of repairing, renovating, and selling the property. The lender is often highly motivated to work with homeowners in these situations.

REMEMBER

A short sale isn't always an attractive option for the lender. Also, you need to talk to someone who can make the decision. Most people who handle the account for the lender are hourly employees who don't have decision-making power. If the homeowners decide to explore this option, encourage them to start early; after the bank has decided on a plan of action, getting it to change course is like trying to stop a fully loaded freight train traveling at top speed.

Assisting Homeowners in Assessing Their Refinance Options

Distressed homeowners often overlook the power of the equity they've built up in their properties over the years. They experience a temporary financial setback, fall behind on their property tax payments to the tune of a few thousand dollars, and resign themselves to losing their home in foreclosure, even though they have tens of thousands of dollars in equity built up in it.

Sit down with the homeowners, as explained in Chapter 9, and calculate the amount of equity they've built up in the home. They may be able to refinance their loan, consolidate their debts, and establish affordable monthly payments that get them out of trouble.

REMEMBER

Refinancing out of foreclosure isn't always an option. If the homeowners have bad credit, have no foreseeable increase in income, and can't refinance with a loan that provides affordable monthly payments, refinancing may simply put them back on track to face a future foreclosure situation.

Suggesting the Option of Selling the House before Foreclosure

One of the best decisions many distressed homeowners can make is to scale back: sell their home and buy a more-affordable home with lower property taxes, lower utility bills, and less maintenance. By selling the home, they can often pull out most, if not all, of the equity they have in it, salvage their credit, and have a chunk of money to use as a down payment on their next home.

This option isn't open to everyone, of course. If foreclosure is only a couple weeks around the corner and the home is located in an area that has no redemption period, the homeowners aren't likely to have sufficient time to market and sell their home. If the homeowners have plenty of equity in the home and several months to act, however, this option usually is the best one.

REMEMBER

I'm a real estate agent, so I can list and sell a home and profit from the transaction even if the owners choose not to sell it to me. You may not be in the same position, but you should always present the homeowners all their options and let them decide what's best. If you're a real estate agent, you need to make sure that you disclose this fact to the homeowner many times, in writing and verbally, even if you represent yourself.

Bringing Up the Bankruptcy Option

I'm not a big fan of filing for bankruptcy because it's usually a lose-lose situation for everyone involved. Even if the homeowners qualify for bankruptcy, it rarely erases their credit card debt and simply delays an inevitable foreclosure. Creditors can simply wait until the bankruptcy stay is lifted and then proceed with foreclosure.

WARNING

As a foreclosure investor, however, you should always present bankruptcy as an option and inform the homeowners that they have a right to seek professional advice from an attorney. Attempting to discourage a homeowner from seeking legal counsel is illegal, not to mention just plain wrong. Don't even try to explain bankruptcy to them. Provide them the names of several qualified attorneys, just in case one doesn't work out and the homeowners attempt to pin the blame on you.

Offering a Helping Hand

When you're working with distressed homeowners, think of creative solutions to assist homeowners in digging themselves out of their financial hole. I once met a homeowner facing foreclosure who was a hard worker — the kind of guy who always has a little grease under his fingernails, the guy you want working for you. I referred him to my friend at the job placement office, and my friend called me later that afternoon. He said, "You know that guy you sent me?" And I said, "Yeah, what about him?" My friend replied, "He showed up here in stained overalls and a beat-up ball cap with grease under his fingernails. His résumé was on a folded-up piece of lined loose-leaf paper with the names and phone numbers of where he worked and descriptions of what he did at all those places — all handwritten, of course."

"No, I didn't know that, but it doesn't surprise me," I said.

"Wait a minute," my friend said, "You sent me over the roughest-looking guy who has ever walked into my office, and you know what? He's absolutely perfect! An employer just gave me an opening for some sort of specialty hydraulic work, and this guy has ten-plus years of experience in that very field. I called the references on that tattered résumé, and each and every one said the same thing: 'If I could have kept him on, I would have. He'll be your top worker; there aren't many like him.'" My friend went on to say that the guy was starting his new job the next day.

Later, I received a call from the homeowner, and he couldn't thank me enough. He was sorry that I wasn't going to make any money, because now he wouldn't need my help saving his house, but he was very thankful. He said, "You just got me a new lease on life. Things are going to be okay." And they were.

I didn't make money on the deal, but my name was gold to that man, and when his mother passed away and he wanted to sell her house for cash, whom do you think he called? Well, he didn't actually call; he came to the office to see me. He said he wouldn't think of working with anyone else. Win–win situation? I think if you look up the definition, this story is right there.

Revealing the Option to Walk Away

Few lenders will pursue homeowners who simply vacate the premises, but I never recommend that someone just head out of town when they're facing foreclosure. Walking away without a trace usually leaves a trace on the homeowners' credit history, which makes obtaining future loans much more difficult.

A better way to walk away from a property is to sell it to an investor who can deal with the lenders or offer the lenders a deed in lieu of foreclosure with the agreement that the foreclosure won't show up on the homeowner's credit history and that the homeowner won't be responsible for any deficiency that might arise after the sale of the house. (Some states allow for deficiency judgments in which the lender can pursue the homeowner after the sale for a portion or all of the money the lender lost when the homeowner defaulted on the loan.) I discuss this option in greater detail in Chapter 2. Deed in lieu of foreclosure is usually an attractive option only for homeowners who have negative equity in the property and no investor who's willing to pay them to move on.

TIP

If the homeowners have no equity or negative equity in their property, crunch the numbers to see whether you can come up with an offer that's better than a deed in lieu of foreclosure. The homeowners can still walk away from the property, but they walk away with some cash in their pockets, and you end up with the property — after paying off the senior lienholder, of course.

» Turning up your nose at get-rich-quick schemes

» Verifying facts and figures with vigilant research

» Investing with your head, not your heart

» Creating win–win transactions by dealing aboveboard

» Coping with guilt and blame

Chapter **22**

Ten Tips for Avoiding Common Foreclosure Minefields

I f foreclosures were risk-free, easy money, everyone with a little cash and motivation would be buying and selling foreclosures. The risks are very high, however, and one minor misstep can tip the balance from glowing success to financial failure.

In this chapter, I point out the most serious and common problem areas in an attempt to steer you clear of buried mines, including get-rich-quick schemes, misleading information, the natural impulse to let emotions drive decisions, the common temptation to take advantage of distressed homeowners, and the disappointment and guilt that often paralyze even the most empathetic foreclosure investor.

Steer Clear of Foreclosure Investment Scams

Every segment of the real estate market seems to attract con artists. Most of these fraudsters are quite intelligent and more than capable of making an honest living in real estate. In fact, a wide majority of them would make more money putting their energy, knowledge, and experience into more productive and honest pursuits. Instead, they prefer to exploit vulnerabilities in the system and to prey on distressed homeowners.

WARNING

When you're starting in foreclosure investing, you too may be vulnerable to the silver-tongued promises of the slick, fast-talking con artist who promises quick, easy profits.

Research the Title Yourself

Buying any property is first and foremost a legal transaction. To ensure that everyone involved in the transaction — including the seller, buyer, and lender — is protected and that the transfer of property from one owner to the next is legal, county offices record several documents that are publicly accessible, including the deed, title, mortgage (and note), and city records.

REMEMBER

Before buying a house directly from a homeowner or from another investor, have your title company supply you a title commitment, and examine it carefully so that you know what you're getting yourself into. See Chapter 8 for details on researching the paperwork.

Inspect the Property with Your Own Eyes

You wouldn't buy a used car without test-driving it, kicking the wheels, and taking a peek under the hood. Yet, many novice foreclosure investors do just that. They walk into a foreclosure auction and plop down tens of thousands of dollars for a property they've never even glanced at, often without knowing where it's located. They'd probably have a better chance of making a profit by buying lottery tickets.

REMEMBER

As a real estate investor, "My eyes or no buys" should be your credo. Until you see a property with your own eyes, you don't know what it is or what kind of condition it's in, or the condition of the properties on the same block.

Know What You're Bidding On

Novice investors often purchase "properties" at foreclosure completely unaware that for $30,000, they just bought a second mortgage that's almost guaranteed to be wiped off the books when the first mortgage is foreclosed on. They buy what almost assuredly will become a worthless piece of paper.

When you decide to buy a foreclosure property at an auction, realize that you may be bidding on any of the following:

>> Senior liens (first mortgages)

>> Junior liens (second mortgages or other claims against the property)

>> Tax liens (for unpaid property taxes)

REMEMBER

Before an auction, research the title carefully so that you're aware of all lenders and other parties that have a claim against the property. That way, you'll know whether the lien being auctioned is a senior, junior, or tax lien, and you can bid accordingly. When you're starting out, bid only on senior liens or tax liens.

Set Realistic Goals

I don't want to be a wet blanket choking out the fire of your enthusiasm, but I do want to encourage you to start slowly. Set a realistic goal of buying one or two foreclosure properties in your first year. Next year, you may want to buy one every quarter. The following year, you may be prepared to buy a property once a month or even more frequently if you have a strong support team and the necessary financial foundation in place.

TIP

Do your first foreclosure right; focus on one property from start to finish. See how it goes, log your mistakes, and then, when you're ready for your next property, repeat the process — without the mistakes this time. If a transaction flops, don't give up. The knowledge you gain in a failed attempt can only improve your chances of future success.

Muffle Your Emotions

When you're dealing directly with distressed homeowners, empathy is the most effective and appropriate response. As a real estate investor, however, this process is business, so avoid becoming too emotionally involved. The following list provides specific emotional guidelines to follow:

» **Avoid emotional connections with distressed homeowners.** Desperate homeowners often take desperate measures to remain in the home, trying to play your emotions against your business sense. You've arrived to help them out of the hole they're in, not to have them drag you into the same hole.

» **Leave your emotions at home when you attend an auction.** If your love for a property or your obsession to outbid the competition leads you to pay more for a property than it's worth, you lose.

» **Funnel frustration into determination, not anger.** You need others to help you gather the information you need and perform the work required to turn a profit. Anger only turns the people you need against you. Every problem has a solution. Solve the problem rather than blame others.

» **Don't despair.** Despair is so totally not cool.

Invest with Integrity

Some con artists who call themselves real estate investors seem to believe that anything they can do to get their grubby little hands on a house is good business. They justify their immoral and often criminal actions by saying things like these:

"Everybody's doing it."

"I didn't twist anybody's arm. They could have said 'No.'"

"If they had paid their mortgage and taxes, they never would have had to deal with me."

Admittedly, these statements are true, but certain actions cross the line that divides good from bad, ethical from unethical, and legal from illegal. Here are some practices that clearly cross the line:

» Withholding information from the homeowners that could enable them to sell the house themselves and extract some equity from the property.

» Misleading homeowners into believing that the only option they have is to sell the property to you.

» Befriending the homeowners to persuade them to sell the property to you, even when that's not in their best interest.

» Buying the tax lien and then persuading the homeowners to move out because now you own the property, even though they could pay the back taxes and retain possession of the home.

» In a state that has a redemption period, buying the property at auction and then informing the homeowners that you bought the property and that they need to move out immediately without informing them of their redemption rights and the amount of time they have to redeem the property.

» Cheating the homeowner out of overbid money. An *overbid* occurs when an investor pays more for the property at auction than what is owed on the property. The overbid amount is used to pay off junior lienholders first (assuming that they file a claim for what they're owed), and any remaining money belongs to the homeowners if they claim it. Con artists often try to charge the homeowners as much as 50 percent to help them claim the overbid money; other con artists simply take it all.

REMEMBER

If you feel that what you're saying to homeowners isn't in their best interest, you're probably doing something wrong. You want to make a profit, of course, so what's in your best interest counts too, but not to the point of misrepresenting the facts.

Anticipate Delays

Many of the most experienced and successful real estate investors refuse to deal with foreclosures, because foreclosures can be messy and drawn-out. In a way, that's good for you — you have less competition from the high rollers — but you have to prepare yourself for the messiness.

Because the successful foreclosure buyer must be patient, you need to calculate delays into your formula. Realize that any of the following delays often result in your having to wait to realize your profit:

>> Homeowners taking their sweet time to make a decision

>> Courts or trustees taking their sweet time to resolve the issue

>> Homeowners changing their minds at the last minute

>> Redemption periods that can last from several months to a year

REMEMBER

Don't count on quick-cash deals when you're investing in foreclosures. If you're investing part-time, keep your day job. You need steady income, so you can afford to be patient. If you need the profit from a foreclosure property to pay the bills, the stress of waiting may be enough to persuade you that investing in foreclosures isn't exactly the best option for you.

Foresee Unforeseen Expenses

Investing in real estate isn't rocket science. You can't calculate to the penny how much a property is going to cost because of all the variables involved. Although you can't prevent unforeseen expenses from sinking your budget, you can reduce the risk by creating a buffer and at least considering the following expenses:

>> Purchase price. This is something you control, so set the price with the goal of making a profit of 20 percent or better.

>> Repair and renovation expenses.

>> Holding costs, which include property taxes, interest on loans, insurance, and utilities for the duration of the project or the redemption period (if applicable in your area), time to repair and renovate the property, and time to sell it.

>> Real estate commissions, if you hire an agent to sell the property.

>> Transfer tax (sort of like sales tax), which varies from one locale to another.

>> Research fees for the title work and any other documents you need.

>> Recording fees, particularly at closing.

>> Miscellaneous expenses, including mileage and phone calls.

TIP

Underestimate your profit and overestimate your expenses. See Chapter 10 for guidelines on how much you can afford to pay for a property to be fairly certain of a profitable investment.

Deal with the Blame and Guilt

In some people's eyes, foreclosure investors are the scum of the Earth, stealing homes from poor, unfortunate homeowners and old ladies. As a foreclosure investor, you'd better be able to deal with the contempt you're about to face. Many real estate investors simply can't handle it and they look for the exits after investing in only one or two properties.

To steel yourself against the disdain you're likely to face, keep in mind that you didn't cause the predicament the current homeowners are in. They're in this predicament due to their own foibles or because of some unforeseen, financially stressful event that's outside their control. You've arrived on the accident scene with a possible solution to their current problem.

Appendix

Foreclosure Rules and Regulations for the 50 States

When you're playing the foreclosure investing game, you need to play by the rules. Here, I provide the rules and regulations governing foreclosure in each of the 50 United States as well as the District of Columbia, and I offer some additional research resources where you can obtain more detailed information.

To decipher this information, keep the following definitions in mind:

>> **Deed type:** Deed of trust, mortgage deed, or both. A *deed of trust* is a mortgage contract that places control of the deed in the hands of a third party: a trustee. The trustee has the power to foreclose on the property in the event that the borrower defaults on the loan. A *mortgage deed* is a contract between the lender and borrower that gives the lender the right to foreclose on the property in the event that the borrower defaults on the loan.

>> **Foreclosure process:** Judicial, nonjudicial, or both. A *judicial* foreclosure process is followed when no power of sale is provided in the mortgage or deed of trust; lenders must file a lawsuit to obtain a court order to foreclose on a property. A *nonjudicial* foreclosure process occurs when a power of sale is preauthorized in the mortgage or deed of trust, in which case the lender is given the right to foreclose on the property and sell it to pay off the balance of the loan in the event that the borrower defaults on the loan.

>> **Process period:** The average amount of time that the foreclosure process takes from the time a foreclosure notice or notice of default is presented until the time that possession is transferred to the new owner.

>> **Notice of default:** A notice that some states require be sent to homeowners, notifying them that they have failed to fulfill their payment obligations as borrowers. Here, I specify whether a notice of default is required by the state.

>> **Notice of sale:** An official announcement that specifies the time, place, and terms of a foreclosure sale and typically includes a description of the property,

the names of the mortgagor and mortgagee, and other information. In most states, such a notice must be published and posted in a public location and sometimes at the property for several weeks before the sale.

>> **Redemption period:** Most states have a mandatory redemption period after the sale, during which time the foreclosed-on homeowners have a right to redeem their property by paying off the loan along with any interest and penalties. Here, I specify whether the state has a mandatory redemption period and, if it does, the length of that redemption period.

WARNING

The information provided here offers a general overview of the rules and regulations governing foreclosure in each state. These rules and regulations may vary from one county to another, so consult your real estate attorney and the county clerk or register of deeds for additional details and clarification.

Alabama

Deed type: Deed of trust and mortgage deed
Foreclosure process: Judicial and nonjudicial (more common)
Process period: 60–90 days
Notice of default: Not required by state but may be required by mortgage
Notice of sale: 3 weeks in a local newspaper and posted at the courthouse and 3 other public places, or as specified in mortgage
Redemption period: 12 months

Alaska

Deed type: Deed of trust and mortgage deed
Foreclosure process: Judicial and nonjudicial (more common)
Process period: 90 days
Notice of default: Varies
Notice of sale: 4 consecutive weeks in local newspaper and also in 3 public places, including the closest U.S. Postal Service office, 30 days before the sale date
Redemption period: Judicial, 12 months; nonjudicial, none

Arizona

Deed type: Deed of trust
Foreclosure process: Judicial and nonjudicial
Process period: 90 days
Notice of default: None required
Notice of sale: 4 consecutive weeks in local newspaper, with the last notice appearing no fewer than 10 days before the sale; mailed to the borrower and all

other lienholders at least 3 months before the sale; posted on the property and at the courthouse at least 20 days before the sale
Redemption period: 6 months

Arkansas

Deed type: Deed of trust and mortgage deed
Foreclosure process: Judicial and nonjudicial
Process period: 120 days
Notice of default: Required to be filed with county (nonjudicial only) and mailed to the borrower
Notice of sale: 4 consecutive weeks in local newspaper, with the final notice appearing at least 10 days before the sale, and posted in the office of the county recorder
Redemption period: Judicial, 12 months; nonjudicial, none

California

Deed type: Deed of trust and mortgage deed
Foreclosure process: Judicial and nonjudicial (more common)
Process period: 90–120 days
Notice of default: Required to be filed with county and mailed to the borrower and other parties who have a claim against the property
Notice of sale: 3 consecutive weeks in local newspaper, starting at least 20 days before sale; recorded with the county at least 14 days before sale; and posted on the property and in one public location at least 20 days before sale
Redemption period: Judicial, 365 days; nonjudicial, none

Colorado

Deed type: Deed of trust
Foreclosure process: Judicial and nonjudicial (more common)
Process period: 60–150 days
Notice of default: None required
Notice of sale: 5 weeks in local newspaper and mailed to the borrower
Redemption period: Senior lienholders may redeem the foreclosed home 15 to 19 business days after the sale, but no later than noon of the final day. Each subsequent lienholder has an additional 5 business days and must redeem by noon of the final day. Redemption periods are not shortened if someone redeems early.

Connecticut

Deed type: Mortgage deed
Foreclosure process: Judicial

Process period: 150 days
Notice of default: None required
Notice of sale: Attorney assigned to sale publishes sales notice
Redemption period: Court decides

Delaware

Deed type: Mortgage deed
Foreclosure process: Judicial
Process period: 210–300 days
Notice of default: None required
Notice of sale: 14 days, posted in public places, on the property, in two local newspapers (no more than 3 times per week for 2 weeks before sale), and delivered to borrower (at least 10 days before the sale)
Redemption period: None, although the borrower can contest the sale before the court's confirmation of sale

District of Columbia

Deed type: Deed of trust and mortgage deed
Foreclosure process: Nonjudicial and judicial (rarely)
Process period: 30–60 days
Notice of default: Required to be sent to borrower
Notice of sale: Required, must be mailed 30 days before the sale date to the homeowners by certified mail, recorded with the county, mailed to the mayor or mayor's agent, and sent to any other lienholders. Notice of sale must also be posted as specified in the mortgage deed or deed of trust or advertised in the local newspaper at least 5 weeks leading up to the sale.
Redemption period: None

Florida

Deed type: Mortgage deed
Foreclosure process: Judicial
Process period: 150–180 days
Notice of default: Not required by state but may be required by mortgage
Notice of sale: 2 consecutive weeks before the sale, in a local paper or legal news publication, with the second notice published at least 5 days before sale
Redemption period: None

Georgia

Deed type: Deed of trust and mortgage deed
Foreclosure process: Nonjudicial and judicial (rarely)

Process period: 60–90 days
Notice of default: Not required by state but may be required by mortgage
Notice of sale: 4 consecutive weeks before the sale in a local news or legal publication and sent to borrower at least 15 days before the sale
Redemption period: None

Hawaii

Deed type: Deed of trust and mortgage deed
Foreclosure process: Nonjudicial and judicial
Process period: 180 days (nonjudicial), 330 days (judicial)
Notice of default: Required by the sale clause in most mortgages
Notice of sale: 3 consecutive weeks before the sale in a local newspaper, with the last notice appearing at least 14 days before sale; sent to borrower at least 21 days before the sale
Redemption period: None

Idaho

Deed type: Deed of trust and mortgage deed
Foreclosure process: Nonjudicial and judicial (rarely)
Process period: 150–180 days (nonjudicial), 330 days (judicial)
Notice of default: Mailed to borrower and anyone who has requested notification and filed with the county recorder
Notice of sale: 4 consecutive weeks, with the final notice appearing at least 30 days before sale; notice of sale must be mailed to the borrower 120 days before sale
Redemption period: Judicial, 365 days; nonjudicial, none

Illinois

Deed type: Mortgage deed
Foreclosure process: Judicial
Process period: 300–360 days
Notice of default: None required
Notice of sale: 3 consecutive weeks before sale in the legal notice and real estate sections of a local newspaper, with the first notice appearing no more than 45 days before sale and the last notice appearing no fewer than 7 days before sale; notice must be sent to the borrower and others who have a legal claim to the property
Redemption period: 90 days

Indiana

Deed type: Mortgage deed

Foreclosure process: Judicial
Process period: 150–270 days
Notice of default: None required, but most lenders deliver a notice of default to the borrowers
Notice of sale: 3 consecutive weeks before sale in a local newspaper, with the first notice appearing at least 30 days before sale, and in at least 3 public places, in the county courthouse, and delivered to the borrower by the sheriff
Redemption period: None

Iowa

Deed type: Mortgage deed
Foreclosure process: Judicial and nonjudicial (by request)
Process period: 120–180 days
Notice of default: Required
Notice of sale: 2 weeks before sale in a local newspaper, with the first notice appearing at least 4 weeks before sale, and in at least 3 public places, including the county courthouse, and delivered to the borrower (if still residing in the property) at least 20 days before the sale
Redemption period: 12 months

Kansas

Deed type: Mortgage deed
Foreclosure process: Judicial
Process period: 90–150 days
Notice of default: Required
Notice of sale: 3 consecutive weeks before sale in a local newspaper
Redemption period: Up to 12 months

Kentucky

Deed type: Mortgage deed
Foreclosure process: Judicial
Process period: 150–180 days
Notice of default: None required
Notice of sale: 3 consecutive weeks before sale in a local newspaper
Redemption period: 12 months

Louisiana

Deed type: Mortgage
Foreclosure process: Judicial
Process period: 60–180 days
Notice of default: None required, but mortgage may require it

Notice of sale: 2 times before sale in a local newspaper (in the parish where the property is located) and personally served to the homeowner by the sheriff; must be advertised for a minimum 30 days
Redemption period: None; deficiency judgments are allowed

Maine

Deed type: Mortgage deed
Foreclosure process: Judicial
Process period: 180–210 days
Notice of default: Required to be delivered to homeowner before foreclosure
Notice of sale: 3 weeks before sale in a local newspaper
Redemption period: 90 days

Maryland

Deed type: Mortgage deed and deed of trust
Foreclosure process: Judicial
Process period: 60–90 days but usually takes longer
Notice of default: Not required but usually provided
Notice of sale: 3 consecutive weeks before sale in a local newspaper; notice must be sent to the borrower and any other lienholders at least 10 days before the sale
Redemption period: Court decides

Massachusetts

Deed type: Mortgage deed and deed of trust
Foreclosure process: Judicial and nonjudicial
Process period: 90–120 days
Notice of default: Not required by state but may be stipulated in the mortgage
Notice of sale: 3 consecutive weeks before sale in a local newspaper, with the first notice appearing no fewer than 21 days before sale; notice must be sent to the borrower and any other lienholders at least 14 days before the sale
Redemption period: None, but the borrower is entitled to any overbid proceeds (money paid at the sale in excess of what the borrower owed)

Michigan

Deed type: Mortgage deed and deed of trust
Foreclosure process: Judicial and nonjudicial
Process period: 90–120 days
Notice of default: Not required by state but often stipulated in the mortgage
Notice of sale: 4 consecutive weeks before sale in a local newspaper or legal publication, with the first notice appearing no fewer than 28 days before sale; notice

must be posted on the property for the same period during which the publication appears

Redemption period: 6–12 months, 30 days if vacant

Minnesota

Deed type: Mortgage deed and deed of trust
Foreclosure process: Judicial and nonjudicial (more common)
Process period: 30–90 days
Notice of default: Required
Notice of sale: 6 weeks before sale in a local newspaper or legal publication; notice must be given in person to the borrower at least 4 weeks before sale
Redemption period: 6–12 months

Mississippi

Deed type: Mortgage deed and deed of trust
Foreclosure process: Judicial and nonjudicial (more common)
Process period: 90–120 days
Notice of default: Required 30 days before sale
Notice of sale: 3 weeks before sale in a local newspaper; notice must be posted at the county courthouse
Redemption period: None

Missouri

Deed type: Mortgage deed and deed of trust (more common)
Foreclosure process: Judicial and nonjudicial (more common)
Process period: 60–90 days
Notice of default: Required
Notice of sale: 3 weeks before sale in a local newspaper (where the property is located); in counties that have a city with more than 50,000 residents, the notice must be published for 20 days before sale with the last notice appearing on the day of the sale; in other counties, the notice must be published once a week for 4 weeks, with the final notice appearing no more than 1 week before sale; notice must be sent to the borrower and other lienholders at least 20 days before sale
Redemption period: Applicable only if the buyer at action is the lender and the borrower expresses the intent to redeem at least 10 days before sale. Then the borrower must post bond within 20 days after the sale in an amount that covers the mortgage interest, secondary loan interest, expenses, damages, and 6 percent interest. Assuming that the borrower can meet these conditions, the borrower has 12 months from the time of sale to redeem.

Montana

Deed type: Mortgage deed and deed of trust
Foreclosure process: Judicial and nonjudicial
Process period: 120–180 days
Notice of default: Not required unless required by mortgage
Notice of sale: 3 consecutive weeks before sale in a local newspaper; mailed to the borrower at least 120 days before sale; posted on the property at least 20 days before sale
Redemption period: 12 months

Nebraska

Deed type: Mortgage deed
Foreclosure process: Judicial
Process period: 120–180 days
Notice of default: Required
Notice of sale: 5 weeks before sale in a local newspaper, with the final notice appearing 10–30 days before sale (for out-of-court foreclosure); 4 weeks before sale in a local newspaper (for court foreclosure)
Redemption period: None

Nevada

Deed type: Mortgage deed and deed of trust (more common)
Foreclosure process: Judicial and nonjudicial (more common)
Process period: 90–180 days
Notice of default: Required
Notice of sale: 3 weeks before sale in a local newspaper; in 3 public places at least 21 days before sale; and mailed to the borrower and any other lienholders
Redemption period: Out-of-court foreclosure, none; court foreclosure (which is rare), 12 months

New Hampshire

Deed type: Mortgage deed and deed of trust
Foreclosure process: Nonjudicial
Process period: 60–90 days
Notice of default: Required by most mortgages, giving the borrower 30 days to pay
Notice of sale: 3 weeks before sale in a local newspaper, with the first notice appearing at least 21 days before sale; delivered to the borrower at least 26 days before sale
Redemption period: Out-of-court foreclosure, none; court foreclosure (which is rare), 12 months

New Jersey

Deed type: Mortgage deed
Foreclosure process: Judicial
Process period: 90–270 days
Notice of default: Required to notify borrower at least 30 days before initiating foreclosure
Notice of sale: 2 local newspapers, one of which is the largest municipality in the county or the county seat; posted on the property and in the county office; and given to the borrower at least 10 days before sale
Redemption period: 6 months

New Mexico

Deed type: Mortgage deed
Foreclosure process: Judicial
Process period: 120–180 days
Notice of default: Not required by state but may be required by mortgage or deed of trust
Notice of sale: 4 consecutive weeks in a local newspaper, with the final notice appearing at least 3 days before sale
Redemption period: 9 months

New York

Deed type: Mortgage deed and deed of trust
Foreclosure process: Judicial (more common) and nonjudicial
Process period: 120–240 days
Notice of default: Not required by state but may be required by mortgage or deed of trust
Notice of sale: 4 weeks in a local newspaper
Redemption period: None

North Carolina

Deed type: Mortgage deed and deed of trust
Foreclosure process: Judicial and nonjudicial (more common)
Process period: 90–120 days
Notice of default: Required
Notice of sale: 2 weeks in a local newspaper; mailed to the borrower at least 20 days before sale, with the last notice appearing not more than 10 days before sale; posted at the county courthouse at least 20 days before sale
Redemption period: 10 days

North Dakota

Deed type: Mortgage deed
Foreclosure process: Judicial
Process period: 90–150 days
Notice of default: 30-day notice of intent to foreclose
Notice of sale: 2 months in the county legal news, with the last notice appearing at least 10 days before sale; delivered to the borrower
Redemption period: 60 days

Ohio

Deed type: Mortgage deed
Foreclosure process: Judicial
Process period: 150–210 days
Notice of default: Required
Notice of sale: 3 weeks in a local newspaper
Redemption period: Until confirmation of sale

Oklahoma

Deed type: Mortgage deed and deed of trust
Foreclosure process: Judicial and nonjudicial
Process period: 90–210 days
Notice of default: Required
Notice of sale: 4 consecutive weeks in a local newspaper (in the county in which the property is located), with the first notice appearing at least 30 days before sale; recorded in the county
Redemption period: Until confirmation of sale

Oregon

Deed type: Mortgage deed and deed of trust
Foreclosure process: Judicial and nonjudicial
Process period: 120–180 days
Notice of default: Required 4 months before sale
Notice of sale: 4 consecutive weeks in a local newspaper, with the last notice appearing at least 20 days before sale
Redemption period: No right of redemption with advertisement and sale, up to 180 days for in-court foreclosure

Pennsylvania

Deed type: Mortgage deed
Foreclosure process: Judicial
Process period: 90–270 days

Notice of default: Required 4 months before sale
Notice of sale: 3 consecutive weeks in a local newspaper and local legal newspaper; posted on the property at least 30 days before sale; delivered to the borrower
Redemption period: None

Rhode Island

Deed type: Mortgage deed
Foreclosure process: Judicial (rarely) and nonjudicial
Process period: 60–270 days
Notice of default: Not required by state; usually required by mortgage
Notice of sale: 3 weeks in a local newspaper and local legal newspaper. with the first notice appearing at least 21 days before sale; borrower must be notified at least 20 days before public advertisement
Redemption period: Up to 3 years

South Carolina

Deed type: Mortgage deed
Foreclosure process: Judicial
Process period: 120–180 days
Notice of default: Not required
Notice of sale: 3 weeks in a local newspaper and local legal newspaper; posted at the county courthouse
Redemption period: If lender reserves the right to file a deficiency judgment, 30 days; if lender waives the right, none

South Dakota

Deed type: Mortgage deed and deed of trust
Foreclosure process: Judicial (more common) and nonjudicial
Process period: 190–270 days
Notice of default: Not required by state but often required by mortgage
Notice of sale: 3 weeks in a local newspaper; delivered to the borrower and any other lienholders at least 21 days before sale
Redemption period: Up to 12 months

Tennessee

Deed type: Mortgage deed and deed of trust
Foreclosure process: Judicial (rarely) and nonjudicial
Process period: 60–90 days
Notice of default: Not required by state but often required by mortgage
Notice of sale: 3 times in a local newspaper, with the first notice appearing at least 20 days before sale; although not required to do so, the trustee often mails a notice to the borrower

Redemption period: Usually none, as specified in the deed of trust, but can be up to 720 days

Texas

Deed type: Mortgage deed and deed of trust
Foreclosure process: Judicial (rarely) and nonjudicial
Process period: 30–90 days
Notice of default: Required
Notice of sale: Posted at the county courthouse; filed with the county clerk at least 21 days before sale; and mailed to the borrower at least 21 days before sale
Redemption period: None

Utah

Deed type: Mortgage deed and deed of trust
Foreclosure process: Judicial and nonjudicial (more common)
Process period: 120–150 days
Notice of default: Required
Notice of sale: 3 consecutive weeks in a local newspaper, with the final notice appearing at least 10 days but not more than 30 days before sale; posted on the property at least 20 days before sale; posted in the office of the county recorder at least 20 days before sale
Redemption period: Court decides; none for out-of-court foreclosures

Vermont

Deed type: Mortgage deed and deed of trust
Foreclosure process: Judicial and nonjudicial
Process period: 7–10 months
Notice of default: Required
Notice of sale: 3 weeks in a local newspaper, with the first notice appearing at least 21 days before sale; delivered to the borrower at least 60 days before sale
Redemption period: Up to 6 months

Virginia

Deed type: Mortgage deed and deed of trust
Foreclosure process: Judicial and nonjudicial (more common)
Process period: 30–90 days
Notice of default: Required
Notice of sale: Delivered to borrower at least 14 days before sale; mortgage and state statutes may stipulate other advertising requirements
Redemption period: None

Washington

Deed type: Mortgage deed and deed of trust
Foreclosure process: Judicial and nonjudicial (more common)
Process period: 120 days
Notice of default: Required for out-of-court foreclosures
Notice of sale: Must be recorded at least 90 days before sale and mailed to the borrower and any other lienholders; published in a local newspaper at least once between the 32nd and 28th day before sale and once between the 11th and 7th day before sale
Redemption period: 12 months unless redemption rights have been precluded

West Virginia

Deed type: Mortgage deed and deed of trust
Foreclosure process: Judicial
Process period: 60–90 days
Notice of default: Required for out-of-court foreclosures
Notice of sale: 2 weeks in a local newspaper unless specified otherwise in the trust deed; mailed to the borrower and other lienholders at least 20 days before sale
Redemption period: None

Wisconsin

Deed type: Mortgage deed and deed of trust
Foreclosure process: Judicial (most common) and nonjudicial
Process period: 6–10 months
Notice of default: None, but the lender typically warns the borrower before filing with the court
Notice of sale: Varies according to court's ruling or county or local laws; in most cases, the property can't be advertised for sale until 10 months following the court's ruling, although the lender and borrower can agree to an earlier date
Redemption period: None

Wyoming

Deed type: Mortgage deed and deed of trust
Foreclosure process: Judicial and nonjudicial
Process period: 60–90 days
Notice of default: Required to notify borrower at least 10 days before advertising the sale
Notice of sale: 4 consecutive weeks in a local newspaper
Redemption period: 3 months

Index

A

accepting cash offers, 164, 182

accountants, 64–65

adjustable-rate mortgage (ARM), 89–90

adjustment period, 89

advertising

  creating, 102

  for foreclosure properties, 114

affidavits, for expenses, 283

Alabama, rules and regulations in, 354

Alaska, rules and regulations in, 354

amortization, as a feature of hard-money loans, 82

amount owed, calculating, 176–177

anger, handling in pre-auction stage, 44–45

angst, handling in pre-auction stage, 44–45

anticipating delays, 349–350

appliances, kitchen, 302–303

Arizona, rules and regulations in, 354

Arkansas, rules and regulations in, 355

ARM (adjustable-rate mortgage), 89–90

"as is" condition, 16

"as is" market value, 176

assessing

  ability to deal with pre-auction scenarios, 45–46

  amount owed, 176–177

  homeowner options, 181–182

  homeowners' credit health, 179–180

  homeowners' equity, 174–177

  return on investment (ROI), 293–294

  top cash offer, 177–178

  wants of homeowners, 180

assessor's office, obtaining information from, 138

assets, selling through chapter 7 bankruptcy, 242

assigning positions, to junior lienholders, 327–328

attorneys

  bankruptcy, 112, 122–123, 249–250

  divorce, 112, 121

  foreclosure, 111

  homeowner-centered, 250

  probate, 112, 119

  real estate, 111

  self-interested, 249

  teaming up with, 119–123

  value of, 243

auctions

  acquiring properties after, 52–54

  bidding at foreclosure auctions, 197–201

  finding dates, times, and places for, 190–191

  following up after, 202–206

B

backup buyers, 201–202

balloon payments, as a feature of hard-money loans, 82

bank addendum, 223

bank foreclosures. *See* Real Estate Owned (REO) properties

bankruptcies

  about, 241–242

  attorney's specializing in, 60

  delays and, 251–253

  filing for, 36, 167, 182

  finding houses in bankruptcy, 245–248

  gatekeepers, 248–251

bankruptcies *(continued)*
  knowing when to purchase, 244–245
  laws on, 242–243
  suggesting, 341–342
bankruptcy attorneys, 112, 122–123,
    249–250
bankruptcy notices, 246
bankruptcy trustees, 249
basements, renovating, 300
bathrooms, renovating, 299
bedrooms, renovating, 299–300
bidder's packet, from county treasurer's
    office, 237
bidding
  about, 49, 189–190, 347
  agent commissions and, 193
  closing costs and, 193
  estimating holding costs, 192–193
  estimating property values, 192
  estimating repair and renovation costs, 192
  finding auction dates. times, and places,
    190–191
  following up after auctions, 202–206
  on junior liens, 335
  opening bid, 190
  poker face for, 51–52
  preparing maximum bids, 191–197
  process of, 197–201
  on properties at auctions, 13–15
  pros and cons of buying at auctions, 50–51
  role of backup buyers, 201–202
  sealed bids, 199–201
  on second mortgages, 335
  setting maximum bids, 23–24, 51
blame, dealing with, 351
BPO (broker's price opinion), 208
brokers
  mortgage, 61–62
  real estate, 112

REO, 211
  waiting for, to list REO properties, 219–220
broker's price opinion (BPO), 208
budgets, for renovations and repairs,
    294–296
building permits, 138–139
bullet loan, 83
business cards, 100–102
buybacks
  about, 252
  financing through insurance-policy
    proceeds, 323
buyer's agent, 71
buyer's financing, 313
buying
  junior liens, 269–272
  properties after the sale, 15–16
  properties in probate, 120–121
  properties of divorce, 122

C

California, rules and regulations in, 355
calling homeowners, 156–159
CARES (Coronavirus Aid, Relief, and
    Economic Security) Act (2020), 14
case number, on Notice of Default
    (NDO), 127
"cash back at closing" deals, 314
cash calls, as a feature of hard-money
    loans, 82
cash needs, estimating, 78–79
cash offers, accepting, 164, 182
cash-out strategies. *See also* selling and
    leasing
  about, 26–28, 319
  assigning position to junior lienholders,
    327–328
  equity stripping, 322
  financing buyback, 323

leasing to foreclosed-on homeowners, 324–325

life insurance, 324

offering lease-option agreements, 325–327

refinancing, 320

reselling to previous owners, 320–324

chain of title, 63

chapter 7 bankruptcy, selling assets through, 242

chapter 13 bankruptcy, restructuring debt through, 243

Cheat Sheet (website), 4

checklist, for properties, 142–144

choosing

point of entry in foreclosure process, 41–55

renovation strategies, 292–293

seller's agents, 73–74, 308–309

church affiliations, using for networking, 113

closing costs

as a feature of hard-money loans, 82

subtracting, 193

closing date, 314

closing deals

about, 185, 316–317

on pre-auction purchases, 280–281

on REO properties, 224

before sales, 48

closing papers, 280

clubs, using for networking, 113

code violations, 139

Colorado, rules and regulations in, 355

commercial foreclosure information services, using for finding Notice of Default (NDO), 117–118

communication, importance of, 103–104

communities, building, 100

comparable properties, renovations and, 294

comparing offers, 313–315

competitiveness, cash and, 18

completing paperwork, 24–25

computers, importance of, 102

conditional clauses, 314

confidence, cash and, 18

congratulating homeowners, 155–156

Connecticut, rules and regulations in, 355–356

construction (mechanic's) lienholders, 257, 267

contact information, managing, 104

contacting

homeowners, 145–171

lenders, 145–171

senior lienholder, 170

continency planning, 88

contracting, with contractors/subcontractors, 68–70

contractors, 66–71

conventional loans

about, 80, 88–89

recordkeeping, 90–93

types of, 89–90

Coronavirus Aid, Relief, and Economic Security (CARES) Act (2020), 14

cost overruns, planning for, 88

costs

holding, 192–193, 333

of renovations, 294

counteroffers, negotiating, 313–316

county sheriff's office, 54, 128

county treasurer's office, 237

craftsmanship, quality of, 100

Craigslist, 114

creating

ads, 102

communities, 100

leads, 96–97

teams, 16–17, 59–75

creativity, cash and, 18

credibility, cash and, 18

credit cards, as a source of investment capital, 86–87

credit reports, 91–92

credit scores, improving, 92–93

credit-card loans, 80

creditors, getting on your side, 250–251

cross-collateralization, as a feature of hard-money loans, 82–83

D

date recorded, on mortgage/mortgage note, 136

deal analysis
  about, 173
  assessing credit health of homeowners, 179–180
  assessing homeowner options for, 181–182
  assessing wants of homeowners, 180
  calculating amount owed, 176–177
  calculating homeowners' equity, 174–177
  calculating top cash offer, 177–178
  closing, 185
  determining gross monthly income of homeowners, 180
  determining options based on LTV, 178–179
  logging loan status, 178
  purchase agreement, 183–184
  worksheet for, 174–180

debt
  restructuring through chapter 13 bankruptcy, 243
  suggesting negotiations, 340

debtor in possession stage, of bankruptcy process, 244

deed in lieu of foreclosure, 36, 166–167

deed warranty names, on foreclosure information sheet, 135

deeds
  recording, 203, 215
  types, 353

Delaware, rules and regulations in, 356

delays
  anticipating, 349–350
  from bankruptcy, 251–253
  planning for, 88

delinquent, as a loan status, 178

delivering
  follow-up letters, 152–155
  letter of introductions, 151–152

Department of Housing and Urban Development (HUD), 53–54

Department of Veterans Affairs (VA), 53–54, 89

designing business cards, 100–102

determining
  homeowners' gross monthly income, 180
  options based on LTV, 178–179
  worth, 91

discount points, as a feature of hard-money loans, 81–82

District of Columbia, rules and regulations in, 356

divorce
  finding properties of, 121–122
  properties from, 97

divorce attorneys, 112, 121

divorce court, as source of finding properties of divorce, 121–122

documentation, investigating, 20–21

dontwanners, 114–115

DOT (state department of transportation), 53, 237–239

down payments
  about, 223
  lease-option agreements and, 325

drive-by inspections, 140–142

drug enforcement agency, 53–54

due diligence
  about, 125
  acquiring title, 126–127
  assessor's office, 138

checklist for, 142–144

collecting information about properties, 126–140

drive-by inspections, 140–142

inspecting properties, 140–142

miscellaneous information, 139–140

Notice of Default (NOD), 127–132

performing, 19–23

property worksheet, 138–139

red flags, 144

Register of Deeds office, 132–137

taking pictures, 142

walk-around inspections, 140–142

E

earnest money, 314

earnest-money deposit (EMD), 184

emotions, muffling, 348

Equifax, 91

equity, cashing out, 28

equity stripping, 322

estimating

"as is" market value, 176

cash needs, 78–79

holding costs, 192–193

needs of lenders, 220

property value, 192

repair and renovation costs, 192

value of properties, 22

eviction

about, 39

process of, 287–289

exit strategy

about, 279–280

closing on pre-auction purchases, 280–281

evicting residents, 287–289

investors and, 284–287

maintaining property status quo, 282–283

planning repairs and renovations, 287

redemption period and, 282–287

securing properties, 283–284

tying up loose ends after auction, 282

expenses, expecting unforeseen, 350–351

Experian, 91

exteriors

renovating, 297–298

staging, 309

F

family, using for networking, 112–113

Fannie Mae properties, 231–234

FDIC properties, 234

Federal Deposit Insurance Corporation (FDIC), 234

Federal Housing Authority (FHA), 89, 226, 316

filing for bankruptcy, 36, 167, 182

financial advice, providing basic, 338

financing

about, 77

buybacks through insurance-policy proceeds, 323

conventional loans, 88–93

estimating cash needs, 78–79

finding private lenders, 83–84

foreclosure investing and, 17–18

with gap loans, 81, 83

with hard money, 81–83

options for, 79–81

partnering with investors, 84

planning for contingencies, 88

securing, 97–98

shopping for low-cost loans, 93–94

using your own resources, 84–88

finding
  contractors, 68
  foreclosures, 18–19
  for FSBO properties, 115–116
  government-seized properties, 234–239
  houses in bankruptcy, 245–248
  HUD homes, 227–229
  Notice of Default (NDO), 116–118
  private lenders, 83–84
  professionals, 98
  properties, 133–134
  property tax sales, 273–274
  REO properties, 210–216
  seized properties, 18–19
  skilled laborers, 70
  subcontractors, 68
  unskilled laborers, 70
  VA repos, 230–231
first-mortgages
  lenders, as lienholders, 266
  loan amount, on mortgage/mortgage note, 136
  protecting, 271–272
fiscal calendar, for lenders, 218
fixed-rate mortgages, 89
Florida, rules and regulations in, 356
following up
  after auctions, 202–206
  delivering follow-up letters, 152–155
for sale by owner (FSBO) properties, searching for, 115–116
forbearance
  about, 35
  as an option for homeowners, 170
  negotiating with lenders for, 162, 181
foreclosure attorneys, 111
foreclosure investing
  about, 9–10
  attorney's specializing in, 60
  building teams for, 16–17
  cashing out, 26–28
  finances and, 17–18
  finding properties for, 18–19
  performing due diligence, 19–23
  postsale stage, 15–16
  presale stage, 12–13
  process of, 10–12
  sale (auction) stage, 13–15
  scheduling activities, 146–149
  setting maximum bid, 23–24
  starting, 12–16
  taking possession of properties, 24–26
foreclosure notices. *See* Notices of Default (NODs)
foreclosure process
  about, 29–30, 353
  deeds in lieu of foreclosure, 36
  eviction, 39
  filing for bankruptcy, 36
  forbearance, 35
  junior liens, 38
  missed-payment notice storage, 31–32
  mortgage modification, 35
  notice of default, 32
  pre-auction stage, 42–46
  redemption period, 37–38
  reinstating mortgages, 34–35
  repayment plan, 35
  sale stage, 32–33
  selecting point of entry in, 41–55
  stopping, 33–38
  types of, 30–31
foreclosure wholesalers, 54
45-to-60 days' notice, 31
Freddie Mac properties, 231–234
friends, using for networking, 112–113
FSBO (for sale by owner) properties, searching for, 115–116
funds, insufficient, 331–332
future value, 61

G

gallery, 211

gap loans, 81, 83

general contractors, 67–68

General Service Administration (GSA) Auctions, 238

Georgia, rules and regulations in, 356

goal-setting, 347–348

government loans, 80

government properties
  about, 53–54, 225–226
  Fannie Mae properties, 231–234
  finding government-seized properties, 234–239
  finding HUD homes, 227–229
  finding VA repos, 230–231
  Freddie Mac properties, 231–234

government-seized properties, 234–239

governor, 197

greed, 336

gross monthly income, determining for homeowners, 180

GSA (General Service Administration) Auctions, 238

guilt, dealing with, 351

H

hard-money loans, 79, 81–83

Hawaii, rules and regulations in, 357

helping
  homeowners in job searches, 338
  offering, 342–343

hiring general contractors, 67–68

holding costs
  estimating, 192–193
  underestimating, 333

home equity, as a source of investment capital, 86

home inspectors, 65–66

home-equity line of credit (LOC), 90

home-equity loan, 90

HomeInfoMax, 134

homeowner-centered attorneys, 250

homeowners
  accepting cash offers, 164
  assessing credit health of, 179–180
  assessing options for, 181–182
  assessing wants of, 180
  assisting in assessing refinance options, 340–341
  assisting in job searches, 338
  calling, 156–159
  congratulating, 155–156
  contacting, 145–171
  contacting after sales, 284–285
  convincing to seek help, 161
  deed in lieu of foreclosure, 166–167
  delivering follow-up letters, 152–155
  delivering letter of introductions to, 151–152
  determining gross monthly income of, 180
  encouraging move-on of, 26
  encouraging to contact lenders, 339
  equity stripping and, 322
  filing for bankruptcy, 167
  getting on your side, 250
  guiding in pre-auction stage, 43–44
  inspections and, 168–169
  investigating, 22–23
  lease-option agreement, 165, 182
  leases, 166, 182, 251
  leasing properties to foreclosed-on, 324–325
  listing properties, 163–164
  mail campaigns for, 151–156
  negotiating with lenders for forbearance, 162
  options for, 160–168
  profile for, 159–160

homeowners *(continued)*

  redemption period, 167–168, 216

  refinancing mortgages, 162–163

  refinancing through you, 164–165

  reinstating loans, 162

  short sales, 164

  suggesting help from family/friends to, 338–339

  teaming with, 261–262

  telephone number of, 139

  tracking down, 150–151

  trusting, 336

homeowners' equity, calculating, 174–177

homeowner's insurance, exit strategy and, 281

HomePath, 233–234

HomeSteps, 232

HUD (Department of Housing and Urban Development), 53–54

HUD bid site, 202

HUD homes

  about, 226, 227

  finding, 227–229

HUD Homes, 229

HUD repos, 53

I

icons, explained, 4

Idaho, rules and regulations in, 357

identifying personal lead generators, 110–113

Illinois, rules and regulations in, 357

improving credit score, 92–93

Indiana, rules and regulations in, 357

Individual Retirement Accounts (IRAs), self-directed, 86–87

inner circle, 103

insertion date, on Notice of Default (NDO), 127

inspections

  about, 140

  drive-by, 140–142

  exit strategy and, 281

  homeowners and, 168–169

  mistakes with, 334

  of properties, 21–22, 346–347

  REO properties, 216–217

  walk-around, 140–142

insufficient funds, 331–332

insurance

  financing buybacks through proceeds from, 323

  obtaining, 203, 283

  paying, 25–26

  proof of, 70–71

integrity, acting with, 99, 337–343, 348–349

interest rate caps, 89–90

interest rate of loan, on Notice of Default (NDO), 129

interest rates

  as a feature of hard-money loans, 82

  on mortgage/mortgage note, 136

interiors

  renovating, 298

  staging, 310–311

Internal Revenue Service (IRS)

  buying properties from, 236–237

  as a lienholder, 258, 265–266

  notifying, 265–266

Internet resources

  Cheat Sheet, 4

  Craigslist, 114

  credit reports, 91

  Federal Deposit Insurance Corporation (FDIC), 234

  General Service Administration (GSA) Auctions, 238

  HomeInfoMax, 134

HomePath, 233

HomeSteps, 231

HUD bid site, 202

HUD Homes, 229

IRS properties, 236

Michigan's DOT, 238

National Association of Certified Home Inspector (NACHI), 65

Oregon's DOT, 238

Real Property Utilization & Disposal, 238

Realtor, 73

U.S. Department of Agriculture (USDA) Real Estate for Sale, 239

U.S. Treasury Real Property Auctions, 239

USA People Search, 151

Vendor Resource Management (VRM), 230

Vistaprint, 100

investigating

documentation, 20–21

homeowners, 22–23

titles, 20–21, 333–334

investing with integrity, 348–349

investment capital, sources of, 85–87

investors

buying properties from other, 54

financial attractiveness of, 210–211

partnering with, 83–84

Iowa, rules and regulations in, 358

IRAs (Individual Retirement Accounts), self-directed, 86–87

IRS (Internal Revenue Service)

buying properties from, 236–237

as a lienholder, 258, 265–266

notifying, 265–266

J

judicial sale, foreclosure by, 31

junior lienholders

assigning positions to, 327–328

contacting, 171

junior liens

about, 13–14, 38, 49

bidding on, 335

buying and selling, 269–272

K

Kansas, rules and regulations in, 358

Kentucky, rules and regulations in, 358

kitchens, renovating, 298–299, 301–303

L

landlords, becoming, 317

laws, bankruptcy, 242–243

leads

generating, 96–97

maximizing, 337–343

rewarding, 104–105

lease-option agreement, 165, 182, 325–327

leases, 28, 166, 182, 251, 324–325

leasing and selling

about, 305

assets through chapter 7 bankruptcy, 242

becoming a landlord, 317

closing deals, 316–317

junior liens, 269–272

marketing for, 312–313

negotiating offers/counteroffers, 313–316

properties, 27

staging for, 309–311

suggesting, 341

through qualified real estate agents, 306–309

your position to other lienholders, 28

legal lot, subdivision, and city, on Notice of Default (NDO), 128

lenders
  contacting, 145–171, 267–269
  encouraging homeowners to contact, 339
  estimating needs of, 220
  fiscal calendar of, 218
  negotiating with, for forbearance, 162, 181
length of redemption period, on Notice of Default (NDO), 129
letter of introductions, delivering, 151–152
liber
  on mortgage/mortgage note, 136
  on Notice of Default (NDO), 129
lienholders
  dealing with, 259–260
  hierarchy of, 256–259
  negotiating with, 265–269
liens
  defined, 49
  obtaining information about, 137
  unpaid, 137
life insurance, 323–324
lifetime cap, 89
line of credit (LOC), 86, 90
liquidation stage, of bankruptcy process, 244
listing agents. See seller's agents
listing properties, 163–164, 181
loan officers. See mortgage brokers
loan to value (LTV)
  determining options based on, 178–179
  as a feature of hard-money loans, 82
loans
  bullet, 83
  conventional, 80
  credit-card, 80
  gap, 81, 83
  government, 80
  hard-money, 79, 81–83
  home-equity, 90
  logging status of, 178

personal, 80
rehab, 90
reinstating, 162, 181
shopping for low-cost, 93–94
LOC (line of credit), 86, 90
local publications, using for finding Notice of Default (NDO), 116–117
logging loan status, 178
Louisiana, rules and regulations in, 358
low-down-payment mortgage, 90
LTV (loan to value)
  determining options based on, 178–179
  as a feature of hard-money loans, 82

M

Mackay, Harvey (author)
  Swim with the Sharks, 103
mail campaigns, for homeowners, 151–156
mailing lists, using for finding Notice of Default (NDO), 117
Maine, rules and regulations in, 359
managing contact information, 104
margin, 89
market demand, renovations and, 294
marketing
  properties for sale/lease, 27, 312–313
  yourself, 100–104
Maryland, rules and regulations in, 359
Massachusetts, rules and regulations in, 359
maximizing
  leads, 337–343
  values, 27
maximum bids, setting, 23–24, 51
mechanicals, renovating, 300–301
Michigan, rules and regulations in, 359
Minnesota, rules and regulations in, 360
missed-payment notice stage, 31–32
Mississippi, rules and regulations in, 360
Missouri, rules and regulations in, 360

mistakes
  avoiding, 345–351
  common, 331–336
  planning for, 88
money, using your own, 85
Montana, rules and regulations in, 361
mortgage brokers, 61–62, 112
mortgage company's attorney, on Notice of Default (NDO), 129
mortgage fraud, 136
mortgage modification, 35
mortgage notes, obtaining information from, 136
mortgage payoff information, 316
mortgage sale date, on Notice of Default (NDO), 129
mortgagee
  on foreclosure information sheet, 135
  on mortgage/mortgage note, 136
mortgages
  adjustable-rate mortgage (ARM), 89–90
  first-mortgages, 136, 266, 271–272
  fixed-rate, 89
  low-down-payment, 90
  obtaining information from, 136
  refinancing, 86, 162–163, 181
  reinstating, 34–35
  second, 271–272, 335
  variable-rate, 89–90
mortgagor names, on foreclosure information sheet, 135
Multiple Listing Service (MLS), 22, 98–99, 176
must-sell ads, 110

N

name of the mortgage, on Notice of Default (NDO), 129
name of the mortgagee, on Notice of Default (NDO), 129

name of the mortgagor, on Notice of Default (NDO), 129
National Association of Certified Home Inspector (NACHI), 65
National Association of Realtors (NAR), 307
Nebraska, rules and regulations in, 361
negotiating
  counteroffers, 313–316
  with lenders for forbearance, 162, 181
  with lienholders, 265–269
  offers, 313–316
  short sales, 256–269
neighbors, using for networking, 112–113
networking
  about, 95
  acting with integrity, 99
  bankruptcy and, 247–248
  building communities, 100
  communication, 103–104
  craftsmanship, 100
  finding foreclosure properties using, 110–114
  finding professionals, 98
  generating leads, 96–97
  inner circle, 103
  managing contact information, 104
  marketing yourself, 101–104
  Multiple Listing Service (MLS), 98–99
  power of, 96–99
  rewarding leads, 104–105
  securing financing, 97–98
  tools for marketing, 101–102
Nevada, rules and regulations in, 361
New Hampshire, rules and regulations in, 361
New Jersey, rules and regulations in, 362
New Mexico, rules and regulations in, 362
New York, rules and regulations in, 362

newspapers
  as a source of finding properties in probate, 120
  as source of finding properties of divorce, 122
90-day limit, 31
non-redemption certificate, 286–287
North Carolina, rules and regulations in, 362
North Dakota, rules and regulations in, 363
notice of sale, 354
Notices of Default (NODs)
  about, 31, 32, 46, 353
  benefits of waiting for, 47
  closing deals before the sale, 48
  drawbacks of waiting for, 48
  finding, 116–118
  obtaining information from, 127–132
notifying Internal Revenue Service (IRS), 265–266

O

obtaining
  credit reports, 91
  properties after auctions, 52–54
  properties in probate, 119–121
  property insurance, 203
  title insurance, 203
  titles, 126–127, 134
offers
  comparing, 313–315
  to help, 342–343
  lease-option agreement, 325–327
  negotiating, 313–316
  pitching for REO properties, 220–224
  putting in writing, 222–223
  timing for REO properties, 217–220
Ohio, rules and regulations in, 363
Oklahoma, rules and regulations in, 363
opening bid, 139, 190
Oregon, rules and regulations in, 363

organizations, using for networking, 113
Other Real Estate Owned (OREO), 15
overbidding, 203, 285, 333
overestimating property value, 332

P

page number, on mortgage/mortgage note, 136
paperwork, completing, 24–25
partnerships
  with investors, 83–84
  pros and cons of, 74–75
paying
  insurance, 25–26
  property taxes, 25–26, 282
payment caps, 90
payoff amounts, obtaining, 262
Pennsylvania, rules and regulations in, 363–364
performing due diligence, 19–23, 125–144
periodic adjustment cap, 89
personal lead generators, identifying, 110–113
personal loans, 80
phones, importance of, 102
photos, taking for inspections, 142
PIN (property identification number), 138
pitching offers for REO properties, 220–224
planning
  for contingencies, 88
  renovations, 287
  repairs, 287
  repairs and renovations, 293–296
point of entry, selecting in foreclosure process, 41–55
points, as a feature of hard-money loans, 81–82
poker face, at auctions, 51–52
positions, assigning to junior lienholders, 327–328

possession, taking for properties, 24–26

postliquidation stage, of bankruptcy process, 244

postsale stage, 15–16

pre-auction stage
about, 42
anger and angst, 44–45
assessing ability to deal with, 45–46
closing on purchases in, 280–281
guiding homeowners, 43–44
pros and cons of, 42–43

preparing maximum bids, 191–197

prepayment penalties, as a feature of hard-money loans, 82

presale stage, 12–13

previous mortgagors, on foreclosure information sheet, 135

price paid
on foreclosure information sheet, 135
in offers, 313

printing business cards, 100–102

private lenders, finding, 83–84

probate attorneys
about, 112
acquiring properties in, 119–121
as a source of finding properties in probate, 119

probate court, as a source of finding properties in probate, 120

process period, 353

professionals, finding, 98

profit, realizing, 26–28

proof of financing, 223

proof of insurance, 70–71

properties. *See also specific properties*
about, 109–110
acquiring after auctions, 52–54
acquiring properties in probate, 119–121
advertising for, 114
bankruptcy attorneys, 122–123

bidding on at auctions, 13–15
buying after the sale, 15–16
buying from other investors, 54
deciphering foreclosure notices, 118
estimating value of, 22
Fannie Mae, 231–234
FDIC, 234
finding, 18–19, 133–134
finding dontwanners, 114–115
finding FSBO properties, 115–116
finding Notice of Default (NOD), 116–118
Freddie Mac, 231–234
government, 53–54
homes of divorce, 121–122
identifying personal lead generators, 110–113
inspecting, 21–22, 346–347
leasing to foreclosed-on homeowners, 324–325
listing, 163–164, 181
mailing lists, 117
marketing for sale/lease, 27, 312–313
networking to find, 110–114
Real Estate Owned (REO), 52–53
renovating, 27
repairing, 27
reselling to previous owners, 320–324
securing, 283–284
selling, 27
subscribing to commercial foreclosure information services, 117–118
taking possession of, 24–26
taxable value of, 138
teaming up with attorneys, 119–123
using local publications, 116–117

property history, 21

property identification number (PIN), 138

property list, from county treasurer's office, 237

property tax collector, 257

property tax formula, 138

property tax sales
about, 272–273
finding, 273–274
golden, 274–275
redeeming tax deeds, 275
tax certificates, 275
tax deeds, 275–276

property tax status, 138

property taxes
paying, 25–26, 282
unpaid, 137

property worksheet, obtaining, 138–139

purchase agreement, 183–184, 223, 316

R

real estate agents
about, 72
approved for HUD homes, 228
selling through qualified, 306–309
as a source of finding properties in
probate, 119
as source of finding properties of
divorce, 121
subtracting commissions, 193

real estate attorneys, 60–61, 111

real estate brokers, 112

Real Estate Owned (REO) properties
about, 52–53, 207–208
brokers for, 211
closing deals, 224
drawbacks of, 208–209
estimating lender's needs, 220
financial attractiveness of investors,
210–211
finding, 210–216
fiscal calendar for lenders, 218
inspecting, 216–217
pitching offers for, 220–224

process of, 209–210
redemption period and, 216, 218
reevaluating your needs, 221
timing offers, 217–220
waiting for brokers to list, 219–220
writing offers, 222–223

Real Property Utilization & Disposal, 238

realtor, 72

Realtor (website), 73

receiving forbearance, 35

recording deeds, 203, 215

recordkeeping, for conventional loans, 90–93

red flags, 144

redemption period
about, 15, 24, 37–38, 167–168, 216,
282, 354
effects of, 54–55
maintaining status quo, 282–283
timing and, 218

reevaluating your needs, 221

reference number, on Notice of Default
(NDO), 127

refinancing
about, 28
assisting homeowners in assessing options
for, 340–341
as a cash-out strategy, 320
mortgages, 86, 162–163, 181
through you, 164–165

Register of Deeds, 116–117, 132–137, 203

regulations and rules
from county treasurer's office, 237
by state, 353–366

rehab loan, 90

reinstating
as an option for homeowners, 170
loans, 162, 181
mortgages, 34–35

REJ - Redemption, as a loan status, 178

Remember icon, 4
renovations and repairs
  about, 27, 291–292
  adding valuable features, 303–304
  basements, 300
  bathrooms, 299, 303
  bedrooms, 299–300
  choosing strategies for, 292–293
  estimating costs for, 192
  exterior, 297–298
  interior, 298
  kitchens, 298–299, 301–303
  mechanicals, 300–301
  mistakes with, 335
  planning, 287, 293–296
  quick makeovers, 297–301
rent, lease-option agreements and, 325
REO managers, 222
REO (Real Estate Owned) properties
  about, 52–53, 207–208
  brokers for, 211
  closing deals, 224
  drawbacks of, 208–209
  estimating lender's needs, 220
  financial attractiveness of investors,
    210–211
  finding, 210–216
  fiscal calendar for lenders, 218
  inspecting, 216–217
  pitching offers for, 220–224
  process of, 209–210
  redemption period and, 216, 218
  reevaluating your needs, 221
  timing offers, 217–220
  waiting for brokers to list, 219–220
  writing offers, 222–223
repaired value, 61
repairs and renovations

about, 27, 291–292
adding valuable features, 303–304
basements, 300
bathrooms, 299, 303
bedrooms, 299–300
choosing strategies for, 292–293
estimating costs for, 192
exterior, 297–298
interior, 298
kitchens, 298–299, 301–303
mechanicals, 300–301
mistakes with, 335
planning, 287, 293–296
quick makeovers, 297–301
repayment plan, 35
repos. *See* government properties
requesting forbearance, 35
researching
  bankruptcy filings, 246–247
  titles, 134–135, 346
reselling properties to previous owners,
    320–324
resources, tapping your own, 84–88
restructuring debt, through chapter 13
    bankruptcy, 243
retirement savings, 323
return on investment (ROI), calculating,
    293–294
rewarding leads, 104–105
Rhode Island, rules and regulations in, 364
rules and regulations
  from county treasurer's office, 237
  by state, 353–366

S
sale (auction) stage, 13–15, 32–33
savings, as a source of investment capital, 86
scams, 346

schedule
  for foreclosure activities, 146–149
  for renovations and repairs, 294–296
sealed bids, 199–201
second mortgages, 271–272, 335
securing
  financing, 97–98
  properties, 283–284
seized properties, finding, 18–19
self-directed IRA, as a source of investment
    capital, 86–87
self-interested attorney, 249
seller's agents
  about, 71–74
  choosing, 308–309
selling and leasing
  about, 305
  assets through chapter 7 bankruptcy, 242
  becoming a landlord, 317
  closing deals, 316–317
  junior liens, 269–272
  marketing for, 312–313
  negotiating offers/counteroffers, 313–316
  properties, 27
  staging for, 309–311
  suggesting, 341
  through qualified real estate agents,
      306–309
  your position to other lienholders, 28
senior lien, 13–14, 49
senior lienholder, 170
setting
  goals, 347–348
  maximum bids, 23–24, 51
shopping, for low-cost loans, 93–94
short sales
  about, 28, 164
  as an option for homeowners, 170
  as a homeowner option, 181

  negotiating, 256–269
  suggesting, 340
skilled laborers, 70
South Carolina, rules and regulations in, 364
South Dakota, rules and regulations in, 364
staging, for showings, 309–311
state department of transportation (DOT),
    53, 237–239
stopping foreclosure process, 33–38
strategies. *See also* cash-out strategies
  about, 255–256
  buying and selling junior liens, 269–272
  negotiating short sales, 256–269
  property tax sales, 272–276
subcontractors, 66–71
submitting sealed bids, 199–201
subscribing, to commercial foreclosure
    information services, 117–118
subtracting
  agent commissions, 193
  closing costs, 193
Swim with the Sharks (Mackay), 103

T

tax assessors, contacting for homeowner
    information, 150
tax certificates, 49, 275
tax deeds, 275–276
tax ID number, 138
tax liens. *See* tax certificates
tax sales
  buying properties at, 235
  gurus of, 236
teams
  about, 59–60
  accountants, 64–65
  attorneys, 119–123
  building, 16–17, 59–75
  buyer's agent, 71

contractors, 66–71
home inspectors, 65–66
mortgage brokers, 61–62
partnerships, 74–75
real estate attorneys, 60–61
seller's agents, 71–74
subcontractors, 66–71
title companies, 63–64
temporary restraining order (TRO), 289
Tennessee, rules and regulations
    in, 364
terminal, as a loan status, 178
termite inspection report, 316
Terms and Conditions, lease-option
    agreements and, 325
Texas, rules and regulations in, 365
30-day notice, 31
timing
    offers for REO properties, 217–220
    redemption period and, 218
Tip icon, 4
title commitment, 63
title companies, 63–64
title history, 20
title insurance
    about, 63
    exit strategy and, 281
    obtaining, 203
titles
    acquiring, 126–127
    investigating, 20–21, 333–334
    obtaining, 134
    researching, 134–135, 346
tools, for marketing, 100–102
total owed on property, 139–140
TransUnion, 91
treasurer's office, 150, 237
TRO (temporary restraining order), 289

trustee sale, foreclosure by, 30–31
trustees, bankruptcy, 249
trusting homeowners, 336
two-week notice, 31

U

underestimating holding costs, 333
unskilled laborers, 70
U.S. Department of Agriculture (USDA) Real
    Estate for Sale, 239
U.S. Securities and Exchange Commission
    (SEC), 98
U.S. Treasury Real Property Auctions, 239
USA People Search, 151
Utah, rules and regulations in, 365
utility companies, 280–281

V

VA (Department of Veterans Affairs), 53–54,
    89, 226
VA repos
    about, 53, 226
    finding, 230–231
value
    "as is," 176
    of attorneys, 243
    estimating, 139, 192
    estimating for property, 22
    maximizing, 27
    overestimating for property, 332
    taxable, of properties, 138
value-add renovations, 292
variable-rate mortgages, 89–90
Vendor Resource Management (VRM), 230
Vermont, rules and regulations in, 365
Virginia, rules and regulations in, 365
Vistaprint, 100

W

walk-around inspections, 140–142

walking away, as an option, 343

Warning icon, 4

Washington, Rules and regulations in, 366

websites

  Cheat Sheet, 4

  Craigslist, 114

  credit reports, 91

  Federal Deposit Insurance Corporation (FDIC), 234

  General Service Administration (GSA) Auctions, 238

  HomeInfoMax, 134

  HomePath, 233

  HomeSteps, 231

  HUD bid site, 202

  HUD Homes, 229

  IRS properties, 236

  Michigan's DOT, 238

  National Association of Certified Home Inspector (NACHI), 65

  Oregon's DOT, 238

  Real Property Utilization & Disposal, 238

  Realtor, 73

  U.S. Department of Agriculture (USDA) Real Estate for Sale, 239

  U.S. Treasury Real Property Auctions, 239

  USA People Search, 151

  Vendor Resource Management (VRM), 230

  Vistaprint, 100

West Virginia, rules and regulations in, 366

white-box strategy, for renovations, 292

Wisconsin, rules and regulations in, 366

word-of-mouth networking, 110

worth, determining, 91

writing offers, 222–223

Wyoming, rules and regulations in, 366

Y

yourself, marketing, 100–104

About the Authors

Ralph R. Roberts's success in real estate sales is legendary. He has been profiled by the Associated Press, CNN, and *Time* magazine, and has done hundreds of radio interviews. Ralph is a seasoned professional in all areas of house flipping, including buying homes, rehabbing, and reselling them quickly and at a handsome profit. He has penned several successful titles, including *Flipping Houses For Dummies* (Wiley), *Sell It Yourself: Sell Your Home Faster and for More Money Without Using a Broker* (Adams Media Corporation), *Walk Like a Giant, Sell Like a Madman: America's #1 Salesman Shows You How To Sell Anything* (Collins), *52 Weeks of Sales Success: America's #1 Salesman Shows You How To Close Every Deal!* (Collins), *REAL WEALTH by Investing in REAL ESTATE* (Prentice Hall), and *Protect Yourself Against Real Estate and Mortgage Fraud* (Kaplan).

Foreclosure investing is one of Ralph's many specialties. For over 35 years, he has personally worked in the foreclosure arena, purchasing pre-foreclosures directly from homeowners, buying foreclosure properties at auction, and often helping homeowners dodge the foreclosure bullet and retain possession of their homes. In *Foreclosure Investing For Dummies*, Ralph reveals his unique win-win approach to investing in foreclosures.

Joe Kraynak is a freelance author who has written and co-authored dozens of books on topics ranging from slam poetry to computer basics. His most recent *For Dummies* titles include *Oceans For Dummies* with Ashlan and Philippe Cousteau, *Cannabis For Dummies* with Kim Ronkin Casey, and *Bipolar Disorder For Dummies*, 3rd Edition, with Candida Fink, MD. In this new edition of *Foreclosure Investing For Dummies*, Joe and Ralph join forces once again, this time along with Ralph's son, Kyle, to deliver the definitive guide to profitably investing in foreclosures — without selling your soul. You can find Joe on the web at JoeKraynak.com.

Kyle Roberts works in the field of human resources and in this capacity has supported teams such as field operations, talent management, and talent development. Like his father, he also has a passion for flipping houses and has recently sold his fourth investment property (following many of the same principles found in this edition of *Foreclosure Investing For Dummies*).

Dedication

From Ralph: To the many investors and Realtors I've worked with, trained, consulted, and coached who have made investing in foreclosures both successful and rewarding.

From Joe: To the investors who use our book, not only to build wealth in real estate but also to assist distressed homeowners and build stronger communities.

Author's Acknowledgments

Although we wrote the book, dozens of other talented individuals contributed to its conception, development, and perfection. Special thanks go to acquisitions editor Jennifer Yee, who chose us to author this book and guided us through the tough part of getting started. Tim Gallan, our project editor, deserves a loud cheer for acting as a very patient collaborator and gifted editor — shuffling chapters back and forth, shepherding the text and graphics through production, making sure any technical issues were properly resolved, and serving as unofficial quality control manager. We also tip our hats to the production crew for doing such an outstanding job of transforming a loose collection of text and illustrations into such an attractive bound book.

Throughout the writing of this book, we relied heavily on a knowledgeable and dedicated support staff, who provided expert advice, tips, and research so that we could deliver the most comprehensive and useful information. We owe special thanks to our technical editor, accomplished real estate pro Blanche Evans, for ferreting out technical errors in the manuscript, helping guide its content, and offering her own tips and tricks.

Publisher's Acknowledgments

Acquisitions Editor: Jennifer Yee
Development Editor: Tim Gallan
Copy Editor: Keir Simpson
Technical Reviewer:
  Blanche Evans (previous edition)

Production Editor: Tamilmani Varadharaj
Cover Image: © zimmytws/Shutterstock